# CONQUEST OF THE NEW WORD

University of Texas Press, Austin

# CONQUEST

Experimental Fiction

# OF THE

and Translation

# NEW WORD

in the Americas

## JOHNNY PAYNE

# The Texas Pan American Series

First edition, 1993

Requests for permission to reproduce material from this work should be sent to Permissions, University of Texas Press, Box 7819, Austin, TX 78713-7819.

⊗ The paper used in this publication meets the minimum requirements of American National Standard for Information Sciences—Permanence of Paper for Printed Library Materials, ANSI Z39.48-1984.

### Library of Congress Cataloging-in-Publication Data

Payne, Johnny, date
Conquest of the new word : experimental fiction and translation in the Americas / Johnny Payne. — 1st ed.
    p.    cm. — (The Texas Pan American series)
Includes bibliographical references and index.
ISBN 0-292-76546-0 (alk. paper)
1. Argentine fiction—20th century—History and criticism.
2. Uruguayan fiction—20th century—History and criticism.
3. Experimental fiction—Latin America—History and criticism. 4. Latin American fiction—20th century—Translations into English—History and criticism. 5. Literature, Comparative—Latin American and American. 6. Literature, Comparative—American and Latin American. 7. Politics and literature—Latin America. 8. Politics and literature—United States. 9. Dictatorship in literature. 10. Latin American fiction—Women authors—History and criticism. I. Title. II. Series.
PQ7703.P39   1993
863—dc20                                                      93-6537

# Contents

# Acknowledgments

Culmination provides one kind of pleasure; process provides another. It gratifies me doubly to culminate the writing of this book by expressing my gratitude to those people who shared in the process of its making. First among them is Miriam Payne, whose imaginative sympathy extends to every area of our life in common. Miriam's patient, unstinting support in all practical and impractical daily matters has allowed me time to research and write. Her genuine enthusiasm for the life of the mind is matched by her ability to cock a skeptical eyebrow. Cat Stevens knew whereof he spoke when he sang "If I find me a hard-headed woman, I know the rest of my life will be blessed."

I also owe very special thanks to John Felstiner, who gave me guidance at many stages of my writing of *Conquest of the New Word*. I found him exemplary at every turn in his gentleness of manner and toughness of mind, in his gifts as a translator, and in his attention to minutiae combined with a generous intellect. John's book, *Translating Neruda: The Way to Macchu Picchu*, and his essays on Paul Celan set standards for scholarly care and engaging style.

Marjorie Perloff's literary histories of European and U.S. avant-garde literature helped me early on to frame many of the larger questions that arose in trying to describe an "other tradition" in Latin America. Mary Pratt introduced me to the work of Ricardo Piglia and Nelson Marra in the context of recent political oppression. Gilbert Sorrentino cued me in to generative devices and Oulipo.

The Stanford Humanities Center gave me a congenial, supportive time and place in which to work for a year. The fellow members of my reading group there—Laura Rigal, Carolyn Williams, Mary Gluck, and Elizabeth Hansot—offered considered, lucid readings of early drafts of two of my chapters, along with the timely advice that I give my work a more historically specific turn. Stanford's extensive holdings of Argentine and Uruguayan texts that would be otherwise hard to come by facilitated my research, and its Latin American librarians are to be commended for their responsiveness.

Eden Quainton, an intellectual companion, fellow editor, and kindred spirit, has been of inestimable importance to me in the myriad unaccountable ways that friendship can take. In particular, his rigorous editing of some of my Teresa Porzecanski translations helped me re-enter the domain of her writing with a clearer understanding. In both our correspondence and our personal contact, Teresa Porzecanski herself has gone out of her way to make her work and thought available to me. Mary Kinzie, whose thoroughgoing knowledge of Borges makes me think she must have spent some time doing research in the Library of Babel, provided eminently helpful, exacting, and detailed criticism of chapters 4 and 6. Thanks also are due to Helen Deutsch and Jules Law for their considered readings of my introduction on short notice.

I am grateful to Stephen-Paul Martin at *Central Park* for his early editorial support of my writing. Portions of *Conquest of the New Word* have also appeared, in somewhat different form, in *boundary 2, Black Warrior Review,* and *TriQuarterly,* as well as the anthology *Anxious Power,* and I appreciate the thoughtfulness that the editors of those publications brought to my work in the form of scholarly articles. Theresa May, at the University of Texas Press, has been conscientious in expediting the various stages of the editorial process, and she made her enthusiasm for my project clear early on. The designated readers of my manuscript performed their tasks with both celerity and care, and I availed myself of their constructive criticism in the process of revision.

Finally, I want to thank my daughter Sonja, who daily provided me with needed perspective on my priorities by remaining utterly oblivious to my scholarly prerogatives and insisting that I turn my attentions to the more humble paternal tasks at hand. I dedicate this book to her and to Miriam.

# CONQUEST OF THE NEW WORD

# Introduction

*Literature is an art that has learned to prophesy that time when it will have turned silent, and to gorge itself on self-regard, and to become enamoured of its own dissolution and to court its own demise.*

JORGE LUIS BORGES

The epigraph to my book is taken, both appropriately and perversely, from a 1930 essay by Borges entitled "The Superstitious Ethic of the Reader." In it, he decries the narrowness of received notions of style and makes ironic use of what he considers the ultimate exemplary novel, the *Quixote,* as a polemical example of works that might arguably be excluded by the prevailing standards of his time. "The truth is, it suffices to rewrite a few paragraphs of the *Quixote* to feel that Cervantes wasn't a stylist."[1] Borges did, however, actually make good on his promise to improve upon this "exemplary" style of the *Quixote.* He and his alter ego Pierre Menard accomplished this task a few years later by "recomposing" some paragraphs from it verbatim and allowing history to do the rest. Borges, both in earnest and at play, was very much alive to the historical contingency of defining what it means to be a stylist and never entertained the matter as self-evident.

For the other Latin American writers considered in this study, the question of the efficacy of received notions of style took on a renewed urgency in the seventies and eighties, chiefly because the prevailing, exclusionary standards of their time happened to be imposed by military dictatorship. Governmental constraints on open expression were especially severe in Uruguay and Argentina at that time. In both of those countries, a body of experimental fiction came into being which emphasized its own artifice and in doing so explored a different modality of style. The perpetually prophesied demise of literature that Borges spoke of with irony in 1930 by 1970 threatened to become a concrete reality, at least as a short-term proposition. Because of this circumstance, style, rather than offering itself as a given, a passively received notion, or even an unstable make-it-new aesthetic category, functioned as a dialectically contingent and specific response to oppression. Nor did the writers from that time limit themselves to simply satirizing the dictatorships, which had dedicated their energies unequivocally to shattering social and intellectual spheres. Whatever its purported subject, much of this experimental fiction called into question, directly or obliquely, the socially constitutive, self-legitimating rhetoric of dictatorship.

I say I have chosen my epigraph appropriately because the pages that follow deal largely with this historical relation between literature and dictatorship in modern Argentina and Uruguay, and the year of Borges' essay, 1930, is a pivotal reference point in Argentine history, marking the beginning of dictatorship as an unmistakable and resilient force in Argentine life. I say *perversely* because the sui generis Borges, despite the deep impact he has made on Latin American letters, doesn't fall easily or naturally into any single grouping of writers, including my own. Borges, that avatar of the tortoise, came to belated prominence in the 1960s, in English translation, as an international figure of the Latin American "boom" in fiction—in spite of the fact that he prefigures his ostensible Latin American compeers in the boom by at least a generation. His inclusion within that canon, especially as it exists in translation, suggests at the least its logical inconsistency as a phenomenon. The widespread appearance of Borges in English translation at roughly the same time as Julio Cortázar, Mario Vargas Llosa, Manuel Puig, and José Donoso created a sense of his simultaneity with these authors, but this simultaneity, with regard to Borges, is a construction of literary history.

As an illusion of critical revisionism, or as a temporal appearance of a cultural archetype, Borges can perhaps be said to be synchronous with these "compeers," and yet, as in Zeno's paradox, they cannot truly overtake him. His presence, as an enticing Borgesian conundrum, allows one to puzzle over questions about the relation between dictatorship and contemporary Latin American fiction in a manner that his absence would preclude, since his absence would allow the periodizing metaphor of "boom" to stand more easily unchallenged. Thus, I think of the elusive Borges as the household spirit hovering over my study of boom and post-boom authors in Argentina and Uruguay. His inclusion here also has suggestive relevance to the fiction of some of his other "counterparts" in contemporary fiction writing in the United States, whose fiction I will also be discussing.

Borges is accurate in his pronouncement about literature's morbid fascination with prophesying its own silence and demise, a tendency which has reprised in contemporary North American criticism as well and which I detail in the first chapter of this study. Cultural impasses tend to invite doomsaying. But if anyone has turned out to be prophetic, it is Borges, by his phantasmagorical, shape-shifting, yet enduring presence, and not the prophesiers of literary dissolution—not even those who bore witness to dictatorship. The boom, if anything, is too much with us in the United States. In spite of the dire straits of literary publishing at the present time, there are probably more different titles of Latin American fiction in English translation in print than at any moment in the past.

But notwithstanding its literal inaccuracy, contemporary literature's love affair with its own dissolution has its reason for being and even its usefulness as a cultural rhetoric. The case of U.S. culture is particularly instructive in this regard. For the puzzling question remains of why the upsurge in translation that began in the sixties has not, by and large, provided Latin American literature's U.S. readership with a substantively more complex view of Latin American history and politics. If translation, in this historical instance, were conceived of as a solution to cultural misapprehension, it would have to be described as on the whole a failed solution. The boom, as a phenomenon, incredibly appears to have reinforced many long-standing exotic and essentializing stereotypes about Latin America. My own emphasis, therefore, in the pages that follow, is on reading a selection of modern fiction from South America carefully against its political and cultural grounding, in the hope that the boom, as well as myriad extra-boom and post-boom experimental writers who fall, strictly speaking, outside that phenomenon, will thereby be read less phenomenally—less as a series of brilliant but ephemeral after-images or flashes on consciousness than as an aggregate of great diversity, unified conceptually in its desire to find a way out of the cultural impasse imposed by dictatorship.

Doing so effectively, in the context I am elaborating, has also entailed situating Latin American writers vis à vis U.S. writers who are compatible with them in terms of genre, philosophy, or method—artistic doppelgängers, so to speak. Setting up this sort of rough congruence between writers in each individual instance allows both the similarities and disparities in their respective cultural grounding to become more salient. The "conquest of the new word" in my title refers to the tendency to read Latin American fiction in a manner which exaggerates its magical, exotic hues, while assiduously glossing over the grittier social aspects that become evident when the works of fiction are considered more closely in relation to the cultures which engendered them.

My argument, however, is that the conquest of the new word is not the product of simple cultural dilettantism on the part of U.S. readers but rather the result of a complicated attempt to appropriate Latin American fiction as a "solution" to a particular crisis of confidence in contemporary U.S. society and its fiction—a yearning that nonetheless inevitably leads to reductivism. My hope is that *Conquest of the New Word* may serve, among other things, as a modest corrective to the ahistoricizing proclivities of readers who have, in other respects, been hugely appreciative of Latin American fiction in translation. As for Latin Americanists already steeped in the fiction I undertake to explicate, I hope that I may persuade those who are disposed to exclusively "macro" social analyses to reconsider the virtues of close reading as it occurs within a theoretical matrix.

My study takes Montevideo and Buenos Aires, the capital cities of Uruguay and Argentina, as its cases in point. Their modern literatures, because of the historical, cultural, and social affinities of the two urban areas, are often referred to in conjunction as "literatura rioplatense"—literature of the River Plate. Argentine and Uruguayan writers have long been accustomed to speaking of the two countries in the same breath. In writing about the relationship between dictatorship and literature in Latin America, one might, because dictatorship has been so widespread, arguably take almost any of its nations, and any number of its authors, as points of departure.

But because of the widely disparate ways in which many of those countries' post-independence republican histories have led them into periods of dictatorship, I have found it prudent, in order to make my claims as focused and particular as possible, to limit myself not only to two specific countries, but to a specific area of those countries (most of the writing and publishing, in any event, has been centered in the capital cities). As I will detail in my first chapter, there are decided problems in trying to speak of Latin American or South American literature as a conceptual whole, and one quickly comes up against the limits of the generalizations that can safely be made about an entire continent. By this token, the authors discussed in these chapters are not presented as microcosmic representatives of Latin American consciousness. Some of my analysis of the political dilemmas of Argentina and Uruguay is doubtless pertinent in varying degrees to crises of literature and dictatorship in other Latin

American countries, particularly Chile. But I seek only to delineate the specific cultural configurations taken up in this book.

The particular Argentine and Uruguayan authors I have selected for discussion argue the necessity of their inclusion in different ways. While a few of them, such as Jorge Luis Borges, Manuel Puig, and Ricardo Piglia, have already been canonized as key figures of their respective eras by Latin American scholars, other less decisively established writers, such as Nelson Marra and Luisa Valenzuela, serve as especially suggestive focal points for a detailed analysis of a particular cultural nexus. As for Teresa Porzecanski, I will categorically say that I consider her one of the most talented and subtle writers of her generation.

Silvia Schmid is probably the least known of all these writers, but her use of the epistolary conceit complements her compatriot Puig's use of it, as well as matching uncannily Fanny Howe and Lydia Davis' approaches to the question of letters and psychoanalysis. Though Schmid's contribution is doubtless slighter than Puig's, the inclusion of her "Viva Freud!" for discussion helps to clarify one's understanding of the epistolary as a *genre* of social satire in a manner that could not be accomplished by a consideration of Puig in isolation. In any event, one of the objects of *Conquest of the New Word* is to call into question the notion that any single selection of texts and authors can be truly or fully representative of that apocryphal political and literary entity called Latin America. Instead, I offer individual instances of authors who connect in the kinetic enterprise of trying to locate a viable common cultural ground.

Beginning in the sixties, the apparently definitive failure of both liberal democracy and revolutionary movements in Uruguay and Argentina heralded a degree of militarization unprecedented in those two countries. The domination and reshaping of the urban cultural sphere by dictatorial force and by regressive military social policies couched in the rhetoric of democracy gave impetus to experimental fiction writers in those countries to use their writing to reflect on, and sometimes challenge, the violent duplicity of dictatorial rule and its verbal manifestations. The fiction of these writers exhibits their strong desire to reclaim the social sphere (or at the least to keep it intact) and a desire to discover forms of collective life more resilient to tyranny. Yet the authors of this fiction, mostly written during the seventies and eighties, are equally skeptical of the established, apparently discredited alternatives to dictatorship and are acutely aware of strong ideological and historical continuities between dictatorship and democracy. Thus, they remain hesitant about embracing either armed revolution or the ethical tenets of liberal modernity as solutions to the political impasse they are caught in and are reticent in the main about proposing solutions of any kind.

U.S. writers from the sixties onward, in a simultaneous yet rather different cultural configuration, have been experiencing the apparently wholesale capitulation of liberalism and left politics to a consumer society. That consumer society seems bent on making dissent appear irrelevant by claiming progress and democracy as natural states of affairs and by using the rhetoric of liberalism, tolerance, and the open society as a normative tool. The response of U.S. experimental fiction writers to this historical situation has taken various forms, some writers openly endorsing the normative thesis of happy democracy or indirectly endorsing it by complaining of its symptomatic effects while yearning for a return to the "lost" causes (e.g., the sanctity of marriage and the patriarchal family as microcosms of the blissfully hierarchical society) of those degraded symptoms. Others have bitterly satirized consumer democracy as dystopian and violently oppressive in its attempt to force individuals out of the realm of social engagement and back into the artificially "separate" sphere of private woe. Like their Argentine and Uruguayan counterparts, most U.S. writers in this latter category have stopped short of suggesting either political or aesthetic solutions to social malaise and have concentrated instead on finding a fictional idiom to critique democracy's "constitution" of subjectivity and to express the desire for eventual social regeneration.

My account of the fictional strategies of the U.S. writers examined here is guided in part by the cultural context of sixties and seventies political activism, mainly that espoused and practiced by the New Left. This intellectual frame, however, is obviously less encompassing than that of dictatorship, and I have tried not to push it beyond its limit of suggestive relevance. The writers I consider are on the whole as "politically" or "socially" motivated, in the broadest sense, as any of the Latin American writers, and part of my wish in this study is in fact to call into question the false dualism of "aesthetic" versus "political" writing. U.S. experimental writers have tended to be evaluated mostly in formalist terms, while the emphasis on Latin American writers inevitably seems to fall back on their political and social perspectives. Boom writing, as I have indicated, has too often served as a political other for the U.S., a medium onto which our collective political anxieties could be displaced. Nonetheless, the social dimension and ground of U.S. writing are not any less, though they are less categorical.

Translation is one of a number of visible preoccupations in this book but should not be taken as my principal subject or single, guiding metaphor. Nonetheless, my engagement with certain writers, such as Teresa Porzecanski and Nelson Marra and to a lesser extent Ricardo Piglia, began with my translating some of their fiction into English. And in the cases of the first two, I do devote some extended attention to the process of translating their work, in order to address the discrepancies in the ways different cultures constitute such concepts as aesthetics and politics.

However, to present my transformation of a work of fiction as simply an exercise in successful (or unsuccessful) artistic or linguistic problem solving strikes me as a diminishment of that fiction and, moreover, a misrepresentation. The attention given over the past few decades to defining translation as the sum of a set of "cultural equivalencies," such as the thesis put forth by Eugene Nida in the sixties in *Toward a Science of Translating,* has been crucial to pointing out the structural relationship of languages and dialects to their respective cultures. But the continued preoccupation of translation "theory" with the minutiae of texts, or even with systematic methods of accounting for them, to the exclusion of questions about the changeability of history (and of translation as a biased intervention within history), paradoxically can encourage the filtering out of those minutiae. Positing culture and history as static fields more or less available to disinterested borrowings situates translation and translation theory in a privileged, ostensibly neutral position at the center of a bustling marketplace of linguistic exchange. Its tenets, taken too far in this direction, begin to sound like a workaday version manqué of Claude Lévi-Strauss' questionable dictum, in "The Structural Study of Myth," that even the *worst* translation preserves the "essential" features of a culture. One might instead begin by asking how what is deemed essential in those features comes to be defined within the culture at large in the first place, and by whom, and for what purposes.

Given the broader conceptual emphasis of *Conquest of the New Word,* translation has had to find its proper place among a group of concerns. I do not in any way wish to suggest that the practice or theory of translation will "resolve" social contradictions. At their best, they instead make those contradictions more apparent. Insofar as translation and translation theory appear in these pages, they take various forms, sometimes, as described above, as a close reading of my translation of a story or novel, simultaneous with an explication of the political events coming to bear on what Walter Benjamin, in "The Task of the Translator," has referred to as the work of art's "afterlife." Sometimes translation appears as an exercise in method, analogous to the author's, an attempt to force an awareness of the ideological assumptions latent in different kinds of social rhetoric. Sometimes I address translation as it appears explicitly or implicitly in the work of an author as a metaphor for obliteration or oppression—or in some cases, resistance to those things. In many instances, translation can be taken as the transposition of theoretical concepts from one social tradition to another.

Though my presentation of writers does not obey chronology, there is a logic to the progression of chapters. Chapter 1 describes the reception given to the boom authors in English translation. It details how the critical myths that sprang up in both the popular and scholarly press emphasized the tropicality of Latin American fiction and facilitated U.S. writers' and critics' need to project their own sociocultural anxieties about the impendng dissolution of U.S. literature onto another literary tradition. This emphasis ultimately resulted in erroneous rumors of the "death" of Latin American literature. To give a different account of the boom and post-boom period, I first reject that periodizing economic metaphor as the standard by which Latin American literature should be judged.

I then begin, in chapter 2, with the publication leading to Nelson Marra's imprisonment in Uruguay, in the midst of the oppression that had intensified with the military dictatorship's 1973 ascent to power, in the wake of its decisive defeat of the Tupamaro urban guerrillas. The formal period during which the Uruguayan dictatorship held power antedates the Argentine one by three years and ends six years before the Argentine military officially relinquishes power in its country, so it seemed to make sense to begin with the Uruguayan case and end with the Argentine one.

Chapter 3, an incursion into the fiction of Teresa Porzecanski, presents the stylistic verso of oppositional writing in Uruguay. Marra's satire is overtly, directly, and ferociously topical. Porzecanski's writing, at the other extreme, is deliberately non-topical. Though Porzecanski is highly acclaimed in her country and to a growing extent abroad, and though Marra has achieved a peculiar kind of notoriety, I would not necessarily make the claim that they are Uruguay's most revered writers. But I can make the specific argument that these two writers, taken together, do in key ways serve to define the parameters of oppositional writing under the Uruguayan dictatorship. My discussion of them, in chapters 2 and 3, in conjunction with U.S. writers Donald Barthelme, Gordon Lish, and Harry Mathews, marks out a range of aesthetic positions along a continuum, with respect to the question of how to represent history in literature. The question of historical representation is central for all the writers I consider in this study—even those who wish to deny or gloss over historical complexities—and is also central to *Conquest of the New Word*.

The remaining three chapters are devoted to Argentina, although the political contexts of the two countries have, as I have mentioned, strong continuities, and my inquiries into them are not strictly separate matters. Chapter 4, in its reading of Ricardo Piglia's 1980 novel, describes the narrow channel of intellectual life permissible under dictatorship and, as the analysis of Marra does, suggests some of the historical precedents and causes of the contemporary political situation. My analysis of the use of the epistolary conceit, in both Piglia's and U.S. novelist John Barth's fiction, is at the same time an analysis of the formation of the modern democratic-republican state and of the ways in which that formation, from its beginnings, has defined the public sphere in a fashion that leaves it extremely vulnerable to being shattered repeatedly.

Chapter 5, an appraisal of the epistolary fiction of Manuel Puig, Silvia Schmid, Fanny Howe, and Lydia Davis, focuses on how that public sphere can be transposed into the language of domesticity. These four writers, in critiquing a patriarchal state's attempt to restrict feminine identity to the private sphere and in consciously exploring the interrelation between the public and the private, take up where Piglia and Barth leave off.

Chapter 6, in considering the fiction of Jorge Luis Borges, Luisa Valenzuela, William Burroughs, and Kathy Acker, spans the time period of a modern epoch that comes into being under the sign of dictatorship. I refer to their collective attitude as "radical skepticism"—the justifiable attempt to find a place of hiatus from the vicissitudes of social violence, a place where contemplation about alternatives to it may occur. The quixotic quandary of Borges, who both desires and fears modernity, reaches back into the end of the nineteenth century. That quandary is rooted in the waves of European immigration that helped fuel the proto-militaristic, nationalist definitions of modernity that Borges, in his quiet way, repudiated. Luisa Valenzuela, for her part, in her topical 1982 book of fiction, tries to sort out the lingering, grim legacy of that dictatorial modernity. In a 1986 travesty of the Cervantine tradition, Kathy Acker also attempts, with more mixed results, to portray an impending apocalypse driven by the misogynistic social relations that seem to characterize consumer society. And in a vein similar to Borges, Burroughs in the fifties is already pessimistic about the prospects for social radicalism under consumer capitalism.

Chapter 6 as a whole is an inquiry into the reasons for this contemporary radical skepticism, at a time when relief about the official "end" of dictatorship is accompanied by a pervasive gloom toward a supposed return to democracy. Radical skepticism, a state of mind shared by the society at large, has its roots in the origins of democracy and continues in Argentina up to the present moment. The dilemmas that have resulted in this skepticism have yet not been resolved in society, but at least they have been addressed with subtlety and intelligence by an appreciable number of experimental writers, rather than being taken as self-evident and thereby perpetually self-fulfilling. This effort, with all its inconclusiveness, seems to me clearly preferable to the heady, monumental, but finally ephemeral conquest of the new word rumored to have occurred, decisively, sometime before the dark decade of the seventies had even begun.

# 1. Conquest of the New Word: U.S. Experimental Fiction, Gabriel García Márquez, and the Latin American Boom

Though the words never actually stopped being manufactured for an instant, there came a pause in the late 1960s when some novelists and literary critics in the United States began to wonder, in print, whether it was still possible to continue to write. In 1968, in "The Literature of Exhaustion," one of the most widely cited literary essays of that decade, John Barth makes clear that "I don't mean anything so tired as the subject of physical, moral, or intellectual decadence, only the used-upness of certain forms or exhaustion of certain possibilities." This impasse, in his estimation, provides no cause for alarm. It provides, rather, a possible point of departure for new, metafictional possibilities. Still, despite his calculated, cavalier assertion that "whether historically the novel expires or persists seems immaterial to me," he acknowledges that "if enough writers and critics *feel* apocalyptic about it, their feeling becomes a considerable cultural fact."[1]

From all indicators, if they never became a numerical majority, enough of them did feel this way to constitute at least a critical mass. Discussions of the "death" of fiction and appraisals of its prognosis became especially intense in the literary media during these years. I don't pretend that these appraisals in any way negate the proliferation of writing during that time. Just as the current vehemence of the rhetoric about "cultural illiteracy" and the collapse of the humanities doesn't imply that the humanities are in actual dissolution, neither did these earlier accounts of the state of fiction necessarily indicate literal concern that letters or the profession of literature were in danger of perishing; the collective anxiety was instead about what form their continuation would take. The stark scenarios invoked by such a rhetoric allow the various interested parties within the culture to put forth sharp, competing claims about the shape of the transformation and renewal. Many of these participants may also, as happened in the case of the "death" of fiction in the sixties, gravitate toward a consensus.

Typical of the critiques of the late sixties is a piece by Stephen Koch, published a few months before Barth's. The apocalyptic tone of Koch's inaugural essay of a *TriQuarterly* number, billed as the "Under 30 Issue," proposes to "talk, however uneasily, about a rebirth" but would seem to negate the heraldic purpose of the issue in which it appears. Instead, Koch devotes his opening words to the question of literary silence.

> Is American writing moving toward another rebirth? At the moment, our literature is idling in a period of hiatus: the few important writers of the earlier generations are dead, silent, or in their decline, while the younger generation has not yet produced a writer of unmistakable importance or even much work of very great interest. . . . Even though there is a large body of new work, nothing thus far has been heard on the highest levels except an eerie silence.
>
> The most important critical question to be asked now concerns how and when this silence will be broken; it asks whether it is the silence that precedes the speech of art. The question is purely speculative, and hence unanswerable; but is also so urgent that I, for one, cannot help asking it. Despite the ignorance and lethargy working against the creation of serious work, I think that it can be broken and that—to put it grandly—the history of late twentieth century literature in English has yet to begin. Indeed, unless the language is to fall into complete artistic desuetude . . . it *must* be broken, for in the past fifteen years writing in English has touched bottom and survived what in my opinion will eventually be regarded as the lowest and most impoverished point in its history since 1870.[2]

John Barth is less tentative than Koch in his belief in a way out of this impasse, yet without ever denying that the prevailing sense of used-upness and attendant anxiety are, as he puts it, "cultural facts." He believes the ultimacy can result in a productive tension for writing in English: "Beckett has become virtually mute, musewise, having progressed from marvelously constructed English sentences through terser and terser French ones . . . and 'ultimately' to wordless mimes." But since language consists of both silence and sound, "silent figures aren't altogether ultimate . . . Nothingness is necessarily and inextricably the background against which Being et cetera;

for Beckett . . . to cease to create altogether would be fairly meaningful: his crowning work, his 'last word.' "

Barth's own proposed solution tends in the inverse direction of this approach to the limit of silence and involves, instead, an attempt to "rediscover validly the artifices of language and literature—such far-out notions as grammar, punctuation . . . even characterization! Even *plot!*" in a fashion as self-conscious as possible about the literary past.[3] His formulation of the famous, diminished final phrase in Samuel Beckett's *The Unnamable* would require a different, more Shandean emphasis, and thus a different punctuation: "I can't go on? I'll go on!!" It is significant, though, that whatever the particulars of the proposed way out of the present, his solution presupposes a shared understanding that a novelistic stasis and muteness has made itself fairly widely felt throughout the U.S. and Anglo-European literary scenes. Silence is one of the key terms in the debate about the possibility of continued literary innovation. The late sixties stages the drama of the struggle of Being to (re) emerge against a created backdrop of silence.

Susan Sontag, too, reflects in 1969 on "The Aesthetics of Silence," and her characterization of that specifically modern aesthetics is more ascetic, recasting "art," in this era, as a spiritual project. Her description implies that she is less certain than Barth of immediate answers to the difficult dilemmas this aesthetics poses for artistic consciousness.

> Whereas formerly the artist's good was mastery of and fulfillment in his art, now the highest good for the artist is to reach the point where those goals of excellence become insignificant to him, emotionally and ethically, and he is more satisfied by being silent than by finding a voice in art. Silence, in this sense, as termination, proposes a mood of ultimacy antithetical to the mood informing the self-conscious artist's traditional serious use of silence . . . as a zone of mediation, preparation for spiritual ripening, an ordeal that ends in gaining the right to speak.[4]

This right to speak, this mastery and fulfillment, it would seem, have already been gained, been tried and re-tried, taken for granted even, but to what avail? Fulfillment appears to have been succeeded by surfeit and then by counterfeit fiction. The uncomfortable feeling of verbal glut is not, in Sontag's formulation, simply the perennial complaint that "it's all been said before." It is rather the trope used to describe the collective verbal anxieties that vex a particular era, define it as an era.

But this movement toward ultimacy nonetheless marks, I would argue, the desire for a culmination that *will* result in some form of renewal, the illusion if not the fact of starting afresh. Writing as such never ceases, but here, the ambivalent attraction to silence gives silence the power to shape a guiding myth of contemporary U.S. culture and its fiction. Says Sontag:

> Silence and allied ideas (like emptiness, reduction, the "zero degree") are boundary notions with a very complex set of uses, leading terms of a particular spiritual and cultural rhetoric. To describe silence as a rhetorical term is, of course, not to condemn this rhetoric as fraudulent or in bad faith . . . the myths of silence and emptiness are about as nourishing and viable as might be devised in a . . . time in which "unwholesome" psychic states furnish the energies for most superior work in the arts. Yet one can't deny the pathos of these myths.[5]

Nor can one deny, it may now be added, the effect of the myth of silence upon the way that the body of experimental fiction being produced in the U.S. (both by U.S. writers and in English translation) during the sixties and seventies would come to be read and critically received, nor the myth's effect on the predispositions, yearnings, and sensibilities of the writers of that fiction.[6] Sontag's more general description expresses the cultural paradox, underlying experimental fiction, which came to a head in the late sixties: "The art of our time is noisy with appeals for silence. A coquettish, even cheerful nihilism. One recognizes the imperative of silence, but goes on speaking anyway. Discovering that one has nothing to say, one seeks a way to say *that*."[7] The desire expressed in the rhetoric of silence—partaken in not by all but by an influential "critical mass"—is for a literary energy to rush into the void from afar, allowing the continuation of speech, even after the possibilities of speaking seem to have been exhausted once and for all.

Right about the time that Barth's "The Literature of Exhaustion" was making its first appearance in print in *Atlantic Monthly* and Koch's "Premature Speculations" in *TriQuarterly*, a single novel by a Latin American author was published in Spanish, was ecstatically received, and quickly began to forge critical and cultural myths of its own, to such an extent that within a decade it had practically come to stand, by way of synecdoche, for all of Latin American literature. The novel, it almost goes without saying, is Gabriel García Márquez's *Cien años de soledad*—or, as it would soon and fondly come to be known among English-speaking readers, *One Hundred*

*Years of Solitude.* Many others in Latin America were writing too, some of them publishing, many of them not. But abdicating or by-passing, in favor of silence, that "ordeal that ends in gaining the right to speak," which Sontag says rightly belongs to a prior era of artistic endeavor, is exactly what Latin American fiction writers could not do and did not wish to do. Many were struggling through a repressive silencing of the social sphere as a whole, where the legal possibilities of speech became almost nil, at the very moment Sontag, Barth, and many of their U.S. and European contemporaries felt their own or-deal of silence to be located at the nether limit of verbal profusion.

Just as with the critical terms modernism and *modernismo,* whose conflation usually ends up effacing the concerns of the latter, there appears here a historical disjunction—not in the neo-colonialist sense of so-called emerging literatures, of playing literary catch-up, but rather in the sense of two sets of writers with different (albeit related) and differently formulated sets of historical concerns and thus a different relationship to the question of the aesthetics of si-lence and speech. Latin American fiction writing was by no stretch of the imagination an incipient practice in the sixties, but the guid-ing myths articulating those writers' collective malaise were ex-pressed in terms of recuperating a being and a voice that had been wrested away or forced into stagnation and silence. The single voice of military dictatorship had attempted, with fairly good success, to silence all others. The concerns of Latin American writers had va-lences somewhat other than the U.S.-European trope of a vacuum of aesthetic silence brought on by too many writers with too little to say.

It is in this context that the boom of Latin American fiction in English translation, which began in the sixties, and the specific form of reception—and often distortion—it has taken in the minds of U.S. writers and readers can be understood. An equally self-conscious and experimental but more vigorous, fertile, and "organic" Latin Amer-ican fiction rushed, by most accounts, into the sterile vacuum of impoverished U.S. writing. An infusion of the tropic staved off the entropic. My interest here is not to employ *boom* as a critical term for explicating the individual works of the authors normally grouped under that heading. Their writing, both individually and collec-tively, has already been described and anatomized at wearying length; discussion of them has dominated Latin American literary criticism for the past two decades. To continue to focus on this exact same group of writers is simply to reduplicate the prevailing notion that they are, finally, the be-all and end-all of Latin America's fictional endeavor. I attempt, instead, to offer a broader set of conclusions about the relationship between fiction, democracy, and military dictatorship than those same few questions and answers which have been invoked again and again in the name of "magical realism."

The excitement that greeted the seemingly sudden influx of Latin American fiction in the sixties and seventies makes itself felt in the often ecstatic accounts of that fiction by U.S. writers and critics. In fact, the first epigraph to Barth's "The Literature of Exhaustion" (the other one taken, significantly, from his own fiction) is culled from the *Labyrinths* of none other than Jorge Luis Borges: "The fact is that every writer *creates* his own precursors.[8] His work modifies our conception of the past, as it will modify the future." The implications here are clear: Barth, in a self-consciously Adamic authorial act of self-(re)creation, will, by arbitrary and revisionist force of will, nationalize the full-blown Borges—who is, however, a relative newcomer to U.S. literary consciousness at large—into the literary tradition of Barth's legitimate precursors. This gesture reconfigures the past, situating contemporary U.S. experimental fiction within a fresh tradition that suddenly seems to offer itself for purposes of discovery and reinvention. The "tradition" is both used-up and new and as such allows Barth to "rediscover validly the artifices of language and literature."

He comments with unabashed optimism on Borges' "Pierre Menard, Author of the Quixote," a story about a turn-of-the-century scholar who, "by an astounding effort of imagination, produces—not *copies* or *imitates*, mind, but *composes*—several chapters of Cervantes' novel."

> The important thing to observe is that Borges *doesn't* attribute the *Quixote* to himself, much less re-compose it like Pierre Menard; instead, he writes a remarkable and original work of literature, the implicit theme of which is the difficulty, perhaps the unnecessity, of writing original works of literature . . . he confronts an intellectual dead end and employs it against itself to accomplish new human work.[9]

"Pierre Menard," first published in 1939, precipitously takes on a renewed and powerful currency in the context of the U.S. cultural rhetoric of the late sixties, partly because of its recently and retroactively becoming part of the incipient translation boom and partly because its former lack of currency among English-speaking readers now makes it available as one ahistoricized, "fresh" solution to the increasingly thorny and frustrating problem of originality. The bizarre inappropriateness of Barth's Pollyannaish sanguinity about

Borges' rather despairing parable of intellectual and political dead-ends in another place and time becomes apparent when "Pierre Menard" is read in its 1930s Argentine historical context, as I undertake to do in the final chapter.

But it is for *One Hundred Years of Solitude* that Barth reserves the honor, a dozen years later, in his 1980 follow-up *Atlantic* essay, "The Literature of Replenishment," of standing as the "exemplary postmodernist" novel, the contemporary successor to *Finnegans Wake*. His praise of the novel is as gushy and unqualified as a back-cover blurb. It is "as impressive a novel as has been written so far in the second half of our century, and one of the splendid specimens of that splendid genre from any century," a "synthesis of straightforwardness and artifice, realism and magic and myth, political passion and nonpolitical artistry, characterization and caricature, humor and terror. . . . Praise be to the Spanish language and imagination!"[10]

The emergence of this imagination marks the "discovery" of a new literary continent, and García Márquez's novel, which in this version of its success is unrestrained by the effeteness of North America's exhausted possibility, can "magically" recover the conventions and artifices of the past, while at the same time cross-fertilizing U.S. writing with its organic originality. The attribution of organic properties to a text seems to reduplicate uncritically one of the very categories that experimental fiction on both continents has been intent on calling into question. But because of the cultural myth being written around *One Hundred Years of Solitude* and the relative silence implied to have preceded it, it apparently can speak freely in a way that U.S. fiction can't.

This kind of cultural mythologizing, however enthusiastic, can't help but efface and restrict the variety and historical complexity of the literature being embraced, not to mention oversimplifying the question of the aesthetics of silence and the recovery of the word, the more so when the myth relies, as I'll shortly demonstrate, on an appeal to exoticism. On reading García Márquez's novel, Barth says—perhaps too readily—"the question whether my program for postmodernism is achievable goes happily out the window, like one of García Márquez's characters on flying carpets."[11] Flying carpets! Such recommendations as Barth's are, of course, largely the result of personal enthusiasms, pleasant rhetorical excesses, but it is prudent to take heed of Tzvetan Todorov's caution about New World (or here, New Word) otherness, in *The Conquest of America*: "Even if the discovery of the other must be assumed by each individual and eternally recommenced, it also has a history, forms that are socially and culturally determined"[12]—a caveat especially applicable when the personal enthusiasms are cast as reflections about the state and future of the novel-at-large.

Despite the massive readership of this singular novel (over twelve million copies in thirty languages as of March 1983),[13] John Barth's elaborate praise of *One Hundred Years of Solitude,* his account of the New Word and the direction it advocates for post-sixties fiction, might still plausibly be restricted to a personal aesthetic rather than a general cultural aspiration if it didn't find its echo so precisely in other quarters. Larry McCaffery (who has written widely on, among others, William Gass, Donald Barthelme, and Robert Coover) clearly gives *One Hundred Years of Solitude* the premier place in his introduction to the compendious *Postmodern Fiction: A Bio-Bibliographical Guide* (1986), which runs the international gamut from Walter Abish and Kathy Acker to sci-fi writer Roger Zelazny:

> If a single work may be said to have provided a model for the
> direction of postmodern fiction of the 1970s and 1980s, it is
> probably García Márquez's *One Hundred Years of Solitude,* a
> work that admirably and brilliantly combines experimental
> impulses with a powerful sense of political and social reality.
> Indeed, [García] Márquez's masterpiece perfectly embodies a ten-
> dency found in much of the best recent fiction—that is, it uses
> experimental strategies to discover new methods of reconnecting
> with the world outside the page, outside of language. In many
> ways, *One Hundred Years of Solitude* is clearly a nonrealistic
> novel, with its magical, surreal landscape, its dense, reflexive
> surface, its metafictional emphasis on the nature of language . . .
> Yet for all its experimentalism, *One Hundred Years of Solitude*
> is a highly readable, coherent story, peopled with dozens of
> memorable characters.[14]

The desire expressed, here somewhat nostalgically, is for a means by which experimental fiction can recuperate such formerly suspect concepts as an objective reality outside of language, unitary ego ("memorable characters"), seamless narrative, without coming into conflict with the demands of experimentation. These wished-for components are pretty much of a piece with the ones that Alain Robbe-Grillet, already in 1957, was lambasting as "Several Obsolete Notions"—character, atmosphere, form and content as separable entities, message, narrative ability, "true" novelists.[15] García Márquez's novel, apparently untroubled by these conflictual demands between realist and experimental conventions, effortlessly achieves the wished-for synthesis. *One Hundred Years of Solitude,* the New Word, the "single work," looms large as a continent, invigorating all post-1960s fictional innovation. McCaffery, much in the vein of Barth, refers to the synthesis as an "organic form of experimentalism." This organic form is especially appealing because "authors today are less interested in innovation per se than they were ten or fifteen years ago—especially innovation in the direction of reflexive, nonreferential works."[16]

The declining authorial interest in more unrelenting self-reflexivity and non-referentiality favors a fiction able to synthesize previous methods without slavishly reproducing them. "Organic experimentalism" is called upon to situate contemporary fiction in relation to some reviving tradition without naively succumbing to its dictates. This wish can plausibly be read as at least symptomatic of a more general sense of cultural failure. The apparent frustration with fictional innovation per se may lend some weight to Andreas Huyssen's "hypothesis that postmodernism always has been in search of tradition while pretending to innovation." He views this renewed search, whose quickening he locates at the end of the 1960s, as issuing out of "the fragmentation and the decline of the avant-garde as a genuinely critical and adversary culture," and even speaks, in a phrase that echoes Barth's, of "the exhaustion of the tradition of the avantgarde." According to him, "The 1970s search for roots, for history and traditions, was an inevitable and in many ways productive off-shoot of this [Western, industrial, cultural and political identity] crisis." This "search for the past (often for an alternative past) . . . in many of its more radical manifestations, questions the fundamental orientation of Western societies toward future growth and toward unlimited progress."[17] In making this analysis, Huyssen assumes a strong continuity between that literature which succeeds the crisis of exhausted possibility and that which precedes it. But like Sontag, he is interested in exploring hypothetical boundary notions—in his case, a "great divide." He is careful to distinguish a careful reappraisal of the type he describes from a "simpleminded rearguard assertion of traditional values."

Importance should indeed be attached to the form such a search takes, to prevent the renewal of U.S. fiction from becoming an enterprise that merely recapitulates, in various guises—some contented, some rebellious—that essentially realist story of future growth and unlimited progress, with all its accompanying notions about the coherent categorical subject living out that story. Even the writerly obsession with establishing a linear, paternal genealogy raises prickly doubts about the viability of embracing an alternative tradition. Just as troublesome is the potential relationship to history of such a nostalgic version of replenishment. Such leading terms of cultural rhetoric as silence can have, as Susan Sontag has suggested, a very complex set of uses—among them, and not least, that of filtering out the bothersome static of historical nuance.

It should be remembered that the boom took place on the heels of another momentous event that brought the two Americas, and many of their artists and intellectuals, face to face: the Cuban Revolution. The effects of the Cuban Revolution came to be felt in various ways—most concretely, its success inspired guerrilla movements throughout Latin America, including Uruguay's Tupamaros and Argentina's Montoneros, who became convinced that the overthrow of oppressive government by guerrilla warfare was possible, viable, and even imminent. The two above-mentioned guerrilla groups, acutely conscious of the political particulars of their own respective situations, made clear their rejection of many of the specific tactics of the Cuban Revolution, insisting on autochthonous strategies more suitable to the urban terrain on which their battles would have to be fought. But the revolution in Cuba did provide a powerful and explicit inspirational example, suggesting that guerrillas in each country, while expressing solidarity for the general ideal of communist or socialist revolution, could make the ideal of self-determination come to pass according to their local exigencies.

The guerrilla insurgency in Cuba inspired others as well who possessed a more archetypal cast of mind. Most of the boom novelists have written at least one novel of epic sweep chronicling the collapse of a patriarchal tyrant into the ruins of his megalomania, and some of the boom novelists, Gabriel García Márquez and Julio Cortázar in particular, shared the buoyancy following the Cuban Revolution, openly expressing sympathy for its aims. In the United States, not only student radicals, but a number of left-oriented artists and intellectuals likewise looked to the Cuban Revolution—and to one of its presumed progeny, the Latin American "new novel"—as sources of political energy in a generalized struggle for a just society.

Even those in the U.S. who positively opposed, or remained indifferent to, the example of Cuba were not exempt from the growing general fascination toward the newfound dark continent which lay past the Caribbean gateway, somewhere to the south. In his famous essay "Caliban," Roberto Fernández Retamar says of the new Latin American novel that "its circulation beyond our borders is in large part owing to the worldwide attention our continent has enjoyed since the triumph of the Cuban Revolution in 1959."[18] For the first time, Latin America began to be perceived on a worldwide scale as a force to be reckoned with, both politically and aesthetically.

Fernández Retamar's strategic claiming of Caliban as Latin America's historically appropriate symbol illuminates some of the causes and effects of the creation, across the U.S. and European ideological spectrum, of the exotic myth of the New Word during the 1960s. Decrying the nature of the esteem which replaced former obliviousness toward the region, he says that

> the notion of [Latin America as] an Edenic creature comprehends, in more contemporary terms, a working hypothesis for the bourgeois left, and, as such, offers an ideal model of the perfect society free from the constrictions of that . . . world against which the bourgeoisie is in fact struggling. Generally speaking, the utopic vision throws upon these lands projects for political reforms unrealized in the countries of origin. In this sense its line of development is far from extinguished. Indeed, it [also] meets with certain perpetrators . . . in the numerous advisers who unflaggingly propose to countries emerging from colonialism magic formulas from the metropolis to solve the grave problems colonialism has left us and which, of course, they have not yet resolved in their own countries. It goes without saying that these proponents of "There is no such place" are irritated by the insolent fact that the place *does* exist and, quite naturally, has all the virtues and defects not of a project but of genuine reality.[19]

The projection, by U.S. and European artists and ideologues of various stripes, of their own irresolvable social dissatisfactions onto the "Edenic" sphere of Latin America does ignore crucial events subsequent to 1959, such as the sharp disagreements among the denominated boom writers about the significance of the Cuban Revolution. Carlos Fuentes and Mario Vargas Llosa exhibited ambivalence toward its example as early as 1961, and Vargas Llosa began to criticize all forms of left-oriented politics with growing vehemence. In fact, one of his key strategies in his 1990 campaign for the presidency of Peru was categorical rejection of left politics, in favor of an authoritarian "free market" economy. Even those Latin American intellectuals who continued to identify with Cuba could not fail to remark the crushing defeats of one promising guerrilla force and socialist project after another throughout Latin America during the sixties and seventies (Chile, Peru, Argentina, Uruguay, the Dominican Republic) and the fierce consolidation of military dictatorships throughout the hemisphere.

The particular example of Uruguay's Tupamaros (Movimiento de

Liberación Nacional, MLN) proves instructive, since their passionate and determined militancy precedes the era of generally more muted political expectations that I will give most of my attention to in the chapters that follow. The Tupamaro movement, initiated in 1962, only three years after Castro's victory in Cuba (and one year after his declaration of adherence to Marxist-Leninist principles), had great, and seemingly somewhat justified, faith in its armed militants' ability to "generate revolutionary consciousness" by providing Uruguayan workers with an exemplary vanguard of direct action. The high, long-stable level of unionization among laborers and state employees, and the intensity of economic and political crisis in Uruguay, made it seem feasible to the MLN guerrillas to build an alliance with the unions, then to use strikes to paralyze the state badly enough that they could conduct a successful urban guerrilla war against the armed forces, most of whom were concentrated in Montevideo, the country's capital.

The movement gathered enough force and weaponry, sank far enough into public consciousness, and staged enough sporadic assaults that by 1969 it publicly and succinctly declared, in a clandestine interview published in an Uruguayan magazine, "We're indestructible." As late as 1970, with the conditions for a "justifiable" coup fairly accomplished by the military and the dissolution of virtually all representative institutions of government already in process, the Tupamaros still could confidently and plausibly declare that

> Montevideo is a city sufficiently large and polarized by social struggles to give protection and shelter to a vast contingent of active guerrilla fighters. The conditions for urban warfare are much better here than other revolutionary movements have had. . . . Any organization that expects to last through an urban struggle has to have built patiently the material bases and the wide movement of support and shelter necessary for an armed contingent to operate or subsist in the city.[20]

Though from the perspective of the present, their claims appear exaggerated and overconfident, from a militant perspective in the late 1960s, the Tupamaros could not be dismissed out of hand as boastful, for even more than Castro, they seemed to have accomplished to a visible degree the "patient building" and "material bases" to make at least thinkable a struggle like the one they envisioned. But even by 1969, some of the most experienced MLN leadership appeared uncertain about its prospects for success and its direction and began to explore other avenues of voicing political dissent. Despite their trenchant opposition to the "anti-revolutionary reformism" of communist and socialist parties in Uruguay, the Tupamaros agreed to participate in a united left front in the 1970 electoral campaign. The fraud-ridden elections resulted in the presidency of the ultra-conservative Bordaberry, who would prove so instrumental in overseeing and legitimating, in the course of three devastating years, the absolute and unconditional surrender of civilian government and all its prerogatives to the military.

Disillusioned, the Tupamaros took up arms again, but the "historical conditions" appeared by then to have deteriorated beyond immediate revolutionary repair. In a brief, full-scale urban struggle, the Tupamaros effectively were overpowered by military force. By 1972, with most of their main leaders imprisoned or dead, they were reduced to conducting secret negotiations with "progressive" elements within the armed forces, trying to eke out promises of social reforms from the governmental heirs apparent, in exchange for total surrender. Even these negotiations were abruptly halted by the military officers involved, without any explanation being given, and the MLN extracted absolutely nothing in exchange for its forced capitulation.

Subsequent to the coup, nine of the remaining MLN militants were literally buried alive. In a document of "self-criticism" issued two months after the dictatorial coup, the veteran leadership of the Tupamaros critiques itself as having failed after 1968 to build the necessary popular and political support, due to its overemphasis on the armed aspect of its struggle and due to its overly optimistic faith in the logic of vanguardism. Also, the sixty years preceding the MLN's movement, given a tradition in Uruguay of democratic republicanism with periods of (relative) prosperity and openness, ironically provided all the right precedents for the military dictatorship, in part by adopting the rhetoric and some of the institutions of "progressive" democracy, to neutralize militant opposition.[21]

The brief flickering of buoyancy on the part of guerrillas and intellectuals during the sixties, though not extinguished utterly, gave way to a very different and much more cautious temperament among Latin American writers and dissenters, as revolutionary movements were squelched and even the much more modest social initiatives of liberal democratic governments disintegrated. Those in the U.S. who insisted on perpetuating the New Word myth—whether political radicals, utopian aesthetes, or reform-minded liberal capitalists eager for hemispheric "progress"—had to remain largely oblivious to "insolent facts" such as these in order to maintain their utopic visons of Caliban intact.

The distinct potential arises, in the New Word cycle of fiction-making, cultural mythologizing, and critical reception, to generate a thin, unreflexive account of the historical processes that have been underway since the 1960s, an account which at its most extreme could become a kind of comfortable and comforting reader's digest, a heterogeneity pared down to its most seamless and undemanding form. Novelist and philosopher William Gass, in his acerbic late-sixties reflection, in *The Nation*, on "The Medium of Fiction" offers a powerful indictment of this relatively "transparent" type of critical reception:

> For most people, fiction is history; fiction is history without tables, graphs, dates, imports, edicts, evidence, laws; history without hiatus—intelligible, simple, smooth. Fiction is sociology freed of statistics, politics with no real party in the opposition; it's a world where play money buys you cardboard squares of colored country; a world where everyone is obediently psycho-logical, economic, ethnic, geographical—framed in a keyhole and always nude, each figure fashioned from the latest thing in cello-see-through, so we may observe our hero's guts, too, if we choose . . . For truth without effort, thought without rigor, feel-ing without form, existence without commitment, what will you give? for a wind-up world, a toy life?[22]

The penchant for utopian projection was exacerbated by the hos-tility in the U.S. toward the more exacting intellectual demands raised by experimental fiction as an aesthetic and historical practice within our own borders. This anti-intellectual (and still widespread) hostility is epitomized, a decade later, in John Gardner's normative, widely read and discussed *On Moral Fiction* (1978). Gardner's dia-tribe stages a direct attack on artifice, metafiction, and self-con-sciousness in favor of what is essentially a wholesale return to con-ventional, and mythic, realism.[23] But Gardner and Co. weren't the only ones to feel those yearnings, since many of the U.S. advocates of experimental fiction I have alluded to already remained at best ambivalent about their own allegiance to innovation, preferring to look elsewhere for solutions.

Mass-media critics and reviewers have proven just as diligent in homogenizing and synchronizing the innovations and subtleties of boom writing, and as adept at representing it in its mythic-realist dimension, as they have been eager to give it coverage. A review from *Time* in 1983 (the year after García Márquez won the Nobel prize) bears the catchy title "Where the Fiction is *Fantástica:*

Gabriel García Márquez spearheads Latin American writing." It begins by chastising North Americans because they "neither know nor care to know too much about Latin America, unless, of course, someone shouts 'The Russians are coming!' " And, promisingly, it offers the caveat that the denomination *El boom* is not quite right, because "the term suggested the sudden discovery of Latin American talent rather than its slow growth." It briefly cites other, already more familiar names of poets such as Neruda, Mistral, Vallejo, and Paz, along with more recently well-known names such as fiction writers Donoso, Fuentes, Vargas Llosa, Cabrera Infante, and previous Nobel winner Miguel Angel Asturias, to give a sense of precedents and diversity. But, despite his good intentions, the reviewer soon gets down to the business of framing the continent's writing as a whole in terms of its gargantuan "spearhead," García Márquez. "*One Hundred Years of Solitude* struck with incalculable force . . . the novel was hailed as an epic and a metaphor for the outsize realities of Latin America. . . . civil wars and banana fevers . . . Despite the heavy overtones, *One Hundred Years of Solitude* was great fun to read."[24] While the novel does concern itself "heavily" with a kind of mythic tropicality, what is significant here is the way in which the reviewer presents this Nobel-worthy epic as truly encompassing and expressing the manifold artistic aspirations and historical realities of an entire continent. It is noteworthy too how this work of supposedly magical, mythical enchantment is casually reinscribed within the less "heavy," more pedestrian (and more powerfully operative) mythical topos of the Latin American exotic: "civil wars and banana fevers." The title of the article implies that *all* contemporary Latin American fiction is steeped in the exotic, the fantastic, that it is naturally and necessarily a representation of actual "outsize realities" beyond the ken of Anglo readers.

In an article for *Publisher's Weekly* celebrating García Márquez et alii and the bestowal of the Nobel prize on "the personification of *El boom*," Sarah Crichton remarks on the cover design of the original Avon paperpack edition of *One Hundred Years of Solitude*, which "found its way into hundreds of thousands of knapsacks in the 1970's"—"a couple embracing in the jungle." In fact, most of the covers of the Avon Latin American translation series, and those of many others, have contained features which evoke Edenic, mythic tropicalism in one way or another. The effect of such connotative packaging on the perceptions of readers and reviewers is apparent in Crichton's own review. She makes the flat assertion that "nearly every Latin American author uses the techniques of magical realism, but each, of course, has his or her own way of expressing it" and describes García Márquez's writing style as reality tempered with "folkloric lushness." As if this tourist's-eye view of Latin America weren't reductive enough, she goes on to make a statement which reveals startling geopolitical assumptions. "The political and social upheaval of Latin America may wreak havoc on lives, but it is very good for literature. The only major country south of the Rio Grande not to have produced an important writer is Venezuela—the only stable democracy on the subcontinent."[25] This frightening logic implies that a few good coups might be advisable to bring Venezuela into the fold of the literary renascence.

García Márquez, though he would no doubt be taken aback by a statement such as the latter, has himself—in his Nobel acceptance speech and in an essay translated and reprinted in a 1985 issue of *Harper's*—helped to foster notions about the "outsize realities" which Latin America is said by reviewers and critics to possess. The essay, originally printed in a Mexican newspaper and entitled "Fantasy and Artistic Creation in Latin America"—but retitled by the editors of *Harper's* "Latin America's Impossible Reality"—begins by making a distinction between *fantasy* and *imagination*. In García Márquez's definitional scheme, "fantasy has nothing to do with the reality of the world we live in: it is a purely fantastic invention, an inspiration, and certainly ill-advised in the arts." Imagination, his preferred category, "is the particular faculty artists possess that enables them to create a new reality from the one they live in." The peculiar problem faced by Latin America's artists, he says—in a formulation that has by now been repeated so often by critics and novelists in the U.S. that it has become the emblematic phrase of Latin literature—is that "in Latin America and the Caribbean, artists have had to invent very little. In fact, their problem has been just the opposite: making their reality credible. It's been this way since our historical beginnings."[26] He goes on to regale the Anglo reader with tales and details which reinforce the reader's sense of a reality which, by its very fecund, organic, prodigious nature, represents an El Dorado for the imagination (rather than a mere Ferlinghettian Coney Island), lying in wait with riches beyond belief.

García Márquez is fairly aware of the implications, and possibly some of the ironies, of the image he is constructing. He begins historically, in fact, with Columbus' voyage to America and with examples of the calculated, flagrantly exotic representations that Columbus made of it to royalty back in Europe for purposes of financing further expeditions. García Márquez also mentions "gullibility on the part of the conquistadors," partly due to "the literary delirium surrounding the novels of knighthood." But then he goes on to help encourage a contemporary literary delirium of his own, with direct implications for experimental fiction—the delirium of the New Word. "To encompass completely the breadth of our reality we would have to make up a system of new words. There are endless examples proving this need." They include a Dutch colonial explorer's account of traveling, in the Amazon, "through an area where speaking out loud would set off downpours"; a Caribbean village whose inhabitants were all buried under lava except for a sole prisoner, "protected by the indestructible cell that had been built to prevent his escape."[27] The reader is given, ultimately, to understand that however much Columbus might have exaggerated the specifics of this place of "primitive myths and magical conceptions," there really did exist, then as now, actualities that could easily rival, and even surpass, Columbus' wildest concoctions. This "Believe It or Not" quality, furthermore, is not restricted to odd rarities but makes up the fabric of everyday life.

García Márquez makes it very clear that these exotic everyday phenomena are not only exceedingly difficult for Latin Americans to articulate but are, in his estimation, by their very prolific nature almost beyond the imaginative grasp of Europeans (and by implication, of North Americans).

> When we write the word *storm*, Europeans think of lighning and thunder, but it's not easy for them to conceive of the phenomenon we mean to represent. The same thing happens with the word *rain*. In the mountains of the Andes, according to a description by the Frenchman Javier Marimier, there are torrential rains that can last for five months. "Those who haven't seen these storms," he writes, "can't conceive of the violence with which they develop. For hours on end, bolts of lightning quickly follow one another like a waterfall of blood, and the atmosphere quakes beneath the continuous claps of thunder, whose crashes echo in the vastness of mountains." The description is hardly a masterpiece, but it would have been enough to make the least credulous European shudder with horror.[28]

The connection García Márquez fails to make, though he mentions the lineaments of it quite prominently in this description, is that the unbelievable "phenomena" he feels to be beyond the imaginative grasp of Europeans have been lifted by him directly *from* the descriptive accounts of those same Europeans. There are no natural phenomena here. There are only his representations of European representations, replete with the standard topoi of frightening primitive fecundity, savage violence, waterfalls of blood. One can remark of such colonializing accounts in general what Todorov asserts about Columbus—that his " 'knowledge' is obviously a decision made in advance," and that "his vision in this respect is facilitated by his capacity to see things as it suits him." Despite his partial self-consciousness, García Márquez nonetheless participates in the elaboration of a contemporary cultural myth, taken up by U.S. writers and critics, whose rhetoric derives in part from the old narrative of colonialist expansion and assimilation. And even though this exoticist dimension of the largely cosmopolitan fiction boom is certainly not a function of indigenous ethnicity, Todorov's gloss on Columbus is at least rhetorically suggestive if the phrase *Latin American fiction* is substituted for the phrase *the Indians* in the following remark: "This image can be arrived at," says Todorov, "only at the price of the suppression of every feature of the Indians that contradicts it— a suppression in the discourse concerning them."[29]

But what of the power of "imagination" as conceived by García Márquez and its transformative role in the U.S. cultural debate about the literature of replenishment? By linking the New Word myth to its more patently economic dimension, as I mean to do in the remainder of this chapter, one can see how, discursively, such a myth might conform uncritically to the expansionist narrative of unlimited Western progress and to the contours of U.S. capitalist consumer culture. For, as Todorov suggests, "spiritual expansion, as we now know, is indissolubly linked to material conquest."[30] The boom, as a wildly successful publishing phenomenon of selected imported writing, becomes a U.S. spoil of world culture, a fact with drastic consequences for the power of Latin American fiction in its aggregate to represent otherness with more than a bare modicum of success.

The title page of García Márquez's *Harper's* essay is preceded on the facing page—whether by conscious editorial fiat or simply by one of those illuminating metonymic coincidences—by an advertisement entitled, oddly enough, "The Quality of Imagination." The ad, sponsored by United Technologies, consists wholly of "excerpts from a speech given by Harry J. Gray, chairman and chief executive officer of United Technologies." It functions, in effect, as both an advertisement and an encapsulated counter-essay on "imagination." The essay begins on a note of concern. "American business is facing stiff competition from the rest of the world. We read that one reason other countries have had success is that they have adopted American technology. That's true. But it's not the only reason. I believe it's also because they have adopted American [i.e., U.S.] virtues." Gray goes on to list those virtues—dedication to learning, hard work, patriotism, helping others, perseverance, leadership, respect for the individual—all of which, he says, have recently and falsely been copied from our own long tradition by others. Still, despite this virtual counterfeit and theft of "our" national virtues, "there is one American virtue that other people can never fully adopt. It is our imagination."

This counter-definition, in its literal proximity to García Márquez's own attempt to fashion a serviceable definition of imagination, fairly begs to be taken as one of the complex sets of uses to which the leading terms of the general cultural rhetoric of replenishment can be put. Gray, as much as García Márquez, Barth, Sontag, and the various other rhetoricians of experimental fiction, is eager to give his interpretive spin not only to "imagination" but even to the concept of experimentation: "We live in an open society. Throughout our history we have always shown a willingness to entertain new ideas, a tolerance for experimentation, an eagerness to try something different." Though availing himself wholly of the literally shopworn phrases of xenophobic, nationalist, commonsense, individual-based, free-enterprise, positivist capitalism, Gray makes very clear that he is tolerant and open to, and even passionately advocates, experimentation as such. He appears, in fact, much less ambivalent about it than his more literary counterparts. Endless experimentation, it seems, can be endlessly "used" or assimilated by capitalist consumer society and even contributes to the proliferation of that society.

The specific rationale behind Gray's unflinching advocacy becomes apparent in the anaphora with which he rhetorically closes his pitch:

> Our capacity for imagination has led us to expand the American frontiers across the continent.
> Our capacity for imagination has brought about technological achievements which have changed our lives dramatically, irreversibly, for the better.
> Our capacity for imagination has given America its competitive edge.[31]

In this version, imagination is a utilitarian concept with little potential for representing otherness in its manifold nuance and historical fullness. It is, rather, imbued with the rhetoric of expansionism—colonial exploration, Manifest Destiny, the Monroe Doctrine. History only goes one way, inexorably and "irreversibly" advancing. This encapsulated essay is a ringing example of Gass' "history without hiatus—intelligible, simple, smooth." There exists only one imagination—our national one, whose destiny is to always already encompass all imaginations into a United imagination. Its formulations are decidedly not part of that search for an alternative tradition, as posited by Huyssen, attempting to question the fundamental orientation of Western societies toward future growth and unlimited progress. Its assumptions are meliorist, part of the story of progress which, in the Americas, begins with Columbus. The name United Technologies itself sounds like a bad joke, something lifted out of a vicious and reductive satire of capitalism by a Latin American writer, perhaps García Márquez himself in a weaker moment. It is, unfortunately, no joke. Gray's evocation of imagination as that which has led "us" to expand the American frontiers across the continent (and, it is implied, the world) demands, in Todorov's words, "spiritual expansion . . . indissolubly linked to material conquest." The new word is *imagination,* and the story of United Technologies is that of the conquest of the New Word.

This explication of the myth in its more economic aspect has a broader context of its own. The critical process of enshrining García Márquez, Mario Vargas Llosa, Carlos Fuentes, Julio Cortázar—generally acknowledged as the "big four" of the Latin American boom—along with the recuperated Borges, a kind of fifth horseman, and a handful of other (male) Latin American writers as international literary icons, owes its economic beginnings, as Angel Rama (among many others) points out, to the dissemination of their novels by publishing houses throughout Latin America and the world. While arguing against the often acid interpretations of the boom that wish to reduce it purely and simply to a cooked-up commercial enterprise, Rama nonetheless gives some attention to that important and undeniable aspect of it. The coinage, he says,

> has its origins in the terminology of modern North American marketing, designating a sudden jump in sales of a particular product in consumer societies. It postulates the prior existence of such societies, which began to be noticeable in the post-war era in the most developed enclaves of Latin America, where a boom had already occurred in toilet articles and would soon follow in calculators and household appliances. The surprise was its application to a product (books) which . . . was on the margin of such processes.[32]

This etymology suggests with respect to Latin America's literary culture in the 1960s what has already been endlessly documented about its material culture—that it is beginning to be incorporated intensely into the capitalist consumer world marketplace. The inevitable historical distortions resulting from this process are described by Rama as "the reductionism which came to bear on the rich literary flourishing of the continent, and the progressive incorporation of publicity techniques, and the merchandising which the business infrastructure was led to when the traditional editions of three thousand copies were substituted by massive editions." This impact, significant enough within the Hispanic continent, was greater still within the international marketplace, where "the attention given to translations in the United States, France, Italy, and finally in West Germany . . . contributed to a synchronic flattening out of the history of Latin American narrative."[33]

The newfound enthusiasm on the part of U.S. and European publishing enterprises could, because of the self-imposed structural constraints of those large, commercial houses, do little more than create a handful of privileged successes, mega-authors who were capable of sustaining, as professional writers, the prolific pace of literary production demanded after the success of their current hits had diminished and their previous works had been published retroactively in translation. A sufficient monetary return on this stable of authors also required their conversion into international celebrities, whose acquiescence in mass-media interviews and other forms of massive publicity would help assure the sale of the equally massive editions. Most of these authors, especially Mario Vargas Llosa, Carlos Fuentes, and Gabriel García Márquez, proved more than willing to assume the role of celebrity, allowing the shift to mega-authorship to take place with maximum efficiency and even more quickly than it might have otherwise. At the same time, one of the upshots of celebrity participation is that this type of publicity medium takes from the novelist's public remarks "elements that serve its own purposes, fragmentary elements out of which it constructs a different discourse, adequate to its own ends." Rama points out that the Latin American novelist's "recently accomplished professional autonomy, so coveted or envied in remote lands, implies a visible restriction of his liberty and an integration into the mechanisms whose wheels may easily crush him."[34] This commercial publishing logic follows the shift from an elite literary market of smaller editions to a mass one of large editions of fewer works. Multinational publishers, as a rule, says Rama,

> attend exclusively to economic profit, and if they have incorporated into their catalogs practically all the saleable works of the boom authors, they've stopped paying attention to new inventions . . . not because of anticultural perversity, but

because of the imposition of a massive system which permits them to handle only books with a predictably high sales margin.[35]

Alastair Reid, linking the El Dorado trope more directly to the actual economy of publishing, says in a review of the boom writers that "their emerging novels caused publishers in this country to look to the Andes with the narrowed eyes of prospectors." Publishers, he believes, don't "appear to go to much trouble to assemble lists of works in other languages which deserve to be translated. As a result, the whole business of translation remains something of a lottery, and the choice of Latin American works has been characteristically haphazard . . . The search for stars has obscured the firmament."[36]

The remedy to such haphazard neglect is not the mere addition to publishing lists of a few extra, equally "deserving stars" but rather an inquiry into a U.S. society so celebrity-struck that it insists on giving a vast array of history and culture, whatever its sources, the synchronic status of "event," and into that society's relationship to the continent that has long provided the U.S. with much of the promising "material" demanded by its incessant consumerism. Alastair Reid's wry trope of publishers as mineral prospectors becomes chilling rather than merely witty when one considers the actual history of the material relationship between the two continents. That relationship, in many respects as dark and crude as petroleum springing from the drilled ground, is outlined in Eduardo Galeano's biting book of political economy, *Open Veins of Latin America*. Half of U.S. investments there, Galeano says, "are dedicated to the extraction of petroleum, and to exploiting mineral riches." And he cites a remark by the U.S. president of the International Council of the Chamber of Commerce, that "our need for raw materials continually grows as our population expands and the standard of living rises. At the same time, our domestic resources are running out."[37] Scarcity at home means prospecting abroad.

In light of Rama's economic analysis of the boom—a term which is, after all, as he points out, derived directly from marketing—the analogy between the processing of Latin American minerals and that of Latin American authors does not seem especially strained or fanciful. In "After the Boom," Robert G. Mead alludes to the fact that many Latin American intellectuals "saw the boom as another manifestation of the dependency theory."[38] For despite the genteel, artistic, quasi-philanthropic veneer trade publishing has managed to accrue over the years—as though profit-making were only of secondary importance to its aims—international publishing at present fundamentally differs little from any other international capitalist venture. The world, in its manifold nationality, ethnicity, and variety of languages, represents for it different "markets," which offer certain supplies, depending on their location, and make different sorts of consumer demands and thus require different strategies—"target marketing."

Galeano describes how one of the "fathers" of space technology, shortly after the moon-landing, waxed prophetic in a press conference about other cosmic possiblities just on the horizon. He proposed the installation of a space station, claiming with enthusiasm that "from this observation platform, we'll be able to examine all the riches on Earth: unknown oil wells, zinc and copper mines . . ." Large publishing concerns, though their product is slightly different, partake of this worldview. A 1981 *Publisher's Weekly* article entitled "Daisy Goes Latin" offers a suggestive parallel to the Latin American boom in its description of the status of writers and audiences as interchangeable commodities and targeted markets, in a consumer logic of successive "booms." The article's sub-heading is telling: "The Krantz novel in Spanish translation is the first of a series of paperbacks with which Bantam hopes to penetrate the huge Hispanic market in the U.S."[39] As drill bits penetrate the ground, so does Bantam penetrate the Hispanic market.

This article, in its enthusiastic, rosy description of Bantam's strategy for mass-marketing two of the U.S.'s acknowledged "pulp" novelists (Judith Krantz and Louis L'Amour) to U.S. Hispanics, outlines a commercial strategy which demonstrates only minor variations in the earlier marketing, during the seventies, of the ultra-erudite writings of the Latin American boom authors (due to the different "target" audience), but which otherwise sounds depressingly similar.

> By the late seventies, the market had changed. Sales showed signs of peaking. The era of explosive paperback growth appeared to be ending. If it were to continue, new readers and new markets would have to be found. So why not aim for Hispanic communities that offered both, especially given vocal sales enthusiasm? The question was how to best tap their resources.[40]

The specifics of the product involved matter little to the publisher in aesthetic, historical, or political terms. After the fashion of United Technologies, what is of greatest importance here is that unlimited growth be sustained, that, even in the absence of any intrinsic need for expansion, "new readers and new markets" be found for

a particular consumer item. The slowdown in the growth of the paperback trade is, of course, unacceptable, since expansion is taken
for granted as an absolute value. The U.S. Hispanic market, like the
petroleum-rich South American Hispanic soil, is a "resource" to be
"tapped."

Having established a priori the need for growth and having identified the potential area in which this growth might occur, the publishers turned to defining the particulars of the product in question.
The problem, as they saw it, was that "the market was culturally
diversified." But, like all the most successful entrepreneurs, they
found a "creative" solution to this dilemma. The head of Bantam's
international division explains that "Bantam opted for an international blockbuster as the spearhead book. Judith Krantz's *Princess
Daisy* seemed like a natural, a novel full of romance and high living
on an international scale. . . . It was the strongest candidate, if we
wanted a book that could move rapidly through the existing distribution system." If the word "spearhead" sounds familiar, it's because the *Time* reviewer uses the identical term to describe García
Márquez and "his" boom's impact on his American readership. Bantam's publicity director, Stuart Applebaum, adds about *Princess
Daisy* that "a novel of that stature is more acceptable in the marketplace. It has built-in celebrity value."[41] Krantz and García
Márquez are both conceived of as the authorial "spearheads" of a
marketing phenomenon designed to have international flair and a
"natural" appeal. A system of distribution is in place, needing only
a particular product, preferably penned by a "star" with "celebrity
value," and a good sales campaign to prove its ever-functioning
efficacy.

The dissemination of Latin American fiction in translation nonetheless has produced many positive results in terms of bringing a
modicum of world attention and, it should be said, a reasonable
amount of discriminating appreciation to Latin American literature.
Likewise, my project here has not been to present the boom as nothing more than a calculated instance of economic opportunism but
rather to suggest how a body of literature, selectively produced and
disseminated in conjunction with certain cultural crises and the economic demands of consumer culture, becomes subject to extremely
limited possibilities of interpretation within that culture.

Only a fundamental misapprehension of Latin American fiction,
in its first massive influx into the highly industrialized consumer
societies of Europe and the U.S., could result in opinions about its
fictional future such as those expressed, for instance, in a 1984 issue
of *World Press Review*. In an article with the sanguine title "Latin

America's Golden Age," the reviewer praises *One Hundred Years of Solitude* as "still the model by which the international public redis-covered its lost taste for the art of storytelling" and speaks glowingly of Fuentes, Vargas Llosa, and Cortázar—only to conclude pessimis-tically that "the Hispanic-American novel does not seem likely to engender new authors capable of such landmarks as those of 1940–70 . . . people do not quite believe in the Hispanic-American novel now; they are standing back." Making an exception for the contem-porary Argentine novelist Manuel Puig, the review ends on this maudlin note: "The dream is short but it is happy [*sic*], [the author] says in *Kiss of the Spider Woman*. That could serve as an epigraph for the state of the Hispanic-American novel."[42]

A similar sentiment is reported in the opening sentence of Rama's retrospective on the boom: "With the same lack of solid arguments with which people began in the sixties to praise and consecrate the so-called 'boom' in Latin American narrative, around 1972 various reports on writers and journalistic articles indicated that its extinc-tion had begun to be decreed."[43] Scarcely four years after its arrival on the U.S. scene, Latin American fiction, like the domestic fiction it was supposed to invigorate, becomes subject to identical rumors about its "death."

The erroneous, tendentious critical myth of this literature's brief, organic efflorescence, followed by its abrupt death, after being last seen in the company of U.S. fiction, can be dispelled, or at least modified, by a consideration of some contemporary social history. In their aggregate, experimental fiction writers of recent decades, however cosmopolitan and ripe for becoming international com-modities, have demonstrated in their writing a concern with the po-litical topography of their respective native cosmopolises at a partic-ular point in time, rather than with the creation of a mythic, enchanted, unified continent. The writers I have chosen to focus on in the succeeding chapters give their attention to such issues as the formation of the modern state and the close relationship between dictatorship and liberal republicanism, and I try to delineate the myriad ways in which repression and oppression come to be repre-sented in the different types and genres of fictional experimentation recurred to by these writers. Worth considering, too, is how various writers formulate the effects of state repression not only on concep-tions of history but on identity, gender, political ideology, utopian-ism, belief in origins, the loss of language, and the dissipation of being. Their fiction ranges freely and coherently across this concep-tual terrain, sometimes in strikingly similar patterns, but no two writers do so in precisely the same way.

During the seventies, the Uruguayan and Argentine fiction writers I am concerned with were not inhabitants of a lush realm of tropical enchantments. They were having to contend with an "exhaustion" and silence of their own. Their social and intellectual spheres had been shattered, largely as a consequence of the unprecedented militarization taking place in varying degrees throughout the South American continent. Many intellectuals found themselves in unwilling exile, or in an internal "exile" where editorial activity atrophied and the constraints on open expression were severe. Magical realism represents only one of the myriad styles and forms these fiction writers explored at the time, in their efforts to counter, or at least to examine, the pseudo-democratic, self-legitimating expressions set forth by their countries' military governments. These styles range from Nelson Marra's grotesquerie and mock epic, to Silvia Schmid's mordant satire of psychoanalytic manipulation, to Manuel Puig's cannibalization of *cursi* pop culture, to Luisa Valenzuela's stark or blackly comic tales of obsessive sexual and political brutalization, to Ricardo Piglia's allegorical and philosophical epistolary novel of shattered identity, to the plasticity of Teresa Porzecanski's oblique imaginative writing.

Given even the range of writing alluded to here, many stories about its intersections with history could likewise be told, in many different ways. The story I wish to tell begins with a writer in Montevideo named Nelson Marra, who, by winning a writing contest sponsored by a newspaper, provoked an aesthetic of silence, the kind handed down by government decree.

# 2. Primers of Power: Nelson Marra's "El guardaespalda" and the Uruguayan Military

The brief paragraph devoted to Nelson Marra in the *Diccionario de literatura uruguaya* gives a rather terse, dry account of the well-known incident which, for many Uruguayans, epitomized their country's full-fledged entry into an epoch of dictatorship unusual in the republic's history. Marra's story "El guardaespalda" ("The Bodyguard"), says the dictionary, "is sadly famous among Uruguayans, since its publication in *Marcha* in 1974 (as winner of the fiction contest organized by the newspaper) provided the excuse for the definitive closure of that weekly. Marra is jailed for four years; having served his time he leaves the country."[1] These denotative sentences, these bare facts, leave a vast context to annotate.

The story is the first-person account of a lumpen bodyguard who has been ambushed by guerrillas and who lies in his hospital bed, filled with bullet wounds, fending off death just long enough to catalogue a life comprised of his climb from paltry thug and neighborhood soccer star to torturer for the state and privy protector of a powerful political don. In a trite but unrelentingly ferocious lingo, as riddled with cliches as his body has been with bullets, he recounts his adulteries, gratuitous petty cruelties and vicious sadism; his megalomania undercut by a painful awareness of his lumpen character; his tear-jerking sentimentality about his daughter and the early romance with his wife. The attempt to yoke these verbal fragments into a coherent, restorative narrative crumbles in the course of the story, undermined by the contradictions of his monologue, which is essentially patterned on, and derived from, the legitimating discourse of a repressive military state.

Marra, whose literary output is decidedly modest and sporadic, seems in some respects ill-suited to occupy the infamous place he occupies in Uruguay's literary history. He is certainly no prolific, epic, protean Gabriel García Márquez or Carlos Fuentes; before his ill-fated selection as prize winner by a committee composed of such literary luminaries as novelists Juan Carlos Onetti and Eduardo Galeano, Marra was scarcely famous, not even "sadly famous," among his fellow Uruguayans, much less the lightning rod of an international literary phenomenon. The year he wrote "El guardaespalda," buffered by what surely came to seem in retrospect—after four years of imprisonment and torture—benign critical neglect, García Márquez's world-famous novel was taking several countries by tropical storm.

The closest link between the two is the fact that Marra, in his first book of fiction, *Vietnam se divierte*, wrote a story, an homage dedicated to García Márquez "with respect and admiration," entitled "José Arcadio Buendía" and based on the earthy character of that name in García Márquez's *Cien años de soledad*. Buendía, in Marra's story, rises from the dead one hot December morning only to find that mythic, enchanted Macondo has undergone some significant and unpleasant changes. "New gringos had arrived in Macondo, and were surely there to stay." Buendía's retina is flooded with signs bearing such unfamiliar words as "Sugar" and "Drugstore," and the spot where cock fights used to take place has come to be occupied by an immense gas station, attended by men wearing red caps and gray uniforms. When he consults a map to orient himself, he finds that the seven letters MACONDO have been replaced (in a kind of colonial-imperialist cartographer's version of Hangman), by the seven letters AMERICA. This story, "José Arcadio Buendía," seems eager to propose García Márquez's celebrated character—and by implication, his magical, mythic writing—as the prototypical liberating textual force cried out for by a gringo-subjugated South America. Yet, the representational map of America which is to guide Buendía in this supposed upheaval bears the telltale marks of the same colonializing, gender-bound figurations of America that are supposedly being renounced and overthrown. In this respect, Marra, like García Márquez, recapitulates the utopian version of Caliban, as described by Fernández Retamar, that the more "sympathetic" U.S. or European critics and writers wished to ascribe to the South American continent. The epic man's-man Buendía, after perusing the new map, discovers that its outline forms the stylized figure of a woman. The lusty, lumbering hero exclaims to himself that

America is a woman, a broad [*una hembra*], an amazing broad who waits for me and needs me. Macondo is, perhaps, her center, her moist vagina which I must preserve. "America" he said again, and relished the seven letters, as before, in that other time, he'd relished the seven letters of Macondo.[2]

By imagining America as female, and Macondo as her moist vagina, Marra has put his finger (so to speak!) on one of the more troublesome aspects of evoking a Macondo-ized America as the alternative to rapine and plunder. America here, in Marra's remarkably crude formulation, is conceptualized as no less passive, vulnerable, and willing than in any European or other "gringo" representations. In fact, this map of a feminized America, ready accomplice to her own despoliation, dates precisely back to the maps made by Renaissance (Dutch, English, Italian, Portuguese, and Spanish) cartographers during the colonialist conquest of the Americas in the sixteenth century. One of countless possible examples is that of the half-savage and exotic, half-classical America draped with a gown and holding a cornucopia in Giovanni De Vecchi's 1574 western hemisphere of a world map with allegories of the continents. There, "she" appears as an exotic, irresistible land, waiting to be taken, hungrily assaulted, and assimilated into a European familiarity. She could, indeed, easily be speaking the words of groveling Caliban in *The Tempest:*

> Hast thou not dropp'd from heaven? I'll show thee every fertile inch o' th' island; and I will kiss thy foot. I prithee, be my god. I'll show thee the best springs; I'll pluck the berries; I'll fish for thee, and get thee wood enough. A plague upon the tyrant that I serve! I'll bear him no more sticks, but follow thee, thou wondrous man.[3]

Whether the map is labeled Macondo or America, its feminization begets machismo in the strain of colonialist recrudescence and in the guise of Latin American liberation (à la Che Guevara) from gringo exploitation. In either case, the mythic allegory seems to lead to the same male mastery, the same gas stations, the same Macondominiums.

The story ends when José Arcadio Buendía, standing somewhat sentimentally as the figure of revolutionary salvation, goes to waken from the dead his *compañero* and *compadre* Pedro Páramo, the protagonist of Juan Rulfo's classic Mexican novel, so that the two of them together can incite the continent to revolution. This unremarkable short story doesn't provide many portents for how Marra's later composition, "El guardaespalda," could come to prominence as a sharp, effective criticism of dictatorial, patriarchal force. Yet the latter story does undertake, as I will argue in my translation-reading of it, a very different critique of the relationship between power and gender than that which informs (or, rather, doesn't inform) "José Arcadio Buendía." The later force of Marra's writing results in part from his abandoning the abortive attempt to take García Márquez's writing as prototypical and his concentrating instead on the actualities unfolding before him. The earlier story (which is, it must be said, a cartoonish takeoff on García Márquez's variegated novel) is marred not least by Marra's well-intentioned filial pietism.

Despite this homage, it was Marra's own fiction, not García Márquez's, which provoked some counter-inciting of a very direct kind, by happening to be situated in the midst of a larger, more pervasive cultural and economic militarization of the Uruguayan state. I don't undertake an analysis of "El guardaespalda"/"The Bodyguard" in the interest of proving that Marra's writing is "better than" (or "worse than") any of García Márquez's own writings, or those of anybody else. It is not a matter of evening up the literary score, of trying to make a case that writers more "deserving" than those already lavished with attention have been ignored (most critics of the boom have used similar judgements as the basis for their complaints). To take an obvious Uruguayan example, Marra cannot compare, in terms of literary output, or perhaps even "quality," with an established, canonized modern Uruguayan fiction writer such as Juan Carlos Onetti. But even in relation to Onetti, the significance of Marra's "El guardaespalda" must be acknowledged.

It must not be forgotten that Onetti was one of the jury members who selected Marra's story as prize winner. "El guardaespalda" thereby came to be for Onetti, as for numerous other prominent literary lights, a pivotal point of reference, the mnemonic device that would summon to Onetti's mind (and to Eduardo Galeano's and to Jorge Ruffinelli's) the forcible closure of *Marcha*, the ordeal of Onetti's own imprisonment, and his subsequent exile.

Juan Carlos Onetti, probably Uruguay's single best-known modern writer, made his living for many years, like so many Latin American authors, as a journalist. By 1974, Onetti had been writing for the weekly *Marcha* under pseudonyms (Periquito el Aguador, Grucho Marx) and/or had been involved editorially with it over the course of thirty-five years, since its inception. In many ways, *Marcha*, its editors and writers, remained throughout this period at the center of his cultural and intellectual life. The closure of it became a kind of personal truncation.

His selection of Marra's story, in the weekly's final weeks, can serve in some ways as the logical apotheosis of the values that Onetti held dear in his philosophy of writing. Looking at the inaugural issues of 1939 and then at the end of *Marcha*'s life-cycle, it appears that Marra in many ways came to fulfill the requirements for a "national" writer that Onetti had set forth so many years before. In the

Periquito el Aguador column of June 23, 1939, Year 1, Number 1, under the literally portentous title of "Sign," Onetti complains of the "insufficiency" of Uruguayan letters and pleads instead for a writer who will provide a "bolt of boldness, firm, sheer, intellectual daring."[4]

The following week, his disgruntlement not abated, he elaborates on his request, under the insistent title "A Voice That Hasn't Yet Spoken."

> In the article that appeared on this page, in the first issue of *Marcha,* the problem of the stagnation of our letters was set forth. We'd like to take another step in this direction, outlining a desirable future for Uruguayan literature. . . . We still don't have a literature of our own, there's no book in which we may find ourselves. . . . The language taken up is, in general, a grotesque travesty of what's used in Spain.[5]

Expanding on his plea, he asks for a writer who

> knows nothing of our poor [current] rhetoric, of our tropical remains, nor of the false, transcendent anxieties that hound us. This, without a doubt, is what the literature of the Río de la Plata needs. A voice that simply says who and what we are and is able to turn its back on an irremediably useless artistic past and accept, without fretting over it, the title of barbarian.[6]

What is notable about Onetti's clarion call for a new artist is how he formulates it in terms that complicate the standard, centuries-old topos of an undiscovered literary continent. In the first column, he had, indeed, referred to nascent Montevideo as the "virgin literary territory of the city, which offers its narrow but deep emotional riches to the newest sojourners." In these pat phrases lurks the potential for an uncritical version of New Word writing. But in the follow-up article he asks, paradoxically, that this hypothetical new literature should shy away from the "tropical remains" of current writing practices, seeming to reject, rhetorically, the kind of impulse toward exoticism that would later lead Latin American letters to the cultural impasse of the New Word, as in the case of Marra's abortive would-be García Marquesian story.

At the same time, Onetti vindicates a modified, anti-utopian model of Caliban by asking (as Fernández Retamar was to ask of all Latin American writers some twenty years later) that an Uruguayan writer willingly accept "the title of barbarian." It is at this juncture that Marra, an otherwise unlikely candidate, seems to begin to fit Onetti's ideal type.

Onetti, as many such artists do when they issue clarion calls, doubtless had himself in mind as first choice for the post of barbarian. But in a quirkier yet profound sense, Marra seems to lay equal claim to that title, thirty-five years later, through no fault of his own and with Onetti on hand to bear witness to the occasion. Marra is, in the most palpable sense of the word, a literary barbarian, but one should not think the less of him for that. Like many of the writers in the thirty-five-year interval of *Marcha*'s literary life, he decidedly rejected, in his language, the "grotesque travesty of what's used in Spain," the land of the conquistador, in favor of a more local, Uruguayan language. His singular contribution was not, however, originality per se. Rather, Marra employed, instead of the effete unconscious parodies of peninsular Spanish decried by Onetti, a deliberately grotesque travesty of Uruguayan Spanish. Seizing on the barbaric, lumpen, *lunfardo* idiom that is considered by many to be the quintessential lingo giving the Río de la Plata its identity, he debased it to the point that it became art. Marra was willing to forego Europhilia with a vengeance and likewise put aside his failed García Marquesian tropicalisms, in the interest of forging a dystopian Caliban. In this pursuit, grotesquerie and travesty were to become not his liabilities but his fortes.

Thus, in evaluating the merits of "The Bodyguard," I will not describe it, as in the ever-invoked (and speciously constructed) dualism of aesthetic vs. political, as a personal political gesture on the author's part and worthy of note solely on that score—of "historical" interest, as the slur often goes. To describe "El guardaespalda" as merely a celebrated "experimental" story is to relegate it, as in the case of the dictionary entry, to the status of a minor taxonomical oddity. But, as the odd history of Marra's story proves, taxonomical headings such as "political" or "experimental" themselves have a history, a cultural conditioning, one which becomes even more apparent and laden with problems when a reader or a translator attempts to bring such a story over into another, seemingly equivalent cultural tradition. In this chapter, I read Marra's story not only against the South American military grain but against the fiction of contemporary U.S. fiction writers Donald Barthelme and Gordon Lish, to demonstrate what radically different effects can be created by fiction which is often grouped under a single, misleading heading such as "experimental" or "postmodern."

Yanking fiction such as Marra's out of its historical context and accommodating it to a slick ahistoricizing "postmodern" aesthetic such as that promulgated by Lish's novel *Peru* tends to flatten out the political pungency of Marra's writing, taming its significant otherness into the kind of circumscribed consumer's sense of history one might get by visiting a theme park. Its oppositional relation to a particular configuration of repressive government thus drops more or less out of sight. The multivalent pastiche of Barthelme's story "Paraguay," in contrast, in its parodic, travestying treatment of the genre of travel literature, offers a pithier, more interrogative analogue to "El guardaespalda." Any translation problem is part of the broader question of reading culture attentively, and here my effort is to represent "El guardaespalda" in a manner which retains the historically specific texture of its adversarial character, rather than lending it a vaguer, more generic, south-of-the-border "political" quality.

Even the immediate impact of Marra's story, for instance, can't sufficiently be accounted for under the outsize-reality rubric of personal heroism in literature, but rather, the story stands as a somewhat unintended provocation of the authorities, conditioned and limited by the social moment in which it appeared. The publication in 1974 of "El guardaespalda" in *Marcha*—which had fiercely criticized various governments throughout its trajectory—was not, as has sometimes been asserted, a calculated act of political defiance, at least not on the part of those who published it. Hugo Alfaro, one of the editors of the weekly, makes this clarification in his memoir of *Marcha*. "Though it's hard to believe, none of the editors had read that story before its publication on February 8." In fact, Alfaro says, many of those associated with the newspaper and its long tradition of opposition, would not have approved of its "risking its life—an exemplary life of 35 years—for the publication of a story in the literary pages." Both the reproaches and the praises, of "those who believed the publication of 'El guardaespalda' an act of civic courage and a voluntary holocaust, need to be retracted definitively."[7]

Alfaro details, in an account black with the irony of historical circumstance, Marra's nervous visits in the week before the story's publication, to try to collect his payment and to ask various editors how they'd liked the story. The author's uneasiness, though he never said so overtly, seemed to derive from doubts about the possible consequences of a story so blatantly and satirically critical of the excesses of military power. But the editors had other things on their collective mind, such as figuring out how to fill the extra eight pages they had on their hands, due to a sudden reversal in governmental policy concerning price restrictions on weekly and daily newspapers—one of the means by which the new, militarized government exercised a more direct financial control over the free flow of information. The extra pages, the editors hastily and casually decided, would be filled by a combination of Marra's story (which had languished in a drawer until then) and an expanded entertainment section. Marra, who returned to the offices right about then to try to speak to the editor-in-chief about the fate of his prize-winning entry, was congratulated on the forthcoming publication of the story that none of those doing the congratulating had read. Its author was brushed aside so that more pressing matters such as deadlines could be attended to.

The Thursday before the story appeared, Marra and his wife, who "had no doubt calculated the risks lying just ahead" and had begun to have second thoughts, phoned to ask that the publication of the story be postponed—a request to which the answer was a definitive and harried "Are you crazy?" There was no way to fill the extra four pages now occupied by "El guardaespalda." Alfaro laments that "Marra paid a terrible price for not going personally to the press on Thursday to say to the typesetter . . . 'It's clear you haven't read the story either! Take the trouble to read it—it's not so bad!—and see if you still want to publish it.'" Two days later, says Alfaro, "we were all wearing hoods in Department 6 of Security, Maldonado and Paraguay."[8]

The story thus found a rapid readership, one unfortunately given to close reading. Alfaro, the elderly editor-in-chief Carlos Quijano, Onetti, and several others were detained by the police for shorter periods of about three months, Marra imprisoned for a longer one, and *Marcha* shut down for good. The corporeal scattering and linguistic shattering which began in Montevideo (many of whose victims would regroup eventually under the broad aegis of the diaspora) seems to have been accomplished swiftly by those exercising power. But though the turn of events at *Marcha* may, in some respects, have caught the editors quite by surprise, in other respects they had for a long time been anticipating something of its nature, in one guise or another. The newspaper had suffered forcible and temporary closures on many previous occasions. Other newspapers around it, throughout the early seventies, were being shut down—*Epoca, Extra, Democracia, De frente, Ya, Izquierda*—in an atmosphere of increasing intimidation. A season of militarization was in full flower. A coup long in the making had been staged in Uruguay in 1973, the same year as Pinochet's Chilean coup. Argentina's 1976 coup was being prepared for. Marra's story can only fully resonate if it is re-inserted in the larger historical process which produced its silence. The infamous *Marcha* edition of February 8, 1974, does not represent a static point in time. Just as that day issues eventually into the far-flung diaspora, it also marks a gathering, a point of political, literary, and historical convergence.

The analysis in historian Selva López Chirico's *The State and the Armed Forces in Twentieth-Century Uruguay*, of the Uruguayan military's gradual movement toward the center of power during the sixties and seventies would help even the most geopolitically misinformed observer come to the conclusion that the old 78-rpm joke—Why is South America like an old phonograph record? Because they both have 78 revolutions per minute—won't suffice to account for what happened in Uruguay. López Chirico begins his book by asking "How [has] Uruguay, the country of exemplary democracy, civilian-oriented, almost exceptional in a continent where military decrees have carte blanche . . . fallen into a military dictatorship?"[9] Though the question may be a rhetorical overstatement, overemphasizing both Uruguay's previous "exemplary" liberality and its singularity among Latin American republics, it is true that Uruguay has been governed in the main on the model of the bourgeois liberal state and not by the generic succession of dictators evoked by the Time-Life Inc. version of South American history as a perennial cycle of "civil wars and banana fevers." The second part of López Chirico's study of the military, covering the years 1955–1973, is called, significantly, "From the Periphery to the Center."

This relatively liberal republic, in López Chirico's account, historically has fomented many of the kinds of programs, both economic and social, that characterize a welfare state. In states of this kind, the armed forces tend to play only an indirect role in the maintenance of governmental power, and the distinction between civil and military roles remains fairly clear. But as Uruguay after World War II became more heavily dependent on the increasingly harsh impositions of industrial capitalism and its representatives—the World Bank and the International Monetary Fund, who imposed rigid "stabilization" programs requiring wage freezes, elimination of protectionism, liberalization toward the fluxes and influxes of the world market, devaluation of currency, elimination of subsidies—then the welfare state, unable to support its own internal programs, began to collapse, and the resulting intense political strife led the Armed Forces to reformulate their own role in the structure of power, in ways that began to blur the civilian-military distinction. During the first months of 1973, the crisis of hegemony reaches such a severity that, finally, "the June coup signifies the passage of the coercive apparatus to the center of the State and the declaration of open war on all representative institutions."[10]

Many of the repressive measures taken could certainly be described as "open"—the dissolution of Parliament; the unification of primary, secondary, and university teaching into a single entity under the "Teaching Law" ("sticking them all in a single bag, the better to beat them"[11]); the prevalence of torture; the suspension by the mid-seventies of habeas corpus and of the rights of assembly, association, privacy, correspondence; suspension of the right to keep private documents, to move about freely within and outside the country, of freedom of the press, of most other provisions of the constitution, and of all political activities. Yet despite the "openness" of these measures, it is, instead, the masking language, the naturalizing ideology, of the military's reformulation which helps illuminate the oppositional rhetoric of Marra's "El guardaespalda" and suggest why both the story's intrinsic stylistic features and its almost coincidental historical positioning catalyzed such hostility on the part of the military authorities.

An analysis of this military coup that attempted to describe it as the musclebound exercise of sheer naked power would fail to acknowledge that governments (even military ones), like stories (even prize-winning ones), eventually have to contend with a critical reception and thus have the continual need to manufacture a consensus. This need explains, for instance, what in 1980 led the military dictatorship, despite its premonition that its initiative would lose, to hold a constitutional plebiscite in which it proposed certain political and economic "reforms." François Lerin and Cristina Torres remark that, "after seven years of exercising power, promoting a social and political model foreign to the democratic matrix in which they had forged themselves," the dictatorship "at the moment of seeking 'legitimacy' did so by reproducing older forms," namely "the strong remnants of the democratic ideology which was [formerly] the source of the country's main currents of thought."[12]

Lerin and Torres indicate 1968 as the year in which the increasingly repressive civilian governmental powers entered into the era of their de facto dissolution, by "recurring permanently to the [quasi-constitutional] mechanism of *medidas prontas de seguridad*" (expedient security measures). This gradual abdication of the constitutional, civilian forms of government (brought about by the ironic measure of *invoking* a particular provision of the constitution) had led by September of 1971 to a "new logic," when "the Armed Forces took over conducting the anti-subversive fight [against the Tupamaro guerrillas], leading to an increasing intervention of the military in public matters" and to the "definitive closure of the old institutional system and the country's long democratic-representative tradition."[13]

Then-President Bordaberry, in order to retain his nominal share of power, signed an agreement with the military, known as the Boiso-Lanza Pact, which virtually ensured the collapse of representational government. He then sent to Parliament, in order to achieve the "consolidation of peace," a project to enact a law known as *La ley de estado peligroso* (Law of Danger to the State), which López Chirico describes as cast

> in a patently totalitarian style; it refers to political crime, without being the least bit specific; creates the crime of opinion, etc., under the pretext of "substituting exceptional regimes, expedient security measures and the suspension of individual liberty; guaranteeing the State's security against the danger of subversion, and protecting men from subversive organizations, in the desire to consolidate the peace which has been achieved at such great sacrifice."[14]

This "new logic," this sophistry, whether earnest or cynical or both, represents a sustained and elaborate (though not necessarily subtle) exercise in verbal construction, necessary in order to rationalize the continuing will to power. The Uruguayan military's self-legitimating ideology, with its strong quasi-religious and apocalyptic overtones, is tellingly laid out in López Chirico's description. The military, he says,

> tends to take upon itself the salvation of a situation compromised by the "power vacuum" propitiated by civil irresponsibility . . . The ultra-leftist project, under these conditions, appears as an unacceptable alternative between chaos, catastrophe, and the power vacuum, on one hand, and on the other, the structuring of a new order which doesn't contemplate the military as an element of power. . . . [The military's] definition of new roles and objectives is presided over by the Armed Forces' messianic instinct.[15]

This salvational rhetoric rings clearly in a secret internal document of the Armed Forces, eventually given as a speech before the Parliament, and ultimately printed in—where else?—*Marcha*. The document states that "the Armed Forces have taken conscience of the national reality, a national reality which leads irremediably to the country's destruction if there isn't an immediate and vigorously energetic reaction at every level. There exists a vast deterioration in moral values, a stagnant, backward-sliding economy."[16] The apocalyptic language of chaos, stagnation, and decay is both generated and counterpoised by the Armed Forces, whose "vigorously energetic" response is put forth as a necessary rescue, moral in nature, rather than merely expedient.

At the same time that the boom writers, within the myth of the New Word, were being heaped with praise in the U.S. for their organic experimentalism, President Bordaberry, in direct concert with the Uruguayan military, was proposing an organic style of his own, one which set itself in direct opposition to artifice. Lawyer and historian Oscar Bruschera, in his political analysis of Uruguay's "infamous decades" (1967–1985), describes the antinomial language of Bordaberry's political philosophy, as expressed in the president's advocatory primer of power, *Las opciones*.

> The force of the natural prevails over rational artifice; the concept of three powers with civil authority balanced among them is, definitively, artificial, given that there is no authority without force. It's not possible to imagine authority without force, because then it would cease to be so, but rather one must ask that force be used with justice. Given the bankruptness of artifice, natural and authentic authority breaks forth.[17]

The legitimation of brute and arbitrary force designed to crush any alterity or opposition masks its own construction by directly opposing itself linguistically to artifice and presenting itself as natural and organic: "the force of the natural." As it happens, the resolution on national security made by the Commanding Military Junta defines national security as "the state in which the cultural patrimony, in all its forms, and the process of development toward national objectives, finds itself sheltered from internal or external interferences or aggressions"— and that resolution, whose date of enactment comes only a few days after the detention of Marra and his publishers, is taken from article 4 of the aptly-named Organic Military Law. It would follow from this peculiar logic that Marra's story, as part of the national cultural patrimony, is being protected from Marra's story, an instance of internal aggression. The closing down of *Marcha* and the imprisonment of Marra are—naturally—an attempt to protect Marra from himself. Carlos Quijano, editor and director of *Marcha*, exclaimed in a 1969 editorial, during the transition toward dictatorship, that "as far as the Executive Power was concerned, the

Constitution had been reduced to number 17 of article 168, the one which authorizes the adoption of [expedient security] measures."

And Bruschera observes, in a chapter entitled "The Theories of the Process," that in the military's self-legitimating (and alterity-destroying) logic and rhetoric,

> the nation is set forth as a natural fact, which manifests itself as organic, unitary, and vividly within history . . . The nation shows its organicity and unity in the State and in the government . . . The mission of the Armed Forces is to supervise the integrity of the nation's organic unity, and to control the government, to ensure that the latter doesn't deviate from accomplishing these objectives.[18]

In the military's self-conception, it "responds to the nature of things, and remains above the spurious forces which distort it."[19] It should come as little surprise, then, that military authorities in this State of Exception found themselves in a state of exceptional anger at the artifices, deviations, travesties, and distortions of Marra's story, which challenged, both directly and indirectly, this organic and univocal self-conception.

Outside the extreme political context of the Uruguayan dictatorship, the patently "artificial" narrative of "El guardaespalda"— vernacular to the point of cliche, dominated by vitriolic posturing, stereotypical characters (if a long-suffering wife, a demented political don, a 100 percent tits-and-ass mistress, etc., can be called characters), and the familiar topos of fascistic violence—can make for a problem. Its effect, when I transfer it into English, might easily become one of unmitigated, "natural," and not especially horrific (or even significant) banality. The fact that the bodyguard speaks from a position of absolute impotence, bedridden, full of metal shards from Tupamaro bullets, does provide an ironic counterpoint that runs through the entire story, a large textual clue that his narration is not to be read straight. But there are also a number of scenes that could be read as attempts to "naturalize" him, either by humanizing him or, on the contrary, by making his exaggerated rhetoric more sinister, to bring out what Hernán Vidal suggests is true about at least one type of torturer, who lives

> his life as a simple office routine, which he later abandons to return to the bosom of an apparently normal family; who enjoys amusements and other daily activities in a radical contrast that renders them the antipodes of his subterranean labors.[20]

But though the bodyguard in Marra's story does indeed embody "the force of the natural," he is a mock-heroic exemplar of that force, dystopian and barbaric. As narrator, he creates his own brand of "organic" narrative, one which masks and rationalizes, after the fact, his ardent participation in state-sponsored violence. This "organic" monologue comes in the form of a romanticized sentimentality toward his daughter, Cecilia, and hazy, soft-focus memories about his early romance with his wife, Rosa. One of the troubles with those scenes is that given the exaggerated conventionality of some of the story's features, an attempt to treat the bodyguard/torturer as a full-fledged "character" has the unfortunate effect of merely sentimentalizing him. It becomes easier thus to perceive the nostalgia and the insistent lyrical rhapsodies about the "better" self who takes daughter Cecilia to an amusement park or about the little ragamuffin who hangs around the fisherman's shack as clues that the bodyguard could have turned out a devoted father and husband, if not led astray by his environment and his darker proclivities. If such is the perceived intention, then his boss Don Carlos' ludicrously inappropriate remark to the man he's about to hire as bodyguard and assassin— "that the bad local crowd had led you into petty theft, that you were a good kid who just needed help"[21]—would beg to be taken as spoken in earnest, or at least as a truth.

If that is the case, then the tone of the entire story and the authorial stance become highly troubling when one starts to consider the reduction of his mistress, Beba, to a pair of giant breasts and a white ass, the aestheticization of violence in the celebration of male sadism on the soccer field and elsewhere, and so forth. The famous statement that Hitler was once a little boy playing in the fields may be true but, once said, doesn't take one very far in the depiction and appraisal of a ruthless mentality. One of the bodyguard's observations, in a flicker of self-awareness, belies his descriptions of the tenor of that supposed "better" self: "You always chose worse, no help for it, that's you all over, besides it did pay and now there's no time to ask yourself what combination of things led you down that path."[22]

Sentimentality has its place in other fiction being written against the Cono Sur militaristic grain around this time, as Manuel Puig's *El beso de la mujer araña* (*Kiss of the Spider Woman*) so deftly demonstrates. But the imprisoned homosexual Molina's weepy, gushy retelling of Nazi romance and wicked French resistance, or of the plantation owner's son who joins the guerrillas and discovers his mother's shameful affair with the wicked, etc., etc., depends on the undercutting existence of his tough-minded cellmate Valentín, on the prison setting, on the Freudian footnotes (as well as the camp stylization of Molina's own narration), for a full comprehension of its place in the total narrative, which manages to be both pop and serious. Imagine if the entire novel consisted of sentences like the following description of the Nazi officer and his beloved from occupied France:

> He says he's in charge of German counterespionage operations here in Paris, and he's come personally to offer his apologies for the trouble she had to put up with that morning. She asks if the flowers come from his country, and he answers yes, they come from the Upper Palatinate, where he was born, near a marvelous lake set between snow-capped mountain peaks.[23]

Puig, of course, is drawing on the facile, glossy, romantic purpleness of a certain genre of Nazi novel and film, one of many stylistic facets of his novel's construction. Marra's story doesn't present clear multivocality in this sense, rather it is a monologue, narrated from first to last by a sharply and deliberately curtailed consciousness. The potential for the entirety of "El guardaespalda" to be read in sentimental terms remains high. I can minimize this potential through the cues I provide in my English version, "The Bodyguard." But the translation of Marra's story requires a somewhat different approach than the one required by the translator of Puig's novel.

The romantic scenes in the story occur after the narrator has been given an anesthetic injection to kill pain, and his frequent references to them as part of "the world of dreams" suggest one plausible interpretation of them as his willed romanticized distortion of his past, his artificial construction of a self that never existed as he now presents it. My approach as translator has been to foreground and exaggerate those elements in Marra that call ironic attention to the romanticization and artifice the narrator engages in. A simple change of punctuation, from statement to interrogative, and a dash to separate the final phrase of the following utterance, call into question his ability to recall or imagine a time when his love for his wife Rosa was pure and free from violence.

> La casa del Buceo . . . donde te acostaste por primera vez con Rosa, con su cuerpo blanco, fresco, sin moretones aún.[24]

> The diver's shack . . . where you slept for the first time with Rosa, with her fresh, white body—still without bruises then?[25]

The change is strongly interpretive on my part, but just as Puig's parody of the genre of Nazi literature needs to be acknowledged in translation, so does Marra's playing off of a literary tradition of megalomaniac, heroic evil, which finds its more recent expressions in novels such as Carlos Fuentes' *La muerte de Artemio Cruz* (*The Death of Artemio Cruz*). Unlike Puig, Marra does not provide framing parodic devices such as footnotes or film synopses. He makes much more muted, but equally ironic, use of those conventions of dictatorial heroics that have been elevated by the New Word mythos into the essentialized features of an exotic continent full of evil archetypes, leaving Marra much more open to being read "conventionally" in English translation. This vulnerability sometimes requires of the translator measures to heighten Marra's ironic reappropriation of these conventions, to make it apparent in another cultural context.

In a later part of the passage cited above, the "carnada fresca y jugosa" that the young version of the narrator hands up to the fishermen and the pants he wears, "de color indeciso, de color carnecita sucia e irresponsablemente magullada" turn into "fresh juicy bait" and pants "of an undecidable color, the color of jailbait, dirty and irresponsibly bruised." This pun further points up the possibility that in the now undecidable accuracy of his memory, his sexual encounter with the young Rosa might as probably have been violent as not.

The use of insistent alliteration and as much soft assonance as possible in English, to render the sounds and rhythms of these innocent nights of passion even more "poetic," makes it more difficult for a reader to take the anaesthetic, "organic," self-sentimentalizing litany only at its stated value. In my English version of the following passage, initial and internal soft sounds *s*, *m*, *n*, *r*, and to a lesser degree *f*, *w*, predominate (along with harder sounds for *confused cries* and *bad boy*).

Respetuosas otras noches . . . sobre la arena empapada, entre los humildes faroles encandilando el mar, con algún brevísimo grito de algarabía que apenas alertaría a los peces en su nocturna y ritual derrota. Noches de pescadores, con el chico que no conoce aún su destino de policía, tira, milico, chivato.[26]

Respectful other nights . . . over the soaked sand, among the modest signal lamps making the sea sparkle, with the briefest of confused cries that would scarcely alert the fish in their nocturnal routs and rites. Fisherman's nights, many monotonous, beau-

tiful nights, with the boy still ignorant of his destiny as a
policeman, hired gun, soldier boy, bad boy.[27]

In "The Bodyguard," these alliterations help recreate Marra's self-
consciously artificial, mock-heroic style, and I use them to some
degree throughout the story. Also, the exaggerated consonance of
"routs and rites," especially given their connotations in context
here, confuses copulation with annihilation, as do the confused cries
of the supposedly still-unbruised Rosa. Finally, the repetition of the
defining term of innocence, "boy," in stock phrases for what he,
"still ignorant of his destiny," is to become—"soldier *boy*, bad
*boy*"—casts doubt on how ignorant the "boy" was to begin with.

This impulse toward mock epic, pastiche, and hyper-convention-
ality characterizes Donald Barthelme's writing as well. Barthelme,
in a manner analogous to Marra, reconstitutes the detritus of language and narrative conventions into a parodic commentary on the
stale rhetoric of official culture. Much experimentation took place
in U.S. writing during the sixties and seventies with a type of fiction which came to be known as trash writing. Appraising Donald
Barthelme's fiction as "The Leading Edge of the Trash Phenomenon," William Gass describes Barthelme's method in these terms:

> First he renders everything as meaningless as it appears to be in
> ordinary modern life by abolishing distinctions and putting every-
> thing in the present. He constructs a single plane of truth, of rel-
> evance, of style, of value—a flatland junkyard—since anything
> dropped in the dreck *is* dreck, at once, as an uneaten porkchop
> mislaid in the garbage.[28]

This description strikes me as only partially accurate. While it is
true that Barthelme, like Marra, works on a flat synchronic plane,
with the dreck of language as his plastic medium, the effect of
Barthelme's reduction of language, like Marra's, is often to evoke
multiple planes of truth, relevance, and style. Out of the artifice of
homogenization, heterogeneity emerges. Barthelme's short story,
"Paraguay," is a case in point. Imaginatively and geographically,
both the distance between and the proximity of Barthelme's "Paraguay" and Marra's Uruguay suggest them as fitting analogues of one
another. Lying alongside each other, yet not quite flush, these make
for a map which, unlike colonialist ones, foregrounds the flaws in
its power to represent. Barthelme's "Paraguay," from a translator's
perspective, can stand as a Para-Uruguay.

"Paraguay" begins with a journeyer's description of crossing the

"Sari Sangar Pass, 14,200 feet," leading a pony and accompanied by guides as they pick their way among the rocks. At the summit, where "it is customary to give payment to the coolies," the narrator says, "I paid each man his agreed-upon wage, and, alone, began the descent. Ahead was Paraguay."[29]

The Sari Sangar Pass? Coolies? At the borders of Paraguay? At the conclusion of this brief first section, a footnote indicates that the description is a "slightly altered" quotation of Jane E. Duncan's 1906 *A Summer Ride through Western Tibet.* Not only have the geographical markers quickly become suspect, but so has the quality of the straightforward narration itself. The narrator seems a combination of explorer crossing the mountains, anthropologist, and casual alpinist-tourist, outward bound for adventure. The epic figure of the heroic conquistador is undermined, made mock-epic, from the start. Barthelme deflates the conventions of explorer-traveler writing, which have persisted from the beginnings of the conquest up to modern ethnography and beyond. In a reading of various ethnographers' writings, Mary Pratt describes this tradition of the descent to encounter the natives as "a utopian scene of first contact that acquired mythic status in the eighteenth century, and continues with us today in the popular mythology of the South Sea paradise (alias Club Méditerranée/Fantasy Island). Far from being taken for a suspicious alien, the European visitor is welcomed like a messiah by a trusting populace ready to do his or her bidding."[30]

Barthelme also quickly complicates the possibility of taking this "strange country" as representative of any geographical entity the reader might have had in mind. Proceeding, under the heading "Where Paraguay Is," in a style that is half explorer's notebook and half mundane grade-school anti-history textbook, the narrator informs his reader that "This Paraguay is not the Paraguay that exists on our maps. It is not to be found on the continent, South America; it is not a political subdivision of that continent, with a population of 2,161,000 and a capital city named Asunción. This Paraguay exists elsewhere."

Yet his disavowal is not made in the interest of giving the author license to create an exotic, romanticized Paraguay of the imagination. For the place described, while in many respects exceedingly strange and fantastical, appears at the same time, ultimately, disappointingly and pervasively flat. The narrator's tone reinforces this sense of anticlimax. A woman in conventionally "exotic" dress—"a dark girl wrapped in a red shawl" with fringed ends and dangling silver bobs—meets and embraces him at the edge of the city, only to take him to "her house, a large, modern structure some distance from the center of the city; there I was shown into a room containing a bed, a desk, a chair, bookcases, a fireplace, a handsome piano in a cherrywood case."[31] The accommodations seem pleasant enough, but the household furnishings ticked off are mundane, not the trappings of an El Dorado or even a homely but mysterious Guaraní hovel.

Descriptions of the inhabitants remain just as devoid of the aura and verbal grandiloquence on which explorers' journals (and militaristic bombast) depend. Barthelme's whimsical, arbitrary categories of logical, abstract analysis, applied in the driest of ways, makes for a "new logic," a sophistry of a different kind than that which appears in the official pronouncements of the Uruguayan regime: one heterodox rather than reductive. "The temperature-dependent pattern of activity is complex. For instance, the males move twice as fast at 60 degrees as they do at 35 degrees, but above 60 degrees speed decreases."[32] Larry McCaffery says that such multifariousness comes from "Barthelme's uncanny ability to mimic worn-out styles and conventions while totally undermining or trivializing the easy assumptions they make."[33]

This visitor to Paraguay, walking through gold and silver leaves, accompanied by his hostess's husband, one Herko Mueller, describes an affective state of mind which could perfectly apply to Marra's bodyguard. The leaves, says the narrator, are awarded "to those who have produced the best pastiche of the emotions. He is smiling because he did not win one of these prizes, which the people of Paraguay seek to avoid."[34] A pastiche of emotions, as in the case of Barthelme's "characters," is just what the quasi-characterization in "The Bodyguard" consists of. Read against the background of Marra's story, "Paraguay"'s own experimentation with such artifice and superficiality reveals a darker quality in Barthelme's story, much in the spirit of Marra's portrayal of the military's attempt to displace and replace what is thinkable and imaginable.

Herko Mueller, for example, tells his guest that he is, "professionally, an arbiter of comedy . . . more what you would term an umpire. The members of the audience are given a set of rules and the rules constitute the comedy. Our comedies seek to reach the imagination. When you are looking at something, you cannot imagine it."[35] This gloss on indirection and its rule-bound arbitration could almost be used to describe article 3 of the decree dissolving Parliament, handed down by the Uruguayan military dictatorship on the day of the June 27 coup. This article

prohibits the divulgation by the oral, written, or televised media, of all types of information, commentary, or recording which directly or indirectly mentions or refers to the dispositions of the present decree, attributing dictatorial motives to the Executive Power, or which might disturb tranquility or public order.[36]

Oscar Bruschera, lawyer and historian, keenly aware throughout his political analysis of the irony, contradictoriness, and black humor of the pseudo-legal decrees which paralyzed his country, describes this June 27 decree as a "delicious text." And he calls the crippled pseudo-institution which replaced the Parliament, and served only to "keep the dictatorship from being called by its true name," an antiquated little organ, an *organito de marras*—a phrase which becomes an equally delicious pun only in the context of my own discussion here about Marra as an oppositional figure. Bruschera recounts how Quijano, the chief editor of *Marcha*, in an issue published right after the coup, simultaneously complied with and skirted the perpetual gag order and made a devastating comment on the military decree by means of a simple, savagely ironic indirection: "he published the decree, giving it the impeccable title 'It's Not a Dictatorship.' "[37]

The likewise gagged Marra seems the antithesis of the state-sponsored artists described in the most offhand, faux-naif (but wildly ironic) manner in Barthelme's "Paraguay" under the heading "Rationalization."

> The problems of art. New artists have been obtained. These do not object to, and indeed argue enthusiastically for, the rationalization process. Production is up. Quality-control devices have been installed at those points where the interests of artists and audience intersect. Shipping and distribution have been improved out of all recognition . . . The rationalized art is dispatched from central art dumps to regional art dumps, and from there into the lifestreams of the cities. Each citizen is given as much art as his system can tolerate. . . . each artist is encouraged to maintain, in his software, highly personal, even idiosyncratic standards.[38]

The stale, affectless language of rationalization (read repression, dependent on the hollow, concocted illusion of "idiosyncratic" diversity—what Noam Chomsky refers to as "the manufacture of consent") here strikes the ear in a similar fashion as the tinny, off-key, technocratic, and liberal-democratic language adopted by the Uruguayan regime in the years both before and after the coup, as it spoke to questions of economic and social policy. When the Uruguayan military in 1972 issued the renowned communiques number 4 and 7—their first blatantly direct intervention of this type in the civilian realm—in order to distance themselves from the civilian government's own economic policies, the singularity of this action derived as much from its *lack* of linguistic novelty as it did from its political novelty. López Chirico observes that

> the communiqués took people by surprise. In spite of the fact that they didn't contain anything earthshaking as such, the mere fact of hearing the armed forces express their opinions about the country's severe economic problems—something Uruguayans weren't accustomed to—and the perception that they didn't do it in terms very different from those of the popular movements, disconcerted the masses.[39]

But in this new economy, where, à la Barthelme, "shipping and distribution have been improved out of all recognition," the main product being dispensed to the populace is silence. Barthelme's "Paraguay" again approximates the language of Marra's Uruguay, in a section entitled "Silence." The narrator-traveler remarks how

> in the larger stores silence (damping materials) is sold in paper sacks like cement. Similarly, the softening of language usually lamented as a falling off from former practice is in fact a clear response to the proliferation of surfaces and stimuli. Imprecise sentences lessen the strain of close tolerances. Silence is also available in the form of white noise. The extension of white noise to the home by means of a leased wire from a central generating point has been useful, Herko says.[40]

The dictatorship's antidotes to the troublesome, subversive, polyvocal "proliferation of surfaces and stimuli" and the political "strain of close tolerances" have been, precisely, the harsh imposition of silence and the "softening" of language: the manufacture of imprecise sentences and white noise in the form of its pseudo-liberal, official decrees. Marra's "El guardaespalda" goes in for a softening more designed to expose the sogginess of the dictatorship's own self-romanticizing language, as in Marra's alliterative description, cited earlier, of the bodyguard and his wife Rosa at the seashore, lying "over the soaked sand, among the modest signal lamps making the sea sparkle." The story also opts for a white noise, one much less soft and more violent than the crashing of waves against a fisherman's wharf.

"The Bodyguard" creates much of its impact using a vernacular as ferocious as it is trite. It speaks the language of an authority that insists on reducing the many voices of the social organism to a single voice; that attempts, in its monomania, to encase its own internal contradictions in a fossilizing rhetoric. Hernán Vidal's "paradigm of locution and silence" can help explain Marra's narrative technique. Citing Bakhtin, Vidal gives the analogy of society as a group of voices that represent different cultural projects. Fascistic power, he then says, "presents itself as a constant locution which projects itself from the heights in a vertically descending direction . . . a soliloquy insofar as other voices . . . have been silenced." This theatrical single voice must stage itself in orchestrated situations, tones, and postures that accentuate "the expansive thorax, histrionic symbol of the epic, the heroic, with precise and energetic movements." Tone and posture attempt to project "an image of personal charisma . . . endowed with supernatural, superhuman, exceptional qualities or powers."[41]

The bodyguard's soliloquy stages him in various situations that will accentuate his omnipotence and charisma. In his recreated day on the soccer field, the crowd roars its approval of his irresistible appeal ("with a little footwork, to make the fans roar, to make the local broads swoon over you . . . the neighborhood boys surrounded you . . . they imitated you even in the way they walked, and the trainer . . . guarding you like a jewel"[42]) in a cult enthusiasm and personal devotion similar to Vidal's description of that which a fascistic leader attempts to evoke in order to interiorize and lend outward credence to his sense of being called to act by destiny.[43] This wished-for sense of inevitable ascent to power is underlined by expressions of the bodyguard such as "Now you were growing. That was the thing: you felt yourself grow. Grow." Or, there is his observation of the significance of his homosexual encounter with his boss Don Carlos—"nothing entered your head except that you were the stronger, and that strength would pay you dividends."[44]

There are several ironies in the presentation of this theatrical soliloquy. In terms of vertically descending rhetoric, the bodyguard and his locutions (addressed, in the story's present, to a cult following imagined instead of actual) occupy a rather low status. His relatively minor power and its precariousness and dependency are facts which, in spite of the self-aggrandizing bombast, make their way at various times into the soliloquy—"when you were in charge . . . with your look of a lumpen climbed out of his class . . . friend of presidents and queers." Also, the hospitalized physical posture of the speaker is anything but epic; instead of an expansive thorax, we're presented with "the head that won't turn . . . eyes clouded by a cloth that blocks out your surroundings." Instead of the heroic, precise, ener-getic movements of a superhuman leader, we get "I can't even move and don't even recognize my body among these bandages." Given these contours of his situation, the bodyguard's tough, street-talk imitation of the rhetoric of power becomes a parody of it. The solilo-quy exaggerates in its failing attempt to silence or overpower the contradictions in the bodyguard's situation.

"El guardaespalda" is not merely a satire of Uruguay's militariza-tion. The bodyguard's ambush can be taken as a clear reference to the Tupamaro guerrillas who staged attacks of that kind as part of their escalating assault on the Uruguayan government between 1962 and 1972. But given the fact that the Tupamaros had recently dis-solved as a political force at the time Marra wrote the story, it seems questionable to describe Marra's project as the symbolic, fictional re-enactment of one of these assaults in order to reaffirm its salva-tional potential for Uruguay at that time. Instead, Marra's story em-bodies the linguistic codes of a dictatorial state and makes them over into literary codes, in this case a stylized lumpen vernacular that parallels the kinds of worn-out cliches that make up the locutions of the Uruguayan military. The bodyguard's observation, after his boss Don Carlos explains the political situation to him in tough street language, is significant in this respect: "It surprised you to hear him speak that lingo—you who thought it was specific to your circles and who'd always heard Doctor C. use the big words."[45]

One of the difficulties of translating the vernacular of Marra's Spanish into English is that the cliches, in order to be perceived as such, must be made familiar in terms of assimilating them to the cultural resources of U.S. English. These equivalents won't neces-sarily express the relationship of popular speech under military rule to the rhetoric of power and its will to univocality. Pop cliches, one of the resources of so-called postmodernism, do have a high potential for promoting univocality, for commodifying and de-historicizing Marra's literary locutions (like one of Barthelme's cement sacks of silence) in such a way that the reception of the translation could become like that of, say, images of South African police brutality in one of several music videos shown simultaneously in a dance bar, or a Latin American military parade taking place on a television on display in a shopping-mall department store.

Gordon Lish's 1986 novel *Peru* is a case in point of minimizing South American otherness out of existence, through pop culture and popular speech. The novel, which takes its name—as in the case of Barthelme's story—from a South American country and similarly disavows any connection with the known geographical entity, is nonetheless an enterprise of a totally different kind from Barthelme's. The tenuous connection with turbulent Peru provides Lish with a mere pseudo-exciting occasion, a many-times-removed shock effect which is meant to lend the poignancy of historicity to his narrator's own emotional vapidity and his pointless self-absorption.

The novel is a reconstruction of the events surrounding one child's cold, sensationalistic killing of another child in a sandbox. The most common device used by Lish and his various less-than-zero protégés, often referred to as "minimalist" writers, is to narrate melodramatic, "nihilistic," and "decadent" events (drug abuse, casual sex, random violence) drastically undercut by a narrative tone of ultra-alienation and disaffection. I killed somebody. Yeah? So? Typically, the page is filled with the detritus of contemporary consumer culture, brand names proliferate, and the language is one of slangy, studied illiteracy—an emotional pidgin English. The style, ostensibly, is language squeezed to a sinewy dryness, one which refuses to acknowledge, much less be shocked by, the horrific dimensions of the violence and horror it so laconically recounts.

One of the drawbacks of this style, certainly from the perspective being elaborated here, is that, like the more slipshod of hard-boiled detective novels, its tone and concerns more often than not bottom out into unself-conscious sentimentality. Despite the brave, world-weary, stoical front this style of writing presents, it's sad and nostalgic about the lost golden world which hovers at its borders. It's squeamish about acknowledging the social causes of its degradation and rarely willing to think beyond the confines of its depressingly obsolescent family unit, which the narrators typically blame for all their personal psychological dysfunctions. But this type of writing truly aspires to grand opera instead of soap opera. And it mistakes a flat description—of, say, a character flipping between one television channel and another with a remote-control stick—for a brilliant critique of the fragmented modern ego and the collapse of high culture into consumer culture.

The "novel proper" of *Peru* begins with the relentlessly circumscribed, almost amnesiac, I-based lament of the former child-murderer:

> I do not remember my mother. I do not remember my father. I do not remember anyone from back before when I killed Steven Adinoff in Andy Lieblich's sandbox. What I remember is the sandbox, and anybody who had anything to do with the sandbox, or who I, in my way, as a child, thought of . . . I cannot tell you

what I thought about the other people, about almost all of the
other people. I cannot even tell you who most of the people
were, except to give you certain highlights of them when I think
of them.[46]

The unflinching toughness of this rambling, like that of a suspect
resisting police interrogation, in no way negates its sentimental
evocation of orphanhood adrift in a world bereft of meaning. As a
point of departure, as a narrative stance being staked out, there is
nothing necessarily limiting about this kind of curtailment of consciousness. The bodyguard's own reflections are in many respects,
as I've pointed out, highly circumscribed and doggedly unreflexive,
especially his fixation on the moment he is pinned in his car and
being riddled with bullets. The choice to restrict a narrative view-
point to a childish or child-like consciousness can be extremely powerful. Yet little or nothing in Lish's novel, besides the monotonous
note of somehow being above his own material, suggests any escape
or differentiation from this paratactic, solipsistic, self-identical,
child's-eye view of violence and "other people." The distinction between the child and the voice remembering the child remains minimal. Instead, there is pop psychology, infantile titillation, anal fixation, and the child-murderer's childish wish that mommy will
make it all better.

I wanted to be [my teacher] Miss Donnelly's hankie, Miss
Donelly's lilac, Miss Donnelly's bodice. . . . I wanted to be able
to sit on the toilet and really do something. I wanted to never
have to get down off the toilet and go downstairs and have to
talk to Mrs. Adinoff when she came over to my house to make
my mother make me get down off of the toilet and go downstairs and have a good talk with her and let her get a good look
at me and ask me the question of what kind of boy I think it
took to go ahead and kill a person.[47]

This passage, in the aspirations it expresses, could almost be a
manifesto of the unconscious for Lish's group of minimalist pro-
tegés, who so tenaciously eschew too-adventurous incursions into
the big, bad, threatening world of the intellect. In fact, the child-like
(and, of course, terribly serious) epigraph of *Peru*—consisting of the
full text (with full stops) of the Mother Goose rhyme "One, two,
buckle my shoe. Three, four, shut the door."[48]—could easily be replaced by an updated, more Freudian version of another nursery
rhyme, the title of which would have to be "Pop Goes the Superego."

The recalcitrant, infantile quality of the narration, despite two ostensible narrative shifts, never substantially changes in the course of the novel's 222 pages. The supposedly "framing" or counterpoint aspect of the novel, signaled by its title—which is meant to imply a largeness of endeavor and, one assumes, some engagement with history—is limited to the five scant pages of the prefatory chapter which opens the book. And these pages, with their talky, repetitive, insistently banal and pointless conversation, are of a piece with the rest of Lish's monochromatic novel. They concern bickering between a man and a night employee about—what else?—something the man saw on television. The man has called the TV station to find out the location of some violent prison event he has witnessed on the late-night news with the sound turned down.

There is, as might be expected, no one in charge at the station. Everything, in this abandoned, effete, fallen world, is being run by automation and remote control. But the man, who has developed psychological indigestion, insists that the night-employee take some action.

> I said, "Yes, but I don't think you really understand me yet. . . . How could they show a thing like that, people doing things like that? Didn't you see it yourself? Didn't you yourself see it yourself? It was so unbelievable. I'm telling you, you have to do this for me, you have to go find somebody and ask. . . . How can I sleep after this? You think people can sleep after this? Oh, come on, you must have been listening, they must have said, you must have heard, somebody there must have heard them say. One of your announcers probably, or what about an engineer?" I said, "All I am really asking for you to do is just to please do something, please go ask."[49]

How, in fact, could they show a thing like that? It is a question worthy of asking, once it is clarified exactly who "they" might be; but such asking, unfortunately, is here tantamount to helpless whining. Somebody has to "do something" in this wacky, depressing, incomprehensible world, because somebody's doing something terrible to somebody somewhere, wherever that is. But whoever does that something, it is not going to be the man, or anybody like him. However bewildering the rest may be, that much is made unambiguously clear from the start. Nor does Lish, in his narrative, feel compelled to undertake the difficult task of elucidating, or even suggesting, what historical and political configurations of power might underlie terrible, upsetting "things like that." He is too busy afford-

ing the reader the cheap thrills provided by the "knowledge" that
somebody—you know, whoever—is asleep at the wheel.

The vignette ends when the man's question finally gets answered.
The woman at the station, as full as her interlocutor is of infinite
solipsism, says to him,

> "I already told you, it was just some footage on the news. A
> prison thing—a thing in prison—it was just some prisoners loose
> in a prison somewhere, some hostage thing in a prison some-
> where, some kind of trouble somewhere with a prison."
>
> I said, "Where? Where was it trouble with a prison? Which
> prison, where?"
>
> "Oh," she said. "Where," she said. "So you only want to know
> where," she said.
>
> I said, "Yes—that's it—I want to know where. That's right," I
> said, "tell me where the prison was."
>
> "Peru," she said. She said, "They said Peru."[50]

Lish's condescension toward his dull-witted, television-benumbed
characters implies that they ought to know more than they do. The
answer, at last, to the man's vehement desire for particulars, for
whens and wheres about this "hostage thing," this "prison thing,"
seems to indicate that the revelation of the country's specific name
will provide a possible point of departure for an inquiry, a contextualization, and thereby make that remote geographical tag meaningful. The dramatic flourish of the final two sentences, the lingering
resonance of this chord, the revelation of the secret name which was
withheld, promises that "Peru" is to stand at the imaginative center
of this investigation into the abyss of violence.

But despite the imminence and intimation, neither the word
"Peru" (in what is obviously a conscious deletion), nor any prose
which might connote a country, real or imagined, of that name ever
appears in the novel beyond this pronunciation of it twice. Peru disappears from the map. The selection of it as the secular talisman is
presented, like every other act in the novel, as random. The news
about the prison massacre of Peru's Shining Path guerrillas happened
to flicker onto the news screen during an instant when someone
happened to be looking (even if the sound was turned down). It could
as easily have been Honduras, or Zaire, or any other foreign place in
which "they said" violence occurs. The novel immediately "cuts"
to the story (or rather, item) of the sandbox murder. The rather predictable, and highly questionable, conclusion *Peru* seems to put for-
ward is that there is no appreciable difference in the ways violence

occurs or in the reasons for it. We all have a similar capacity for violence, a lord-of-the-flies heart-of-darkness, and the differences among its various manifestations are negligible. The monochromatic TV representations of it, though unsatisfying and depressing, can't really be improved on. All we can do is pilfer through the slag heaps of unreclamated language.

Fredric Jameson points out the fascination of postmodernisms with the "whole degraded landscape of schlock and kitsch . . . of the late show and the grade-B Hollywood film" and describes some of the features that constitute postmodernism as "a new depthlessness, which finds its prolongation . . . in a whole new culture of the image or the simulacrum; a consequent weakening of historicity, both in our relationship to public History and in the new forms of our private temporality."[51] I don't mean to suggest that this depthlessness is inherently negative—thus my distinction between Barthelme's "Paraguay" and Lish's *Peru* in relation to the possibilities they offer toward a translation of Marra's story. I am suggesting, rather, that this depthlessness can, quite easily, promote in readers/consumers of "The Bodyguard" a very different sense of private temporality than the "routines profoundly violated, mutilated, and altered" of the Uruguayan context, given the potential of this depthlessness for cannibalizing world culture into simultaneity and homogeneity. As Jameson points out, the culture of the simulacrum has the propensity for replacing a sense of history (including, I would add, current "history") with a mere sense of the historicity of aesthetic styles. One of the examples he gives is "some Disney-EPCOT 'concept' of China."[52] When this phenomenon occurs, what is often referred to as postmodern "self-consciousness" turns out in fact to be a very limited kind of consciousness. Like those who attend the swimming-pool party dressed in Hawaiian shirts and listen with pleasant irony to Don Ho records, it is understood between such interlocutors that they are not really tacky, or really Hawaiian.

My approach in translating Marra's story has been to make the soliloquy of cliches in "The Bodyguard" as theatrical as possible, giving its violent fossilizing impulse fullest expression, while using every opportunity to foreground the contradictory impulses as they appear in the text. I take my cue from the bodyguard's ambivalent self-description in the phrase "even though a body would like to feel like a twenties movie hero, instead of the garbage he actually is,"[53] and I attempt to evoke neither distanced, depthless irony nor an expectation of identification with the story's "realism"; neither fish nor dreck-encrusted porkchop. Rather, I strive for a recognition that the exaggeration of a rhetoric of power which seems a parody of itself to begin with is based on linguistic codes of a military consciousness which must, finally, be taken in absolute seriousness.

Taking my impulse from Barthelme's more effective and critical attempts at mimicry and travesty of worn-out styles, I have drawn on the diction of the "movies of the twenties," on the tough talk of the detective novel, and to some degree indiscriminately on various, sometimes incongruous, sources of American vernacular. The words are thus less the speech of a realistic character than dead language with a strange, violent life of its own.

> You clotheslined him and broke his leg, but you felt good and when three or four came on like gangbusters . . . you laid into them and brought on the general strike . . . but you left no mistake about your personal machismo.[54]

Or,

> giving them a left right left right in the liver until they're pulverized or just a little electric prod up the ass, in the balls . . . and afterwards ice water so the faggots tough it out like men and don't faint, and another left right, another prod . . . yeah you're going to grab them one by one.[55]

At the same time the use, in my English version, of humor to conflate the worn-out turns of speech helps create the sense of a human consciousness equal to the seemingly outrageous violence of these turns of speech, as in the narrator's insistence that he's "a live one and kicking, okay not kicking but a live one," or this almost-metaphor of landing and cleaning a fish, when he imagines his revenge on the guerrillas who ambushed him.

> Los vas a ir pescando uno a uno como a chorlitos, como giles que son, en tus garras van a caer y ahí que los vas a hacer de trapo.[56]

becomes

> You're going to reel them in like flounder, like the jerks they are, they're going to struggle on the hook, you're going to clean their clocks.[57]

The wordplay among *flounder, jerks, struggle,* and between cleaning fish and cleaning clocks, attempts to yoke together the cliches in a way that emphasizes the latent force in the banal utterances that go together to make up a militaristic worldview. The bad joke I work in about his learning, as a torturer, to distinguish between "communist apes and guerrillas" (which plays off Marra's animalistic imagery in the same passage) would remain nothing more than a bad joke if it weren't in some way representative of the hostile, crude taxonomy of torture.

One of the areas of a competing voice within this monologue is in the language of sexuality, in the bodyguard's homosexual encounter with Don Carlos. In *Male Fantasies*, his thoroughgoing study of the "inner life" of soldiers of the proto-fascist German *Freikorps*, Klaus Theweleit makes the crucial distinction that the attraction of the fascist male soldier to scenes of violent sodomy is not because they are "homosexual" acts. Rather, the attraction serves as a "maintenance process" for ensuring the soldier's own psychic and physical integrity. Such acts may perform for the fascist male the same end as participation in torture, whose "primary product is the totality of the experience of the tormentor, his absolute physical omnipotence." Threatened by the constant vulnerability that he will disintegrate into the "bloody miasma" of the feminine mass, the torturer-sodomizer must assert his control. But, according to Theweleit, "nor is the advantage of being able to stop [inflicting punishment] a distinguishing mark of the torturer. And he only calls a halt when the victim's loss of contours has allowed [the torturer's] own body to gain definition . . . as armored body-totality."[58] His latent longing for fusion with the political and erotic mass is countered by his intense fear of the self-disintegration that would follow in the wake of such a fusion, which he staves off by displacing his longing onto other acts, such as sodomy.

The scene between the bodyguard and his employer appears in some ways the inverse of the bodyguard's sentimentalized description of the night in the diver's shack with his wife Rosa. In the homoerotic encounter, Don Carlos is depicted in terms as repulsive as possible—"slobbery hands . . . thick, unctuous lips"—and the overt rationalization for the sodomy is as a straightforward power ploy, no different from any of the bodyguard's other violent acts. But this scene may be read as in fact the moment at which the assertion of omnipotence becomes most vulnerable, closest to disintegration into the "bloody miasma," and thus omnipotence must be unflinchingly maintained.

The repetition of the phrase "y no te dió asco," just as the kisses, caresses, and embraces (*not* the kicks and slaps) begin, suggests the bodyguard's surprise that the experience has dimensions beyond the homophobic disgust, assertion of force, or simple indifference with which he means to recall it. The repeated phrase "y no te dió asco" is articulated as a negative, to submerge its implications, but I have chosen to translate it not as "it didn't make you nauseous," or "it didn't disgust you," but as "it didn't repulse you," in that the repetition of this latter implies its antonym—the positive phrasing "it attracted you"—in a way that the former two don't. When Don Carlos asks to be taken to bed, the bodyguard speaks of that request as "obviando un mundo de sobreentendidos que nunca te cuestionaste," literally "obviating a world of hints you never asked about," which I translate as "letting surface something always implicit between you," to help make the quality of repressed desire resonate through the entire passage. Once the intercourse begins, he is again surprised, this time by "la insólita facilidad de abrazar sus falsos senos"—"the unexpected ease of hugging his false breasts."[59]

The word "ease" at this point is significant. It is important to indicate that following Theweleit's analysis, I read (and translate) this scene not as one of degradation-through-homosexuality or even of simple sexual desire. This temporary, libidinal "dissolution" in memory can be read as the bodyguard's (failed) attempt to supersede the more profound physical and ego dissolution that is taking place in the story's present, as he lies in the hospital bed. The memory is his attempt to reinforce the boundaries of his ego and his "body-armor." The appeal of this memory to him must be understood in relation to a disintegrating body in almost constant pain. That body is the principal counterpoint to the soliloquy of omnipotence throughout "El guardaespalda." As Elaine Scarry succinctly puts it in *The Body in Pain: The Making and Unmaking of the World:* "having pain may come to be thought of as the most vibrant example of what it is to have certainty."[60] The certainty here is of death and the cessation of his megalomaniac monologue.

The transition between the "homosexual" scene and the anesthetic dream sequence about the bodyguard's early days with his wife and daughter is achieved by the explicit equation of the bodyguard's ejaculation with the temporarily soothing injection he receives. (Note the implications of his not only giving but receiving the "injection.") Both, in some sense, are "ease," momentary liberations from the violent world of his making and its unmaking of him. And although ultimately the various arenas of his assertion of force crumble into one another, in this instance the bodyguard, in futile search of respite from the libidinal violence which has done him in, distinguishes these "injections" from an earlier, sadistic reference to scenes of torturing victims, where "the injection served another purpose, to keep them alive." But here:

> Le vaciaste el semen que le llegó a las entrañas más ocultas, según su grito de puta desenfrenada, el doctor. La inyección había cumplido su función . . . su efecto y ahora era el descanso. El descanso.[61]

> You emptied the semen that reached into his most hidden places, all the way with his unbridled whore's cry, doctor, see; the injection accomplished its function . . . its effect, and now there was rest. Rest.[62]

The bodyguard's ecstatic, ejaculatory "union" with his superior Don Carlos follows an unconscious logic similar to Theweleit's concept of the sadistic, basic-training-induced "blackout," which, he says, characterizes the fascist soldier's "relationship to the commanding officer, or to the person for whose sake he makes physical effort." In this union, not only does the soldier achieve "ejaculation and release of bodily tension," but also the flow "pours across the sensory perception of the man and extinguishes it." Theweleit asks, "Could it be then, that this hallucinatory union with the superior (even with the Kaiser himself) occurs in the state of blackout? That the forbidden loving penetration of man into man takes places imaginarily in this blackness?"[63]

I have played off the familiar name for Don Carlos I have the narrator use throughout, Doctor C., to achieve a transition similar to Marra's, and one that will emphasize the cathartic, fluid qualities in the rest-giving ejaculation and rest-giving injection. "Doctor, see" can be read as both the locution of the health-care worker watching the patient succumb to anesthesia and the bodyguard's ecstatic crying out of Don Carlos' nickname, to match the latter's "unbridled whore's cry."

Note that these choices are not the same as the perennial translator's dilemma of finding equivalents for culture-specific language, say the Uruguayan slang "tartamuda" (stutterer) for a machine gun, or "mina" (mine) for a woman. Rather, the challenge is to evoke in the story's readership a sense of the relation of such culture-specific language to the discourse of power that it scrutinizes. This language does not correspond neatly to geographical concepts such as national literatures and in fact goes to some lengths to question the very sense of "nationalism" to which the military dictatorship continually appeals for purposes of self-legitimation. So the relative ease or difficulty of translating is not limited to the question of differences between languages or dialects. The rhetoric and counter-rhetoric of power are not "Uruguayan" in the same way the word *mina* is, except to the extent the latter participates in the former.

*Mina* is a common vernacular term in Uruguay and Argentina. If I approach its translation as merely the task of finding an acceptable equivalent in American English, I may choose among *chick, gal, babe,* and the like. But the word appears in "El guardaespalda" as part of the bodyguard-narrator's extremely restricted consciousness. His field of discourse is dominated by the language of three areas: militarism, sports, and sexuality. These are the arenas in which the bodyguard plays out his violence and in which the fate of the body (both his and his victims', as well as both the physical body and the body of power-language) is decided. One or more of these three arenas is almost always present in the narrative, and there is a great deal of overlap in the terminology characteristic of each field of endeavor, in part reflective of the bodyguard's attempted reduction of all he confronts to a single urge to overpower it.

I don't mean to suggest that a word or phrase will always have specific double or triple connotations applicable in a given context, although it sometimes does, but rather that this is the kind of speech most available to the speaker and that, regardless of how it comes to bear on an immediate context, it has a cumulative effect in the story as a whole. *Mina* can be an explosive device, a mine in the military sense, in addition to its sexual usage: "vulgar—woman, especially young, with whom one has amorous relations."[64]

An article on "Montevidean Popular Speech" also defines it as, "in tango lyrics, an 'exploited woman.' " And tango lyrics are, of course, the musical-verbal expression of the Argentine and Uruguayan gangsterish, *lunfardo* underworld, the linguistic source of much of Marra's aesthetic travesty. The article on Montevidean popular speech and its glossary were compiled to reflect *"lunfardo* slang," the "linguistic torrent in the metropolises around the Río Plata."[65]

The author-compiler of the article, whose presentation is made in the interest of advocating the richness and complexity of this low-life slang and to justify its use in fiction writing, mentions the language of sports and that of the tango as two of the important areas of speech which predominate in *lunfardo.* Even a glance at both the glossary and at "El guardaespalda" makes it clear that Marra's story, which is set in Montevideo, draws heavily on this variety of underworld popular speech.

The first appearance of the word *mina* in the story, "las caras de aquellas minas," is at a moment when a group of young Tupamaro guerrillas, some of them identified as women, are filling the bodyguard's body with bullets from a machine gun. In a scene a little later on—"las minas te seguían de lejos . . . que se mueran un poco más"[66]—he is full of his own masculine prowess, having just broken the leg of a fellow soccer player, and decides to let his swooning female admirers "die a little more" before he grants them his sexual presence. Here, sports and sexuality are confused with the language of sadism and slow torture. Because of its wide usage in male speech, *mina* appears in many vernacular short stories without any such effect, and even here the connotations of an explosive device are not conjured up in any direct way. But, as I have said, their significance is often less a word-play that a reader will instantly pick up on than a subconscious trace.

In some instances I have chosen *broad* for *mina* because of the clumsiness, if constantly repeated, of other possible equivalencies that suggested themselves. But overlap between discursive fields occurs throughout the entire narrative, so there are many opportunities for compensation, and the translator's semantic constellation will not necessarily match the author's. One instance of a successful match-up is in the description of sex with the well-endowed Beba, the desirable, exploited character who emerges as little more than a cipher out of a sentimental tango.

> Qué mina, con aquellos pechos imponentes . . . poniendo en juego todo tu aguante varonil para no tener que acabarle en seguida, qué hembra.[67]

> What a bombshell, with those imposing breasts . . . and it took all your staying power not to finish her off at once, what a piece.[68]

Here, "mina" becomes "bombshell," a word that shares the sex-as-violent-explosion associations and is appropriate to the physical description of Beba, who appears in the text only as a voluptuous body to be ravished. "Bombshell," coming out of a movie diction as hackneyed as that of any tango, the kind of term often applied to female stars like Jane Russell or Ann-Margret, works as part of my translative strategy of turning the bodyguard's barrage of reductive vernacular, with which he attempts to suppress a growing awareness of the vacuousness of his narration and his existence, into a collage of North American cliches.

The next instance of overlap, "finish her off," might come out of the mouth of a movie gangster and picks up the nuance of "acabarle" and the bodyguard's inability to distinguish between his penis and other types of weapons. I have chosen to turn the animalistic reference to Beba, "qué hembra," into "what a piece" to foreground the awareness of his own painful body which the narrator wishes to suppress. It emerges a few sentences later in "ese trozo de cuerpo quemado de tanto fuego . . . tanta bala," which becomes "that piece of flesh burned from so much fire . . . so much bullet," a reference both to himself and his fantasy of Beba. In this way, the "pieces" begin to fit together.[69]

It is essential to set up echoes to parallel Marra's, and not only locally. A few pages later, in the scene where Don Carlos "extendía el revólver que, ahora sí, podías llevarlo tranquilo, como si fuera una prolongación de tu cuerpo," a punning interpolation can again underscore the attempts, with ever greater inadequacy, to silence the gaps that have been opened in a disintegrating body. I make the phrase into "the piece that from now on you could carry in peace, as if it were an extension of your body." This rendition not only gives a gangsterish-tango slang for a revolver which is at once confused with the kind of weapon he prefers to use on Beba, who is herself a piece as well as a bombshell, but also continues to emphasize the paradox of a bodyguard obsessed with bodies in pieces.[70]

The references to body parts are frequent: "mové esa mano que no podés," "ese dolor . . . casi vacío de sentido . . . debe partir de alguna parte de tu cuerpo," "le metiste una bala entre las piernas" ("move that hand but you can't," "this pain . . . almost empty of meaning . . . must originate in some part of your body," "you planted a bullet between his legs"[71]). The most obvious translation of the title "El guardaespalda"—"The Bodyguard"—is one of those felicitous chances that translators live for, and I have tried to exploit its possibilities for the story to the fullest, given the body's predominance in Marra's text as the locus and object of suppressions, repressions, mutilations. The repetition of the pronoun *nadie* (nobody) in the opening line of the story provides the first opportunity for the presentation of the authoritarian body—made up of hackneyed speech habits—which, even as it speaks to maintain the integrity of its consciousness, already begins to reveal its disintegration.

> Like this, with twenty slugs in my body, I'm nobody, you're nobody, it's no body. There's no such thing as nobody, not even that pack of sons of bitches who boxed me in on the coastal road with several cars and gave it to me good.[72]

The choice of "nobody" as pronoun rather than the equally avail-able "no one" plays off the title and helps set up the myriad allusions to and functions of corporeality, particularly since its third occur-rence is broken into "no body" to draw attention to the surface of the text. In the story's final paragraph, just before the guerrilla am-bush occurs, the simple substitution of the informal "a body" (i.e., one, a person) for "uno" helps prepare for the narrator's imminent and explicit recognition that the monologue is useless and played out. Thus, "a body drives like always, with equanimity and without waking suspicions . . . a body steers his red auto among the other cars that pass him fast . . . a body lights up the first cigarette of the day."[73] These seemingly unimportant choices provide a direct par-allel between these sentences and the first two of the story.

It is, of course, ultimately the bodyguard's own body which falls to pieces, unable to support the shards of bullets and the weight of its own illusions and linguistic contradictions. In the closing lines of his death throes he at last admits to himself that

> any attempt at defense is pointless, because now the machine guns and revolvers are emptied into your body . . . it would be adherence to a stupid idea, because now everything's blood, the smell of burned, scorched, rotting flesh, and clinging to an idea different from that reality is gratuitous, like it is now to cling to sleep, to the worthless anaesthetic.[74]

And in that recognition, he expires. One wishes that the Uruguayan dictatorship itself could have vanished into oblivion in such a clean and definitive literary coup. It did, in fact, relinquish formal power on February 12, 1985. History, however, especially the history of dictatorship, has a troublesome way of lingering, with threatening overtones of reprisal, as evidenced by the declaration that one of the most powerful Uruguayan military men, Lieutenant General Medina, made at the time of the "democratic" transition, when he was asked for assurances by a reporter about the military's view of its proper role in society. His answer:

> You want me to say something I shouldn't say and don't want to say. You're asking me if we're of a mind to stage another coup. I tell you that we're in no way thinking about it, nor do we want one. What I do want to say is that if they oblige us to do so, if things take the same course as they did in 1973, we won't have any choice but to stage one. I fervently, clearly hope that with

God's help matters won't reach that point, because we don't
want to stage another coup.[75]

One hopes that, with "God's help," what arises from the pieces is
not another messianic military state covered with the stigmata of
its "scorched, rotting flesh," but rather a body politic capable of the
kinds of contradictions that don't lead, inevitably, to its predictable
demise and resurrection.

No matter how carefully and consciously a translator tries to re
create multivalence in a translation, it would be naive to maintain
that the particular resonances I have tried to elaborate (elaborately)
here will necessarily make themselves evident to a given reader, or
set of readers. As Marra's own case eloquently proves, one can adopt
certain writerly strategies, write against the grain, but the impact
they will have in the end is as much influenced by historical circumstances, and by chance, as by any conscious or unconscious effort.
At the same time, a piece of writing, however compact or relegated
to an editor's drawer, has a potentially explosive power precisely
because of its embeddedness in historical process. That power is not,
however, entirely contingent and derives in part from qualities intrinsic to the story or novel. As I have tried to suggest in my analysis
of two U.S. writers analogous to Marra, Barthelme's "Paraguay" in
this instance shares that potential (which has nothing to do with
Barthelme's "intent"), while Lish's novel does not—and it would be
difficult to imagine how it could. From the translation point of view,
the two are not equally "available" to the translator.

In any event, the vital interdependency between Marra's work of
fiction and its labyrinthine historical context suggests that the latter
does not provide mere "background" and that the making manifest
of this context, along with translation "proper," is an integral part
of that cultural process of re-forming reading habits which sometimes goes by the name of translation.

One of the exemplary instances of translation understood in this
way, in the medium of poetry rather than fiction, is John Felstiner's
book *Translating Neruda: The Way to Machu Picchu*. This book-
length study of Pablo Neruda's "Alturas de Machu Picchu"
("Heights of Machu Picchu")—a twelve-part poem inspired by
Neruda's visit to the Inca fortress in the southern Andes of Peru—
represents for me an antithesis of Lish's *Peru*. Felstiner's book consists of an introduction, five chapters, and, at the end, a bilingual
facing-page edition of Neruda's remarkable poem and Felstiner's
equally remarkable translation. In the first chapter, which raises and

entertains a variety of questions about translation in general, Felstiner remarks that "doing without translations . . . might confine us to a solipsistic cultural prison."[76] His project makes it difficult to succumb to such solipsism and makes it inviting not to. In a sentence that could equally describe several of the Latin American writers I undertake to examine in this book, he says of Neruda that, in the U.S. of the seventies, "for most people, if his name sounded at all it was like the name of some remote city whose location and precise importance remain on the fringes of consciousness."[77]

The first four chapters of *Translating Neruda* trace the formative experiences of Neruda's poetic career, but never in a fashion which lets the book become the mere biography of a "great man." Instead, the reader is taken through a careful study of Neruda's early love poetry, to the "dynamic form" engendered later by his breakthrough poem "Galope muerto," to the poetry written out of his contact with the Spanish Civil War, with Mexico, with his mining constituency when he returned to Chile to become a senator, and eventually with Machu Picchu. The study moves deftly among various kinds of contextualization, including: Neruda's biography, evocation of the Spanish Civil War, analyses of versions by others who have translated Neruda's poetry, the full or partial text of Felstiner's own translations of various Neruda poems, the proposal of poems by Whitman and Eliot as analogues of certain poems, the full bilingual (Neruda-Felstiner) text of "Galope muerto" ("Dead Gallop") and "Entrada a la madera" ("Entrance into Wood")—two poetic milestones in Neruda's poetic journey toward the heights of Machu Picchu. All these forms of inquiry are interlaced with one another in such a way that they have an equal bearing on Neruda's definitive poem, which, even as a culmination, does not supplant or diminish the poems one has encountered along the way, but rather hearkens back to them.

In the fifth chapter, "Translating *Alturas de Machu Picchu*," Felstiner presents a detailed reading of his own process of translating each of the poem's twelve sections. By the time one has arrived at the bilingual translation of the poem, the book's broad endeavor in situating the poem historically and aesthetically has made it highly unlikely that either Neruda or Machu Picchu will there be perceived, as in the case of Lish's televison-engendered *Peru,* "like the name of some remote city whose location and precise importance remain on the fringes of consciousness."

Yet the making visible of these vital historical intersections need not always take the form of fully reconstructing a social moment or a textual journey. In a brief note, entitled "Aftermaths of Translation," at the end of his last chapter, Felstiner tells an anecdote which points to the convergence of chance with historical change. In his translation of a Neruda poem ostensibly written to denounce Pinochet and Nixon just after the September 1973 coup in Chile, Felstiner says, he rendered the line "máquinas hambrientas de dolores" as "machines starving for pain." After his translation was published on the Op-Ed page of the *New York Times,* Felstiner discovered that the poem had actually been written "twenty-five years earlier, about Central American dictatorships backed by the United States." And the last word in the aforementioned line he had translated, which had been misprinted in the edition he worked from, turned out to be *dólares* (dollars) not *dolores* (pain). "But," concludes Felstiner—in a phrase that speaks directly to the importance of acknowledging the role of mutation and chance in historical change—"the mistranslation had its own truth, and I let it stand."[78]

Felstiner's perceptive appreciation of the truth of his mistranslation is in stark contrast to the categorical insistence of Norman Thomas di Giovanni, Borges' principal English translator, that translation always be governed by an objective standard immanent in the original text. Giovanni asserts that

> only to someone for whom the act of writing is a frivolity could a mistranslation seem interesting. If Borges wrote, "The sky is blue," and by slip or design I typed, "The sky is glue," and then thought the result greatly interesting, I should be a candidate for the madhouse. I'm still on the side of meaning in literature.[79]

Giovanni's rejection of mistranslation supplies, in the strictest sense, a much-needed caveat about shoddy, haphazard translation. Yet Felstiner's example of unintentional misspeaking, due to the garbling inherent in the chancy medium itself, bespeaks an equally necessary attention to those forms of literary practice governed by chance and to the role of chance itself in contemporary history.

Though explicitly political in content, Marra's story became, as I described earlier, subject not only to deliberate social pressures but to an appreciable element of coincidence. And other novelists writing at the same time, such as U.S. novelist Harry Mathews and Uruguayan Teresa Porzecanski, were exploring the aleatory possibilities of fiction and history in a very different and much more self-conscious way. Their writing, rather than being threatened by chance processes, embraced those processes as the key to an adequate comprehension of historical change.

# 3. Cutting Up History:
# The Uses of Aleatory Fiction
# in Teresa Porzecanski and
# Harry Mathews

If the myth of the New Word has trouble accommodating the awkward stitches dropped in seamless history by Nelson Marra, whose
satirical story played a specific and clearly discernible role during
the collapse of Uruguayan culture under dictatorship, the myth
seems even less capable of giving a satisfactory account of the writings of an author such as Teresa Porzecanski, whose more occult use
of artifice seems to lose the thread of Uruguayan history altogether.
Porzecanski's fiction rarely refers explicitly to her country's political
or historical events. No Garcia Marquesian dictators appear in her
work, nor even any Marran bodyguards. Instead, her stories and novels remain populated by the likes of manikins, idiots, ancestral
totem poles, unkempt old men in rented hotel rooms, ant colonies,
and larval beings. The inanimate and the animate vie for attention.
As often as not, ciphers take the place of characters, anecdote and
speculation stand in for story, and the particulars of her geographical
landscape (as opposed to a psychic one) remain indistinct, less a
vivid, continuous dream than the quickly sketched contours of a
casual daydream. This quality no doubt prompted one reviewer to
assert of Porzecanski's 1986 collection of stories, *Ciudad impune*
(Unpunished City), that "the book's title can be a little disconcert-
ing. It suggests that the very center of this narrative world is the
urban space where the stories occur ... Porzecanski's gaze dwells
much more on beings—and especially the society of their wander-
ings—than on an atmosphere."[1]

In her fiction, the events and landscape of Uruguay seem to have
been snipped with sewing scissors into such unrecognizable remnants that one begins to question whether they came from the fabric
of history to begin with and whether they could be reassembled no
matter what the effort. Porzecanski's means of representing the
"unpunished city" are succinctly stated in at least negative terms in
the concluding story of *Ciudad impune*, "Inoportuno" (Inoppor-

tune), in which a narrator aboard a city bus begins her monologue by declaring "Now I don't want anybody telling me what life is. I don't want a long explanation/recipe/repertory that presents things as comprehensible."

This apparent change in the mind of this reconstructed but unregenerate narrator has been brought about by her listening to the ravings of a "lunatic" aboard the bus, who describes aloud, to no one in particular, in "words without meaning," a "country that had lost its memory, an indeterminate country where things impossible to remember had happened. . . . The entire history of that country had becomed fragmented, dissolved into volatile anecdotes."[2] Only in this patently artificial, cut-up, stitched-together form—as "volatile anecdotes"—does history appear in Porzecanski's fiction. The story pulls up short of allegory even; the piecemeal investigation of those pieces which pass for a unitary conception of the world—rather than that "world" itself—is the subject of Porzecanski's writing.

Though her emphasis on process differs somewhat from that of U.S. poet Charles Bernstein, his description of writing as "dysraphism" or "mis-seaming" gives a reasonable approximation of Porzecanski's violently stitched-together language. Bernstein, in "Blood on the Cutting-Room Floor," conceptualizes his method as

> knitting together pieces of deanimated flesh until, like the monster in Mary Shelley's *Frankenstein,* they come alive. . . . The description of a poem's making as a kind of psychic surgery emphasizes that poetry is a *technology* . . . like a *flesh* made of words. If *flesh* seems too organic a metaphor, it is not intended to oppose a *social* construction with a *biological* one but to point out how *self* is as much a social construction as a poem.[3]

Porzecanski, too, seeks the meeting place where the "deanimated flesh" of self and language—once alive and then fossilized into an inorganic, mineral existence—becomes knit together again, consciously constructed rather than flowing into organic being. In her story "Construcciones" (Constructions), just such a "psychic surgery" and commentary on her artistic method takes place, in a ceramics class where the narrator is working with clay.

> I kneaded . . . a bland unformed paste that sank beneath the subtle weight of my palms, marking it with fingerprints and the vestiges of humanoid forms; sometimes an error or a wrong move wrought havoc, an undesired or sloping well in the most volatile mass ever achieved by any being; flexibility, in the end, of

matter that didn't resist me but rather took on my powers, making possible the endless diversity of form. More potent than a mirror, even more than a mere reflection, the clay was total receptivity, so alive and trembling that properly human flesh had delegated cerebral qualities to it, but without desires or goals, awaiting my knife—my life—my palm in order to succumb and be transformed.[4]

The image presented here is not of matter springing into miraculous anthropomorphic being, of Adam and Eve springing from lifeless clay, but of the reanimation and conscious *reshaping* of a substance to which human flesh has "delegated cerebral qualities." What remains in question is the specific form that it will take in the process of its manipulation. Form, construction, manipulation—these are paramount in Porzecanski's work, and in most of her fiction she is specifically concerned with offering alternatives to the manipulation of ideas and thought into oppressive, confining systems of logic and rationality. A sharp distinction must be made between the transformations in her work and those supernatural, "magical realist" metamorphoses in the fiction of a writer such as García Márquez. Rómulo Cosse, in a review of a story in *Ciudad impune*, points out that in Porzecanski's fiction "everything partially contradicts the laws of nature, but nonetheless the metaphoric discourse weakens the denotative function and hinders one from defining the vision as extraordinary. The narrator expressly says 'I reconstructed.' "[5]

The ease with which contemporary explosions of Latin American fictional innovation have been assimilated under the New Word aegis of enchantment has kept certain strains of experimental writing from being understood on their own terms—in particular, those exploring the methods and subject matter of "chance" combinations of language. Even in her own country, Porzecanski's failure either to represent clearly the grim social realities of Uruguay (as in the fiction of Juan Carlos Onetti, the most dominant force in contemporary Uruguayan letters) or to transform them in recognizable ways (whether in the vein of Marra's grotesque satire or as a variant of Colombian García Márquez's magical realism) has caused some critics to question the historical validity and importance of her writing in relationship to the culture of opposition to the recent Uruguayan dictatorship.

One could argue, of course, that her writing need not be judged by such criteria at all. But Porzecanski herself has staked claims for her writing on this terrain, and I would argue, like her, that her fiction explores a less acknowledged but equally important lacuna of aesthetic response to dictatorial logic and raises interesting possibilities for shattering unitary notions of history—whether those notions derive from military dictatorship, or from a literary left too eager to narrow the possibilities of what constitutes worthwhile, "committed" literature in a time of oppression.

Of all the Latin American writers under consideration in this book, Porzecanski is the one whose writing I have worked with most extensively as a translator. I am therefore also intrigued by the possibility of finding writing practices analogous to hers in the context of contemporary U.S. fiction—not in order to offer an exact model of her writing (an impossible and even questionable task), but rather, as in my comparison of Marra to Barthelme and Lish, to offer suggestive translative parallels for Porzecanski's methods and practices as they might exist in a different cultural sphere.

When the work of a writer in Spanish is brought over into English, it enters into a dynamic relation with all writing which already exists in English. George Steiner, in describing the translation process, which he refers to as "the hermeneutic motion," says that one of its crucial movements—the dialectic of embodiment—"is incorporative, in the strong sense of the word . . . the embodiment is not made in or into a vacuum. The native semantic field is already extant and crowded."[6] If this relation is to be fruitful for the translator then s/he must be able to draw as freely as possible on the practices offered by the various writings occupying this native semantic field. The ability to do so effectively is enhanced by an awareness of the aesthetic and cultural/historical affinities and disparities among authors that seem to have parallel approaches to writing. My attempt in these pages will not take the form of the "close reading" of my own translation of Porzecanski's prose, as I did in the case of Marra, but will suggest an alternative, broader, more provisional form of translation, suited to her emphasis on process, in which I look at various possible ways of meshing the prose of herself and U.S. novelist Harry Mathews. For the translator, this interpretive process is always taking place at many levels, of which the written translation is only the most visible and (seemingly) final product. But the translator can aptly be described as first and foremost a specialized kind of reader, looking with avidity for all available and credible cultural parallels.

In citing the poet Charles Bernstein, I have already suggested one such possible parallel. Thinking of his writing here, and in connection with that of the other "Language" poets he is often associated with, brings to mind Fredric Jameson's peculiar cultural characterization of Language poetry—a characterization similar to the criticisms leveled against Porzecanski in Uruguay. Jameson's description of Language poetry as a degeneration of modernism into postmodern "schizophrenia," in which "the experience of the present becomes powerfully, overwhelmingly vivid and material," is a blatant attempt to deny the cultural and historical validity of those poets' methods of "cutting up" and reassembling the linguistic practices of official culture into almost unrecognizable shapes.[7]

Identifying a more appropriate object for Jameson's accusation of cultural irrelevancy, Bernstein refers to the dominant rhetorical mode of official culture, rather than Language poetry, as "close to being merely a *style* of decorous thinking, rigidified and formalized to a point severed from its historical relation to Descartes and Bacon. It is no longer an enactment of thinking or reasoning but a representation (and simplification) of an eighteenth-century ideal of reasoning."[8] The Language poets, in a barrage of manifestos and aesthetic position papers, and in their poetry, have defended their practices, and many of them (especially Steve McCaffery and Barrett Watten) have asserted their writing as a militant form of cultural activism.

Yet an even more interesting parallel might emerge out of the comparison of Porzecanski's writing with that of fiction writer Harry Mathews, who has allied himself with a school of writing that, like the Language poets, employs "cut-ups" and other "schizophrenic" generative devices but whose rhetoric is quite different. The ultra-aesthetic orientation of Mathews' prose seems to leave it much more open to accusations of the kind of cultural and historical quietism that has sometimes been attributed to Porzecanski's fiction, as well as make him a more vulnerable candidate for the culturally "schizophrenic" practices decried by Jameson. The two fiction writers have, granted, taken different approaches to inhabiting their respective national cultures: the U.S.-born Mathews has long lived in France, often publishes in French, and maintains a much stronger group identity with French writers and intellectuals than with any sort of United States literary or cultural scene; Porzecanski made a conscious decision to remain in Uruguay during the dictatorship. She has said that "everybody was leaving Uruguay; I felt that somebody had to stay."[9] But the aestheticism of the expatriate and very unpolitical Mathews can help illuminate the particular, subtle political quality of Porzecanski's fiction and her redefinitions of unitary concepts of history. One might begin by asking this question, applicable to both writers: Isn't it possible not only that history explains random mutations and those thought processes which exceed logic but that random mutations and the excesses "outside" logic could also explain history?

Mathews has been associated since 1960 with the Parisian group of experimental writers known as Oulipo, or *Ouvroir de Littérature Potentielle* (Workshop of Potential Literature), as the only American among them. This group explores the game-like aspects and structures of language, imposing an array of preconceived formal constraints on their writing, which they describe as "plagiarism in advance." They reject the notion that "constraining structures such as the acrostic, spoonerisms, the lipogram, the palindrome, or the holorhyme (to cite only these five) are mere examples of acrobatics," and propose that "literature ought to become the object of numerous and discerningly conceived prostheses."[10] Their irreverence toward a unitary conception of history is evident in the preface to a collection of their "exhumed documents" from 1960 to 1963. With a title deliberately more suspicious than auspicious—"And Thus Was Born the Workshop of Potential Literature"—the preface lampoons millenarianism, and Oulipo's own "historical" significance, with ironic bombast.

> Oulipo has the habit of measuring its decades of existence as millenia. Not that it wishes to swell in the least the millenarian wave that always foams over at the end of ten centuries of an era no more or less arbitary than another. Let no one see here either the mockery of minds inclined to facetiousness—a judgement often made by those who mistake seriousness for pleasantry, brains for beards. . . . Like those goddesses of ancient civilizations, Oulipo recovers the totality of time, embraces past, present and future: in a word, all eternity.[11]

Teresa Porzecanski has allied herself in Uruguay with a group of writers who cultivate what they call "narrativa de imaginación," opting for a writing that self-consciously explores the plastic possibilities of language, and they, like the Oulipians, prefer an oblique approach to questions of semantic "content." Porzecanski and the other adherents of "narrativa de imaginación," though their participation in Uruguayan cultural life has often been overtly political, frequently eschew direct political subject matter in their fiction, in favor of a "matter" that is more palpable and suggestive.

Imagine writing a historical interpretation of a particular completed Scrabble game left lying on a table or of a mathematical equation lifted at random from the *Bulletin of the American Society of Mathematics*, and you have some idea of the problems inherent in bringing Fredric Jameson's unitary Marxist assumptions of history to bear on the Oulipian productions of a writer like Harry Mathews.

The nature of the potential, or "charm of introducing duplicity" that Mathews imagines for literary practice becomes clear in his essay "Mathews's Algorithm." In it, he proposes a method called S + 7, which, as the Oulipo handbook explains, "consists in taking a text and replacing each substantive with the seventh following it in a given dictionary."[12] Mathews begins by stating that

> the most practical work of prose, no matter how sturdy it may seem in its apparent uniqueness, will prove . . . fragile just as soon as one thinks of subjecting it to the procedures of S + 7 . . . Beyond the words being read, others lie in wait to subvert and perhaps surpass them . . . every word has become a banana peel. The fine surface unity that a piece of writing proposes is belied and beleaguered; behind it, in the realm of potentiality, a dialectic has emerged.[13]

This emergent dialectic doesn't appear to be quite the same one that drives history in Jameson's account of culture. Jameson's method might fertilely be employed to interrogate the historical "schizophrenia" of Harry Mathews' algorithmic prose, but it is just as easy to turn the tables in order to see what other kinds of "truth" might emerge. One can imagine subjecting Jameson's claims, in *Syntax of History*,[14] about "the priority of Marxist analysis" over other interpretive codes as the "ultimate and untranscendable semantic horizon . . . of the *social*," to the procedures of (my own variation on) the Oulipian method S + 7 in order to arrive at a radically different syntax.

> As to the final state, like a baby's fist holding an orange—in all the poststructuralist critiques of interpretation (like a barber's cat, all wind and piss)—in which allegorical writing, like a dose of salts, always presupposes some privileged form of *representation*, like a one-armed paperhanger with crabs, in the present instance, presumably, the representation of History itself, like a spare prick at a wedding—we can merely assert here, like bats out of Hell, that it is precisely in this respect that a Marxist hermeneutic, like Christmas beef, can be radically distinguished from all the other types enumerated above, since its "master code," or transcendental signified, like fury, is precisely not given as a representation, like Old Gooseberry, but rather as an *absent cause*, like something the cat brings in of a wet night, as that which can never know full representation, like the story of the Pharoah's daughter. History is not in any sense itself a text

or master text or master narrative—like trying to open an oyster with a bus ticket—but it is inaccessible to us, like a bird, except in textual or narrative form. We approach it only by way of some prior textualization or narrative (re) construction.

It is precisely because of Jameson's insistence that History can only be approached through narrative reconstruction that it seems so appropriate to subject his own closed, if subtle, account to the disruptions and figurations bodied forth by the alternative, competing interpretive code brought about by S + 7. The resulting paragraph raises questions about Jameson's own hermeneutic, his claims that it isn't merely a "place of truth" but a movement which leaves the subject of history decentered. The juxtaposition of his nuanced, hypotactic prose (seemingly capable of containing and processing all, and *justly*) with phrases culled from a page, opened to at random, out of the *Dictionary of American Slang* lays his assertion of Marxism's primacy over other interpretive codes, whose "strategies of containment" it ostensibly serves to demystify, open to the very same reservations it expresses about mystification and self-sufficiency.

First there is the parenthetical aside that poststructuralist critiques of interpretation are "like a barber's cat, all wind and piss." Doesn't this interpolated slip of the tongue foreground how Jameson's writing's claims to legitimacy depend on a rhetorical strategy of measured thought, one which must needs refrain from bare invective and name-calling, in order to appear balanced and credible? And yet, in order for his Marxist analysis to assert its primacy, competing interpretive strategies must ultimately be characterized as wind and piss, except to the extent that they allow themselves to be subsumed by Jameson's preferred historical method.

Then there is the question of the ways in which each account depends on "some ultimate privileged interpretive *code* in terms of which the cultural object is allegorically rewritten"—a form of representation he claims Marxism doesn't engage in, since its transcendental signified is "not given as a representation but as an absent cause."[15] But some of the myriad absences and exclusions left unaccounted for by that absent cause begin to assert themselves in interesting ways, when the subversive words lying in wait become, à la Mathews, banana peels. What happens to Jameson's account when that absent cause is given sudden, concrete, representation—when it is like something the cat brings in of a wet night? Is this bedraggled thing, dangling from the cat's mouth, the transcendental signified of which we'd heard so much and seen so little? And why

can't the story of the Pharoah's daughter ever know full representation in this modern process of exegesis? Is it because a story about
Moses being found in a basket, with its attendant millenarian,
forward-looking, transcendent overtones, comes too close for comfort to the quasi-nostalgic, quasi-mystical strain in the closing
chords of Jameson's essay and its euphoric evocation of "Alain
Tanner's film *Jonah Who Will Be 25 in the Year 2000*—with its play
of postindividual collective relationships around the absent center
of birth and of a new subject to come"? Or maybe this was another
pharoah's daughter, come to think of it. What does Old Gooseberry
(Mephistopheles, Lucifer, Nick, Old Scratch) have to do with this,
and why *can* he be represented? How is a Marxist hermeneutic like
a Christmas beef? What makes History like a spare prick at a wedding? What do you get when you cross a privileged form of representation with a one-armed paperhanger with crabs?

Riddles, some of them cryptic, possibly unanswerable, and suspi-
ciously inane, begin to proliferate. It can be argued that although the
Oulipian juxtaposition creates some humorous effects through the
disjunctions it produces, the whimsy and "charm" (and, in this case,
earthiness or vulgarity and outright ludicrousness) of these riddles
are a flimsy basis on which to mount an inquiry into historical
method. And yet, the very cryptic and seemingly absurd yet endlessly suggestive quality of such simile-ridden riddles, like the famed
Sphinx's riddle, suggests the trivia of process, the "by-products" of
history, as a dialectical alternative to the Syntax of History and the
imperative toward definitive knowledge as a decentered form of
thinking. Riddles are a form of hermeneusis. The particular strands
I have plucked out of the passage might easily give way to other,
equally viable ones, and it goes without saying that another generative device or another passage of Jameson's writing (or someone
else's) might produce a very different kind of text to be read and very
different concerns. But the point is that Oulipian formal constraints,
often described as sheer play, fun, ultra-aesthetic, disengaged from
anything outside their own effete synchronicity, are not, in fact,
necessarily a- or anti-historical. My purpose in "using them on"
Jameson's sentences is not to negate his dialectic but rather to engage fully and textually that process of historical thinking which he
describes as "narrative (re) construction" and to acknowledge its lacunae and its banana peels. And if a certain quality of ludicrousness
is a by-product of this endeavor, it's not amiss. The attempt to pry
from any master or "not fully representable" narrative of History
(especially one that starts with a capital *H*) a fuller account of that

which it conceals seems to me like nothing so much as like trying to open an oyster with a bus ticket.

Even such influential Marxist intellectuals as the Frankfurt School's Theodor Adorno (to whose writing Jameson devotes the first chaper of *Marxism and Form*) have expressed reservations about the potential for dialectical method to become too systematic a system of thought. Adorno's book of micro-speculations, *Minima Moralia*, is comprised of the kinds of "volatile anecdotes" favored by Porzecanski. In "Bequest," one of the many philosophical vignettes in *Minima Moralia*, Adorno goes daringly far in professing his skepticism toward the adequacy of the dialectical method in which his own thought is rooted, and in offering a caveat. For him, the rigor of the method leaves it vulnerable to taking a rather ruthless turn.

> Dialectical thought is an attempt to break through the coercion of logic by its own means. But since it must use these means, it is at every moment in danger of itself acquiring a coercive character: the ruse of reason would like to hold sway over the dialectic too.[16]

In a variation on Benjamin's declaration that history should be written from the point of view of the vanquished, Adorno advises that knowledge

> should also address itself to those things which were not embraced by this dynamic, which fell by the wayside—what might be called the waste products and blind spots that have escaped the dialectic . . . all that which did not fit properly into the laws of historical movement. Theory must needs deal with cross-grained, opaque, unassimilated material.[17]

Waste products, blind spots; what is cross-grained, opaque, unassimilated; things fallen by the wayside: these are precisely the leftover areas in the "matter" of history which novelists Mathews and Porzecanski most wish to attend to. One of the facets of their fiction is the attempt to illuminate "the ruse of reason." Porzecanski's novel *Invención de los soles* (Sun Inventions), in which her narrator's project is to construct a parallel universe where the reign of chance operates fully, forges its own extra-logical brand of "necessity," as in this passage from its opening sequence:

And now, look at them sitting over there: bellies prominent, smug in their small logical mediocrities, conscious of their apparent intelligence because they've discovered a vaccine for the thirteenth virus of broxilosis trepidium. But there's always something which in the end betrays them. Something exists which they don't have the spirit to distinguish with a name; which spirits them, at the age of sixty, toward the purest and most genuine terror. Tachycardia, the manner of death, the goods for the potential heirs, the drugs that stave off complaints. And another form of terror: when logic fails, when all but silence fails. Look at them over there: terrified, without crutches, without lightning rods, without swords or breastplates, defenseless in their perplexity, paradoxical in their strength, the men of this world which is yet another world, shaken and dragged to vertiginous spatial speeds, corralling the equations of their daily life.[18]

Mathews similarly toys with logic but in a more genteel, more disarming, almost armchair manner that takes less forceful and less passionate exception to prevailing, oppressive paradigms of knowledge. In his writings, the relation of artistic method to explicit political and historical questions seems a more ancillary or minor concern than it does for Porzecanski. In his "Notes on the Threshold of a Book," he puts forth a highly synchronic and fairly restrictive view of writing's potential for affecting the larger cultural domain. In a demonstration of method of what he calls "performative writing," writing "capable of guaranteeing results," he says

I maintain that what you ask of a book is the possibility of learning—of knowing, in thought or feeling, something new . . . I suggest furthermore that since there is almost nothing that is truly new (and what there is will as soon as it is known become part of what is old) what you ask of a book . . . whether it is a book of poetry or a manual for the repair of air-conditioners, is to be given the satisfaction of experiencing the process of learning . . . that this is what is *common* to all books.[19]

All books, regardless of the specific culture and time in which they are produced or read, will, at least as far as *process* is concerned (that which precedes and exceeds their more perfunctory, utilitarian, task-specific, etc., features), "perform" in a fairly similar way, producing "satisfaction." The corollary to this seemingly old-fashioned assertion is that experimental or avant-garde writing in particular occupies no special status as concerns its potential for social transformation and does not come into being as a reaction to determining historical pressures.

Summarizing Mathews' assertions in the way I just have is a schematic rhetorical device and willfully wrongheaded on my part, especially since the speaker takes pains to problematize the position of his "I" through these very performative statements. He even locates his voice, at the end of the piece, by asserting that "I infer that the genius of . . . all successful writing . . . is to provide you with the materials and space to create me in a way identifiable with my historical reality and with the way I assert that that historical reality should be read."[20]

Still, as a rhetorical option, I find it instructive to characterize Mathews' writing here in a way that resists its being too automatically encompassed within the sweeping gestures of those critics who have grouped a large and disparate body of experimental (and not-so-experimental) writing under the aegis of "postmodernism," a term that is becoming increasingly hackneyed and troublesome as it struggles to account for more and more writing. It is limiting to conceive, even within the U.S. and/or U.S. expatriate–French scene, of contemporary experimental writing as all somehow similarly and equally symptomatic (decadent, schizophrenic) of "late capitalism" (Jameson) and "commodification" or, conversely, as a revolutionary form of transforming consciousness in ways that politically "resist" the culture and society in which they circulate. The assumptions informing Harry Mathews' fiction and poetry, for instance, could arguably be demarcated fairly easily from the assumptions and stated claims of some of the Language poets I have mentioned, who, as I have said, also employ generative devices and formal constraints, such as cut-ups, and share an infatuation with structuralist/poststructuralist thought. Though Mathews' writing, like theirs, is preoccupied with complicating authorial intentionality, the following portentous "economic" account of language's political potential, in poet Steve McCaffery's *North of Intention,* rings alien, in both its rhetoric and its content, to Mathews' linguistic project.

> Language Writing involves a fundamental repudiation of the socially defined functions of author and reader as the productive and consumptive poles respectively of a commodital axis. The main thrust of the work is hence political rather than aesthetic, away from the manufacture of formal objects toward a frontal assault on the steady categories of author and reader, offering

instead the writer-reader function as a compound, fluid relationship of two interchangeable agencies within sign production and sign circulation.[21]

The preceding, especially its tone, seems, in fact, a pretty good description of that which Mathews' fiction is *not:* an intellectually activist frontal assault on language as capitalist oppressor. If one provisionally accepts McCaffery's political/aesthetic distinction, at least as poles of a continuum, Mathews' writing would seem to gravitate toward the aesthetic one, with much closer and more obvious affinities to his Oulipian confreres Raymond Roussel and Raymond Queneau than to Steve McCaffery. To say so is not to criticize either tendency. If "postmodern" writing is to remain something besides that inchoate and indistinguishable raw material which is cannibalized (for whatever purposes) by a master historical narrative of liberation and is to investigate the processes and absences of that narrative, then it needs to be acknowledged that there are many viable, competing variants of experimental fiction and poetry, each bearing its own charge of "potential."

The Oulipians, too, have their manifestos, but as a group, they are intent on investigating their own peculiar modalities of the potential of aesthetic process, as the "First Manifesto" makes evident: "A word at the end for the benefit of those particularly grave people who condemn without consideration and without appeal all work wherein is manifested any propensity for pleasantry. When they are the work of poets, entertainments, pranks, and hoaxes still fall within the domain of poetry. Potential literature remains the most serious thing in the world."[22]

It is this serious pleasantry, a pursuit pursued as if it were its own end, that is one of the chief sources of the "satisfactions" Mathews' *The Conversions* has to offer. In the chapter "The Customs House," the place where the protagonist has gone to track down some clues in order to solve the riddles left for him in a Mr. Wayl's will so he can claim his inheritance, he comes upon a group of "lazing officials . . . soft and old and filled with the resignation of old barflies."[23] En route to providing him access to the shelves of books "*Seized at the request of the Earl of Mar*" and suppressed during the subsequent Earl's rule, they recount to him the history of how the patronage system, of which they are the descended, lazy products, was set up as a compensation for the taxes which the Earl levied on his subjects.

Though an equitably corrupting political system, taxation, and the suppression of books are described in these pages, it would be simplistic to construe these topics as the matter of Mathews' prose.

They are, rather, an occasion to engage in some lipogrammatic play, in the formulaic excision of vowels and consonants from the history being recounted by the nine officials.

> This custms hous (one said) was bult in the sixtenth centry to tax the metl producd by the Silvr Glen of Alva, whch blonged then, as now, to the Erls of Mar.
> The Arls (the second haltingly took up) in llowing his ax to be mposed on the roduce of their orkings, tipulated hat in eturn hey be iven ertain rivileges.[24]

The effect of this passage on a reader is similar to that of the linguistic test in which cognition is demonstrated by this very same method of excising phonemes, to show that certain centers of the brain will compensate by filling in the textual gaps on the page. Here, as part of an artistic venture in narrative, the pleasure of the test is in the "satisfaction of experiencing the process of learning" that Mathews says performative writing will evoke. One would really have to be reaching to invest these pages with any sort of explicit or implicit political or social critique, except of the most indirect and casual kind. The game itself is paramount, and though the fiction is highly self-conscious in its formal concerns, the tone is one of largely untroubled, if mildly decadent, leisure. History, if it appears at all, is simply the sum of all possible permutations of the mental pursuit at hand in the present moment.

Something might be made of the fairly obvious analogy between the formal suppression of letters and the thematic suppression of books, but in the novel, this metaphorical relation is not pursued, and what *is* of interest are, rather, the plastic and algorithmic possibilities of language-in-itself. Georges Perec exclaims with approval of *The Conversions* that they "secrete symbols, allegories, points of contact and discontinuity . . . lexical, verbal, and syntactical deformations, myths and obscurities, none of them having, ultimately, reference to anything beyond themselves."[25] That is not to say that the "suppressions" in the novel could not be pursued and given a more political charge, of the kind that might answer more directly to McCaffery's account of the economy of language. What would interest me, though, are the ways in which the two different charges of "suppression" could modify one another, the way I earlier forced a mutual modification between a Marxist "Utopian" and a seemingly frivolous and rigidly formal "Oulipian," so that the work is neither a political frontal assault nor a plasticity with little or no ultimate reference to anything beyond itself.

But the conversion of *The Conversions* into an allegory of dictatorial thought oppression—one might call this apocryphal book *The Subversions*—or even into a stricter analogue of Porzecanski's *Sun Inventions*, remains "potential." It could be carried out, its oppositional language given a more prominent place in the total authorial strategy, but it doesn't take place within *The Conversions* as it stands, since that is not the kind of project Mathews is interested in turning his brilliant inventiveness on. It would require a more subjective or willful intervention on the part of a reader or re-writer or translator to make manifest those scarcely-hinted-at potentialities. An adventurous translator might contemplate an Oulipian intervention, such as a fold-in or cut-up with a text of a kind designed to emphasize certain kinds of political or historical disruptions. I'll resort again, momentarily, to the trivia of process, folding passages of Mathews' and Porzecanski's novels into one another, as a kind of Ur-translation or meta-translation, to see in what ways each can enhance and beleaguer the other.

Both Mathews and Porzecanski make use of the fantastic or allegorical but in such a way that the sacred quest for knowledge and power is never allowed fully to assert its mystical transcendence. In the chapter "The Otiose Creator" of *The Conversions*, the narrator reads a chapter in one of the books stored in the customs house, in which one character, Gottlieb, narrates to another a dream in which he enters a place, "past the clouds, past the stars," which he believes to be Paradise. On the outskirts, about to enter the shining city, he comes upon a man lying in a ditch, runs to the city for help, and describes the prostrate man's subsequent brutalization by the policeman with whom he returns. Someone in Paradise later explains to him that the billions of people suffering and maimed on the outskirts will never die and that heaven, a "logical" extension of terrestrial life, is a place of rigid hierarchies based on wealth and personal connections.

The satiric dream-view of heaven ends with the chilling evocation of "world without end" and, then, Gottlieb's baffling evocation of someone he refers to as "the fucking Johnstones! the enemies of things as they are! . . . May their Gypsy girl have wicked teeth in her cunt!"[26] This textual clue, which immediately takes precedence over the allegory that has preceded it, leads the first narrator back into his quest for the answer to the three riddles that will make his earthly fortune—a quest which leads, ultimately, nowhere in particular.

In *Sun Inventions*, Ana's idiot, vegetable-like cousin, Isaac, who spends much of his time propped in her shop window next to a manikin, gradually comes to be worshiped religiously by the neighbors and one day ascends to heaven. The "space left absent by divinity," after his beatification, soon comes to be filled by the inert manikin, who, because it is equally object-like, is able to supplant Isaac as "the adored image." Isaac's ascension, though it is built to dramatically, does not mark a culminating moment of transcendence, but simply another motion in the process of manufacturing object-gods. It is one of innumerable "sun inventions."

Combining passages cribbed from the two authors produces new formats of significance, a deadly serious game of Scrabble, fixed, yet subject to capricious interpretations.

> The gods would have no followers without bones about to pierce the skin. Meanwhile, the smell of incense permeated the greasy parchment, had indeed begun to break off Isaac's graceful transformation. Little wheezing groans issued from the door like the potent light of a noonday sun. I ran towards the city about him like a body, sacredness palpitated in his gums, poor creature, grew as opaque as a shriek of horror, then became things. I came upon a policeman, dressed in silk, and with his blond head frightfully tilted before me. We were soon beyond choreographed secrets. Our Fathers no longer breathed. As for the policeman, he was seen to die painlessly in his wheelchair, seemed indifferent to the prostrate man. His image gradually faded into an attitude, struck him a terrible blow on the temple, transcending the precarious weather of that day, attaining an absolute, ultraterrestrial color. Then the policeman saluted, one of many Christs to inaugurate, without meaning to, for a while in a shocked daze. The space left absent by divinity manifested itself.

This sort of operation seems to me quite similar to the completion of the translation process, the hermeneutic motion of which George Steiner speaks. "The hermeneutic act must compensate.... The process of translation, like all modes of focused understanding, will detail, illumine, and generally body forth its object. ... The original text gains from the orders of diverse *relationship and distance* established between itself and the translations. The reciprocity is dialectic: new 'formats' of significance are initiated *by distance and by contiguity* [emphasis mine]."[27] And it further resembles translation in the sense that one is performing operations on a preexisting text, yet this does not preclude—in fact invites—creativity and subjectivity.

The Oulipian operations, if they are to be fruitful, involve conscious effort in terms of what will be selected and exactly how that will be formally restricted. Some combinations will "work" better than others. In describing his algorithmic method, Mathews ends up acknowledging that however much the Oulipian arbitrary procedures may open up a text, they, as much as the method of Marxist dialecticians, run the risk of ultimately sealing off possibilities if pursued with too much rigor. His choice of word is telling, echoing Adorno's caveat about the dialectic's potentially "coercive" nature. Mathews says flatly of his algorithm that "its aim is not to liberate potentiality, but to coerce it."[28] The Oulipo handbook strikes this same paradoxical note, caught between arbitrary process and conscious manipulation, in its description of the S + 7 method: "The result obviously depends on the dictionary one chooses. Naturally, the number seven is arbitrary."[29] These minutiae are important in distinguishing the Oulipians from the surrealist currents in which they partly originated. Mathews (and likewise Porzecanski) cannot be categorized as a surrealist. His "arbitrary coercion" does not elevate his preferred method into a social fetish, nor is it an attempt to access some "unconscious" transcendent state beyond language as a millenarian aesthetic space.

By this same token, my earlier S + 7 combination of Jameson's *Syntax of History* with the *Dictionary of American Slang* relied as much on elements of conscious selection as it did on elements of chance to bring out certain submerged tones of Jameson's essay. The opening to the page of similes was random, but the dictionary, one of several I found in an adjoining building during the writing of this chapter, seemed the "right" dictionary for the occasion, for reasons which only became clear to me later.

The discrepancies between the two writers are as significant as their affinities. A sense of history as the history of social repression and resistance does seem to inform Teresa Porzecanski's fiction in a much more direct way than it does Mathews'. In a polemical essay, she makes the case for, and includes her own writing in, the irrealist current of "narrativa de imaginación." These writers, as she is quick to point out, "aren't militant as such in the sense of treating political or social themes." But she describes the practice of making literature as one of subversion in the sense of arising within, and in opposition to, a specific historical and political situation of dictatorship in Uruguay. This imaginative writing wishes to "carefully disassemble both the formal machinery and content of the ideological rhetoric [and nostalgic, millenarian discourse] through which the dictatorship wished to affirm that Uruguayan culture was moving ahead without any significant fractures" and "to give a perfect image of the then-called 'new Uruguay.' "[30]

She eschews realism, saying its inadequacy has to do with its powerful contemporary co-optation by "an officialist discourse, conventionally 'realist,' but emblematically eluding any approach to truth." The stylistic proclivities of the writers of *narrativa de imaginación*—the central role of fabulation, fantasy, allegory; the "problematic of asphyxia," presented principally through form rather than story—these come out of the pressures of a particular, collectively lived historical situation. She speaks of the psychic results of this cultural moment as a collective "sensation of being under scrutiny" and of "lived fear and a desire to flee." She also speaks of the writer as someone whose literary productions must counteract a dictatorship striving to produce a public of "cautious, prudent, readers."[31]

Despite the disparity in the cultural situations out of which they write and their different impetuses, what unites Porzecanski's narrative with Mathews' is her insistence on "turning back toward the materiality of language itself" and "fiction in its character as artifice," although she goes on to add, as Mathews probably wouldn't, "because ... rhetoric is always the repository of all ideology." But her description of literary imagination's being characterized by "the premeditated distortion of expected contours" and "the systematic contortions of art, designed to erase the careful and precarious distinction by which the world is consensually described," are reminiscent of Mathews' algorithmic insistence, quoted earlier, of other words beyond those being read, lying "in wait to subvert and perhaps surpass them," and of how "the fine surface unity that a piece of writing proposes is belied and beleaguered."

Porzecanski's novel *Invención de los soles* is not "about" dictatorship but, rather, about epistemology, hermeneusis, the possibility of coming to know, and the ineluctable impulse to construct a parallel universe. Many of the connections I have made between Mathews, history, and Oulipian techniques come to mind in a reading of *Sun Inventions*. There are a number of episodes, for instance, in which the protagonist, Ana, a teacher of social science methodology, employs a pedagogy in her lectures which, because of its outbursts and pursued tangents, always seems to end up leading not to useful, practical, applied knowledge, but only to ever-greater uncertainty.

The topic of today's class will be research and questions concerning the resources of a geographic space beginning with short-term practicum objectives but at bottom the question always gnaws at me how to accede to the thing how to pretend this reality I'm teaching is the only existing one: perhaps infinite insects I'm not even faintly conscious of are flourishing beneath the stones of the relief map's heights? And this air I breathe? Doesn't it seem as though exhaled by huge forests of which I'm abruptly ignorant? Perhaps that man in the street about to be surveyed is in short nothing more than a percentage? And besides I can always maintain that those very constructions don't exist, that the image of that place which you imagine in that time I imagine in another place and time and that my time and your time are different and the breach, the terrible breach, is unredeemable.[32]

The questions here are not posed in a way which asks that they be answered or proved by empirical knowledge and rational field-work. They are, once again, riddles as a form of hermeneusis, possibly unanswerable, or endlessly and capriciously refutable. No single interpretive code can ultimately, credibly assert itself. No "redemption" stands at the end of history. The only satisfaction to be had is, to use Mathews' phrase, the satisfaction of experiencing the process of learning itself.

The novel's narrative moves between more purely epistemological passages and Ana's investigation of her personal ancestral origins. The reader is given to understand, through various strands and images that appear, that the relatives on her father's side were from Eastern Europe, many of them direct victims of the Holocaust. This allegorical representation, itself very muted, is as close as Porzecanski ever comes to any mention of the proto-fascistic political situation in her own country. History is not permitted to assert itself as any single, unqualified, subsuming narrative which will give a restorative account of that which has been decimated. To do so would be to fall back into a consensual description of the world. Instead, there is a vacillation between the desire for each piece of "matter" to exist in its own right, to tell its own fragmented, self-identical story, and the simultaneous drive to interpret, to give a coherent account of it. As Ana is examining photos of her dead ancestors, "the capricious finery, the faint smiles," she observes that some died

from old age and others because their lives had coincided with planned destructions, an invasion of Germans or Russians or Latvians or whoever else, men who exerted their power over a silent, humble, sleeping village. . . . my ancestors were a mere measly frail percentage of all who'd actually existed on the face of the earth. A bare statistical sample, you might say, a fleeting and diminished manifestation of all that which proclaimed itself as History, the process constructed by sweat and blood with shreds of humankind, with portions of time, with unfinished chunks of diffuse sequences. And in the final stage of wishing to know the total picture, great amorphous holes remained unfilled.

History seems to be constituted out of the perdurance of shreds of matter, yet this matter is in its turn constituted by the interpretive act. "Matter," says Ana, "persists beyond your whimsy, beyond your fickle and convenient interpretations. . . . No fact truly succeeds in a given manner besides that which you posit and can prove at every moment. Oh damned versatility of slippery history, they use you helter-skelter, they abuse you with impunity and time and again your only worth will be for the uses of the present, which is nothing less than the all of existence." Though Ana affirms that objects, un-like facts, will retain a unitary coherence through time, she also asserts, conversely, that the "uses of the present" are tantamount to the all of existence (a position supported and reinforced, like its antithesis, by many other portions of the novel). Porzecanski, like Mathews, puts forth the synchronic notion that history cannot be known by us except as the sum of all possible permutations of the mental pursuit at hand in the present moment.

The attempt to give a total narrative can only lead into and out of portions of time, unfinished chunks of diffuse sequences, and great amorphous holes. This indeterminate status occupied by language is, I think, part of what Porzecanski suggests in referring to "the turning back toward the materiality of language itself" and "fiction in its character as artifice." It is a gravitation as much toward the purely aesthetic as toward the purely historical or political. It is cut-ting up history.

Porzecanski's method of enacting language as the detritus or trivia of process remains, in specific terms, often quite different from that of Mathews, but there are moments at which the similarities assert themselves strongly and demonstrate how Mathews' prose might serve a translator for adapting Porzecanski's fiction into English (and vice-versa: Porzecanski could as easily, and without priority, serve as a medium for Mathews' entry into Latin American fiction). Porzecanski's narrator in *Sun Inventions*, meditating on a col-league's need for "clear, strict, and ordered pigeonholes," and her own opposing preference for "the spectral power to ask," imagines a gyroscope which constantly mixes up questions' parts and throws back results such as: why doesn't sonorous honeysuckle sound the indissoluble hands of? or: does foolproof honeysuckle offer up musty miniatures?[33]

Such palpable verbal "results," produced by what seems to be an orderly and regulated notion of process, are not unlike the verbal results of Mr. Wayl's worm race in *The Conversions,* the rules of which are explained in detail but the outcome of which is unpredictable. At the end of the worm race, the narrator observes that

> There only remained the trail of triturated food and slime my lost worm had left, broken marks of a shiny blackness among which I recognized certain letters
>       e    as    no    s     ex    rex    noth     Syl i
> Mr. Wayl said . . . to me: That was not what I meant. I tried to lay down the food so that he would spell . . . But the result is nothing—fragments.

In Mathews as in Porzecanski, there is a formal distortion of language that moves it toward non-signification, giving the language the status of sheer artifact. At the same time, this play and foregrounding of artifice is embedded within a more conventional narrative, one in which provisional claims about meaning and coherence can be staked by narrators and characters. The game playing both authors indulge in gambles on or with coherence, letting now one interpretive code, now another assert itself, but never fully displaces coherence. The aesthetic effect of these radical distortions depends on creating the illusion that "the total picture" might be revealed and whetting the appetite for it. Porzecanski's conception of the open, resistant work depends on its intimate relationship to the expectations set up by that which it resists. "Breaking the closed field of a single permitted interpretation, [the open work] approached, in an interminable allusion, the opening up of the presuppositions through which [official discourse] had attempted to erect an axiology of regularity and order."[34] And Eric Mottram, comparing Mathews' fiction to the relentless game narratives of Raymond Roussel, says that Mathews "is restrained, less nihilistic, less brutal in response requirements, and more inclined to engage the reader's imaginative abilities than to glut them with ready-mades . . . Mathews is adept at following . . . the pragmatic protocol of a narrative form in order to expose its creative needs, especially present in descriptions of natural process and in technology."[35]

Such a description, including the obsession with technology and borrowed or invented scientific knowledge, could apply very aptly to Porzecanski's own fiction making. The loving, detailed description of the Oulipian *chromaturge* which the painter Namque uses to generate unusual color schemes in *The Conversions* has at least one counterpart in *Sun Inventions*. Here is just one brief passage from Mathews:

> The image entered the right-hand shaft of tube. Again it was subjected to a series of colored lights, but in distinction to the first set, these infused new colors into the image. The recolored image appeared in the viewer on the right, while the switches below it controlled the second group of lights.[36]

The description of the workings of Porzecanski's *mutandis gyroscope* sounds very much like an Oulipian machine in its own right. One of the chief differences to be noted is that her description, especially given the context of the novel as a whole (and the sensibility Uruguayan readers under a silencing dictatorship might bring to it), does have connotations of a process of radical social transformation.

> Ways of constructing a mutandis gyroscope: take dictionaries strictly approved by the Academy, cut into strips of two centimeters per concept, drop into a heat-resistant container along with two centimeters of oozed cerebral sweat and tears and the hard-bitten wound of the left forearm, cook on a low flame stirring constantly to keep the abovementioned salve from sticking. Take from the burner place it on a steel disk propelled to spin at infinite rpm's. . . . when all the paste has started to evaporate begin again emitting voices: first isolated syllables such as yut ipb nko and then, slowly, invent a new language. Don't be alarmed by the initial sounds which may seem a little strange: rather, let flourish, as if you were a ventriloquist, the voices of organs. Finally, knead the perimeter, rolling it out and, from then on, a like mutation is suggested every two weeks.

The tone of the passage at first appears somewhat millenarian, seeming to imply that the process is leading toward a new, final liberation and utopian transformation, a new society heralded by the invention of "a new language." But any specific formulation of that society as the "end" of history is rejected and undercut by the final suggestion of "a like mutation . . . every two weeks." Social and historical change depend on a continual return to process, the endless permutation of language as a tangible entity. This move is especially important given the desire to shatter the repository of ideology, the concepts "strictly approved by the Academy."

Eric Mottram's commentary on Mathews' fiction speaks with directness to Porzecanski's own project on this score. Those writings have, he says,

> nowhere to go but to our own nostalgic reservoir of needs for riddle, enigma, puzzle, strange games, weird languages, craving for result and resolution by way of speculations and curiosity. They are themselves alone, unique, but fulfill an appetite, like cookery.
>
> They also work for another appetite: for the termination of the destructive dominance of the myth that the central design of knowledge is a quest journey, collecting bits of encyclopedic information which indicate totality—that the sacred journey is the major myth-method to accumulate knowledge and therefore power.[37]

To the extent that a writer in one language may serve as a medium for translating a writer in another language, a dialectical, Oulipian juxtaposition of the two seems to me helpful and justifiable. I have purposely not offered, in the pages of this chapter, the kind of translator's textually specific "close reading" that is often worked through in the form of critical prose. But I do see an Oulipian juxtaposition as a more heightened and concrete, if peculiar, instance of the constant mental act which a translator performs when s/he mentally compares writers of two languages for purposes of the linguistic adaptation which the comparison is supposed to help generate. Thus, a cut-up, fold-in, $S + 7$, etc., is not necessarily the "end" of the translative act—the more so since in many important respects there is no such thing—but rather one among many "means" of translation. It seems particularly helpful to me in seeing two such innovative writers as Mathews and Porzecanski in non-prioritized relation to each other.

# 4. Epistolary Fiction and Intellectual Life in a Shattered Culture: Ricardo Piglia and John Barth

The military dictatorship ruling Argentina from 1976 to 1983 euphemistically proclaimed itself "The Process of National Reorganization." The motto "accomplishments, not time frames," became one of its standard replies to discreet queries about the length of time it intended to remain in power. One of the significant national reorganizations accomplished during that time was the mass exodus of, among other citizens, Argentina's intellectuals and artists, many of whom fled to the United States, Europe, or other countries of Latin America. As many remained as left, however, and this demographic rift widened into a spiritual one, to become one of the most acrimonious of divisive forces even among progressive intellectuals of otherwise similar political sympathies.

This mutual contentiousness between those who went and those who stayed, often reaching the emotional pitch of animosity and extending in time beyond the seven years of the Process, could be characterized as one of the most profound incursions of the military into Argentine cultural activity during the seventies and eighties, as significant in its own way as the banning of books during that time or the decrepitude of the publishing enterprise (until then the most flourishing in Latin America). Beatriz Sarlo, one of her country's most prolific "remaining" cultural critics and founder of the adversarial magazine *Punto de vista,* waves aside the often juvenile polemic of moral superiority between those who left and those who remained and describes the separation in more dialectical and historical terms. "With respect to exile, the dictatorship achieved one of its victories in atomizing the intellectual realm, producing two lines of Argentine intellectuals (those inside and those outside), even fostering resentments on both sides and fracturing a center of democratic opposition."[1]

Understood in that way, this particular polemic among two camps of intellectuals becomes part of a more general failure of communication among the intelligentsia and among the members of society-at-large. For the dictatorship depended for its success on a strategy much more subtle than repression plain-and-simple. Its architects strived to create a pervasive sense of cultural doubt and indeterminacy among Argentina's inhabitants, in which selective repression alternated unpredictably with a seeming liberality. Or, as journalist Osvaldo Bayer puts it:

> Sure, books were burned, but that was at the beginning, to show authority, but later everything was done softly and in the dark. . . . The press tried to be as "pluralist" as possible. That's why the dictatorship's best helpers weren't the exegetes of military power but those who expressed themselves "moderately," those who knew how to leave a gentle wake of criticism. They helped demonstrate "pluralism." Of course, there were "taboos" everyone respected: the unnameables, the exiles, the "subversives."[2]

The effect of this selective pluralism was to encourage the fears of everyone involved in the collective cultural enterprise that they themselves might easily, at any time and without prior warning, become one of the "unnameables" in the taboo category. Such institutionalized unease had a stultifying effect on intellectual exchange of all kinds, especially if it could be interpreted as in any way subversive. Beatriz Sarlo describes censorship as exercised with "great tactical finesse."

> The guidelines for censorship were only partially known by those affected by the censors' operations. It manifested itself in the lack of any precise indication of what one could do or say. By widening the zone of indefinition, the military regime aimed to suggest that any act could possibly be construed as a crime. Thus, teachers and professors knew of the existence of prohibitions (books, authors, presses, etc.) but rarely had access to a complete list. . . . Under such a system of indeterminacy, education and the mass media opted for remaining this side of the danger line, proving the efficacy of a game whose rules were known only to the military chieftain presiding in each specific instance.[3]

Given this climate, it surprises little that so many of the country's writers chose to dwell elsewhere while this somewhat random but calculated Process of cultural suppression followed its course. Yet even those who took up physical residence in other countries could not fully escape the vague, all-encompassing strictures imposed on communication, if they hoped to participate at all in the verbal counterculture to the Argentine Process of National Reorganization.

The concept of exile has undeniably come to be freighted with romantic and sometimes opportunistic overtones, and one might legitimately question its appropriation by some Latin American intellectuals who left their country to seek more lucrative teaching positions abroad, yet who nonetheless wished to acquire in retrospect an aura of subversiveness by referring to themselves as "exiled." Accusations of more or less this type were, in fact, leveled at some of those who left Argentina in the seventies by those who remained in the grim and austere atmosphere of dictatorship. Yet an adequate definition of exile must describe it as first and foremost a coercive phenomenon, rather than a matter of choice. Whether this "option" was consciously created by the state or came about simply as a by-product of a larger social deterioration, its effects must in either case be measured as part of the systematic repression and uncertainty during those years of dictatorship.

Both the title and the tone of Tomás Eloy Martínez's "The Language of Inexistence" suggest that exile, for many Argentines, created not only a temporary dislocation but an ontological problem. Martínez, who lived abroad in Caracas for the duration of the Process, says that the resultant social fragmentation "transformed us into indeterminate beings. . . . The flood which exiled all of us who dissented from those in power, within and without, consigned us to disappearance, obliged us not to exist."[4] The military strategy of "disappearing" people—for which Argentina became famous during this period, in lending to a verb that had always been intransitive a new, sinister, transitive usage—derived as much of its impact from the impossibility of determining whether the person in question was alive or dead as it did from the eventual likelihood of confronting that person's death. Martínez's remark suggests that this physical and verbal uncertainty pervaded even the lives of those who had "escaped" to other places. Just as significant is his implication that inhabitants both within and without the geographical border can justly be grouped under the category of "exile," since the concept refers not to mere physical absence but rather to an ever-growing sense of indeterminacy and ontological doubt. In this, he echoes Sarlo's contention that in addition to the exile of "friends and interlocutors," there must be added "the segregation [within Argentina] of intellectuals and artists in an almost hermetic bubble."[5]

The problem of exile emerges as essentially the problem of

communication. A populace whose members find themselves destined, singly, to a collective and perpetual *incomunicado* have difficulty affirming their own existence. Martínez coins perhaps the
most powerful and telling cultural trope of the years of the Process,
when he searches for an anecdotal language sufficient to convey the
sense of non-being experienced by those on both "sides" of exile
during those years.

> Maybe it's worthwhile to evoke how we felt, those of us in exile,
> at the beginning of our inexistence. The episodes are almost
> trivial, but revealing. Warned that correspondence was opened
> by the authorities, we began to modify our names on the letters'
> return addresses. I didn't find it difficult to change myself into
> simply Martínez.[6] But also on the other end, the end over there
> (or for me, always the end over here), the destinee was obliged to
> pretend: to be just the aunt or cousin receiving the letter who
> would, in her turn, deliver it to the real recipient. After a while
> those who didn't write back proliferated, those to whom we
> sent, desperate with hope, one of our books or told a personal
> story, without their acknowledging receipt. We became resigned
> to it.[7]

The writing of letters and the sending of books, the sustained but
(in many cases) gradually diminishing search for a "correspondence"
that will overcome the paranoia enforced by a censoring dictatorship,
suggests itself as emblematic of what it meant for intellectuals during the seventies and early eighties to try to negotiate the harsh pri-
vatization of the public sphere and the concomitant, equally harsh,
public nature of the private sphere. The ruses that Martínez and his
erstwhile correspondents had to resort to poignantly illustrate the
abdications of identity which became necessary in order for artistic
and cultural dialogue under such extreme circumstances to remain
possible. Martínez's account also suggests the epistolary as the consummate mode for understanding the attempt at giving literary expression to the fragmentation lived by a nation of exiles, both internal and external, during this moment in Argentina's history. Sarlo,
Martínez's "corresponding" voice from the inside, goes so far as to
define exile as "that place from which the letters arrived."[8] The years
of the Process were, for intellectuals, epistolary years.

Such a way of defining the cultural crisis produced by the Process
offers a historical context for the rapt reception given to Ricardo
Piglia's epistolary novel *Respiración artificial* (Artificial Respiration), written and published in the midst of the Process (1980). This

historical novel, while it doesn't undertake to portray the dictatorial excesses of its time, as Nelson Marra's story "El guardaespalda," for instance, does for Uruguay, nonetheless represents the Argentine intellectual zeitgeist of the seventies, which I am analyzing here under the rubric of the epistolary. Piglia's novel has generated a great deal of thematic commentary, much of it historical or political in emphasis. This commentary has almost uniformly failed to address the epistolary dimension of what is patently a novel made of letters. Yet the epistolariness of this novel, which bears in its subject matter only the obliquest of relationships to the explicit political moment, is precisely what can best account for its profound emotional appeal to its Argentine readership. In *Respiración artificial*, intellectuals skeptical of the future and critical of the Argentine past employ letter writing as a form of modest hope, to nourish and sustain themselves in the present toward the eventual possibility of a renewed public life after dictatorship.

In searching among critical writings in English for a general account of experimentation with the epistolary genre in contemporary U.S. literature, the closest one might come is a couple of isolated, almost casual paragraphs at the very end of Janet Altman's study in eighteenth-century fiction, *Epistolarity: Approaches to a Form*. Altman remarks of the letter novel, in closing, that it "is one of the first genres constituted by discovery of a medium and exploration of its potential. In that, it resembles many of the experimental forms of the twentieth century that question the subordination of the medium to the message."[9] This insight, however, appears, in true epistolary style, as a mere postscript to her study—resonant with possibility but not elaborated on.

Altman's aim is "to push a certain kind of formalist reading to its limits on a particularly intriguing 'form.' "[10] She reins in "epistolarity," a suggestive concept, to an investigation into form. Her "working definition" of her neologism is "the use of the letter's formal properties to create meaning." Yet a strictly formalist consideration of contemporary experiments with epistolary fiction will fail to provide much insight into John Barth's use of the letter novel to express his vision of social conservatism. In his widely reviewed epistolary novel *LETTERS*, Barth counters the excesses of political activism during the sixties with adherence to a political via media, which he gives expression to as an orderly dance of epistolary exchange. A study limited to formal properties, in this case, could do little more than replicate uncritically that social conservatism, implicitly offering formal symmetry as a transparent and "well-made" substitute for the resolution of societal ills.

One partial explanation of the relegation of experimental writing in the U.S. to eccentricity, in the past two decades, is the fact that fictional innovation has been discussed almost exclusively as if it were a sophisticated parlor game. But Barth's *LETTERS*, far from limiting itself to an exploration of the problems of form and style and forging an aesthetic credo, offers a very specific view of America as a site of intemperate *social* conflict and proposes to substitute his temperate, effete version of "revolution" as an antidote. Unlike Piglia, for whom the retreat of intellectuals from the public sphere is a temporary effect of political coercion, Barth views this state as natural, permanent, and desirable.

The correspondence in Piglia's *Respiración artificial* begins, a few pages into the novel, with a letter precipitously written by Marcelo Maggi, living in obscurity in an Argentine river town at the border of Uruguay—Entre Ríos—addressing his nephew Emilio Renzi. Renzi has written an amateurish novel, a family saga, misrepresenting the "facts" of an adulterous affair Maggi had years ago with an exotic dancer, and Maggi, who had long since dropped out of sight, writes him in order to set the record straight. But the family saga is a mere pretext for establishing a correspondence between two obscure, failed intellectuals who happen to be relatives and who have never met, nor will ever meet. Though both live within the country and though Renzi travels by train to meet his uncle in Entre Ríos, Maggi, for reasons that never become clear, packs his bags and disappears just before the arrival of his nephew, appointing a Polish exile friend, another failed intellectual named Tardewski, to meet him. Maggi also entrusts to Tardewski the manuscript of a book he is writing about Enrique Ossorio, an exile and a nineteenth-century ancestor of Maggi and Renzi, who was accused of being a traitor and double agent during the republican struggles between opposing politicians Sarmiento and Rosas.

But the novel is no more "about" these events per se than Renzi's novel would be allowed by his uncle to be "about" his affair. Rather, *Respiración artificial* explores the formal means through which a group of Argentine intellectuals constitute a sense of collective identity, in a time when they are relegated to a seemingly terminal informality. Under a dictatorship where intellectuals have been dispersed, virtually no public sphere exists. Intellectual institutions and cultural organs such as universities and publishing houses have been dismantled or shut down, except for a modicum of events specifically designed for the participation in public life of a handful of officially sanctioned intellectuals.[11] Few opportunities remain to the marginal majority, outside small gestures such as writing letters to one another. Though peripheral, failed, and obscure by self-definition, Renzi, Maggi, and Tardewski (and their nineteenth-century counterpart, Ossorio) undertake to examine questions at the center of Argentine life.

The role of letters in this undertaking would need to reflect the task of trying to overcome the hermetic isolation and indeterminacy experienced by Argentines during the Process of National Reorganization, and Piglia, in fact, adapts the epistolary conceits of the eighteenth century to these contemporary concerns. In a chapter of Ruth Perry's study of eighteenth-century epistolary fiction, *Women, Letters, and the Novel,* entitled "Separation and Isolation," she concludes that "the isolation of the characters is essential to the epistolary formula because it throws the characters back into themselves, to probe their own thoughts, their own feelings." This process of self-examination, she says, "gathers momentum and ultimately becomes more important than communicating with anyone outside the room in which one sits alone writing letters."[12]

But while isolation does provide the occasion for written introspection in Piglia's novel, the momentum which gathers is directed, in fact, outside the room of writing and bent on discovering a means of communication which will reshape an identity blotted out by the prevailing, systematic degradation of language in the Argentina of the seventies. Maggi's final letter to his nephew vacillates between skepticism about their correspondence and an intense desire for connnection. Maggi self-consciously reflects (in one of Piglia's countless metafictional maneuvers) on the disparity between his present moment and the traditional heyday of the epistolary novel.

> Diverse complications, difficult to explain in a letter, make me believe that for a time you won't have any news of me. Correspondence, at bottom, is an anachronistic genre, a kind of left-over heritage of the eigthteenth century: the men who lived in that era still believed in the pure truth of written words. And what of us? Times have changed, words slip away with ever grcatcr ease, one can see them drifting in the water of history, mingled amongst the floating islands of the current. Soon we'll find a mode for encountering one another.[13]

The ambiguity of his disappearance (it never becomes clear whether it is forced or voluntary, given the gaps in knowledge the characters possess about one another) might suggest a conscious decision to truncate the exchange of letters with his nephew that Maggi himself has initiated, as a prelude to the dissolution of his being. It is possible that he is in the process of becoming a dead-letter recipient, reluctant to acknowledge receipt, because of complications "difficult to explain in a letter"—the kind of intangible, yet ever-present complications Argentines continually dwelt with in the epoch of "National Reorganization."

And perhaps, in capitulating to this dissolution, he is urging Renzi too (in novelist Tomás Eloy Martínez's phrase) to "become resigned to it." Martínez tells, for instance, of a close relative who, interrogated by Argentine authorities about one of Martínez's early novels, denied the latter's authorship. The relative claimed that "the person who had signed the work was a usurper of names, or perhaps a homonym." Martínez recounts how "without realizing that person had given up on my existence, I sent him a letter asking him to correct the error. . . . I never received an answer."[14]

Yet the final, cryptic sentence in Maggi's letter—"Soon we'll find a mode for encountering one another"—and the earlier qualifier for the cessation of news, "for a time," suggest the equally available possibility that the character's self-conscious, self-abnegating epistles represent, for him, the most adequate expression to be had on the way to finding the ideal mode for reconstructing an atomized collective mental life. Letters may be anachronistic, but such an outmoded artifice keeps dialogue alive in times of artificial respiration. Maggi's sensibility here is emphatically first-person plural. "And what of us?" stands as the ultimate question to be answered, not in this letter perhaps, but eventually.

Renzi, in his reply to his uncle's request that Renzi visit him and to the warning that he may not write for a time, waxes irritably impatient. "Point one: of course I'll come to see you when you like. Point two: What am I to make of the *notice* that for a time I won't receive any news of you? I want to make clear that you have no obligation to write me at an appointed time, no obligation of answering me by return mail, or anything of the kind." But, as he is to discover, the encounter in the flesh turns out to be much more difficult to execute than his appointment for it by "return mail." Renzi complains, in this same letter, much in the vein of Maggi, that "correspondence is a perverse genre . . . it requires distance and absence to prosper. Only in epistolary novels do people write one another when they're nearby; even living under the same roof, they send letters instead of conversing, obliged to do so by the rhetoric of the genre."[15] This statement becomes heavily ironic—one of many ironies in the novel—in retrospect, given that his and Maggi's mutual verbal constructions of identity, their representations of self to one another, derive, in the end, almost entirely from this "perverse," non-obligatory exchange of letters and from second-hand, reported information about one another, rather than from any direct contact.

One of Renzi's keenest insights is his self-conception as a character in an outdated novel genre, consigned (by a dictatorship-manufactured isolation, I would argue) to the status of an intellectual dinosaur among intellectual dinosaurs, striving to weather the present and ward off extinction. Skeptical and cynical as he is inclined to sound at times, Renzi recognizes the necessity of refurbishing the antiquated remnants of the discursive conventions to which his impoverished era has been reduced, if he, Maggi, and their peers hope to overcome their hermetic isolation and re-enter, actively, the larger history lying beyond the more restrictive Argentine Process of National Reorganization. This transformative hope for the epistolary is plain in one of his letters to Maggi:

> The epistolary genre has gotten old, and yet I confess to you that one of the illusions of my life is to someday write a novel made of letters. In fact, now that I think about it, there aren't any epistolary novels in Argentine literature, and of course this is due to the fact that (to confirm one of the theories insinuated in your rather melancholy letter just received) in Argentina we never had an eighteenth century.[16]

This latter remark refers to Maggi's characterization of the eighteenth century as an era in which one "still believed in the pure truth of the written word," before words began to "slip away." Renzi intimates here that, from the perspective of the present, such truth has never seemed tenable but that at least an impure "truth" must be granted to a degraded, worn-out language, if the identity they are reshaping and resurrecting in their letters is to have any viability as an antidote to total, permanent dissolution. This recognition is a mutual one, for despite the "melancholy" nature of Maggi's characterization, he nonetheless uses the letter form to reflect on it in a shared context, and Renzi responds in kind, giving that melancholy characterization a rather biting twist.

Renzi and Maggi often turn self-lacerating or ironic, as in Renzi's description of his naive pretensions about wanting to have "experiences" in his youth. His youthful desire for decadence seems to take Baudelaire and Rimbaud as implicit models. At the age of nineteen, his greatest aspiration was to arrive at the age of thirty-five having exhausted all the possibilities in life. He would then "go to Paris for four or five months to live the grand life (that, to me, was the most spectacular model of triumph, I suppose). To arrive in Paris at 35, saturated with experiences and a body of written work, to wander along the boulevards, like a streetwise fellow, just back from everywhere." He then describes an episode in Buenos Aires where he does seem to aspire to the status of a Baudelarian *flâneur*, tracing his own melancholy map through the city, watching men from State Gas dig a tunnel in the middle of the night. He enters a bar, in a Rimbaudian reverie, observing that "bars are our version of whaling ships." This *bateau ivre* youthful self observes how sentimental, teetering drunks offer one another melodramatic, hyperbolic toasts in the bar, a practice he once identified with but now finds absurdly pompous. Yet for all his self-denigration, Renzi's exchange of letters with Maggi remains invested with significance. Renzi finishes his self-effacing recounting of his youthful naivete with a sentiment that runs the risk, in its seriousness, of emotional indiscretion.

> So now I should continue writing you until daybreak; a letter to keep me company through the night; a letter lasting until daybreak so I can go out to the street afterward to see if Marquitos still stands in the Ramos Bar toasting señorita Giselle in spite of having the threat of the terrible sword of Damocles suspended over his heart. I embrace you, Marcelo, and await news from you. Emilio.[17]

The correspondents' banter masks a deep malaise. Piglia's metafiction does not lapse into endless, regressive, formalistic self-reflexivity, into the cleverness of mere letters about letter writing. Rather, his metafictional reflections are offered in the interest of refashioning the epistolary—the mode expressive of the most paralyzing aspects of cultural doubt and ontological indeterminacy—into a replenishing mode of engagement with the present.

And yet, the present time, in Piglia's novel, cannot in its impoverishment suffice for these intellectuals who wish to embrace it and define themselves within it. In "Epistolary Discourse," Janet Altman has said that for the writer of the letter in epistolary fiction

> the present is impossible . . . as "presence." . . . Epistolary discourse is the language of the pivotal yet impossible present. The *now* of narration is its central reference point, to which the *then* of anticipation and retrospection are relative. Yet *now* is unseizable, and its unseizability haunts epistolary language.[18]

The language of *Respiración artificial* is haunted with just such a temporal unseizability. Renzi and Maggi in their letters, Renzi and

Tardewski in their endless conversation in the second half of the novel, and Enrique Ossorio, the articulate traitor and exile from the nineteenth century, are all obsessed with bringing the recuperated past and the future, by means of letters, into a utopian presence. Their awareness of the impossibility of the present does not deter the various conversants from striving toward a solution to their indeterminate status. This "utopianism" differs from a more classic, Marxist utopianism and from that decried by Fernández Retamar in "Caliban" in that it represents not simply a desire for social transformation, an idealized "new society," but rather an attempt to recover a variegated actuality.

Ossorio's letters and journals, which are being edited by Maggi, attest to a utopian strain of this type. In one of several journal entries, this one dated July 14, 1850, Ossorio, exiled in the United States, hits upon the ingenious notion of exile itself—of the place of banishment, of supposed despair of the impossible present—as utopian precisely *because* of its impossibility.

> I thought today: What is utopia? The perfect place? That's not the question. More than anything, for me, exile is utopia. *There is no such place.* Banishment, exodus, a space suspended in time, between two times. We have the memories that have remained with us of our country, and afterward we imagine how the country will be (how it is to be) when we return to it. That dead time, between the past and the future, is utopia for me. So: exile is utopia.[19]

In this temporal conception of exile, Ossorio achieves precisely what Renzi, Maggi, and many Argentine intellectuals of the seventies such as Sarlo and Martínez were in search of: a means of seizing the present made impossible by exile, of recuperating the past made distant by it, and imagining them together as a credible futurity. Ossorio's notion captures what it meant, imaginatively, to try to transform the doubt-ridden epistolarity of the Argentine diaspora in the seventies (including the domestic "diaspora") into a more habitable brand of epistolarity. Like Martínez with his "language of inexistence," or Sarlo with her "zone of indefinition," Ossorio affirms his lack of existence resoundingly yet believes this recognition to be the necessary first step toward self-re-creation. Piglia's detailing of exiles gazing with a longing that was utopian yet clearsighted and grounded in the specifics of the exiles' own memories, toward an actual home best described as "there is no such place," presents an

intelligent alternative to the utopian projection onto Caliban encouraged by U.S. adherence to the New Word myth.

The literary conceit of the journal entry typically suggests the
most private and inward-directed of forms. But Ossorio's journal,
like the exchanges between Maggi and Renzi, is written in a more
public vein—as letters to the future—and he acknowledges as much
in his continuing ruminations on the appropriate literary embodiment of utopia.

7–15–1850
The utopia of a modern dreamer should differentiate itself
from the classical rules of the genre on one essential point: refus-
ing to reconstruct a non-existent space. So: *key difference:* don't
situate utopia in an imaginary, unknown place. Instead, make an
appointment with one's own country, on a date (1979) which
is, to be sure, at a fantastic remove. There's no such place: in
time. There's not *yet* such a place. This equates, for me, to a
utopian point of view. Imagine Argentina just as it will be in
130 years.[20]

The title Ossorio gives to his projected book is *1979;* its epigraph,
"Each era dreams the past one." The "fantastic" date given falls precisely, of course, in the year of *Respiración artificial*'s present, and
so the journal entry is read by the inhabitants of Piglia's imaginative
dystopia, Renzi and Maggi. This journal entry, read in the context of
the all-too-real and unimaginative dystopia created in Argentina by
the militarized Process of National Reorganization, becomes laden
with satirical effect. At the same time, Ossorio establishes a "correspondence" with the future which articulates precisely the aspirations of his kindred exiled Argentines more than a century later.
He insists on locating any possible utopia, if it is to be, geographically within an actual Argentina—emphatically *not* in an exotic continent elsewhere—and positing Argentina as that shared place of future re-encounter and reconciliation. And the epigraph to *1979*
implies the correspondence between Renzi and Maggi (his spiritual
executors) and Ossorio himself, in their attempt to rethink the relation of the militarized present to the potentially romanticized republican past. Piglia's complex play of temporality makes possible
both a scrutiny of the Process and a skeptical caution about future
resolutions to the existential and political dilemmas it has created
(given the disparity between *1979*'s utopia and 1979's dystopia). But
this scrutiny and caution are not necessarily incompatible with idealism about Argentina's social possibilities. Piglia's treatment of exile is neither romantic nor nihilistic; his novel accurately evokes the

subtleties of intermingled hope and despair which have character-ized the mindset and the writings of Argentine exiles of the seventies and early eighties.

This disillusioned-but-yearning ambivalence, in the framework of Piglia's novel, finds its expression as a doubt reaching back to the very beginnings of modern democracy in Argentina. Ossorio's 1850 journal entries coincide with the nascent Republic of Argentina, its juridical and territorial incorporation as a modern state: the coun-try's national constitution was drafted in 1853. The profound failure of the democratic project is clearly implied in the continual paral-lelism between a present marked by "artificial respiration"—an at-titude of barely scraping through, sustaining life as best as one can—and the era in which Ossorio, son of a colonel who fought in the Wars of Independence and personal secretary to the autocratic presi-dent Rosas, worked as a traitor in an abortive conspiracy to over-throw Rosas.

In *Crisis política y poder armado,* published in 1983, just as the Process was formally ending and Argentina was executing the "dif-ficult transition to the National Constitution," Alberto Kohen elu-cidates some possible causes for ambivalence toward this return to "democracy." He describes the dialectical and cyclical alternation between constitutional and militarized government which has char-acterized Argentine politics since 1930, after two decades, at the cen-tury's beginning, of massive immigration, a huge expansion of the working class, and an increasingly radical government which threat-ened the land-holding oligarchy and the newly ascendant middle class. The promises of constitutional government led, throughout the second half of the nineteenth century, to fervid expectations that failed to be met, and the advent of radicalism, immigration, and syn-dicalism in the first part of the twentieth century resulted eventually in the chronic intervention, beginning in 1930, of the military in direct government—a government legitimated, as in the case of Ur-uguay, by quasi-constitutional means.[21] Kohen remarks that

> the constitutional political system gradually becomes denatural-ized and republican organization eventually gives way to a sys-tem which has been called "pendular." It could be defined as "pendulism," after more than half a century of oscillation between constitutional governments and military regimes, something on the order of a system which consecrates an *unstable equilibrium* in Argentine political society.[22]

This "pendulism" needn't be understood as some essential quality expressive of an inscrutable, volatile national character, as often occurs in U.S. commentary on Latin American politics. Rather, it describes a prolonged political crisis closely linked to the questionable "constitution" of republicanism, the illusory and manufactured quality of a democracy in historical concert with the military regimes which appear to alternate with it. The crisis is one of the representation of "representation." The idea of a return to constitutional forms in 1983 doesn't necessarily imply the change in ontological status sought by those who suffered through the Process. Pendulism, this political going back and forth, like an exchange of letters, does not entail a necessary resolution to one's indeterminacy, only a possible resolution. Even Kohen's interesting choice of verb, "denaturalized," can be read several ways. Not only does the constitutional political system become deformed by its continual slide into militarism, but its form, its "constitution," and its lack of natural, organic, transparent essentiality, become more evident, easier to descry. Sarlo, in another of her essays, speaks of Argentine authoritarian discourse falsely presenting itself as "transhistorical and trans-subjective, in the sense that it only speaks of history when it wishes to refer to a founding past which must be restored, because in it were forged the values whose currency remains unquestioned."[23] It is a sham attempt to elicit belief in "the pure truth of the written word," which is supposed to have engendered and mandated, via the republic, the authoritarian regime.

Also, the other valence of *denaturalize*—to deprive of the rights of naturalization or citizenship—suggests the rather wild but quite accurate notion that constitutionality *itself*, republicanism *itself* is banished from the republic as militarism becomes a chronic fixture of government. This rather bizarre contradiction perfectly describes the philosophical nullity to which exiles within and without were subjected during the military's occupation of "its" republic between 1976 and 1983. Under these conditions, it isn't difficult to comprehend the widespread ambivalence of exiles and Argentine intellectuals about a return to the forms of democratic government.

Osvaldo Bayer, in his "Little Reminder for a Country without a Memory," sounds a skeptical, bitter note about the fervor surrounding the reprise of constitutionality in 1983. "Argentine society, suddenly, had washed itself in democracy by the sole formal act of putting a vote in an urn. I saw them blowing their horns in the Plaza del Congreso on October 30, 1983. They were the same faces and the same horns of March 26, 1976" (the date of the military's formal ascent to power). He ends his reminder with what he deems an appropriate symbol for Argentine culture:

Lieutenant Colonel Gorlieri, the one who publicly burned the books and proudly signed the proclamation in 1976, was promoted to General of the Nation, by the Senate elected by the people, in 1984. From lieutenant colonel to dictator to general of democracy.[24]

Writers and intellectuals, as much as anyone, found themselves mired in what Bayer denominates "the psychosocial and intellectual problematic of our society . . . inveterate schizophrenia." Asking his reader to guess the identities of the authors of two statements, and revealing them afterward, he cites pronouncements by internationally acclaimed Argentine novelist Ernesto Sábato and by the dictator of the Process during the end of the seventies, General Jorge Videla. Which was Sábato's pronouncement? An excerpt from it, in which he lauded the arrival of Onganía's dictatorship in 1966, reads:

> We should have the courage to understand (and say) that they're finished; institutions in which no one seriously believed are finished. Do you believe in the Chamber of Deputies? Do you know many people who believe in that kind of farce? That's why people in the street felt a profound sense of liberation [when the dictatorship came].

On the other hand, an excerpt from military dictator Videla's speech, given in 1978, extolls the ideal of a pluralistic, open society:

> We need a critical humanism to face the multiple messages that the social media impart daily . . . a humanism to promote convivial dialogue among different generations, in which experience intermingles with imagination, in a climate of respect and happiness.[25]

As if Bayer suspected that no one would believe the match between the identities of the authors and their respective pronouncements, he mentions in a footnote that he possesses a photocopy of Sábato's article. But with respect, at least, to incredulity toward the institutions of representative government, most intellectuals and exiles—including Bayer—in answer to Sábato's question, "Do you believe in the Chamber of Deputies?" would probably have to answer an unfortunate, hesitant "No," or perhaps a more solidly ambivalent "Not sure."

Given this intense questioning of the root and basis of republicanism, Ossorio's movement toward epistolarity in Piglia's novel begins to make a great deal of sense. In his July 18, 1850 journal entry, he describes a "discovery" he has made while pacing the floor of his room, reflecting on his projected novel, *1979*, and on the Wars of Independence.

> I suddenly understood what the *form* of my utopian story should be. The Protagonist receives letters from the future (which aren't addressed to him).
> So, an epistolary story. Why that anachronistic genre? Because utopia is already in itself a literary form which belongs to the past. For us, men of the nineteenth century, it represents an archaic species, the way the epistolary novel is archaic.[26]

It is significant that Ossorio, writing from the perspective of the *beginnings* of the Argentine republic, expresses a disbelief in utopia, qualifying it as "anachronistic" in much the same language that his 1970s counterparts of the future would use. The aptness of Ossorio's conceit of "letters from the future" for an analysis of the ideological parallels between the Wars of Independence and the contemporary vicissitudes of Argentine democracy is borne out in Juan Francisco Guevara's 1970 book of political commentary, *Argentina y su sombra*. In its opening pages, Guevara offers a lesson identical to that of Ossorio about the flaws in the founding conceptions of liberation, which replicate themselves in the messianic, dictatorial "utopias" of the sixties and seventies. Guevara even uses the epistolary conceit, and his title could almost have been cribbed from Ossorio: "A message from 1829 that arrived in 1966."

In his analysis, Guevara describes the grim, funereal scene of Onganía's ascendancy to dictatorship in 1966, a misfortune amplified by the widespread enthusiasm that greeted the dictator's arrival on the scene. But this spectacle, he claims, should come as no surprise, because Argentina, from the moment of its birth into political independence, has never offered justice and peace with prolonged political stability, due to the republic's inability to distinguish between freedom and oppressive government. Guevara cites excerpts from a letter written by Argentina's "liberator" San Martín to another general in 1829 during the Wars of Independence and offers these excerpts as a prophetic description of the state of mind of those who embraced Argentina's dictatorial "democracy" in the time of Onganía 137 years later:

> A long time ago [San Martín] said "The agitations of nineteen years of trial in search of a liberty that hasn't come into exis-

tence, and even more, the difficult circumstances our country finds itself in, make the majority of men cry out (seeing their fortunes at the edge of the precipice, and their future path covered in uncertainty)—not for a change in the principles governing them (and that, in my opinion, is where the true evil lies) but for a vigorous government; in a word, a military one, because those drowning don't realize what they've grabbed hold of."

He also said, "One can govern people most securely during the first two years after a great crisis; that is the situation that will prevail in Buenos Aires; people will demand of their leader (after the present struggle) nothing more than tranquility."

Guevara says that a rereading of those prophetic paragraphs shows that "even then, it was necessary to change the principles that incipient Argentine liberalism put into effect in our country." Even San Martín, the "father" of the democracy, voiced pessimism about the prospects of democracy, and liberalism's checkered legacy does not inspire any greater hope by the 1960s. "The Messiah already came a long time ago," says Guevara—referring to the cyclical messianism, beginning with San Martín's arrival and continuing up through Onganía, that has alternately hailed civilian rule as a salvation from the failures of dictatorship and then vice versa—"so we needn't expect another one, not even from from the civilian quarter."[27]

Already, at the advent of the republic, republicanism and the democratic project represented a foredoomed ideal. The seeds of disillusion for the fictional Ossorio's latter-day counterparts had begun to germinate in the nineteenth century. Utopianism, like epistolarity, predates the formation of the modern, "democratic" state, issues into it, defines it in a negative dialectic. The desire for authentic democracy seems doomed, out-of-sync, a letter perpetually updated, postdated, never to arrive at its destination.[28]

Yet this desire persists in the mind of a nineteenth-century representative, Ossorio, as in the intellectuals of the seventies. Out of the fruit of negation, he produces an affirmation. In his journal entry six days later, Ossorio asks himself,

Why have I been able to discover that my utopian romance must be an epistolary story? First: correspondence by its nature is already a form of utopia. To write a letter is to send a message to the future . . . Correspondence is the utopian form of conversation because it annuls the present and makes the future the only possible place of dialogue.

But there also exists a second reason. What is exile but a situation obliging us to substitute with written words the relation among the closest friends, who are far away, absent, disseminated, each in a different place and city? And besides, what relation can we maintain with the country we've lost, the country they've obliged us to abandon, what other presence of an absent place, than the testimony of its existence which letters bring us (sporadic, elusive, trivial) that arrive with news of familiars.

So I think I've chosen well the form of this novel written in exile and *out of it*.[29]

The unseizable present may annul its letter-writing exiles, but they, through the act of writing letters, annul the present. At the same time, letter writing produces the concrete, "trivial" linguistic testimony out of which this "utopian," postponed, postdated future will have to be constructed. The society inhabited by returned exiles will not have to be founded on sheer negation, a void. Likewise, Ossorio's journal entries to the future lay the groundwork for an alternative reconstruction of republicanism. Ossorio even speaks of his projected novel of letters sent from the future as being made "out of" the material of a seemingly ineffable exile, establishing a two-way material correspondence between past and future. The witnessing epistolary gesture attempts to preclude, in the seventies and early eighties, what Beatriz Sarlo calls "a virtual disappearance of the public sphere during the years of the Process, at least until its arduous reconstruction beginning in 1982," from becoming total rather than virtual.[30] The first half of the novel ends with a one-sentence journal entry by Ossorio, reading "I write the first letter from the future." The second half ends with a note, written by Ossorio just before his death and read in the present by Renzi, addressed to "Whoever finds my body." In both instances, his effort has been to bolster the present by leaving "remains."

The epistolary novel brings letter writing and the writing of books together in the mutual, almost archival enterprise of preserving at least the written remnants of a collective social identity. Yet *Respiración artificial* also attests to the fragility of even that modest preservational gesture. The potential for both types of letters to become dead letters remains high. Piglia's novel contains its own dead-letter office in the form of a censor named Arocena, who receives a variety of letters out of which he tries to make a meaningful miscellany, by "decoding" their secret meanings. As earnest as he is misguided, Arocena makes for a figure both absurd and chilling.

His attempt at deciphering a random and innocuous assortment of past and present letters—most from correspondents who don't have the slightest apparent relation to any of the characters in Piglia's novel—by means of a numerological system yields a result reminscent of secret messages in spy thrillers. His interest is in a "reconstruction" of a radically different kind from the social one proposed by Sarlo. He surmises of the received letters that

> the words beginning each paragraph had eleven letters, each starting with a different vowel. The eleven letters marked the order of the sentences and gave the code which deciphered the scrambled message. Arocena worked calmly and an hour later he had reconstructed the hidden text.
>
> *No news. I'm waiting for the contact. I'll be staying in the Central Park Hotel, 8th and 42nd. If there's no news before the 10th, I'll follow the instructions from 8–9. If I have trouble and need to return, I'll wait for a telegram. Have it say: Congratulations, Raquel.*

Since some of the letters in this assortment are supposed to have been sent from Maggi to Ossorio, Arocena believes that the others are cryptic letters, sent in a code name, from Ossorio to Maggi. Arocena seems to be Piglia's character—an unintended recipient of the letters from the future in Ossorio's epistolary novel—though it is equally possible that he exists in the novel's present, intercepting actual letters. Arocena serves as the dystopian counterpart of the utopian addressee of the future whom Ossorio imagined as an ideal correspondent. He embodies the censoring, repressive side of epistolary communication, a breaker of spiritual and ontological chain letters. The epistolary, linguistic code of the past and present is "cracked" by him, boiled down to its most banal "message," one of political opposition in a police-detective vein—a message which, when spelled out, would provide the pretext for harsh, preventive repressive measures. Following out his method, he "decodes" the reconstructed message into the sentence "Raquel llega a Ezeiza el 10, vuelo 22.03" (Raquel arrives at Ezeiza on the 10th, flight 2203). *Raquel,* he assumes, is an anagram for *Aquel* (literally, "That one"). "Who arrives?" he asks himself irritably. "Who's about to arrive? They're not going to trick me, thought Arocena, not me."[31]

Daniel Balderston remarks that the nomenclature *Aquel* was used to refer indirectly to former populist president Juan Perón during the period prior to his return to Argentina from exile in 1973.[32] The internecine violence marking Perón's return and the consequent disillusionment of the Peronist Youth fueled much of the political restiveness preceding the coup that deposed Isabela Perón, which initiated the Process. No one even vaguely familiar with contemporary Argentine politics, least of all an Argentine, could fail to recognize the reference to Perón's infamous arrival at Ezeiza Airport and the riots that directly followed.

Arocena, however, is unusually obtuse. In his obsessive search for hidden meanings, he fails to grasp the referent of *Aquel,* and Piglia in this allusion thus provides his own ironic, parodic, "coded" comment on the manipulations which the written underwent during the seventies and eighties. Not only personal correspondence but the writing of books and articles became subject to systematic violations and deformations. Jorge Lafforgue recounts how a fellow editor at the publishing house Editorial Losada in Buenos Aires, in 1976, had accepted for publication two novels by young Argentine authors. "When the military coup came," he says, "both books were already printed in the graphic workshop Americalée." But the owner of this print shop read the books, prompted by "a recent pronouncement by the Commanding Junta, establishing the criminality not only of authors but of those who might have collaborated in the production of any 'subversive' writing." In his unofficial capacity of censoring both self and others, the printer, having read the books and deemed them subversive, refused to turn over the already-printed books, as promised, to the publisher. Though initially indignant, Editorial Losada eventually capitulated and even agreed to share the costs of the "unnecessary" printing.[33]

This printerly consignment to oblivion also plagues Vladimir Tardewski, the Polish exile and close friend of Maggi in Entre Ríos, whose lengthy conversation with Renzi (a masterpiece of philosophical and literary digression) occupies the entire second half of *Respiración artificial.* Tardewski recounts to Renzi an episode of many years ago when he had first arrived in Buenos Aires, a refugee whose exile was occasioned by Hitler's invasion of Poland. En route to dissolution and inexistence, Tardewski writes an article, printed in a Buenos Aires newspaper, about the relationship between Nazism and Kafka's writing in which he attempts to explain the precarious status of his nation to Argentines. But his attempt to secure his identity in the form of authorship is doomed from the beginning, not only on account of its questionable translation, but because of a printing error in the newspaper.[34] In it, his name has been changed from Vladimir Tardewski to Vladimir Tardowski, a minute alteration which has, for him, profound implications. "The paradox," he says, "was that I wouldn't be able to read the text I'd published, since I didn't know Spanish. Which, if it served for anything . . . served as a metaphor for my situation . . . amid the catastrophic headlines about the advance of Nazi troops I found, on the inner pages . . . an article I couldn't read . . . by Vladimir Tardowski."[35]

This combined linguistic alienation and alteration has the effect of stripping him of his identity. And his "intellectual property," a concept which has by then become seriously undermined, has been rendered inaccessible to him by the fact that he can't read his own writing. Then, on arriving at his rented room, he discovers that thieves have stolen everything he owned, including (the final blow) his volumes of Kafka (collected writings and letters). "I found myself facing a reproduction in miniature, real nonetheless, of Europe demolished by war . . . I'd reached the purest state of dispossession that a man can aspire to: I had nothing."[36]

He also finds himself facing, though he doesn't say so directly, a version in miniature of the intellectual life of Argentine authors and readers under the Process. While in exile, Tomás Eloy Martínez experienced in 1979–1980—the time of *Respiración artificial*'s publication—a loss of "intellectual property" and permutations of his signature, just as profound and ironic as Tardewski's. A few months before the death of Argentine editor and sometime writer Victoria Ocampo, the weekly Buenos Aires magazine *Gente* published an article about her, and its "ideas and stutterings," says Martínez,

> sounded familiar to me. I asked myself if, by chance, it was mine. I discovered that yes it was. I'd published it twelve or thirteen years before. But now it bore someone else's signature.
>
> In 1980 I reread one of my interviews with Perón inserted in someone else's book. The author omitted my name but had at least taken care to respect my errata. . . . Around the same time, a television news program which I'd designed and directed did a retrospective of all those who'd appeared on it at one time and another, editing out the images in which I appeared.[37]

Like Tardewski, Martínez had become a living erratum, writ large, with only the mistakes, the stutterings, the discrepancy between his former signature and his revised one bearing ironic witness to his existence. These unacknowledged errata, as in Tardewski's case, serve as a generalizable metaphor for his and many others' lived situations. But the wish for the restoration of the letters of one's name is not, ultimately, a wish for recuperating intellectual property, a wish for a discrete originality, but rather a desire for the restoration of books—letters—as a realm of social exchange. Epistolarity is a means of exchange by which the most personal of documents become the "property" of another, thus in a limited sense public.

But this public nature, necessary to the survival and reconstruction of the social realm, is precisely what leaves it vulnerable. The character of Tardewski is fairly obviously modeled, in part, on the persona of the German intellectual Walter Benjamin who, like Tardewski, attempted to flee from Nazi oppression into exile.[38] Both men pursue in their writings an intense interest in Kafka. Yet though Hannah Arendt, in her introduction to Benjamin's *Illuminations*, compares Benjamin to Kafka in terms of his "uniqueness, that absolute originality which can be traced to no predecessor and suffers no followers," what unites the character of Tardewski to that of Benjamin is precisely the abdication of "originality."[39] Both aspire to virtuoso originality in the classical European sense of creating masterpieces of ideation, but their experience of exile, the literal loss of many of their books and papers and the derogation of their ideas by a hostile Nazism lead them toward plagiarism as a more attractive and more historically relevant metaphor for thought than originality.

After Tardewski's ruin in Argentina, following a brilliant beginning as a privileged disciple of Wittgenstein in Europe, he eventually ends up transferred, in true Kafkaesque style, to a pointless job in a branch bank in the literal backwater of Entre Ríos. Since he seldom has actual work to do, he spends his time surreptitiously "jotting down the ideas of other people in a notebook." He makes a decision "not to write anything I could think of myself, nothing mine, no ideas of my own. I didn't have any ideas, anyway, I was a Polish zombie." His first entry is a transcription of the quotations he had cited in his abortive newspaper article.

> I copied them from a Spanish I didn't understand, so that it was like reproducing a hieroglyphic; I drew the letters, one by one, without understanding what I wrote, guiding myself by the quotation marks, the international sign. Wasn't that a good image of the situation of the Kafkaesque writer?[40]

In her introduction to Benjamin's essays, Hannah Arendt mentions that Benjamin "was a born writer, but his greatest ambition was to produce a work consisting entirely of quotations."[41] The parallel with Tardewski is most striking here. He represents the intellectual who has come to the realization that one must write out of the purest form of "the state of dispossession"—dispossession by the

State. That brand of writer, resigned to dispossession, and not the illusion of the "original thinker whose writing can be traced to no predecessor and suffers no followers," is the clear image of the survivable intellectual which emerges in Piglia's novel. And if he "cites" Benjamin in the creation of Tardewski, Piglia adapts this creation, and the status of book-ness itself, to the Argentine exigencies of the time.[42]

For the mere possession of books, during the Process, left one open to the severest retributions. The tone of the satisfied, almost complacent Benjamin who collects books in "Unpacking My Library" (first published in 1931, just after the first of the cycle of Argentine dictatorships came to power) would have to be modified, like Tardewski's signature, in significant ways in order to express adequately what it meant to try to "possess" a library within the confines of the Argentine Process, or for that matter in the Germany of the 1930s. In the serene mood of the avid book collector in the midst of reshelving his beloved possessions, Benjamin begins by inviting his listener to

> join me in the disorder of crates that have been wrenched open, the air saturated with the dust of wood, the floor covered with torn paper . . . so that you may be ready to share with me the mood. . . . it is certainly not an elegiac mood but, rather, one of anticipation—which these books arouse in a genuine collector.[43]

There exists in most of his writings another, darker Benjamin analogous to those masses of exiled Argentine intellectuals: the epistolary exile whose privations and dispossessions during the years leading up to World War II help one understand the tender longing in the evocations of this more self-satisfied, and ephemeral, Benjamin. In his correspondence with Gershom Scholem between 1932 and 1940, their thoughts return with an almost obsessive frequency to books, or rather the lack of them, and the chronic difficulty of obtaining them. In fact, their requests for loans of books from one another and for offprints or manuscripts of each other's writings *and of their own* (Benjamin's "archive" is partly housed in Scholem's Jerusalem residence) are as impassioned a subtext in the letters as their inquiries after one another's well being.

In a 1933 letter written in Ibiza, Spain, to Scholem in Jerusalem, lamenting the inaccessibility of his personal library back in Germany, Benjamin observes how an essay he is commissioned to write for a German magazine on the sociology of contemporary French literature "acquires a more or less magical mien by virtue of the fact that I have to write it here, with next to no source material of any kind." Then he goes on to acknowledge the value which loaning books, like writing letters, possesses as a medium of both binding social exchange and personal intellectual survival during the years of German National Socialism's increasing persecution of Jews, when he comments how "I now especially praise the impulse that made me give Brecht's book (and, if I'm not mistaken, several other books on loan) to Kitty to take with her (to Jerusalem), since by doing so I hope they will return into my possession before too long."[44]

An act of voluntary dispossession, of stripping himself of intellectual property, has, in the context of social events, the ironic and unintended effect of increasing the likelihood of its return to him. This comment stands in stark (yet dialectical) contrast to the Benjamin who fretted continually about his work being plagiarized and to the 1931 persona of "Unpacking My Library," who characterizes the genuine book collector by his penchant for borrowing the books of others and carelessly neglecting to read, much less return, them.

But by 1933, the year in which book burnings in Germany began, the difficulty of holding onto one's books had quickened into a historical and ontological urgency tantamount to that of holding onto one's very identity. A letter from Scholem in September of that year stresses the importance of Benjamin's consolidating immediately his intellectual property as best he can, lest he be bereft of it forever. The tone of Scholem's advice fairly equates the failure to do so with annihilation by repression.

> Just today I read the list of the first 35 fortunate ones to be relieved of their German citizenship, and of their assets at the same time. I take this occasion to reiterate my very urgent advice to attend to the transfer of all your papers abroad, and to do so in time, for very soon it could be too late. If you do not have a secure location, I am always prepared to keep as many things for you as possible. Perhaps you can make use of this offer. Your library—for whose housing I admittedly have no advice or proposal to make—should also be exposed for as short a time as possible to the chance of being auctioned off one day for some sin or other committed in your family's past, present, or future.[45]

Benjamin did manage to recover a portion of his library and his papers and have them sent to him abroad, but there was no question of any real and permanent "possession," given Benjamin's constant mobility and the vicissitudes of massive social dislocation. His "private" collection of papers and books, like his "private" letters to Scholem, formed part of the crucial public currency exchanged among exiled German Jews to foster intellectual and spiritual resilience among themselves. The radical changes which transformed Benjamin's happy "disorder of crates that have been wrenched open" from the musing reveries of a book collector to a trope for those forces which threatened intellectual survival can serve as the approximate measure of Argentina's own social dislocations in the seventies. If the "elegiac mood" absent in Benjamin's "Unpacking My Library" were, in fact, substituted for the "mood of anticipation" presiding over the "wrecked crates, wood dust, torn paper" surrounding his disarrayed books, then Benjamin's evocation would suffice as an exact description of the fate of innumerable private book collections after the Argentine military seized power in 1976. Santiago Kovadloff, in *Argentina, oscuro país*, begins an essay entitled "The Hands of Fear" with the description of just such a library "unpacking."

> The news spread: they rapped at the door unannounced. They signaled their arrival with dry authority. Appearing in groups of four or five while their trucks awaited in the street, they said they were looking for prohibited literature. They had orders to search through the house's library, the bookcases, the basement, if there were any. When they found impugned or impugnable works, they carried them off. And along with the works, their readers. They didn't want to hear any explanations or excuses. The sequestered titles were proof enough of the crime.[46]

Not only Marxist materials but almost any work of social science, history, philosophy, economy, or writing of a partisan political nature, had the potential for qualifying as suspect. These wide-ranging, vague criteria had the effect, according to Kovaldoff, of instilling a self-censoring fear in everyone who possessed books.

> With a heart full of anguish, the painful ritual of shame began. In the middle of the night or in broad daylight, we dismantled our libraries . . . we tore into pieces dozens of essays, novels, biographies, stories and poems in which the slightest trace of social conscience or political restlessness might be perceived. At our feet, like the ashes of a better time, accumulated what had before been cherished pages. . . . what had been books were now nothing but shreds of paper.[47]

Wrecked crates, wood dust, torn paper—these relished signs of personal possession have become, in the Argentine context, as they quickly did in Benjamin's Germany, the unwritten prologue to intellectual dispossession. Benjamin remarks with enthusiasm that the book collector's existence is tied to "a very mysterious relationship to ownership," emphasizing the love of objects not as functional, but rather "as the scene, the stage of their fate."[48] The same can be said of Argentina's exiled intellectuals with respect to their necessary abdication of the private objects—both literal and figural—of spiritual and mental life, in favor of a more transitory, epistolary mode of possession and engagement with the scene of their fate. But while the Process lasted (and it continues, in many ways, to last), it became impossible for them to share Benjamin's book-collector's sentiment that

> The most profound enchantment for the collector is the locking of individual items within a magic circle in which they are fixed, as the final thrill, the thrill of acquisition, passes over them. Everything remembered and thought, everything conscious, becomes the pedestal, the frame, the base, the lock of this property.[49]

Instead, the acquisition Argentines sought, the frame of all consciousness and memory, was the acquistion of existence itself, the prerequisite to any other kind of possession. The book and the letter, both subject for a time to the same fate, became interlaced in the epistolary novel. *Respiración artificial* is the timely chronicle of the resolve to transform the language of inexistence into a renewed, if necessarily postponed, presence.


In John Barth's epistolary novel *LETTERS*, published in the U.S. only a year before *Respiración artificial*, presence is just as bedeviled by its relation to inexistence, futurity, and history, but not nearly so difficult to seize. Barth's relentless experimentation is executed with even-handed serenity. The subtitle of Barth's novel—*An Old-Time Epistolary Novel by Seven Fictitious Drolls and Dreamers, Each of Whom Imagines Himself Actual*—suggests a good-humored, Sterneian solidity of self, an ontological safe haven for the "actual" seventh letter writer, the Author. This actuality mitigates the burden of inexistence, a state belied with whimsy by the fictitious "drolls" who imagine themselves into an illusory sense of actuality. Their language has the comforting rondure of existence.

Presence never comes as deeply into question in *LETTERS* as it does in Piglia's novel. In a missive from lawyer Todd Andrews (a character recycled, as are all the letter-writing characters except one, from Barth's previous novels) to the Author, Andrews defines both a political and ontological stance set squarely in the via media. Defining himself as a "Stock Liberal . . . inclined to the Tragic View of history and human institutions," with "no final faith that all the problems he addresses admit of political solutions—in some cases, of any solution whatever," he nonetheless manages to locate himself, in a few quick strokes, with surprising ease. As a devotee of the Tragic View, he adheres to wistful, ironic nonintervention in public life, believing that social violence and violent emotions alike will spend themselves in good time and of their own accord, leaving society as it always was. His professed lack of solutions in no way implies his dissolution, contrary to the experience of Piglia's characters Renzi and Maggi. He believes that "Reason, Tolerance, Law, Democracy, Humanism," all upper-case ethical values and thus out of doubt, are "precious and infinitely preferable to their contraries. He is ever for Reform as against revolution or reaction." In the benign Barthian universe, Democracy and its opposite, dictatorial rule, or Law and its opposite, military decree, seem never to enter into dialectical tension, even for such a "connoisseur of paradoxes" as Andrews.

As for the relation of the present to other times, Todd Andrews subscribes to Augustine's view

> that while the Present does not exist (it being the merely conceptual razor's edge between the Past and the Future), at the same time it's all there is: the Everlasting Now between a Past existing only in memory and a Future existing only in anticipation.[50]

The idea that it might be necessary to abdicate the present in order to reclaim it in futurity, such as in the postponements depicted as necessary in Piglia's novel, appears in *LETTERS* as a quaint and fanciful idea. Though Andrews acknowledges, as in Piglia's Argentina, the inexistence of the present, the present nonetheless stands out as palpable, vividly capable of being grasped, in contrast to the ineffable past and future, which exist for Andrews "only in" memory and anticipation—the two very faculties which Argentine exiles required in order to reconstruct the present. Like the concept of Reform, the present stands ready to serve as the moderator, the affable middleman. Andrews asks, in reference to the paternal-filial conflict between corporate conglomerate owner Harrison Mack and Harrison's stock sixties "revolutionary" son, Drew, why the two can't "simply *shake hands*, like *Praeteritas* and *Futuras* on the Mack Enterprises letterhead, and reason together?"[51] History, here vaguely Rotarian or Masonic, resolves itself in the bonhomie of two hale fellows well met.

To characterize the novel as complacent in its reluctance to grapple with the malaise-inducing subtleties of Democracy is not to locate its narrative attitude in any one of the various "characters." Though Andrews is only one of the multiple personae in *LETTERS*, this attitude of the tragic-viewing but firmly planted observer pervades Barth's novel.[52] And though his tone remains wry and self-mocking, these qualities of irony and self-mockery serve as the very indicators of leisurely expansiveness, faith in one's fixture in a solid time and place from which to experiment at will.

Nonetheless, history, utopia, and "revolution" are the concerns of *LETTERS*. This 1979 novel, written over the course of almost a decade, fills the breach between Barth's 1969 meditation on the "literature of exhausted possibility"[53] and his 1980 reprise meditation on "The Literature of Replenishment." Like Piglia, Barth responds to the social dislocations of the seventies with his own version of epistolary exchange. In a 1979 interview, conducted shortly after the appearance of *LETTERS*, Barth refers to the sixties and early seventies, when he was teaching at riot-besieged SUNY Buffalo, as "a time when people could be forgiven for wondering whether a lot of institutions were falling apart." But his analysis of the "revolutionary" tumult of that time deliberately never goes beyond such platitudes. Indeed Barth, in his distaste for things "political," tends to describe historical events, in the interview, with the combination of dryness and mild boosterism one might expect of a junior high school civics teacher.

> But even if 1968 was the cultural watershed year . . . 1969 wraps up the decade. . . . Although the domestic explosions would continue for a couple of years, there was a genuine feeling that a lot of the uproar was winding down. And there was the happy detail that, although in 1969 no one had really begun to talk about our Bicentennial, the Bicentennial was in the wings.[54]

And in response to the interviewer's question about the possibility of reading *LETTERS* in connection with the "uproar" of the time, he is quick to try to downplay any overt connection between his writing and social events.

I'm not at all comfortable about describing *LETTERS* as a commentary upon the counterculture of that period. The counterculture is there in the novel, but it's there because it figured in everyone's life at that time. I don't know how you could write a book set in 1969 and fail to acknowledge what went on.[55]

Yet what "is there in the novel" must be reckoned with, conscientious objections notwithstanding, particularly since so much emphasis in the novel is self-consciously laid upon the concept of "revolution" and also because the events of the novel are set, just as in Piglia's novel, in two times of republican revolt separated by roughly a century and a half. Barth implies the almost synchronous continuity between eras of revolution when he states of the earlier period that "my interest in the War of 1812 did not derive so much from a historical novelist's interest in past events as from the fact that, when it was going on, the war was frequently referred to as the 'Second American Revolution.' "[56] The strict parallelism of the novel—the dates of composition of all the letters in it fall either in the year 1812 or 1969—suggests that the sixties, for Barth, should be invested with equivalent "revolutionary" significance.

The two most prominent ways in which Barth takes on the subject of sixties dissent throughout *LETTERS* are his depiction of the activism of a largely white student youth and his continual attempt to forge a harmonious view of history that will subsume student revolt, neutralizing its violent excess. Despite the fact that the mostly white college student movement represented only one aspect of a variegated response to societal oppression at that time, one cannot fault Barth for failing to undertake a more broadly based assessment of dissent (resistance to the Vietnam War, the women's movement, black nationalism), any more than Piglia should be blamed for limiting his account of "artificial respiration" to a consideration of marginalized backwater intellectuals, scarcely mentioning the military dictatorship or topical political events. Piglia's success, in fact, derives from his ability to make the "irrelevant" conversations of his failed intellectuals suggestive of what Argentines as a whole experienced psychically and privately during the Process.

Likewise, one can only expect Barth's novel to succeed within the limits of the terrain it stakes out for itself—in this case, college student activism (and the all-important parental restraint of an older generation) overlaid with the parallel activities of revolutionaries (and their parents and progeny, and *their* parents and progeny, et cetera) during the War of 1812. Barth means for this juxtaposition to give depth and scope to his vision of violence and the human comedy, to explain and ultimately resolve, through the Tragic View, the efficient causes of "revolution" and dissent. Though he seems to focus on a younger generation than Piglia's intellectuals, the political guidepost of sanity he erects is in fact the older generation, comprised of tragic-viewing Stock Liberals such as the lawyer and *bourgeois gentilhomme*, Todd Andrews, or the mistress to various renowned literati and acting provost of Marshyhope State University, Lady Amherst. These characters are excessive in their personal (especially sexual) appetites but, in the end, happily complacent in their clubby moderation and relieved to renounce the follies of their salad years for a nostalgic meat-and-potatoes discretion. They, and not the youthful activists, are the standard by which social harmony is ultimately judged. In fact, the chief significance of youthful dissent (a dissent crucial to Barth's enterprise) is to serve as a self-regulating demonstration of how youth is doomed, in Barth's historical view, never to act on its own behalf, but always in loco parentis.

This "truth," which Barth's novel holds self-evident, appears in manifold guises throughout *LETTERS*, like the re-enactments of famous battles that vacationing Americans can witness in "historic" towns throughout the United States: each the same in significance and kind, differing only in locale. This "historical" undertaking is the terrain on which *LETTERS* fails. Barth's portrayal of Drew Mack, for instance, the novel's resident radical, in one of Todd Andrews' letters to the Author, lands squarely (and necessarily) in the category of caricature, its tone droll, jocular, and satirical.

> Having disappointed his parents in the first place by choosing Hopkins and Brandeis as his soul mothers rather than Princeton and Harvard, he now quite exasperates them by dropping his doctoral studies in '63 to assist in the Cambridge (Maryland) civil rights demonstrations—quite as his father had picketed his *own* father's pickle factories in the thirties. When the July 4th fireworks were cancelled that year on account of the race riots, Harrison followed in the family tradition of disowning his son, though not by formal legal action. Drew responded promptly by marrying one of his ex-classmates, a black girl from Cambridge.[57]

All of the actions of this exceedingly tame "revolutionary" are mildly mocked, reduced to an intergenerational conflict between father and son. Dissent is a "family tradition." One is given to understand that his rebelliousness—marrying a black girl, joining demonstrations in a marshy backwater as peripheral as Piglia's Entre

Ríos—remains restricted to the realm of psycho-social adjustment to familial expectations and does not constitute a serious threat to society at large. Even his implied dynamiting of Andrews and two other characters at the novel's end represents the random, isolated action of a malcontent (as defined by the Tragic View), devoid of any larger resonance. Here, the choice of one Ivy League school over another (though a "disappointment" in the patrician familial context) and even the failure to finish one's doctoral studies raise merely a smile rather than a ruckus.

Barth has expressed his awareness of this possible effect in saying he "wouldn't be surprised to learn that any true commune dweller or activist . . . would find my portraits caricatures." He claims that "to some extent they are meant to be caricatures" and that they are not at "the center of the novel." Yet this declaration of intentionality shouldn't suggest that overeducated dissenters are included in *LETTERS* as mere local-color entertainment. Barth, who finds himself drawn to the genres and writing styles of the eighteenth century, uses caricature, as much as do Swift and Sterne, to critique the revolutionary tendencies threatening the skeptical middle way. His lampooning of activist intellectuals in *LETTERS* deliberately recapitulates one of the commonest myths about them, just as his description of Borges and García Márquez as New Word writers purposefully limits itself to drawing on the commonest myths about Latin America. Since Barth's conception of history is largely predicated on using broad comedy to first smooth out the rough complexities of the even broader social questions he raises, his deliberate political misapprehension (of Drew, for instance) calls into question the validity of his entire view of history.

In his "Revolt of the Young Intelligentsia" (1971), Richard Flacks (one of the founders of Students for a Democratic Society, SDS) tries to rectify the simplistic notion that sixties campus turmoil and defiance of authority expressed mere "generational conflict" of the Drew Mack variety, limited to a handful of malcontents. He says that "emphasis on the youth problem and generational revolt obscures the more fundamental sources of the growing antiauthoritarianism . . . among white youth in America."[58] Flacks calls attention to the fact that "student activists are overwhelmingly from affluent backgrounds," professional families in particular, and that in their skepticism about "the self-denying, competitive, status-oriented individualism of bourgeois culture," these intellectuals more or less *resembled* their parents. Unlike Barth, he sees dissent as genuine, serious, and as a mark of intergenerational solidarity, not as a mere phase to be outgrown, a puerile attempt to deny the conformist and complaisant truer self supposedly residing in oneself and in one's parents.

Flacks' view is echoed in Kenneth Keniston's *Young Radicals,* a thoroughgoing study of the sociological traits of a group of activists participating in a social program called Vietnam Summer in 1967. In his admonition about cultural reductionism, he easily could be speaking straight to Barth: "Popular stereotypes . . . confuse the politically pessimistic and socially alienated student with the politically hopeful and socially committed activist." His description of "the protest-prone personality," based on his research with the Vietnam Summer volunteers, is strikingly similar to that of Flacks. "Student activists come from families with liberal political values; a disproportionate number report that their parents hold views essentially similar to their own, and accept or support their activities." Many of the parents, he says, are liberal Democrats, pacifists, or socialists.[59] Keniston finds the majority of these activists explicitly *not* engaged in generational revolt, but instead "living out expressed but unimplemented parental values."[60]

In accounting for the genesis of radical disaffection from the prevailing culture, Richard Flacks reaches conclusions related to Keniston's but emphasizes more of a definitive rupture with parental values, because of the incompatibility of those values with the contradictions of the larger society. He observes that the "intelligentsia . . . those engaged vocationally in the production, distribution, interpretation, criticism, and inculcation of cultural values," far from being an uncohesive rabble, possess "many of the cultural and political characteristics of a class in Marx's sense." An affluent but inequitable "industrializing society was overproducing educated youth; finding a vocation commensurate with one's education and aspirations became an acute problem."[61] The logic of U.S. capitalist society, committed to producing a broader middle-class base of reasonably affluent, educated consumers to sustain an economy based on principles of overproduction and selective distribution, characteristically "overproduces" a substantial number of overeducated intellectuals who can't be fully assimilated, either productively or ideologically, into that economy.

Yet their unprecedented large numbers, their cultural cohesiveness, their immediate personal comfort, their subsequently increasing expectations about the ability of the U.S. to translate its unprecedented material affluence and liberal rhetoric about equality and democracy into a visibly just society, and their increasing disillusionment about the disparity between this rhetoric and the inequitable condition of society as a whole, make these white, bourgeois intellectuals, who might have been expected to remain complacent, into a force of turbulence and dissent. In "Cornucopia and Its Discontents," another white student activist and founder of the New Left, Todd Gitlin, describes this same ambivalence.

> Affluence . . . in the fifties . . . was assumed to be a national condition, not just a personal standing. Indeed, affluence was an irresistible economic and psychological fact in a society that had long since made material production and acquisition its central activities. The boom from 1945 to 1973, occasionally interrupted by recessions only to roll on seemingly undiminished, was the longest in American history. . . . The flush of prosperity and the thrill of victory also translated into a baby boom. . . . the sustained boom took place only in the United States, Canada, Australia, and New Zealand, countries that were left unscathed by the war, blessed with land, robust with confidence, feverish with what Lord Keynes called "relentless consumption". . . . The baby boom was widely touted as a tribute to the national glory . . . babies were the measure and the extension of the economic boom; they were good for its markets; they were its pride; in some ways they were its point.[62]

But a significant number within this secondary, human boom, try as they might, could not share fully that robust confidence. If anything, they took too much to heart the parental and societal dictum that affluence should be a national condition and not just a personal standing. Unlike the characters populating Barth's novel, they were unwilling to accept the premise that their familial situations of material comfort were generalizable as a metaphor for the good life in society as a whole. Many of these questioning minds, as Gitlin describes, coalesced by the early sixties into the New Left and attempted to articulate an alternative set of values.

> In a nation devoted to private pursuits, they believed in public action. In a culture devoted to the celebration of middle-class security, they labelled it smugness and expressed solidarity with people who were systematically excluded from a fair share in prosperity. The revelation that there were people blocked from affluence not only offended them, it discredited the dream—a dream they already felt ambivalent about, estranged from.[63]

However much they may wish to, they can't share the tragically tinged but ultimately benign and self-assured confidence about the democratic republic—"the dream"—that characterizes the historical counterparts of Barth's fictional Stock Liberal. Flacks describes the political stance of this latter "class" as one of "substantial optimism about the direction of society and a wholehearted acceptance of the legitimacy of the national political system, coupled with a strong hostility to those political and cultural elements they could identify as reactionary or regressive"—or, as Todd Andrews puts it in his letter, "ever for Reform as against revolution or reaction." Flacks further describes the adherents of this republicanism with respect to their belief that

> the federal government could be molded into a force for social amelioration, economic progress, and equality. . . . They believed that the new vocations (the service, helping, and educational professions) would be significant in curing and preventing social and psychological pathology, in extending the possibilities for democracy and upward mobility, and in raising the intellectual and cultural level of the people.[64]

But the "young intellegentsia" of the U.S. in the sixties found it difficult to participate wholeheartedly in this "upwardly mobile" ideology of the liberal republic.

I don't suggest that Barth necessarily need endorse the thesis that student activists ultimately broke with the tradition of American liberalism in order for his novel to qualify as substantively historical in its representation of democracy and revolution. In *Being Free* (1970), Gibson Winter suggests that the New Left have incorrectly been "criticized for an almost nihilistic attitude toward contemporary society" and that their failure as an instance of radicalism has much more to do, in fact, with their excessive *continuities* with the tradition of liberalism.

> The New Left limit their negation to the anti-democracy of the American techno-society. . . . The New Left took America's democratic values to heart . . . They are thoroughgoing moralists. They want America to be consistent—to realize the promise of a democratic society. . . . The New Left carry the American ethos of achievement and the technological will to the nth degree.[65]

As part of his evidence, Winter quotes in the appendix portions of SDS's influential manifesto, "The Port Huron Statement," which rings with the freedom rhetoric of the founding fathers. "The search for truly democratic alternatives to the present, and a commitment to social experimentation with them, is a worthy and fulfilling human enterprise . . . an effort rooted in the ancient, still unfulfilled conception of man attaining determining influences over the circumstances of his life." Or: "As a *social system* we seek the establishment of a democracy of individual participation, governed by two central aims: that the individual share in those social decisions determining the quality and direction of his life; that the society be organized to encourage independence in men and provide the media for their common participation."[66] These are tenets of constitutional democracy, updated with a passion.

Whatever position one may take about radicalism, Winter's appraisal has two distinct advantages over Barth's: first, it does not represent American history as a very long and tiresome family quarrel, a human comedy scripted as situation comedy; second, it does not assume capital-*D* Democracy to be a self-evident, self-explanatory value. If anything, Winter's critique of the New Left's failures calls into question (as Piglia's novel does for Argentina) the origin, guiding structures, and supposed consistency of democracy and democratic values. Historian Staughton Lynd, though he gives a somewhat more optimistic prognosis for participatory democracy than Winter, states this thesis even more strongly, tracing a line of revolutionary rhetoric from dissenters in England to the American Declaration of Independence, on up through nineteenth-century abolitionism, all the way to the dissent of the New Left and of black-power militants such as Stokely Carmichael. At the same time, he asserts the ways in which this text of belief in the "natural rights of man" had to be restated in each case to incorporate the historically specific texture of each struggle. Lynd is also extremely quick to claim the non-universality of democratic language and to advise against attitudes that attempt to essentialize democracy. His first chapter is entitled "Truths Self-Evident," and the very first sentences of that chapter have this to say:

> The Declaration of Independence is so familiar that, to use its own language, its propositions seem "self-evident." But the Declaration's assertions were not commonplace and inevitable at the time they were written, nor are they so now.[67]

His description of the intellectual tradition informing contemporary radicalism not only acknowledges that tradition's "democratic" underpinnings. It also directly attributes the deficiencies in attempts at revolution-by-replication to the essentialistic, "natural rights" conceptualizations that serve as the legitimating rhetorical basis for American democracy.

> Any critic of the American present must have profoundly mixed feelings about our country's past. On the one hand, he will feel shame and distrust toward Founding Fathers who tolerated slavery, exterminated Indians, and blandly assumed that a good society must be based on private property. On the other hand, he is likely to find himself articulating his own demands in the Revolutionary language of inalienable rights, a natural higher law, and the right to revolution.
>
> The tradition I have attempted to describe made the following affirmations: that the proper foundation for government is a universal law of right and wrong self-evident to the intuitive common sense of every man; that freedom is a power of personal self-direction which no man can delegate to another; that the purpose of society is not the protection of property but fulfillment of the needs of living human beings; that good citizens have the right and duty, not only to overthrow incurably oppressive governments, but before that point, to break oppressive laws.[68]

One may indict radicals if one wishes, but to do so, one must begin by indicting a self-contradicting United States, and democracy itself. The irony of *LETTERS* is that the materials for making a reasonably compelling and historically based indictment of radicalism (which seems to be Barth's fervent wish) are amply there in the novel, with its profusion of researched detail about various attempts at "revolution" in the eighteenth, nineteenth, and twentieth centuries. It would scarcely have stretched Barth's imagination further to recast his epic familial drama of ideological continuity as a social drama of radicalism redux. In fact, it is an absolute tour de force on his part to have pulled together such a wealth of historical material and still to have produced a tome so utterly devoid of historical nuance. But so profound is Barth's distaste for radicalism, and so strong his dedication to the via media, that he prefers to sacrifice a complex view of history altogether rather than having to indict Democracy. The alternative vision of "history" he offers remains contingent, as I have said, on first reducing radical politics to way-out shenanigans and crazy college capers.

The narrative of *LETTERS* counters the disaffection of the sixties with its immoderate caricature and its measured tone. In the aforementioned reductive portrait of Drew Mack, the lineaments of

Barth's temperate concept of "revolution" begin to emerge. In his gloss on the notion of a" Second American Revolution," Barth cites Marx's "famous observation that important events in history tend to occur twice: the first time as tragedy, the second time as farce."[69] In concurring with such a reading of history, Barth, though avowedly unengaged with the dissent of the Second American Revolution in the sixties, nonetheless participates, like Piglia's "unengaged" intellectuals, in the elaboration of his own counter-version of a utopian desire to make the present habitable. In the case of *LETTERS*, he does so by trying to enact the present (the farcical "second time" of historical events) as a conservative, conservational via media between other, unacceptably radical versions of utopia, which are for Barth dystopian. In "Revolution, Liberation, and Utopia" (an essay in a topical book from 1971 entitled, appropriately, *The New American Revolution*), Paul Kress remarks that both utopianism and the creation of dystopia—flip sides of one another—remain equally "important to the development of contemporary myths of revolution and liberation," but whereas utopia performs a positive function, the overt purpose of dystopia is to satirize. "There is," Kress says, "a profound affinity between satire and dystopia that bears directly on the concept of liberation."[70]

In the case of Barth's novel, the present as dystopia takes myriad forms, criticizing the excesses of violent revolt in its many guises. Not only do Drew and his cohorts range from naive to misguided to buffoonish, but one of the novel's seven letter writers is Jerome Bray, a mad computer researcher—or possibly a large insect representing a "communal" colony of insects somewhere in Maryland—who is/are writing a revolutionary novel on a LILYVAC computer, in a new literary form called "numerature" which, so he/they/it claims, will make literature obsolete. Bray has sworn revenge on various of the other letter writers, whom he/it considers, for various reasons—phrasing it in Bray's computerese—supernumerary. One of Bray's letters of solidarity to Drew, under the title of "LILY-VAC'S LEAFY ANAGRAM" and addressed to "Comrade," begins by vowing

> Death to Jacobins, usurpers, anti-Bonapartists. The King is dead; long live the 2nd Revolution. Beware of Todd Andrews, agent of the pesticide cartel. . . . We last met in February at the funeral of H.R.H. your father . . . when you questioned us closely as to the practicality not to say the authenticity of LILYVAC's Novel Revolutionary Program for which you had twice loyally arranged support from the Tidewater Foundation.[71]

Here, the specter of this blind, mindless, violent, amalgamated revolutionary urge might be frightening if it weren't rendered so ludicrous by Barth's satirization of its rhetorical overload. The prospect of a humorless, Braying, LILYVAC-generated "revolution" comes across as even more dystopian than Jerome Bray's paranoid imaginings about a "pesticide cartel." At every turn of the novel, moderation emerges as the only acceptable alternative. Jacobins, anti-Bonapartists, activists, haters of the tragic-viewing Todd Andrews, and the various historical moments in which they participate are all conflated satirically into a single, synchronic revolutionary force, irrevocably out of context and out of time—out of everything except steam.

The novel's willingness to cast its utopian impulse in the form of a via media remains consistent with its view of the relationship of temporality to history. Charles Harris' description of Barth's treatment of the progression of history in *LETTERS* sounds reminiscent of Piglia's treatment, but the difference lies in Piglia's full, dialectical exploration of this temporality and Barth's impulse toward immediate, synthetic, even a priori resolution. Harris says that

> One of Barth's major concerns in *LETTERS* may be seen as the forms of historical progression. Two forms he considers and then discards [are] repudiation and emulation of the past, because both represent ultimate denials of history. The former apprehends history as linear and causal, locating its utopian dream at the end of history. . . . it attempts to displace, violently if necessary, attendant states of affairs so that man may move closer to his ultimate victory. . . . Emulation of the past . . . takes its place within the archetype of the Eternal Return . . . all moments and all situations remain stationary and thus acquire the ontological order of the archetype. History is apprehended as cyclic, notions of mechanistic causality are rejected, and the utopian dream is located *in illo tempore,* before History began.[72]

These options, however, are presented in Barth as clear, discrete, and discernible choices, rather than, à la Piglia, versions of one another mutually engendering the notion of historical progression. Barth's novel, rather than the specters raised by Harris, is the "ultimate denial of history." As becomes redundantly clear in the novel's final chapters, neither emulation nor repudiation can be accepted, but not because Barth proposes to offer a more engaging view of historical progression. Emulation and repudiation of the past are disqualified, in characteristic Barthian manner, on account of their extremity. What interests Barth, who demands closure and resolution from the outset, is a happy medium, a marriage of true historical minds to which impediments can't be admitted. It is "arrived" at with little effort.

The novel ends with an alphabetical wedding toast, taken from a sixteenth-century hornbook of wedding greetings, to celebrate the (imagined or "real") marriage of Ambrose Mensch and Lady Amherst, two of the letter writers in *LETTERS*. The wedding takes place—Lady Amherst describes it with typical complacent irony, in a letter to the Author—as part of a patriotic film being made in which the British Lady Amherst plays the part of Britannia and Ambrose the role of Francis Scott Key. The wedding march consists of a single patriotic tune sung as *God Save the Queen* by the "British" guests, and as *My Country 'Tis of Thee* by the Americans. Two lyrics, one tune, is Barth's happy contemporary synthesis to the revolutionary acrimony of yore. "Finally, to symbolise the birth of a nation truly independent of both Britain and France, the bridegroom Ambrose/ Key will draft, and all hands sing, 'The Star-Spangled Banner'!"[73] The wry tone in which she recounts these proceedings, the exclamation mark at the end, the self-consciousness of frames within frames (i.e., a movie about a wedding, performed within a novel), are all supposed to mitigate and complicate the heavy-handedness of this patriotic synthesis, but they work in fact, through a sly and complicitous wink, to define the history of "revolution" in civics-textbook fashion, as a modestly modified and updated acceptance of the (essentially unquestionable) lessons of the past.

*LETTERS* accomplishes, to the letter, Barth's claim for it in his subtitle as an "Old Time Epistolary Novel." Barth employs the full repertoire of fictional techniques supplied by modernity to produce the ultimate anti-modern novel. His epistolary novel disputes Alan Friedman's distinction between traditional novels and modern novels—not in the interest of questioning high modernism's ethical legacy (which Barth largely shares) but of coming down gloriously on the side of tradition. According to Friedman, the novel before the twentieth century embodied "the traditional [ethical] premise of a closed experience. . . . The novel traditionally rendered an expanding moral and emotional disturbance which promised all along to arrive, after its greatest climax, at an ending that would and could check that foregoing expansion." But the modern novel, in dispensing with endings, exposes its reader "to an essentially unlimited experience."[74] Barth's novel outdoes the traditional novel's approach to moral closure in ending the novel before it has begun, in checking disturbance and expansion before they occur.

The final paragraph of the novel, part of the Author's "Envoi," simply caps off the closure and synthesis of historical change that have been vigorously pursued all along. In his note to the reader about interpreting both the novel and the data of history, he advises "You read this on (*supply date and news items*). How time passes. *Sic transit! Plus ça change!*"[75] The cyclical and linear views of history—the two ways in which "time passes"—are formally reconciled (as they already had been in narrative tone since the first page of the novel) in a satisfactory and sufficient present, overriding the intervening violence. One might justifiably subtitle the novel *All Ends Well That Begins Well.*

The via media marked out by *LETTERS* constitutes a version of epistolarity. Apart from the specific content of each of the eighty-eight letters, *LETTERS* constructs its epistolary ethos—its Stock Liberal, republican-minded, self-assured, out-of-ontological-doubt approach to both aesthetic and historical questions—through, appropriately, a system of checks and balances. The letters, wildly inventive and idiosyncratic as they are, work collectively toward a formal symmetry that mirrors the measured quality of its narration. The novel is made in a design that involves the repetition of various series of numbers in certain patterns which determine everything from the dates of composition of the letters to the order in which the writers write to the number of sections of the novel and, within the narrative, determine the course of seemingly innumerable, yet carefully numbered, events—for example, Ambrose Mensch's affair with Lady Amherst is meant to have seven stages, which correspond to the seven letters in the title, *LETTERS,* and to a host of other sevens in the novel. Ambrose, for instance, describes a previous affair as "all those seven and sevenths seen together, in an instant . . . on the 7th stroke of the 6th stage of the 6th lovemaking, etc., etc."[76] In gamelike fashion, everything "works out."

Likewise, the exchanges of letters attempt to achieve, in their totality, a similar kind of balance, substituting the satisfaction of complex formal symmetry for the resolution of social conflict, advocating the balance achieved through formal play in this "old-time epistolary novel" as a desirable "old-time" conservative utopia. In his interview with Reilly, Barth defines "the book's true subject, stated simply" as "Reenactment, Recycling, or Revolution—the last in a metaphorical sense rather than a political sense."[77] Stating Barth's project in anagrammatic terms, one could say that the epistolarity of *LETTERS* consists in transposing the conversational into the conservational. The letters in their conglomerate mute the extremest expressions of liberation and utopian desire.

I don't mean to suggest here that formal play and the gamelike quality of narration necessarily result in this sort of neutralizing negation. More purely "aesthetic" and formalist writing of this kind, as I have proposed in my consideration of Teresa Porzecanski and Harry Mathews, may have (or come to have) a quite provocative and suggestive relationship to the language of power. But in the case of *LETTERS*, as I have tried to delineate, Barth's novel works assiduously through artifice toward an ultimately uncritical affirmation of the liberal-republican ideal. Barth and Piglia take inverse approaches to reappropriating the epistolary novel, and the disparities in those approaches cannot be reconciled so easily as such questions usually are for Barth's characters. Unlike Piglia's fiction (also Porzecanski's or Mathews'), in which representations of social and political conflict are oblique yet highly suggestive, Barth's *LETTERS* stakes large and relatively unambiguous claims about history and the political. The aesthetic dimension of these "letters" is equivalent to, and expressive of, an unexamined belief in presence and self-sufficiency, unhampered economic and social progress, et cetera. The relationship of the letters to one another within the novel's structure of artifice serves to reinforce the "natural" appeal of complacent liberalism.

Jerome Bray's diatribe to Drew, for instance, is directly preceded by one of the letters of Andrew Cook IV to his unborn child. Cook, a participant in the War of 1812, plays a role requiring multiple duplicities to various factions, such that his identity remains unclear to those connected with him. Like Ossorio, his Argentine counterpart in Piglia's novel, Barth's Cook is a traitor and double agent. But unlike Ossorio, his letters ultimately endorse republicanism, by helping to construct the liberal fiction of the democratic middle way. Cook's dissolving, "indeterminate" identity remains, in this sense, solidly unitary, out of doubt. He writes at the very end of this letter to his child that

> You will be born into a war. I think no one can now prevent it. I must hope (& try with my life) that no one will "win" it, or all is lost. Andrée & I are pledged now neither to the British nor to the "Americans"—nor, finally, to the Indians—but to *division* of the large and strong who would exploit the less large, less strong. Thus we are anti-Bonapartists, but not pro-Bourbon; thus, for the nonce, pro-British, but no longer anti-"American." No hope or point now in *destroying* the United States; but they must be checkt, contain'd, divided, lest like Gargantua's their mad growth do the destroying. May this be your work too, when your

time comes. Farewell. Do not restart that old reciprocating engine, our history; do not rebel against the *me* who am rebelling against myself.[78]

The system of checks and balances prevails here. The more Cook denies his allegiance to any faction, the more he thereby affirms his allegiance to the besieged ideal of liberal republicanism. His goal is to preserve these United States as an efficiently functioning state. And the closing lines of his letter serve as a check on the Jerome Bray rhetoric ("Death to Jacobins . . . long live the 2nd Revolution") which directly succeeds them on the same page. Barth's novel— filled with repetitions, recurrences, interlacings, interweavings, juxtapositions that "resolve" conflict through the rhetorical reconciliation of opposites—sustains a Point/Counterpoint view of history— two distinct sides to every issue, each of which has something to be said for it and against it—and its eschewal of radical (and, of course, reactionary) perspectives is relentless. But rather than investigate the dialectical tensions and contradictions that underlie the troubled concept of republicanism (Reason, Tolerance, Law, Democracy, Humanism, and their antitheses), Barth's narrative employs counterpoint, as in music, to reinforce the sensation of a harmonic, harmonious relationship between and among its paradoxes. Barth, like Todd Andrews, is a "connoisseur" of those paradoxes.

It is this implausible attempt to substitute sheer formalism—the elegant turns of an epistolary conversation—for a more considered inquiry into the social transformations it so conspicuously alludes to, that make Barth's New American Resolution so unsatisfactory. Gerald Graff has observed that "what makes Barth's narratives hang together . . . is not a vision of historical change but a structure of repeating motifs. For a novel with so much history in it, *LETTERS* is oddly unhistorical." One need not precisely agree with Graff's broader exhortation for a continuance of the ideals of high modernism to concur with his disenchantment with a novel like *LETTERS*, which makes grand and overt historical claims yet is ordered and powered chiefly by repetition, recurrence, and reenactment.[79]

In explaining to interviewer Reilly why he turned to the epistolary form, Barth speaks a phrase that calls to mind Piglia's "artificial respiration." "The epistolary novel," says Barth, "the form that established the novel as the most popular form of literature, was also the first novelistic form to die. . . . I regarded it as part of my literary function to administer a kind of artificial resuscitation to this apparently exhausted form."[80] But if such a resuscitation is to surpass its own artificiality and reprise as a compelling form of literary endeavor, then it must go beyond its artifice and artfulness to the extent of wrestling acutely with the historical questions it raises. There is, as Barth himself suggests in his essay "The Literature of Exhaustion," no intrinsic necessity for the novel as a form to endure, much less a genre of it such as the epistolary novel. Its perceived necessity arises out of its vital engagement with its time.

# 5. Letters from Nowhere: Epistolary Fiction and Feminine Identity—Fanny Howe, Silvia Schmid, Lydia Davis, and Manuel Puig

The compendious, sweeping quality of Piglia's and Barth's epistolary novels, Piglia's range of philosophical speculation and Barth's ambitious artistic invention, might leave one with the impression that between the two of them they've managed, for better or for worse, to exhaust the possibilities of re-exploring the genre. Yet important lacunae remain untouched and virtually unacknowledged in their writing, especially regarding questions of gender. In the epistolary world of *Respiración artificial*, intellectual life, impoverished as it is, remains a male enclave, and epistolary exchange is restricted to "men of letters." Six of Barth's seven letter writers in *LETTERS* are male, and the seventh, Lady Amherst, though she plays a prominent part, serves mainly as the principle of the eternal feminine, as literary mistress and muse, her prolific writing (most of it devoted to recounting her sexual excesses with various renowned literati) clearly no match for her sheer sexual fecundity.

But experimentation with epistolary fiction, on a self-consciously smaller scale, was also taking place among women in both Argentina and the U.S., in ways which Barth and Piglia, for all their imagination, would never have imagined. Argentine writer Silvia Schmid and her U.S. "correspondents" Fanny Howe and Lydia Davis all employ the conceit of the letter to explore the onset of an ontological "inexistence" and indeterminacy which arises, almost symptomatically, in the context of cultural resistance to a normative patriarchy. In the case of these women writers, social and sexual repression become almost synonymous, so that inexistence bears an inextricable relation to gender. The Argentine novelist Manuel Puig, in his epistolary novel *Boquitas pintadas* (*Heartbreak Tango*), while working on a somewhat larger scale, also shows marked affinities with these women writers in his handling of the subject of feminine identity. In the tradition of gay writers such as Jean Genet, Edward Albee, and Tennessee Williams, Puig, from the remove of that perspective, has proven as adept at contemplating heterosexual relations from a "feminine" perspective as he has at portraying homosexual consciousness in other novels.[1] Unlike his celebrated novel *El beso de la mujer araña* (*Kiss of the Spider Woman*), in which one of the two protagonists is gay, *Boquitas pintadas* is devoted to permutations of male-female romance and the ways in which the social conventions of that romance regulate and restrict the permissible range of female consciousness.

The notion of engagement, thus, need not always be framed in terms of a large historical diorama spanning two centuries, as it is in the novels of Piglia and Barth. For "engagement" has many valences, including that domestic, intimate, but ultimately public preliminary social contract made between a woman and a man, often a prelude to the woman's overwhelming sense of her own inexistence. Howe, Schmid, Puig, and Davis have made forays into the epistolary genre to take up questions of social annihilation, locating them on the terrain of domestic betrothals and betrayals.

In the epistolary fiction of these writers, the sending to or receipt of letters from a male is what produces the female's inexistence. Cut off from the social realm at large, the woman seeks approval and affirmation of her being through the more private, yet potentially social, medium of exchange of letters. But unlike the stabilizing correspondences in Piglia's and Barth's novels, the epistolary missives in the fiction of these women, and to some extent Puig, serve, conversely, to reinforce a precarious dependency on a hostile patriarchal social structure which, if unaltered, can only lead to the woman's effacement. The malleability of her subjectivity and the misogynist social construction emphasizing her relationality both foster and preclude her aspiring to possess a unitary ego, that fiction on which liberal republicanism and the modern state are founded. She is asked to believe and participate ardently in the domestic manifestations of a "democratic" society whose very definition depends on her exclusion. The letter thus becomes a hopeless, oppressive, dystopian device, encouraging her "communication," even making it a precondition of her acceptance within the patriarchal social structure, but circumscribing that attempted communication within manipulative masculine designs.

The choice of the epistolary form to explore this relation seems especially apt, considering the status of women experimental writers in the sixties and later. In an essay on "postmodern" fiction by women, Bonnie Zimmerman claims that women in the U.S. have written little experimental fiction in recent decades, opting instead for more realist forms of expression.[2] Though only relatively true, such a statement would not in any event seem surprising, given the misogynistic, masculine-experience-obsessed strains in the prose of most of the vaunted experimental writers of the sixties and seventies (e.g., Mailer, Pynchon, and Barth, as well as their Latin American counterparts Vargas Llosa, Cortázar, and Fuentes) and given the virtual exclusion of women writers from experimental anthologies and critical works. Describing the parallel development of women's studies and experimental fiction through the sixties and seventies and the lack of attention each afforded to women writing in experimental forms, Ellen Friedman and Miriam Fuchs give what appears a more accurate view. They surmise that "each field of activity seemed defined along gender lines. . . . in this segregated atmosphere, the current generation of women experimentalists was lost between the cracks."[3]

Those who continued to write in these forms, despite remaining between the cracks, occupy a status similar to that of the female letter writer whose missives, however passionate, fail to establish a genuine correspondence. In exploring the position and social construction of contemporary femininity through the epistolary form, women writers also critique their own position within the male-dominated "canon" of experimental writing of the sixties and seventies, many of whose proponents and exegetes made radical social claims for such fiction, while reproducing the normative social attitudes they decried. But another of Friedman and Fuchs' contentions—that the stance of women's experimental writing, "on the whole more subversive than that taken by many male experimentalists . . . provides a hopeful alternative (rather than a mournful alternative, as is the case in much male experimentalism) to the failed master narratives"—seems an overly sanguine view, or at least inadequate in its generic infusion of "subversive" hopefulness into this writing.[4] The fiction of the three women authors considered here, and that of Puig, accomplishes a devastating, sometimes bitterly satirical critique of patriarchal society as dystopian, but its utopian "hopefulness" (a questionable prerequisite), although not precisely "mournful," remains, at best, severely muted. The letters attest instead to the lacerating difficulty of the attempt to assemble even a minimal feminine (or feminist) identity and to conjoin it to its social medium in a way that prevents it, like a marriage of true minds gone from disappointing to despairing, from being nullified.

The title of Fanny Howe's *Forty Whacks*, evoking the familiar nursery rhyme about Lizzie Borden's parricide, suggests the literally murderous extremity out of which feminine identity may have to emerge. The "I" of this epistolary novella can only begin to engage in self-refashioning after killing a couple—a researcher in zoology and his wife, whom the narrator self-consciously casts in patently Freudian maternal and paternal roles vis-à-vis her "self." She has lodged with them as temporary research assistant and housekeeper, attempting to recover from an implied psychiatric institutionalization. But despite the novella's domestic setting, an adequate discussion of *Forty Whacks* cannot merely describe it as a fractured oedipal family romance but rather must correlate that romance to the political state within which it exists. Richard Feldstein and Judith Roof, in taking to task feminist psychoanalytic criticism that has remained within the "comfortable, suspicious, but conveniently indeterminate norms of human relations," conclude that "the apparently binary balance of the heterosexual romantic couple masks the brooding omnipresence of multiple 'other' terms, such as the state or religion, which create, sanctify, and otherwise control the couple's existence."[5] *Forty Whacks* stages a local enactment of that omnipresence.

The patient's prescribed "rehabilitation," her recuperation into the familial and social bosom, is contingent on her coming to a normative understanding of how a healthy person should behave. This understanding in its turn depends on, and is framed formally by, a one-way correspondence with her psychiatrist, one Dr. Weed, to whom she sends letters—or rather all the letters in a single packet—describing the "progress" she is making.

Howe's novella consists of two framing letters, to which is appended a month-long series of the narrator's journal entries. But the journal entries function overtly as letters, a public writing meant to allow Dr. Weed to keep a close eye on, and ostensibly control of, his patient's progress from far away. "I enclose my diary to prove to you that I have been doing what you suggested—that is, recording my experiences, not by rote but with an analytical eye." And in case she is prosecuted and he must testify as to her mental competence, "here is my confidential record of the events preceding the tragedy. Do, please, respond."[6]

In his absence, Dr. Weed remains vividly present, "responding" even in his textual silence. The letter, the most intimate of documents, serves as a confession, as proof, making public the most "confidential" of processes to a confidant whose approval (and, of course, chastisement) the woman is compelled to seek if her being is to receive acknowledgment. She values the journal because "it replaces my appointments with Dr. Weed."[7] The structure of Howe's novella implies the withholding or deferral of approval through the absence of letters from Dr. Weed. Yet the vivid austerity of this would-be correspondent becomes apparent (and he a parent) in the constant, anxious references to him in the narrator's letters.

> Above all, I must keep an honest record of events and impressions, according to Dr. Weed's prescription. I do miss him.

> I could identify with Rose as much as I could with Arthur, which was sure proof of my mental health . . . I know that Dr. Weed would approve.

> If I think of what Dr. Weed would say, it only confirms my conviction that sexual repression is unhealthy.

In "Entertaining the Ménage à Trois," Jerry Aline Flieger addresses the question of the "multivalence" of the psychoanalytic situation, the mutual vulnerability of patient and analyst. But she also acknowledges that given "the neurotic origin of the transference" and also its relation "to the experience of normal love . . . the powerful position of the analyst in this drama is obvious. The therapist is parent, original love, and authority object."[8] In *Forty Whacks*, it is the illusion of mutual sympathy and openness between patient and liberal analyst, of an equal, mutual correspondence, which enables the female's epistolary subjugation, encouraging her to equate it with a desirable personal transference.

The second letter, the one which begins (and beguiles) at the beginning, describes the nameless narrator's arrival in California and her adjustment to her new life, in a studied prose meant to convey her cheerfulness and newfound self-control and to persuade Dr. Weed that she can, after all, be trusted to behave the way any woman deserving of the name should behave. The letter begins "Dear Doctor Weed: I guess I should tell you everything," and goes on to recount a plan of action reminscent, in its woodenness, of a list of resolutions, of Things to Do, penned by an overeager high school senior vehemently aspiring to the status of co-ed through taking courses by correspondence. She resolves "(a) to learn from Arthur . . . so that . . . I'd be an able research assistant in biology (b) to read the classic works of literature (c) to apply the information I had acquired in your office to my new life (d) to prove myself independent."[9]

In the pursuit of this "independence," the letter and the journal entries also employ the happy-talk of psychology's "up-front" jargon/discourse—"the new language"—as the narrator strives to manufacture a manageable, acceptable self-presentation on paper, even while she enters ever deeper into the domestic bizarreness and jealousies of Arthur and Rose, the couple she's employed by, and experiences aggressive sexual fantasies about Arthur. The narrator, eager to prove her mastery of self-analysis (thus of self), belabors elementary, "significant" connections which are meant to serve as proof that she possesses enough self-awareness to control her former deviant behavior and parricidal rage. Remembering a hunting trip with her father on the day of her journey to California, she remarks, in what might aptly be called a Dick-and-Jane psychiatric prose, that "only once did I want to kill him and that was when he gave me this pearl-handled revolver as a present, obviously a substitute phallus."[10] Elsewhere, on making a connection between Rose's standing between her and Arthur the way her mother stood between her and her father, she observes that "It's fortunate I can see these things, otherwise I would be the victim of disturbing emotions . . . I will *not* be bogged down by unknown infantile feelings."[11]

But this transparent (or at least translucent) auto-placation serves only to veil, like an onion-skin sheet of tracing paper beneath which the writing remains legible, the epistolary script of patriarchal legitimation in which the narrator remains circumscribed and its exacerbation of her "dysfunctionality." For not only does she participate fully in the supposedly therapeutic letter/journal writing designed to serve as the mechanism of her quiescent acquiescence in the domestic confines of a paternalistic state. She too, in becoming an unbidden reader of Arthur and Rose's personal letters, which she discovers in a closet while cleaning their room, reduplicates the invasive voyeurism that she herself is rendered subject to.

> I sat on the floor to read them and had a flash of anxiety (misplaced sexual tension, no doubt) which I was unable to analyze away at the time. It immobilized me, a sensation of fever and withdrawal. I thought of the two alternative actions confronting me: either I leave the space that created the neurosis (that is, stop reading the letters on the floor of the closet) or else stick with it. I decided on the latter.

Deciding on the latter—on the letter—entails an interpretation of her own reading process which, rather than truly resolve any of the analysand's dim unease about the normative, oppressive confines of her open-letter method of treatment, of therapy-by-correspondence, instead subsumes that unease within the category of her supposedly dysfunctional sexuality. The source of her deviance, in the official-psychiatric explanation, lies not with any flaw in the terms under which her sexual and social identity within a patriarchal state are allowed but rather with her libido and can thus be cured by the onanistic sexual release afforded by the "healthy" act of voyeurism. Only by reproducing the terms of her victimization and subjugation can she furnish herself with a socially acceptable identity. She resolves the dilemma, in this case, in the officially satisfactory manner, emphasizing the woman's relational destiny as a function of "her" man and failing to challenge the ontological basis of her social construction.

> If I left, the closet might occupy my mind excessively and bring on more symptoms of anxiety; whereas if I stayed, I would come to terms with the problem and lick it right there. Consequently, I read every letter. . . . The most stimulating were from Rose to Arthur and vice-versa. . . . I can see now that my so-called anxiety was a reaction of sexuality toward their relationship . . . I would give anything to have a man like Arthur writing me letters like the ones he wrote to Rose. So once again he revealed to me, indirectly, what I will want from a man in the end.[12]

In answer to Freud's question, "What does a woman *want?*" the narrator seems, at this juncture, to answer Someone who will wear the pens in the family. In making this decision, the narrator subscribes to what Shirley Nelson Garner calls "the heterosexual imperative." Garner says that "at its incipience, psychoanalysis defined the 'mature' and 'normal' woman as heterosexual and ready for or a participant in marriage and the family in the role of wife and mother. Its aim—though unspoken, unacknowledged, and perhaps unknown—was to socialize women to suit the ends of patriarchy."[13] Thus, the narrator is compelled to conceive of Rose as an impediment to her rehabilitation, in standing between herself and the consummation of her heterosexual and social actualization. Her energies become increasingly directed toward the "conquest" of both the husband and lover of her competitor, Rose. In the course of a dinner party, amid drunken talk of "the revolution," the narrator reflects on her "feeling of power and . . . a calm sensuality that made me appreciate my femininity. The balance of powers had shifted according to my expectations: I had Arthur's respect and John's sexual interest."[14]

This fervid resolve and striving to become a good girl finds its expression too in the frequent reminders to herself to "Write home." The weekend she is left alone in the house and discovers the forbidden letters begins, in fact, with missives of a more dutiful kind: "I've taken advantage of the weekend (they are in L.A. visiting friends) by writing letters home."[15] As with Dr. Weed, in whom paternalistic authority resides, her filial fulfillment depends on her unfailing execution of the imperative to correspond, to render a full epistolary account of her adjustment to the social structure. Each activity reinforces the other.

Yet for all the self-analytical reassurance, would-be wifely heterosexuality, and self-imposed admonishments to "write home," a profoundly resonant note of irony lingers over the rote proceedings. Her desire to become transparently self-identical with her oppressive medium gives way to the suppressed suspicion that self-annihilation is to be the real outcome of her devotion to the epistolary. As her logic of the homonymous gives way to that of the anonymous, the socialization she is encouraged to accomplish so fully that she will perform its routines automatically—all by rote—gives way to her inkling that she is moving ever closer to the phrase "That's all she wrote." However vehemently she wills herself to participate in her domestication, the narrator cannot completely fend off the uneasy awareness that her dissolution is in progress. The first letter she comes upon, an unmailed one to a friend, written by Rose—"expressing what she calls 'despair' "—awakens a vague discomfort in the narrator in its reference to Rose's marriage.

> [Rose] described her state of mind in tiny, shaky writing—"I'm always scared! We hardly ever touch, and it's probably my fault. I jump awake at least three times a night—one of those catastrophic, electric leaps—but it's really the way I feel all day." What is her problem? She has everything a girl could want. I must say, at that point I felt some confusion myself.[16]

Rose and the narrator, to some extent, share a status as "inklings," as compulsive (compelled) and unanswered letter writers who formulate only vaguely the hunch that they are somehow complicitous in the denial of their own being, or in a tightly hemmed-in definition of it. Rose's taboo letter remains, significantly, unsent, tucked beneath sloppy piles of dishes and papers to be graded. It only finds a destinee by accident, haphazardly. Even then the narrator remains constrained by the parameters of her feminine ideologization. This ideology encourages her contempt of Rose's "despair" (and later, contempt of the "lost identity" signaled by Rose's doodling of lower-case roses on the Yellow Pages). Thus, she fails to interpret the letter's desperate valences fully. In the narrator's misguided interpretation of these written clues, suffice it to say that she, in so many words, ends up cribbing a line from Blake and tries to dispense with her rival by concluding, "O Rose, thou art sick!" Unfortunately, rather than make the connection between Rose's situation and her own, the narrator instead wishes that she, too, might be eaten by the invisible worm, that its dark secret love might her life destroy.

Neither of them, in their dependent relationality to masculine endeavor, can adopt Arthur's cavalier disregard toward the socially induced imperative to participate in the "liberally" oppressive dynamic of epistolarity. The narrator remarks that "every day [Arthur's] mail is filled with requests for reprints, advice, speeches, and people asking to visit the lab. But he remains a recluse to the end."[17] Arthur—scientific trapper of serpents and fluent in the zoologic of the "old style of scientific writers"—participates fully in masculine endeavor. As such, he is conferred a privileged status in the realm of exchange of social relations and need not assert or even acknowledge that privileged status. No R.S.V.P. necessary, in his case. The narrator concludes "the more power to him, the less to Rose," but fails to appreciate the perceptiveness of her own insight or its relevance to her own situation.

But the writing is on the wall, or at least on the closet floor, and its import gradually steals over the narrator. Her instructions to "write home" disintegrate little by little, eventually relegated to the first item of a bizarre shopping list—confusing familial, herbicidal, and drugstore notions—which makes up her October 3 journal entry:

write home
Ortho Novum
familia
stockings
Diorissimo
gum

This note of reminder to herself, with its latinate quality of a poorly "rote" religious litany, signals the coming-apart of the seamless "new language" of epistolary psychiatry which she has employed up to this point. The very next journal entry announces that

I've finally broken all ties with my parents. . . . Mother wrote me a letter signing it with hers and father's names. It's so lazy and just plain insulting of her to do this, I've decided to cut off all communication with them. If they can't even write me separate letters, they are not worthy of my time. I don't care if Dad is a day sleeper, he could write me from the factory at nights.[18]

Her aspirations of establishing a direct, satisfactory correspondence with the absent patriarchal figure; of believing in the sacredness of the oedipal triangle, accepting the enabling claims of liberal psychoanalysis, investing this familial triad with its avowed significance in order to overcome it through an epistolary transference; of circumventing the epistolary mediation of other women, who represent for her obstacles to her full integration as the equal, feminine co-respondent of the masculine realm—all these aspirations are hereby declared null and void, as her selfhood has long since been. Her father, like Arthur and Dr. Weed, has no actual need to respond to or integrate her, since she is doing such an impeccable job of manufacturing her own fictive, illusory sense of participation and acceptable femininity. Her potential real correspondents—Rose and her mother—remain equally distant because they, like her, are busy reduplicating the ideology requiring their feminine malleability and mutual wariness or hostility.

The novella's brilliant understatement is achieved through the narrator's cheerful tone of complacent yet anxious, vaguely wary self-delusion, coupled with her unrelenting, critical "analysis" of others, her wholehearted acceptance of Freudian principles and her reasonable, if elementary, understanding of them, as well as her specious application of them to her own situation. By accepting and even seeming to endorse the premises of a modern, liberal state committed to the psycho-social being and "well-being" of its inhabitants, then carrying them to their absurd, fatal, and plausible extremes, Howe creates a dystopian, devastating critique of power and gender relations. The narrator's "parricide" indeed appears as the inevitable outcome of her rehabilitation. In the patient's wholehearted acceptance of patriarchal Freudian doctrine, with its insistence on the patient's latent wish to slay the father, her act seems a ringing endorsement of that doctrine's characterization of her, a sign that she has completely assimilated, correctly albeit crudely, its fundamental precepts. Or, to put it in the words of the narrator in what is her final attempt at writing her way into normalcy before the murder, in her pen-ultimate journal entry, "All we ever really need is time and silence so we can regain our self-consciousness. However, as Dr. Weed would say, 'You can't escape your unconscious.' "[19]

The murder, at the same time, throws the narrator completely back into the category of the "dysfunctional" patient, since the nightmare of any espoused form of social logic (and that which exposes its contradictions) is the too-literal application of it by an over-zealous disciple. One of the keen ironies in the narrator's relation to Dr. Weed is that her letters, which represent the measure and mechanism of her social control and self-control, neither prevent her from murdering Arthur and Rose, nor are sent to the analyst—to the "authorities"—until after the reprise of "aberrance" has occurred.

The formal structure of the novella, presenting the letters and journal entries as a single packet, a single outburst or outpouring, belies the careful, gradual re-socialization implied by the day-to-day diary installments. Dr. Weed, powerless to change the outcome of the story once it has been told to him, becomes the narrator's captive audience. Out of this reversal—a potential always implicit in the ideological fiction of psychiatric transference as a two-way correspondence—arises the ambiguity of power and mutual vulnerability between analyst and analysand which Flieger attributes to the psychoanalytic drama in its quality as a narrative act. Freud's later explanation of the origins of this psychic drama, she says,

> tends to give the patient the active, creative role of psychic subject, who "leads the analyst on" with her tales, a latter-day Scheherazade who captivates her accomplice in the countertransference. For the analysand . . . is above all a storyteller, and the analyst, however powerful, is an audience, a recipient. Both positions contain aspects of power and passivity—which Freud sometimes elides with masculinity and femininity—and both positions imply mutual implication and mutual vulnerability.[20]

Like the modern state, the psychiatry which helps legitimate it contains the contradictions which hold the potential to subvert it. The letter of confession, once the narrator has completed it—and the rash act in which it culminates—is sent by post, posthaste, but its chastising, paternalistic reply, if there is to be one, can only arrive post-mortem. Therapy-by-correspondence (transference), psychiatry's perfected form of social control, has failed.

The novella's very first letter, which reprises verbatim as its very last—written in the second case as part of the final, October 8, journal entry—presents the narrator and the narration as unrepentant. It is an epistle which negates from beginning to end the self-improving, acquiescent, good-girl prose of the installments which succeed (and precede) it. The novella begins, in fact, with the sentence "I'd do it again." The defiance of this terse announcement signals an emergence of sorts, a reconstruction of selfhood that can only begin "when the sickness is past and the swooning is over."

Yet one need not over-emphasize the text's "subversiveness" of the patriarchal order, its status as, in the words of Friedman and Fuchs, "a hopeful alternative . . . to the failed master narratives." In

its advocacy of the reconstitution of feminine or feminist consciousness, *Forty Whacks* tempers its instant of exuberance (occurring in
the brief, hallucinatory space and time between the carnage of a double murder, not only of Arthur but of Rose, and an implied sure
reprisal) with a consciousness of the agonizing difficulty of any satisfactory transformation issuing out of such a dystopian landscape,
where "the almond tree has withered and the lamps are smashed in
the living room; and my gun is rotting there." The grim, but not
impossible, prospect of refashioning the epistolary dynamic of sexual
and social oppression into a social contract or conjoining which will
not ultimately obliterate feminine identity is succinctly captured in
the first/last framing letter. In it, the narrator employs a stuttering
epistolary prose in order to assert her being, and her rejection of her
status as dysfunctional patient, to her absent interlocutor, Dr. Weed.

> The sun is warm.
> Dear Doctor W
> Dear
> Dearest Doc
> Dear Doctor Weed I am severely
> Dear Doctor Weed
>   I am se
> Dear Doctor Weed
>   I am severely
>
> ALIVE[21]

Her form of address indicates that though Dr. Weed stands as her
designated addressee, she does not necessarily stand still as his designated oppressee. His name remains at the head of the letter but in
flux. Nonetheless, language here, a language under renovation, shat-
ters perforce into its basic, almost inarticulate components, as the
speaker struggles to gather it into the constituents of a tenable, minimal identity. The attempt to abdicate the narrator's former, Freudian, epistolary form of communication gives way to what can almost
be described as aphasia. Yet unlike the Mother Goose mutterings of
Gordon Lish's homicidal *Peru*, in which the nursery-rhyme epigraph
"One two, buckle my shoe," articulates fairly accurately the level
of sophistication and scope of its narrative yearnings, *Forty Whacks*,
in its allusion to Lizzie Borden's refrain, returns its narrator to the
childlike beginnings of speech so that they might, just possibly, serve
as a point of departure for a revivifying encounter with language.

The precarious nature of epistolarity came to bear not only on
Howe's conception of *Forty Whacks* but on her emergence as a

woman experimental writer during the sixties. In her 1985 "Arto-biography," her description of her "excruciating" correspondence with novelist Edward Dahlberg during that time provides another instance of epistolary paternalism, in the form of mentoring through letters, a situation not unrelated to the oppressive transference considered in Howe's novella. Though Howe insists that, in the end, the encounter with Dahlberg proved fruitful, providing her "first conscious encounter with a linguistic morality," the portrait of Dahlberg remains that of a manipulative, misogynist correspondent, who injects into this therapeutic exchange with his vulnerable, youthful literary charge an erotic overdetermination.

> By chance, when I was 22, I wrote a letter to Edward Dahlberg after reading his book *Because I Was Flesh*. This correspondence was to continue over a span of seven years and culminate abruptly and furiously. The letters he sent me were very similar to most of his published letters, except, as he said himself, he had never before attempted to instruct a young woman. This at-the-time young woman had never sought instruction from anyone and took it, when it came, with a surprising lack of suspicion.[22]

But this virgin attempt to "instruct a young woman," whatever its intellectual content, seems to have borne a salacious S.W.A.K. on Dahlberg's part—because he was flesh—which he insisted on equating with his mission as Howe's artistic guru. And the sophisticated, intelligent, inquiring Howe, for her part, was therefore cast in the role of the wary, yet sufficiently trusting, object of literary lust, a kind of Little Red Writing Hood à la Bruno Bettelheim.

> I carried his letters on my person, to jobs, movies, everywhere, devouring them over and over again. I was quickly conscious that I was in the presence of a sexist and racist tyrant. But this awareness did not deter me from perceiving, in his aesthetic credo, an important truth which I was privileged to receive personally. . . . He would try to prove to me, towards the end, the connection between life and art—that is, I must love him, if I loved his work.

Howe remarks that this final sophistry failed, and Dahlberg no doubt felt he had one more sorrow to add to his earlier literary litany of *The Sorrows of Priapus*—the lessons of which the remonstrating author, however, had obviously failed to learn himself. For Dahlberg, in that earlier jeremiad, had employed his linguistic morality to assert that

> man must be classed among the brutes, for he is still a very awkward and salacious biped. . . . Primeval natures wallowed without thought, but as soon as men began thinking how pleasant it was to rub themselves and have deliriums from mud, they employed their minds to achieve what paleolithic mankind did without being lascivious. . . . He is the most ridiculous beast on earth, and the reason for this is his mind and his pudendum.[23]

In the intellectually goatish attitude typical of many such exchanges between older, established male mentors and less-established women writers who are trying to fashion an intellectual identity for themselves in a masculinist-pervaded literary culture, Dahlberg's mental chastity—with its attempt to set up a strict ethical opposition between mind and pudendum—turns out to possess an intimate relation to the thinking-man's licentiousness which he decries. Dahlberg himself emerges as a vibrant example of the "bad writing," symptomatic of "moral torpor, dishonest energy, fraud," which Howe says his espoused ethos was meant to negate. Like the ostensibly neutral or chaste correspondent-therapist, Dahlberg encourages a normative epistolary voyeurism, and stakes overt moral or ethical claims for his intellectual dirty-mindedness, while attempting to relegate his female correspondent to a complementary role in a hierarchical power relationship.

Howe remarks how in the course of this correspondence she was "chided, and even verbally abused by him," and wonders in retrospect "why I had the need or desire for such a harsh instructor."[24] One might answer, without lapsing too heavily into the "artobiographical" fallacy, that Howe, like the nameless narrator of her creation (only with a much more encouraging outcome in the author's case) felt she had to write Dahlberg before she could begin to write him off. This socially induced "need or desire" to enter into a verbally abusive contract, another version of epistolary transference—seeking the validating contempt of an older, avowedly "sexist and racist male tyrant" writer representing a literary culture largely contemptuous of women's experimental writing—fairly begs to be called something like "the hysteria of influence."

This tongue-in-cheek denomination in no way implies the necessity, the legitimacy, or even the tenability of such "influence"; the questionable, even pernicious, concept of acquiring a mentor or guru remains at best a useful fiction, though it is not always clear to whom the usefulness redounds. Nor am I putting forth the critically suspect and ludicrous notion that Howe's early (and to some extent, continuing) admiration of Dahlberg attests to some "real life" familial, oedipal anxiety which Howe worked out through her relationship with Dahlberg. An attempted "psychoanalysis" of Howe would not only completely sink into autobiographical fallacy; it would reduplicate the misogynist underpinnings of the psychoanalytic drama under scrutiny here.

Rather, I am asserting that the consent of women writers, much like the "rehabilitation" of the narrator in *Forty Whacks*, to such self-destructive, quasi-Freudian mentoring arrangements, as a validation of their own writing, draws encouragement from the broader notions of gender and vatic/phallic initiation in contemporary society. The "need or desire" for this epistolary transference, for libidinal investment in a literary relationship of this kind, is manufactured (not inherent or necessary) toward the ultimate end of women writers' exclusion. Even the abbreviated description Howe gives of her correspondence with Dahlberg has overtones of a vatic mentoring that numerous women writers can doubtless identify with.

Experimental novelist Christine Brooke-Rose, in "Illiterations," describes a canon as "very much a masculine notion, a priesthood (not to be polluted by women), a club, a sacred male preserve . . . or a heroic son-father struggle, in Harold Bloom's terms. But a body, a corpus, something owned. And not only a male preserve but that of a privileged caste." But despite the dependence of this libidinal, secular/sacred caste on the periodic entry of outsiders for replenishment, "women's writing does not seem ever to have had that role of 'tonic' or outside remedy, nor does it today."[25]

Still, in a democratic, upwardly mobile society such as the U.S. of the sixties, everybody, even untouchables, had the ostensible right to speak, and to be touched if necessary. The nation's libidinal economy, especially with the advent of something called "women's rights," became increasingly permeable to, even dependent on, "open" exchanges. As was the case with psychotherapy, democracy and literature assumed more up-to-date, therefore viable guises, while retaining their nineteenth-century hieratic hierarchies more or less intact. Thus Dahlberg, in the role of therapist-guru-correspondent, consents to administering to his silent, hysterical literary charge what might be dubbed "the writing cure."

In describing the relation between clinical descriptions of hysteria and women's suffrage in the nineteenth century, Claire Kahane could be providing a gloss as well on the relation between the women's rights movement of the sixties and the masculine appraisal of women's "hysterical" writing of the same time. "Although one was a psychopathology and the other a political movement, these historical developments intersected in their inverse relation to the speaking woman. . . . If hysteria raised the issue of the silencing of women's desire, feminism insisted on speaking it."[26] She describes Freud's familiar initial characterization of hysterics: they suffered from "physical symptoms such as loss of voice," and "reminiscences, first conceived as traumatic memories of seduction by paternal figures which, unacceptable to consciousness, were repressed but continued to manifest their effects in symptoms that enacted the content of the repression."

Dahlberg's diagnosis of Howe's illness might be described as her delusion of herself as a writer, her desire to enter the male canon, a symptom of her "natural" but repressed erotic longings. As a female writer, her version of the Bloomian father-son struggle must find its embodiment as a fantasy of literary-paternal seduction—the hysteria of influence. But as with most illnesses, even serious ones, there is a cure.

> The body of the analyst . . . assumes to itself the symbolic function of the father, compels dialogue, compels the subject to speak itself into being while the analyst listens. The talking [in this case, writing] cure moves the subject away from the body and into language by means of the voice, which participates in both.[27]

But the goal of the writing cure in Dahlberg's case is to initiate the patient into a normative understanding which, despite the movement into language, inspires and compels a chastened silence, a realization that, when it comes to the sacred caste of literature, the way is narrow and few (especially women) may enter the vatic enclave. He transmitted, says Howe, a "message about the sanctity of literature. . . . He set a goal which was literally impossible to achieve. . . . His own style, an atavistic vernacular, was the end result of a seven year self-imposed 'silence,' during which time he immersed himself in reading the classics, Scripture, and studies of the same."[28]

In a homiletic homage to the anti-feminist Milton—no doubt one of Dahlberg's anxiety-producing influences—he recommends to Howe a course of action requiring prolonged silence. The writing cure becomes the negation of writing. But despite these monkish imprecations, including the recommendation that she "take the vow of poverty," Dahlberg's continuation of their correspondence for the biblical seven years paradoxically encourages an eroticization of the analyst-analysand relationship, culminating in his offer of a different paternal cure for the hysteria of influence and a different sort of vatic-phallic initiation. If she loves his work, she must love him. She must not only be his appendage, but love his appendage.

In Dahlberg's autobiography, *Because I Was Flesh*—the book that initiated his and Howe's correspondence—he provides a telling insight into the vatic and sexual nature of his approach to epistolarity in recounting the postscript to his sexual relations with a young woman whom he pursued and finally "conquered" during his college days at Berkeley. After many Sundays during which "Angelica twined about me her chestnut tresses" while "I wanted to fall at her feet and chastely press my lips upon her nude body," Dahlberg precipitously decides to "quit" Berkeley in favor of Columbia, in the process leaving behind his formerly desired Angelica, her nude body, and her chestnut tresses. He remembers the written aftermath with the delicious remorse which only the vatic-phallic conjoining of mind and pudendum can accomplish.

> What epistles did Angelica later pour out of her sweet flesh, and how many times she called me Christ. . . . How shall I atone for the beloved Angelica, the bereaved one, the interred one, save as every Edgar Allen Poe, who must bury his seraph?[29]

Given the exquisite options of Angelic burial or reply mail, the choice is easy. But Dahlberg, the avid albeit mobile student, sets forth an eyebrow-raising version of "writing the body." He learns early on the erotic charge of correspondence, the place where letter meets sweet flesh—a lesson he later wishes to teach Howe. But despite the avowed similarity between his published letters and those he sent to Howe, his correspondence with his male counterparts is of a different order, however similar the language. In his self-conscious literary exchange with Sir Herbert Read, in which Dahlberg devotes himself to skewering and vilifying the work of Joyce, Lawrence, James, Graves, Eliot, and Pound, both he and Read assume the tone of literary oracles making sacred pronouncements from an impermeable enclave, which provides them protection against a diminished, feminized age. The first letter begins

> Dear Herbert:
> It is my fear that in this century of woe and panic literature may pass away, and that after the terrible hecatombs to come, it will be harder to find good books than the body of Osiris. These let-

ters to you are poor oblations to the Muses, for like the Athenian women sacrificing at the tomb of Tereus, I offer you gravel instead of barley groats.

When Dahlberg finds himself among his masculine equals, he executes the real business of epistolary exchange, namely the shoring up of a misogynist priestly literary phallocracy. In this prolonged correspondence with Read, tellingly published under the pious title *Truth Is More Sacred,* he defends his tendency to censure literary works, exclaiming, in overtly phallic prose, "I prefer a virile negation to a comfortable, flaccid yea." Dahlberg does not find it amiss, as he proves in undertaking his long postal "instruction" of Howe, "to give a caveat to the raw apprentices of beauty." But the terms of the tutelary agreement are clear: worship of the vatic-phallic principle. "There can be no just words well arranged without vigor. 'I swear upon my virility,' testifies François Villon." The novels of Flaubert, Proust, Lawrence, Joyce, and James, all of which Dahlberg—himself the writer of a literary autobiography—strangely condemns as "personal memoirs," strike him as too effeminate. Such writing "is an occupation for the lagging ear, and not for a potent intellect." Joyce's *Ulysses,* the worst of the lot, qualifies as "a street-urchin's odyssey of a doddering phallus." Joyce "cannot father a virile sentence," thus his book "is not rich evidence of manhood." Dahlberg concludes his initiating epistle to Read with a fervid resolution that "what we need in America are more chaste books and more whorehouses."[30] As in his exchanges with Howe, the mind, the pudendum, and the epistolary remain inextricable, a holy trinity and a ménage à trois. And in the Read-Dahlberg-Howe triangle I have been describing here, the proper place of each is clearly marked out.

Howe's rejection of this scenario found its expression in her negation not only of Dahlberg's prosaic insinuations but also of his insinuating prose. She began to read authors as heterogeneous as Zora Neale Hurston, Edmond Jabès, Richard Wright, and Flannery O'Connor, "none of whom are on Dahlberg's original list to me." And simultaneous with her mentored correspondence, she also made incursions into the strictly secular, non-vatic realm of popular women's fiction. At the same time as she was writing Dahlberg (and *Forty Whacks*), Howe engaged in writing "pulp books for money"—three of them: *West Coast Nurse, East Coast Nurse,* and *Vietnam Nurse.* The omission of this professional detail in her letters to Dahlberg, like the epistolary narration of *Forty Whacks,* leaves itself open to interpretation as either a rejection of her literary filiality or a timorous reinforcement of it; a local abdication of identity, or part of the process of its reconstitution. "These three books," she says, "were written under the pseudonym Della Field. I never mentioned them to Dahlberg."[31] The pseudonymous and the anonymous can be synonymous, but not necessarily.

The sustained critique of the drama of epistolary transference in Howe's fiction, and in her "artobiography," exposes the pernicious, socially constructed, and potentially paralyzing nature of that drama. It strips the "hysteria of influence" of its essentialism, its talismanic power to characterize a woman's desire and her need to write as a kind of literary dysfunctionality, as a need to slay the father. The writing of "Dear Edward"—the production of a dead letter—does not necessarily stand as a prerequisite to the writing of a live one.

Psychoanalytic mentoring arrangements such as the one that Howe's example represents troubled not only women writing in the U.S. in recent decades, but some of their Latin American counterparts. Argentine playwright and fiction writer Silvia Schmid makes an identical connection between epistolarity, Freudian psychoanalysis, and vatic-phallic oppression in her biting, witty epistolary short story, "Viva Freud!" Part of her 1986 book of short stories, this brief exchange, consisting of three letters, might easily be lost or overlooked among the massive outpouring of highly politicized novels, stories, poetry, plays, films, and testimonials that has taken place during the relative liberalization of the post-Process years.

The book of short stories from which it is taken achieved nowhere near the notoriety of Manuel Puig's wildly popular semi-epistolary novel *Boquitas pintadas* (*Heartbreak Tango*). Schmid, while more modest in scope and in reputation, takes up the question of women's anonymity and lack of identity in the wake of the Process as skillfully and relevantly as Puig does in the years preceding it. A consideration of the two of them enhances one's understanding of the obliteration of feminine identity as a continuing preoccupation in Argentine fiction. Taken together with Piglia, their writing is evidence of the resurgence of epistolary fiction in contemporary Argentina as a particularly powerful sub-genre for social commentary.

Puig's *Boquitas pintadas*, which I will discuss at the end of this chapter, uses the epistolary form to satirize strict religious mores and the popular cultural expressions of women's "romance" (e.g., advice columns for the lovelorn, the cliched ritual exchanges of letters between youthful lovers known as *cartear*) in provincial Argentina of the 1930s and 1940s. His use of epistolarity to explore the social construction of feminine consciousness is often just as biting as Schmid's and Howe's. His writing, however, is also imbued with an affection that makes him draw somewhat different conclusions about "the female condition." Both he and Schmid depict romance as a simultaneous pleasure and torment, but Schmid is more pessimistic about its ultimate viability as a manifestation of the social contract, whereas Puig appears more willing to concede that romance, however lopsided and manipulative, possesses certain inalienable charms.

Schmid's "Viva Freud!" resembles Puig's and Howe's fiction in its eschewal of broadly and overtly political themes. Subjugation takes place within the confines of a manipulative male-female relationship. The parallels with Howe however, in particular the conjunction of the epistolary conceit with the subject matter of psychiatry, are more complete. In "Viva Freud!" the male as lover-therapist-father employs the language of psychoanalysis as a means of exerting his intellectual superiority and masculine prerogative over the "dysfunctional" female.

The female correspondent, named A. (as in *Anonymous*, that famous female author of antiquity), begins the exchange. She attempts to reappropriate language, thus her feminine identity, by negating that of J., her estranged lover, and taking his name out of language.

> I've blotted you out of my address book forever, your name, your address and your telephone number, and, it goes without saying, I've blotted you out of my heart, my feelings, and my mind.[32]

These acts, unfortunately, don't go "without saying," since A. has been compelled to break J.'s significant silence in order to assert her shaky, strictly relational sense of existence. Her ploy is to stage a sarcastic, rage-filled inversion of the Freudian drama, wresting the capacity for language, which the hysteric is denied, away from J. and making him the object of analytic aggression.

> I'm only writing these lines because *I* want to use *you*, me, this time, and not the opposite, not like always before . . . I'm going to lay on you all my shit, *merde, merde*, does it sound better like that? You like it better in French, huh? . . . Well, I'm telling you, shit, and if you don't like it, tough shit. Or caca, if you prefer, more psychoanalytic, more Freudian, isn't it? That way, while you're at it, you can analyze me: but please, don't get it turned around, don't you analyze me, please! It's not caca, a gift, it's not the baby giving its caca as a present to its mother . . . I'm not the baby, and you're not my mommy, or my daddy. I want to dump on you all the shit I have inside.[33]

Just like the narrator of *Forty Whacks*, the "analysand" has internalized the jargon designed to enforce her sexual and social control. But where Howe's narrator presents a smooth surface of seemingly complacent complicity with that language, A. adopts a tone of open hostility toward the scene and semes of psychoanalysis, satirizing J.'s pseudo-intellectual pretension and his self-image as the in-control analyst. She clearly exposes, in this first letter, the misogynist designs of therapy and announces that she now has control, that she now occupies the place of her former tormentor. Years of implied suffering and psychoanalytic abuse have led A. not to the conclusion of rejecting the Freudian drama, and its patriarchal idiom, but rather of believing that her acquired expertise, through a hard-won apprenticeship, now puts her in the controlling position of the analyst.

The vehemence of the epistolary tongue-lashing belies any such possibility of control through inversion. To the extent that she attempts to appropriate the analyst's role on its own terms, she remains enmeshed in its normative logic. Schmid's story restricts itself to savagely depicting the mutual implications of a destructive relationship between a couple—her appropriately Argentine epigraph reads "It takes two to tango"—and doesn't elaborate any larger social context. Nonetheless, her portrayal of the Freudian drama has affinities with more overtly ideological concerns expressed by a group of contemporaneous Argentine psychiatrists, in the years of the seventies leading up to the Process, about the relationship of most strains of psychoanalysis to structures of oppression. In "Psicoanálisis: Institucionalización y/o cambio," Emiliano Galende describes the clinical practice of psychoanalysis as "politically inscribed in the process of recuperation of subjectivities for the [political and social] system. This ideological function is a condition of its development." Its "politically overdetermined" application must be linked "to a particular state of social relations, and its operations *necessarily* contribute to the conservation or modification of those relations."[34]

This recuperation of subjectivities, if unchallenged, encourages, for instance, an institutionalized reinforcement of gender roles, ensuring that women will conform to their prescribed status within the state and the status quo. Psychoanalyst Marie Langer, in describing a diagnosis made by two young women psychoanalysts who accompanied her as "participant-observers" in her treatment of a group of women at a Buenos Aires hospital, remarks how the women psychologists' institutional role supersedes their gender sympathies, causing them to diagnose a young female working-class patient in a manner encouraging her to conform to the social expectations commensurate with her class and gender.

> My observers say exactly what I would have said at an earlier time. Let's see: a young working-class woman in a precarious economic situation, expecting her first child, tells how she's trying to study, so she can escape, in the future, the hard life her mother led. "You wish to surpass your mother," one of the psychologists tells her. This is a "correct" interpretation and apparently nothing more. Since the young woman wants to study medicine, one might have also added something about her transferential rivalry. But latent—and we're specialists in latency—is an ideological, guilt-inducing intervention, because it implies that this wish to surpass mama is bad. . . . That's our superego which ensures one doesn't "surpass" her parents, so that the family and the world will remain just as it is.[35]

The ostensibly neutral psychoanalyst insists on containing within the confines of the oedipal scene even this most benign and individualistic of attempts to question the social structure. She in no way acknowledges the analyst's largely unconscious but patently ideological role in reproducing a complacent populace by helping its members find the "real," familial-bound reasons for their discontent. This institutionally trained habit of "addressing the little girl within the adult woman who continues competing with her mother for papa," says Langer, tends toward the final effect of "transforming a 'rebellious' woman into a submissive housewife and future patient."[36]

Given these general parameters of psychoanalysis in Argentina and the difficulty of negotiating its practice in a way that would do something for its women patients besides reproduce submissive social relations within the fiction of the all-encompassing familial sphere, Silvia Schmid's representation of psychoanalysis in "Viva Freud!" can serve as an acute commentary on how the patriarchal logic of the Process and post-Process came to bear on the microrelations of women and men. Schmid's letter-writing A.—another version of Howe's Little Red Writing Hood—caught in a mentor-apprentice storybook transference, accuses J. of similarly neutralizing interventions and expresses the wary realization that her every passionate remonstrance in language provides her lover-analyst with the linguistic basis for her "normalization."

I hate you, I hate you with all my soul, but no, I don't want to be telling you this. Because I can already hear you. "Hate, hate, the other face of love," with your famous theory about love-passion . . . On and on with your smooth little voice, controlled, academic, with your almost inaudible phrases, so ears would perk up, the better to hear you with. Another beauty of a technique.[37]

Only insofar as A. dedicates herself to devouring J.'s pseudo-analytic concepts, perking up her ears, "the better to hear you with," may she exceed her gender-bound role as the passive analysand. And this devouring, of course, only serves to exacerbate her sense of help-less, inadequate abnormality. The one other area in which lupine voracity is permitted is in the fantasy games of her sexual relations with J. She even signs her final letter to him "Wolfie," her bedroom nickname. But, as it turns out in this lopsided and self-destructive epistolary fairy tale, Wolfie, despite her intention to negate the ne-gater in his own jargon, is the one who gets devoured in the end. Even in the first letter, her negative characterization of her tor-mentor gives way in mid-description to a nostalgic, excited evoca-tion of their perverse and animalistic sexual role-playing.

[I was] always apologizing to you. For what? For what? With your cruel little face and your cold, calculating squirrel's eyes. Squirrel! Big bad squirrel! Remember when I used to say that to you? Remember when I used to hide the treats you loved in my clothes and in the sheets, in the folds of my body, and the big bad squirrel had to search for them, poke around in every corner, sniff, nibble, scratch with his little claws, you're cold, warmer, hot, hot, burning up! Until you found them and broke them open with your sharp teeth? And then sipped their exquisite liqueurs. Remember? Remember?[38]

A.'s attempt to write J. off, to "blot his name out forever," with the ink of her writing, only serves to invite a rejoinder from J., which, in its turnabout of the Freudian lingo, provides A. with another kind of blot, a Rorschachian inkblot in which she is supposed to read and correct her deviance so that she will deviate only in those aforemen-tioned sanctioned ways. She signs off the first letter to J. with the postscript "I beg you, don't speak to me or write me." His calculated reply arrives four days later.

Marie Langer, like Howe and Schmid, makes a link between the language of psychoanalysis and the epistolary genre in an essay that forms part of a volume beginning with the famous exchange of letters between Einstein and Freud, in which Einstein asks the Viennese psychiatrist to "diagnose" the reasons for war. Unlike many of the other respondents in this 1970 volume, who answer Einstein's resuscitated question with sweeping statements about the nature of "war and humankind," Langer, in her "Letter to Einstein," responds to him by raising questions about the political status of psychoanalysis as a practice, describing it as "projective"—her letter serving as a literal postscript to Freud. But this projection, she says, despite Freud's claims for the analyst as a mere "screen," is not onto a neutral medium.

> Even if the analyst abstains from making any reference to himself, and insofar as possible, any personal observation, his or her ideology will become apparent all the same. It shows through in his or her manner of intervention, selection of the content for interpretation, and influences the analyst's tone of voice.[39]

In Schmid's satire, the language of J.'s letter to A. works to restore A. to her former position of inferior, guilty, therapy-hungry subjugation through employing a canny, manipulative, pseudo-Freudian blather. As in the case of the "neutral" analyst, he presents himself as the neutral, dispassionate medium, rather than as a formative participant. His tone of remaining engaged with and yet above the subject at hand is meant to remind A. at all times that although he himself attends therapy, she, not he, is the "patient" under analysis at present. But rather than representing a mere "screen" in Freud's sense, J.'s idiom serves in fact to "screen" his ideology, his self-serving and other-obliterating designs.

> Yesterday I found the letter you slipped under my door. I pay no mind to all your outbursts, I blot them out, I have that capacity, luckily. . . . I believe in the urgent necessity to come to an agreement, that is, to resolve the conflict, establishing once again the limits, and abiding by them without question, that is if both parties are in a condition allowing us to accept limits, and thereafter, see them through.

Such a "mutual" agreement, of course, and the consequent paternalistic bestowal of personhood on the analysand cannot be granted out of hand, but rather depends on

> a sine qua non condition . . . that you return to therapy. It's useless to flee . . . from conflicts within oneself, especially when

they lead you into blind alleys, to lacerating punishments of the beloved, and thereby of one's own ego, all this issuing not only into self-destructiveness but also into an undeserved and troublesome flagellation of the other. . . . The conflicts you must resolve are deep ones, and I've truly arrived at the conclusion . . . that only through a long journey toward the interior of your consciousness, an intense deepening of the consciousness in your case, will you be able to recuperate your self, learn to appreciate your own worth and that of others, and, to say it frank and clear, the way you like it, to stop pissing in your diapers.[40]

The reconstitution of A.'s subjectivity, as in Howe's *Forty Whacks*, depends directly on her acceptance of a paradigm casting her in the role of the infantile bad girl and, as in Howe's mentoring arrangement with Dahlberg, presupposes a continual apprenticeship as a preamble to the conferral of her indefinitely deferred, ever-receding subjectivity. The irony in "Viva Freud!" is that A. has already reached the end of such a long apprenticeship, only to be denied the promised "self," and is invited instead to return to therapeutic mentoring as a renewed novice.

However much J. may emerge as a charlatan, a Freudian quack, his sense of mastery of the psychoanalytic idiom nonetheless remains as confident and absolute as A.'s usage of it remains provisional and contingent. In response to her savaging of his Francophile *merde*, he replies with infinite pedantry, "Pardon, mon amour, but I shall not renounce my manner of self-expression, expression which has garnered me, in any case, the recognition of the country's highest intellectual circles, a fact with which you're well acquainted."[41] For J., who takes the ability to use language as an uncomplicated given, self equals expression and expression equals self.

Psychoanalysis appears ipso facto a masculine preserve, its structure and manner of recuperating subjectivities gender-bound and the pursuit of its language continually illusory for women, who even in the throes of therapy are destined to remain bereft of language by definition and, in J.'s loan words, "melodramatic," possessed only of a "vile, vulgar way of speaking."

In her "Letter to Freud," after trying to reconcile the resultant madness of the pilot who dropped the bomb on Hiroshima with the continuing pacifist lucidity of Einstein, one of the fathers of nuclear fission, Marie Langer significantly qualifies her own fictive epistle to Einstein as melodramatic and vulgar and questions her capacity to manipulate language.

It's difficult for me to write you this letter. It strikes me as awkward and too dramatic in comparison with the epistolary exchange between you and Freud, so measured, profound, and scientific. But sometimes the facts require one to be dramatic.[42]

This feminine calling into question of one's epistolary capacity, coupled with Langer's reservations about the mandate to be "measured, profound, and scientific," suggest that if women are to reappropriate this language, then "hysterical," "melodramatic" vulgarity, the basis of subjugation, must be refashioned into an epistolary vulgate, an alternative to the sacralization of a masculinist Viva-Freudian *langage*.

The brief final letter, from Wolfie to Big Bad Squirrel, suggests the double-edged difficulty of such a vulgate. She capitulates to her seemingly definitive annihilation with an ecstatic glee, the very tonal excessiveness of which allows Schmid to present a wickedly sharp satire of the high potential for misogynistic decimation when analysis is employed, as it predominantly has been in contemporary Argentina, as a form of social control.

A thousand kisses, big bad squirrel! I beg pardon of you, a thousand times pardon, though I know you'll never be able to forgive me . . . But how I want you! How I yearn for you! The silly baby in me will stop pissing in her diapers, I promise you! And I've made an appointment with Freud, with Jung, with Lacan, with all of them together! Transactional, dynamic, orthodox, conductist, whatever you like, whatever you wish. . . . And of course the unconscious, the conscious, all the rest. . . . My wolfie baby, my little wolf, your little wolfie is here waiting for you, filled with howls and growls of anxiousness and passion!! . . . Waaaaaahh! Viva Freud!! Viva Lacan!!! I love you. Wolfie.[43]

In precisely the same manner as Howe's equivalently nameless narrator, A. embraces with a vengeance her renewed infantile status as an almost literally born-again analysand. Schmid's dark humor suggests feminine nullity here as an almost overwhelming certainty, the only brand of certainty to be had at present. But at the same time, the grotesque exaggeration of A.'s response leaves available the reading that A.'s language represents the would-be analysand's (and certainly Schmid's) rejecting, parodic mockery of the attempt to infantilize her. This ambivalent stance between accommodating the denomination of silly, diaper-wetting baby and rejecting it with satiric scorn could be characterized as something like the "return of the re-pissed." Rather than dismiss psychoanalysis as frivolous or irrelevant to Argentina's political crisis, Schmid and Langer instead apprehend and investigate it as central to the social and ideological rigidity of contemporary Argentina, as an overlooked facet of the larger Process. Ricardo Piglia's *Respiración artificial*, important as it is, does not acknowledge the place where epistolarity meets gender, and Schmid's story, in its compelling, suggestive brevity, exists as its mutual and necessary corrective and complement.

Schmid's analysis of social rigidity funneled through romance finds its approximate, somewhat altered reflection in Lydia Davis' equally brief 1976 tale of letter-imperfect love, "The Letter." Both stories feature what Elizabeth Goldsmith calls "a standard *topos* of epistolary literature since Ovid—the female letter of suffering and victimization."[44] But in Davis' story, the unnamed woman, unlike Schmid's A. or Howe's nameless narrator, does not even attempt to write that suffering and victimization into an epistle. Rather, she functions as pure reader, as an anguished, still-aching exegete, reduced, in her search for clues to the failed relationship, to desperate interpretations of an offhand "letter" she receives out of the blue from a callous former lover for whom she still feels deeply the heartbreaking pangs of unanswered love. The failure of her diligent, attentive reading of the "letter"—the body of which consists of "a poem, the poem is in French, and . . . composed by someone else"—to illuminate her situation results not from any fault of perception on her part. Rather, her restriction, as a woman, to a particular, obsessively passionate way of "reading the body," via the discourse of "love," cannot produce a truly satisfactory resolution in a liberal republican social arrangement founded on the masculine negation of such excessive, non-rational forms of exegesis. Patriarchal society's supplying of "love" as her vehicle and domain allows her acuteness, subtlety, intellectual force, and passion to expend themselves in the fruitless (therefore doubly effective in reinforcing her gender-bound role in "permissive" society) endeavor of recovering her faithless ex-lover.

This epistolary topos of female suffering and victimization, dating back, as Goldsmith remarks, to Ovid, can more recently be traced to the cusp of the Enlightenment, to the seventeenth-century love letters of the famous "Portuguese nun," Mariana Alcoforado. Mariana's despair, like that of the woman in "The Letter," seems to emanate from a degraded version of chivalric France, the cradle of love—in her case, in the form of a soldier-lover who has not only loved and left her, to return to France, but who acknowledges her pleading letters, if at all, in the most perfunctory way. Her being, on the other hand, has entirely attuned itself, in its obstinate, self-abnegating, luxurious, incapacitating devotion, to his being. She cultivates what Adrienne Rich has ironically referred to as "fertilisante douleur."[45] In her masochistic, imaginative sympathy toward him, she goes so far as to write that "it would not be displeasing to me, I think, to find that the feelings of other women in some degree justified mine, and I should like it if all the women in France found you attractive." Mariana confesses that

> I realize that I love you as a woman loves who has lost her senses. I do not, however, complain of the violence of my emotions. . . . I could not live without the happiness I come upon in the midst of a thousand sorrows and which remains despite them all—that I love you.[46]

This "senseless" love—this love of a woman "who has lost her senses"—however, has done anything but blunt her interpretive faculties, at least as regards the soldier. In the same missive, Mariana demonstrates that whatever his inattentions, she has trained herself to interpret accurately and carefully his careless, hasty responses: "You alone remain profoundly indifferent; you write me cold letters filled with repetitions, with half the paper blank, and they show plainly that you are anxious only to be finished."[47]

The protagonist of Davis' "The Letter," likewise, is in full possession of selected interpretive senses and exercises them with an equal abandon and futility. But unlike Mariana, she has no recipient to whom she may direct an epistle of her own. Instead, she reads her ex-lover's "missives." Her pathetic, semi-crazed, semiotic capacity for decoding his textual and sexual clues has its origin in the final days of their deteriorating relationship.

> She would walk through the town looking for his car. Once, in the rain, a van turned a corner suddenly at her and she stumbled over her boots into a ditch and then she saw herself clearly: a woman in early middle age wearing rubber boots walking in the dark looking for a white car and now falling into a ditch, prepared to go on walking and be satisfied with the sight of the man's car in a parking lot even if the man was somewhere else and with another woman.
>
> The car is an old white Volvo; it has a beautiful soft shape. She sees other old Volvos nearly every day, and some are tan or cream-colored—close to the color of his—and some are his color, white, but undented and unrusted. The license plates never have

a K in them, and the drivers, always in silhouette, are either women or men with glasses or men with heads that are smaller than his.[48]

The woman's formidable powers of observation, fed and heightened by her unreasonable, self-destructive attachment to her lover, allow her to catalogue with frightening accuracy the types and inhabitants of every Volvo she sees, an exercise which reinforces the self-consuming quality of her cognition. For her, in this Kafkaesque search for her lover, the elusive *K* in the license plate, even if she happens to spot it, provides no keys, neither to the car, nor to enlightenment. Her self-consciousness and hyper-awareness serve only to inflame her sense of absolute helplessness. A year later, she brings this same ferocious, voracious, undiminished sensibility to the "decoding" of the cryptic letter he sends her, even though "she has seen right away that there is no possible answer to it."

The *fertilisante douleur* displayed in Mariana's letters, playing itself out to an apotheosis of ecstatic sadness followed by a morality-tale renunciation of the lover, takes a very different, historically specific, form in its contemporary counterpart. As Marjorie Perloff points out in her commentary on "The Letter," "the question of interpretation is Davis's real subject." The central question posed by the story, says Perloff, is "How can the woman understand what the import of this letter is?"[49] The reprise of the old epistolary topos of feminine victimization and suffering, in Davis' post-1960s tale, serves as a critique of what Iris Marion Young refers to as the "enlightened" fiction of "the unity of the civic public." In a unitary polis such as that of the U.S.—whose gender-exclusionary rhetoric and ideals came under especially harsh attack during the sixties and seventies with the intensification of the women's movement—there exists a "dichotomy between reason and desire." Young attributes the initial institutionalization of this false dichotomy to the ascendancy of eighteenth-century republican philosophy in Europe (coincident with the heyday of the epistolary novel). In this philosophy, there remains a strong distinction between "the universal, public realm of sovereignty and the state" and "the particular private realm of needs and desires."[50] The squelching of a differentiated public, in favor of a universalist state with an "impartial point of view transcending any particular interests," is accomplished, in part, through regulation of the affective lives of women and other groups "excluded from the promise of modern liberalism and republicanism." The often passionate discourses of such groups and their counterculture assumptions, because they were in direct conflict with the notion of a rational, liberal polity consisting of "one nation, indivisible, with liberty and justice for all," needed to be confined to their proper spheres. In her essay, Young centers the contemporary striving for a differentiated public squarely in "the new social movements of the 1960s, 1970s, and 1980s in the U.S."[51] Young puts the state's position succinctly thus:

> Modern normative reason and its political expression in the idea of the civic public, then, has unity and coherence by its expulsion and confinement of everything that would threaten to invade the polity with differentiation: the specificity of women's bodies and desire, the difference of race and culture, the variability or heterogeneity of the needs, the goals and desires of each individual, the ambiguity and changeability of feeling.[52]

This distinction between the publicly sanctioned speech of the body politic (what Charles Bernstein calls "a style of decorous thinking"[53]) and the private, excluded one of "women's bodies and desire" serves to throw the protagonist of "The Letter" continually back into the self-contained, misery-ridden space of lovelorn interpretation, heartsick hermeneusis. By foregrounding the protagonist's status as an interpreter and by providing an analogy to another "language game" (the woman tries to forget her pain by spending much of her time translating a book of poetry)—rather than merely insisting on the poignance and tragic qualities of the woman's undeserved suffering—Davis creates a story that critiques (in a manner similar to Schmid's dismantling of the uses of psychiatry within a militarized state) the excluding assumptions of the liberal, rational, unitary republic. Marjorie Perloff rightly denominates "The Letter" a "hermeneutic parable."

In a manner reminiscent of the letter reading of the closeted narrator of *Forty Whacks,* Davis' nameless woman, immersed in the gut-wrenching details of her process of semiosis, cannot reach a level of interpretation allowing her to dismiss the letter altogether as the contemptuous, egocentric, careless gesture that it is. Only through such a dismissal could she hope to escape the restriction of her language of bodily desire to a "private" domain in which it ceaselessly doubles back on itself, reinforcing its own superfluousness and inefficacy in the realm of public exchange.

Her desire's abject quality is heightened by the protagonist's admission of the "unreasonableness" of her effort. For, as she admits to herself as soon as she opens the letter, "she has seen right away that there is no possible answer to it." The social arrangement between her and her lover precludes her participation as his inter-locutor but not the all-important illusion of her participation. She persists, for only on such impossible, neutralizing terms may her desire and difference and her interpretive capacity stage themselves at all. She believes that if she analyzes passionately and diligently enough, embracing the rational hermeneutic claims of the norma-tive reason which rejects and excludes her, the very ardor of her hermeneutic act will transcend her a priori rejection. So, she inter-prets with a vengeance, right down to the quality of the ink impres-sions on the envelope.

> She examines first the postmark. The date and the time of day
> and the city name are very clear. Then she examines her name
> above the address. He might have hesitated writing her last
> name, because there is a small ink blot in a curve of one letter.
> He has addressed it a little wrong and this is not her zip code.
> She looks at his name, or rather his first initial, the G. very well
> formed, and his last name next to it. Then his address, and she
> wonders why he put a return address on the letter. Does he want
> an answer to this? It is more likely that he is not sure she is still
> here and if she is not still here he wants his letter to come back
> to him so that he will know.[54]

The pathos and the arresting quality of this passage lie less in the love-injury per se than in the intense energy with which the wom-an's mind and imagination strain to reconstruct, from the most triv-ial and impenetrable of clues, her ex-lover's authorial intentionality in such a way that a stray ink blot might yield to her even the most minimal indicator of affection. Willing to settle for even less than a bare phoneme, she reads the sub-phonemic ink. The intellect and passion she lavishes on the envelope's markings become even more pathetic and ludicrous when she opens the envelope and proceeds to the love language. For this language, rather than consisting of some "actual" sentiment or emotion, consists essentially of a facsimile, a poem made "genuine," "personal," "private," and "his" by the mere fact of his having copied it out longhand and superadded the per-functory public conventions of a letter to it. These "personalizing" gestures increase her investment of the letter with significance.

> She notices that he has put her name at the top, with a
> comma after it, in line with his name below the poem. The date,
> her name, comma, then the poem, then his name, period. So the
> poem is the letter.

Having seen all this, she reads the poem more carefully, several times.[55]

The "letter," the mechanism of her affective confinement to the limiting terms of parlance granted to a woman in a modern, enlightened republic, is couched in the softening conventions (and thereby doubly oppressive gesture) of "civil" language. This civil love language (expressing, above all, an "impartial point of view transcending any particular interests") is degraded even further by its having been lifted from the hackneyed conventions of lyric love poetry, rendered absurd in the context of Davis' story. The love language might have been cribbed directly from Mariana Alcoforado's own melancholy seventeenth-century letters, but it seems to derive indirectly, and appropriately, from medieval French troubadour love poetry, one of the chief sources of the lyric conventions of modern romance. Through an effort of sheer will, properly channelled desire, and textual poring-over, the woman manages to imbue these commonplaces, made even more trite by the ex-lover's usage of them, with an illusory sense of poetic and emotional correspondence and authenticity. She thus manufactures her own fictive, hollow resolution to her social and sexual isolation and oppression, a falsely hopeful resolution in perfect sync with the requirements of the liberal, "public" society she inhabits.

What she had seen first and the only words she could remember were *compagnon de silence,* companion of silence, and some line about holding hands, another about green meadows, *prairies* in French, the moon, and dying on the moss. She hadn't seen what she sees this time, that although they have died, or these two in the poem have died, they then meet again, *nous nous retrouvions* we found each other again, up above, in something *immense,* somewhere, which must be heaven. They have found each other crying. . . . She examines the word *retrouvions* slowly, to make sure of the handwriting, that the letters really spell out finding each other again. She hangs on these letters with such concentration that for a moment she can feel everything in her, everything in the room too, and in her life up to now, gather behind her as though it all depends on a line of ink slanted the right way and another line as rounded as she hopes it is. If there can be no doubt, then she can believe that he is still thinking, eight hundred miles from here, that it will be possible ten years from now, or five years, or, since a year has already passed, nine years from now or four years from now.[56]

This aspired-to, speciously arrived-at, happy ending depends, of course, on her willingness to defer indefinitely its coming into being and so continue to assume her current position of vulnerability and feminine submission to the buffeting, humiliating, ego-negating torments of an excessive passion. But the taboo excessiveness, if it is to remain socially sanctioned, must continue to absorb her considerable "concentration" in a private manner expressive of commonly held, self-defeating notions of romantic love. What the handwriting "spells out" is nothing more or less than the dependent, feminine, abject terms of her existence.

She yields to these emotions despite her knowledge that the ex-lover's epistolary self-expression, on which her entire being hangs, most probably thinly papers over a linguistic and ontological void into which she has been groomed to fall. She reflects at the end of the story that "his" poem was, no doubt, "the closest thing he could find to a poem that said something about what he was thinking about companions, silence, crying, and the end of things," or perhaps "he happened on the poem as he was reading through a book of French poems, was reminded of her for a moment, was moved to send it, and sent it quickly with no clear intention."[57]

Nonetheless, she upholds her given role in this modern-day arrangement in a way that resembles, yet goes beyond, Mariana Alcoforado's pre-Enlightenment physical cloistering. For the protagonist of "The Letter" not only must experience feminine victimization and suffering but must give over her entire cognition to a "rational," passionate reading and interpretive process affirming and underscoring, with attention to minutiae and painstaking diligence, that victimization and suffering. Modern normative reason, channeled through the private discourse of love, is the instrument through which "her" realm, the realm of passion and emotion, comes to be segregated from the domain of enlightened public exchange. She enacts the hermeneutic equivalent of *fertilisante douleur*.

The epistles of the Portuguese nun underwent a similar adaptation to the social and textual relations of the late twentieth century in *The Three Marias: New Portuguese Letters*. This experimental epistolary novel[58] co-authored by Maria Isabel Barreno, Maria Teresa Horta, and Maria Velho da Costa and published in Portugal in 1972, rewrites Mariana's letters in a way which forcefully demonstrates how the age-old topos of feminine victimization endures at present, still under the epistolary aegis but in more enlightened and acceptable guises. In this book, the publication of which resulted in banning, confiscation, and the arrest of its authors—on the quasi-

constitutional charges of "abuse of the freedom of the press and out-
rage to public decency"[59]—the Three Marias emphasize the historical contingency of the feminine epistolary subject by creating fictitious letters not only from Mariana and a latter-day counterpart, but
from the old/new Mariana's relatives, psychiatrist, lover, the lover's
friends, and from the authors themselves.

Like Lydia Davis, the Three Marias draw attention to woman as
interpreting subject, rather than simply as bereaved lover. One of the
letters from the Marias declares that "the object of passion is simply
a pretext, a pretext, in or through that object, for defining ourselves
and the meaning of our dialogue by whatever means we have left."[60]
By proposing this definition, they attempt to reconstruct the private
discourse of passion as a viable, public form of interpretation and
intellectual inquiry, explicitly acknowledging and exploring the dialectical, often negative, relationship between the two modes, rather
than upholding the fiction of love's (Mariana's) discourse as an affair
of cloistered, fatal, domestic grief. Another of the Marias' letters asserts that

> inevitably, we proceed from love to history and politics. . . .
> Hence we arrive at the myths surrounding contemporary histori-
> cal and political conditions; because it is not yet possible for us
> to speak of love; because in the relationship between a man and
> a woman, in which the partners each believe themselves to be
> alone . . . what society makes and demands of each of them
> intrudes on this relationship. . . . Tristan is forever separated
> from Isolde, and all the myths of love describe this relation as
> something forbidden and unfulfilled, and all love stories are
> stories of suicides.[61]

One of the ways in which the *New Portuguese Letters* call into
question and demythologize this "forbidden" and "suicidal" paradigm is by juxtaposing, for instance, an apocryphal private letter
written from within the convent by the seventeenth-century
Mariana—in which she complains to a friend that "I lost my life
when I heard the portals of this tomb clang behind me"—with a
twentieth-century public document, a "Medical-Psychiatric Report
on the Mental State of Mariana A." In this way, the historically specific nature of a woman's sexual and social oppression becomes apparent; in the latter case, rather than being represented as the blatant
physical cloistering of a nun, it assumes the guise of benevolent,
democratic modern psychiatry vis-à-vis the heterosexual couple, a

guise strikingly similar to those explored in *Forty Whacks*, "Viva Freud!" "The Letter," and Marie Langer's psychiatric writings.

The wish expressed by the frustrated nun Mariana in the apocryphal letter—"I would willingly marry any man my parents chose, any man to whom they sold me, however loathsome I found him"[62]—is granted to the contemporary Mariana A., with equally disastrous consequences. Mariana A. (like Schmid's A., a reprise of *Anonymous*), married to António, who has left her living, sexually frustrated, with his parents for years while he fights wars in Africa, has been interned "in a state of hysteria" for psychiatric observation in the Hospital of——, after being found in her upstairs bedroom locked in copulation with the family dog. The portrait of her which takes shape reveals direct manipulations much like those suffered by Mariana the nun: Mariana A.'s father-in-law reads her letters to her husband and his to her; her mother has brought her up to believe "the flesh is sinful"; her in-laws don't allow her to leave the house alone or with friends.

But framing the domestic imbroglio is the enabling discourse of psychiatric/state officialdom. The unfortunate facts of Mariana A.'s minimal existence are given in the form of a case history:

> Mariana A. is twenty-five years of age; married; born in Beja . . . it is known that her father committed suicide; her mother, a very religious and puritanical woman, is now fifty years old. . . . The patient had also been living at home until . . . the date of her marriage to António C., who is at present doing his military service overseas. As the patient herself reports, her relations with her mother were very strained.[63]

Rather than chastising Mariana for her bestial sexual deviance or taking the disapproving tone of either a parent, an in-law, or a Mother Superior, the medical-psychiatric report analyzes, dispassionately, the precedents in her private life that might account for "the mental state of the patient." The tone of the case history implies that the mother's unenlightened, "puritanical" religious mores and the strict Catholic upbringing she has enforced for her daughter are anachronistic, inefficacious, belonging to an age of nuns and religious cloisters. The patient need not succumb either to bestiality or to her father's suicidal tendencies. The inadequacies of the seventeenth-century Mariana's romantic paradigm and the language which Mariana A. continues to use, "cooped up there in the house, writing to her husband," have been subsumed by a more progressive, efficacious language: that of rehabilitation. The epistolary genre itself appears anachronistic in this document, superseded by the case study, which speaks for the patient, incorporating her love language in the form of a tape recording and transcription of her monologue to her absent husband. And the domain of the private gives way to a more secular, public form of cloistering known as psychiatric observation, its liberal premises set forth in the concluding statement of Mariana A.'s psychiatrists.

Summary:
1. Mariana A. is not insane.
2. There is no evidence in her case of any sexual disorder.
3. The act that brought her here is probably due solely to a serious nervous imbalance, the causes of which must be further investigated in order to attempt to cure the patient.[64]

For Mariana A., as for Davis' desperate protagonist, the construction of the republican (or, in the case of Portugal, militaristic and quasi-republican) rhetorical ideal of an open society for all depends on the manufactured possibility of a happy ending. It is not enough for authority to refrain from frowning on the excessiveness of her "insane" private torments and passions, as evidenced by her copulation with the dog. Society must absolutely deny, must never acknowledge, these excessive passions. Such forms of extreme, "forbidden" differentiation threaten the ideal of republican equanimity and the strict dichotomy. The cur tale must be curtailed. Mariana A.'s Pasiphaëication must give way to pacification. She has passed— or been passed—from, in Young's phrase, "the particular private realm of needs and desires" into "the universal, public realm of sovereignty and the state."

The Three Marias, while recognizing the problematic nature of private passions, their use and continual co-optation by a patriarchal state, attempt to let the passionate realm of the private speak itself, in its physical and metaphysical extremities, into a shared, public form of critical knowing and positive feminine identity. Rather than simply write Mariana, they bring their own writing into relationship with hers and employ the historically powerless secondary position—that position to which the discourse of the feminine, passion, love, and so forth are consigned—to explode the false founding dichotomy of rational republicanism and to argue for a polymorphous polis. In "A Monologue for Myself, Inspired by Mariana, Followed by a Short Letter," one of the Marias declares, "You are the fruit, Mariana, the product, the prolonged moan of a symptom so often lost sight of, so often re-encountered, so often recurring, all through the course of a pitiful story of powerlessness." But in the concluding line of her short letter, this Maria's recurrence to that prolonged corporeal sound, that *fertilisante douleur,* transforms it into an empowering hermeneusis in the form of bodily knowledge. "A soft moan that escapes you takes possession of me, impregnates me, transcends me and kills me: my writing."[65]

Lydia Davis' formal achievement in "The Letter" is more or less of this secondary type. Her narration, too—though its tone is not at all explicitly self-conscious, didactic, or openly feminist in the manner of the prose of the Three Marias—discursively takes the secondary position and, by filtering through it those forms of thought held to be primary, lays their primacy open to question. Among the protagonist's efforts at interpretation of the masculine idiom are her labors as a translator of poetry. Translation serves in the text both as her means of trying to "decode" the lover's words and intentions and as her effort to mute or resist them. In playing upon translation's traditional status as a supplementary, ancillary art, second to the claims of the "original," Davis foregrounds the story's concern with the intertwined questions of interpretation and feminine subjugation. The role of translation here underscores Davis' use of the narrative strategy of free indirect discourse as a filter for the letter. The letter never appears integrally, in its own right, but rather as a function of the narration and of the woman's process of interpretation. Everything in the story must first be subject to the translation process before it can come into being, and thus the letter's (and its "composer's") ontological status remains as much in flux as the woman's.

The woman attempts initially, with very limited success, to use translation as a shield for her suffering, a means of displacing her fruitless semiotic compulsion onto a safer object.

> That spring she was translating a book because it was the only thing she could do. Every time she stopped typing and picked up the dictionary his face floated up between her and the page and the pain settled into her again, and every time she put the dictionary down and went on typing his face and the pain went away. She did a lot of hard work on the translation just to keep the pain away.[66]

She cannot, of course, circumvent the pain, beyond these brief mechanical intervals of respite, because she still remains within the mode of the secondary and all that is aligned with it: woman, submission, feeling, love, superfluous, private, helpmate, translation. As translator, the mere substitution of one object of interpretation for another does not necessarily change the quality of perception, or the resulting sense of abject dependence. Her role, just as when she stumbles about town reading the license plates of Volvos, remains that of reinforcing the primacy of the original at the expense of her own ancillary, or even superfluous, nature.

But Davis' narration complicates notions of translation, secondary status, and supplementarity in a way which makes available another answer, quite different from the one I explored earlier, to Perloff's question, How can the woman understand what the import of the letter is? In her translator's preface to Derrida's *Dissemination*, Barbara Johnson says that the Derridean concept of the *supplément* "means both 'an addition' and 'a substitute,'" that supplements "may add to something that is already present, in which case they are superfluous, AND/OR they may replace something that is not present, in which case they are necessary."[67] As a hermeneutic parable of translation and femininity, Davis' "The Letter" questions the secondary relationship of both to their masculine originals. The woman and her powers of translation are not only superfluous but necessary to an incomplete, partially effaced, masculine idiom.

In *L'Oreille de L'autre*, Monique Bosco, during the round table on translation, likewise invokes the supplement as a way of understanding translation. Bosco refers to a book in which "the beloved woman is a translatoress." She then asks Derrida, "Must woman always be the translatoress of the poet? Stendahl also says to women: don't write, translate, you'll make an honorable living."[68] Her question formulates translation as a peripheral, derivative activity, and she equates this secondary status with the political status of women because of their gender difference.

Derrida, typically, evades discussing at any length the question of translation-and-gender directly in the politically charged terms of Bosco's question, but his answer (a transformation of Benjamin's notion of translation[69]) nonetheless illuminates the suggestive parallel between translation and feminine identity set up in Davis' story.

> If one displaces a little the concept of translation from a perspective which would limit translation to a secondary operation, the position of the translatoress would be effective, even though she's sexually marked. Babel is a man, in effect, an evil God who is not complete; he summons, he desires, he lacks, he calls forth the complement or the supplement or that which will come to enrich him. The translation doesn't come to add itself on like an

accident to a complete substance but rather, it is what the original text needs, not merely the signer of the original text but the text itself.[70]

By making the original dependent on the activity of the "translatoress" for its existence, this conception of translation suggests that neither is prior to the other. It effects a displacement of the privileged term in the hierarchical oppositions original/translation, man/woman. The possibility of just such a reversal is raised in "The Letter." While the woman's attempt to substitute other forms of translation for the persistent, painful image of the ex-lover fails, her skills as a translator—if not her conclusions—open the way for writing, rather than merely helplessly reading, his signs. On the day she receives the letter, the woman again tries to put it out of her mind by working that evening "on a translation, a difficult prose poem. Her [current] lover calls and she tells him about how difficult the translation is, but not about the letter." Eventually, though, she can resist its mute appeal no longer, so "she takes the letter out of her purse and goes to bed to see what she can make of it now."[71]

Her reading of the letter, which I have already described in part, also includes other gestures more closely related to her work as a translator of poetry. The letter consists, after all, of a poem in French. Its originary status, and the ex-lover's authority, are already rendered suspect, as I have suggested, by the fact of the poem's having been copied out longhand and thereby given a "signature." But this already dubious "authority" is further undermined by the woman's interventions as translator, despite her intention to be faithful. The fact of the letter's having been written (in a somewhat illegible) longhand forces her into supplying her own text at certain points.

> There is a word she can't decipher. It comes at the end of a line
> so she looks at the rhyme scheme and the word it should rhyme
> with is *pures* (pure thoughts), so that the word she can't read is
> probably *obscures* dark (dark flowers). Then she can't read
> another two words at the beginning of the last line of the octet.
> She looks at the way he has formed other capital letters and sees
> that this capital must be *L*, and that the words must be *La
> Lune.*[72]

The woman does her best to follow the conventions in order to arrive at the "correct" reading. But in the context of the story, her supplying of *obscures,* while seemingly conventional, yet provides for a masculine/feminine opposition that is ambiguous at best. The "pure thoughts"—which should be aligned with the feminine in a poetic genre based on identifiably sex-specific polar oppositions and their resolution (*nous nous retrouvions*)—are opposed by "dark flowers." But this, too, would seem to be a conventional feminine topos, forcing a reading of its counterpart not as "pure [i.e., unbesmirched] thoughts," rather as something more akin to masculine "pure thought" (i.e., pure reason). In either case, it is impossible to effect a neat resolution of, assign priority to, or even differentiate clearly between, such oppositions as masculine/feminine, pure/impure, thought/intuition, clarity/mystery. Her desire to read his letter in the most straightforward, conventional, "pure" terms possible only serves to "obscure" the language of the letter. She "can't decipher," due to the inadequacy of pure thought. One is forced back onto the woman's process of reading, rather than onto the letter.

Beyond any specific reading of such passages as the one above, the "original" letter and its sender remain elusive, visible only as a kind of epistolary mirage, an effect of translation. The text of the poem is never given, apart from a scattering of French words and phrases as the woman provides her emotional gloss of the poem. One might go so far as to call the woman, ultimately, as much the author of the letter as she is its "translatoress." The originary masculine idiom depends at all points on her "necessary" and active cognition. In Derrida's words, she "comes to enrich" that idiom. It would be stretching the point to claim that the woman's translation process results in a substantial displacement of the abject terms of her secondary mode, but the lineaments of such a displacement are given, just as the potential for mutual vulnerability exists in the manipulative psychoanalytic dramas in *Forty Whacks* and "Viva Freud!" And if this displacement of masculinity were to come to pass, it would come not through abdication of the mode of translation but through embracing it and transforming the prescribed terms of its performance.

Because of Davis' choice of free indirect discourse, sometimes called the "third person limited" point of view, the letter remains at a double remove from the reader, available only as the woman's interior monologue. Though this point of view, like the French poem, might smack of conventionality, Davis' choice of it is quite canny. By appending the title "The Letter" to her story, effectively announcing it as epistolary fiction and then failing to provide the text of the vaunted letter, she reduplicates for the reader, at the level of the story as a whole, the protagonist's dilemma of being "sent" a letter which is in fact not one, which consists wholly of "someone else's" words. Of all the epistolary fiction discussed in this chapter and the preceding one, Lydia Davis' piece of writing is the only one that doesn't supply the text of a single letter within it. Rather, she offers the subtle play of a tormented, letter-constituting, feminine consciousness.

Much in the manner of Davis' protagonist, the various "heroines" in Manuel Puig's *Heartbreak Tango* are avid readers and interpreters of letters. Like Schmid's and Howe's narrators, these women also write letters of their own, using correspondence concerning their lover/brother/son, the small-town lothario Juan Carlos Etchepare, writing either to him or to each other, to reaffirm at every turn their submission to the conventions of romantic love. These conventions require not only that they make an icon out of the selfish, thoughtless, sex-obsessed Juan Carlos, nor is it sufficient for the women simply to behave in a self-sacrificing manner in everything concerning Juan Carlos, blaming themselves for his death by "consumption," his promiscuity, his callousness, his use of their money to support his gambling and debauchery. Following the pop-culture conventions of melodrama, tango, soap opera, and B-movie (and also the origins of the epistolary novel) that Puig manipulates so skillfully, the women are required to despise and blame one another for Juan Carlos' behavior. While he is alive, they scheme against each other as they compete for his (at best) evasive and fleeting devotion to them. Their collective role is neatly expressed in the ironic epigraph of the third "episode," a publicity blurb for a movie starring Jean Harlow and Clark Gable: "She fought with the fury of a tigress for her man! He treated her rough—and she loved it!"[73]

Puig's heroines, like the heroines of the soap operas they watch, seem to thrive on heartache. In keeping with the Catholic imagery and religious leitmotifs that provide much of the novel's atmosphere, they compete to share in the reflected glow of their "martyrdom" of Juan Carlos and derive a lugubrious nourishment from this undertaking. The novel begins with the newspaper announcement lamenting the death of Juan Carlos in the small town of Coronel Vallejos, province of Buenos Aires, where most of *Heartbreak Tango* is set. The announcement is followed, in the novel's first two episodes, by a series of nine letters, dated from May 12 to August 12 of 1947 and written by Juan Carlos' "fiancée" of ten years earlier, Nélida Fernández, better known as Nené. It quickly becomes apparent through this correspondence that Nené derives a doleful ecstasy, in her otherwise dreary married life in Buenos Aires, from the opportunity to offer her condolences to Juan Carlos' mother and to rake over the cold embers of his death: "I knew that he was sick . . . Did he confess before dying? . . . It so happens that Juan Carlos told me more than once that when he died he wanted to be cremated.''[74] In a hilarious subsequent letter, dated June 22, she describes with graphic relish the hypothetical image of Juan Carlos' decomposing body.

> I was just about to write because in the last letter I forgot to ask you if Juan Carlos is buried in the ground . . . or in some family mausoleum. . . . Did you ever get into a pit that someone was digging? Because then if you put your hand against the hard dirt in the hole, you feel how cold and damp it is . . . because that's where the worms are. I'm not sure if those are the worms who later look for what for them is nutrition, better left unsaid, I don't know how they can get into such a thick and hard wooden box. . . . Unless after many years the box rots away . . . I remember that it also seems that we carry the worms inside, I think I read that somewhere, that when medical students have their classes in the morgue they see the worms when they cut up the corpse. . . . Forgive me if this upsets you, but who can I talk to about these memories if not with you?[75]

Through her letters, Nené tries to create a morbid intimacy between her and the mother of the deceased, woman-to-woman, as two members of the cult devoted to Juan Carlos. By initiating this correspondence, she becomes a party to the ultimate corruption of the flesh of the erstwhile libidinous deceased. By the terms of Nené's prosaic devotion, her compositions, which revel in decomposition, have the paradoxical effect of intensifying the incorporeal apotheosis he is undergoing in her mind.

Devotion alone, however, will not accomplish this sanctification. The process is contingent on rekindling, by writing impetuous letters, the smoldering hostilities that Juan Carlos' mother and his sister Celina have felt toward Nené, as well as Nené's own rancor toward Celina. Celina and the mother blame Nené for their brother/son's death from tuberculosis and also for his moral deficiencies, by virtue of the fact that Juan Carlos spent a great deal of time lingering in the drafty passageway outside Nené's parents' house late at night—even though it is clear, especially from Juan Carlos' 1937 letters to Nené, that he aggravated his condition largely by flagrantly disregarding the orders of the doctors treating him at the sanatorium (e.g., sneaking out to go for naked swims in the freezing river at Cosquín).

Notwithstanding these animosities, Nené expresses the desire for a reconciliation in her first letter to the bereaved mother. "This terrible news made me decide to drop you a few lines despite the fact that after my marriage yourself and your daughter Celina had stopped speaking to me. . . . I don't know if you still hold a grudge against me."[76] The probability of achieving a reconciliation, how-ever, is put in doubt early on by a telling epistolary clue. She seems to have an inkling, by the time she has received the second letter from the "mother," of the important fact, revealed much later in the novel, that the reply letters are not written by Mrs. Etchepare. The hated and vindictive daughter, Celina, has been intercepting Nené's letters, reading them for herself, and forging replies. Nené concludes one of her letters by saying, "Well, Mrs. Etchepare, I hope you'll keep writing to me, one thing that surprised me was your steady hand-writing, it seems like a young person's, good for you . . . You don't have someone else write them for you, do you?"[77]

Nené's willful ignorance and obtuseness about what should be painfully obvious is driven in part by her willingness, even eager-ness, to subordinate self-preservation to her epistolary role as the rehabilitator of Juan Carlos. Ignorance is a precondition of her bliss. Letter writing serves as the mechanism and the legible expression of her continued participation in the feminine cult of slavish ad-ulation of an idealized Juan Carlos, even though she previously re-jected the actual man once his disease became too acute and her parents' prohibition too insistent. Her allegiance is as much to an ideal of masculinity as it is to Juan Carlos per se. The fact that this ideal limits her horizons as a woman is part of its attraction, be-cause her hope is that it will also *de*limit her—define her as a woman. As a specific function of Juan Carlos, her existence will be fully acknowledged, and she will have acquired a viable and stable social role. The only way she knows to achieve this goal is by em-ploying, in her letters to Juan Carlos' mother, a cliched language that is equal parts pulp novel and pietà. In one letter to Mrs. Etch-epare, she tells how she often lies in her dark bedroom in the middle of the afternoon and fantasizes "that I'm with you and we go to Juan Carlos's grave and we have a good cry together."[78] In another, she describes how

> I saw a ladybug and asked for two things, do you think God
> won't give them to me if I tell you? Well, first I asked that in the
> next world, if God forgives me after the Last Judgment, because
> I'm sure he forgives Juan Carlos, then could I be reunited with
> him in the other life. And the second thing I asked for is for my
> kids to get handsomer as they grow up because that way I can

love them more, I don't say they should be handsome like Juan Carlos but just not as ugly as their father.[79]

These second-hand sentiments, however stale, are in a fundamental sense genuinely hers. This hackneyed language, making up the very stuff of her consciousness, is indeed the medium through which her metaphysical and ontological groping must take place. Stephanie Merrim comments that "a steady diet of the serial stories, conventional in language and plot, provides [the characters in *Heartbreak Tango*], as did the commonplaces of Romantic works, with a pre-established code for representing to themselves what would otherwise be the existentially charged moments of life: love, sickness, death, poverty, scandal, and the like."[80] As such, neither Nené's language nor her concerns are ultimately trivial. Her words, though they serve to satirize her shallowness, also express the deepest longings of a non-being, a simulacrum in search of authentic being. (One should also keep in mind, parenthetically, the implied social context of this codification, which is as resonant in Puig as it is in Schmid. It has been commented, in an article on Puig's "production of serial literature under militarism," that the pop-culture "mediated, secondary texts that Puig uses to structure his novel . . . are a fundamental element of the middle class's alienation from a military industrial society."[81])

The letters exchanged in the thirties between Nené and Juan Carlos take on a new life as fetishes of their relationship in its "pure" form. She makes bold to ask Mrs. Etchepare for the return of Juan Carlos' letters to her, which she had sent back to him in a fit of pique over the deterioration of their courtship. But upon the announcement of his death, they acquire sudden value as the body and blood of her J. C. As in the case of Mariana Alcoforado, the Portugese nun, the necessary obverse of piety in *Heartbreak Tango* is romance, in its most conventional form. Becoming a renewed novitiate of love, rediscovering it through correspondence, permits the disillusioned Nené to keep at bay the unpleasant sexual politics of marriage, motherhood, and her former relationship with Juan Carlos. As a revisionist writer of letters, she is in control, or so she mistakenly believes, of the chaste image of him that will be created, the apocryphal Juan Carlos who, as she writes at one point, "never hurt a soul." This epistolary role allows her, as a woman who becomes physically ill contemplating the fleshly existence of her own "ugly" progeny and spouse, to become immaculate again. In describing for Mrs. Etchepare/Celina the letters she wants returned, Nené employs with gusto the trite, heartfelt cliches of romantic love, which serve to invest Juan Carlos' earlier missives to her with purity, innocence, and holiness.

> Remember that my letters [from him] are the ones in the sky-blue ribbon, that's enough to know which ones, because they don't have envelopes, when I kept them I was silly and threw away the envelopes, because I felt that they had been handled by other people, don't you think I was right in a way? In the post office many hands touch the envelopes, but only Juan Carlos, poor boy, touched the page inside, and then me, only us two, so the page inside really is an intimate thing.[82]

Commenting on the women's desperate need to establish stable identities, even ancillary ones, for themselves, Alicia Borinsky points out that

> in *Heartbreak Tango* letters become . . . objects through which the characters attempt to create a presence for themselves with the hope of overwhelming the recipient, of according credence to something that might become true if the recipient accepted the invitation to continue the game and respond to the letters. . . . The *fact* of the letter is an *effect* that grants presence to the signature.[83]

This *effect*, however, as Borinsky suggests, is largely illusory. The recipient of Nené's letters does agree "to continue the game," but the correspondence is just that—a game—since the reply letters turn out to be forgeries and since their author, Celina, after tricking Nené into giving out her husband's work address, exacts revenge by sending an anonymous note to him, along with incriminating snippets from some of Nené's letters. In any event, the presence that Nené aspires to was already negated in its first attempted incarnation, a decade before in 1937, when she and Juan Carlos exchanged letters while he was in the sanatorium. Even two years before this exchange takes place, there is clear evidence that Juan Carlos is not exactly the kind of recipient to be "overwhelmed" by the conceits of love letters. The only kind of "conceit" that applies strictly to him is the kind that involves self-regard and self-congratulation. His "Memo Book 1935" is a wickedly revealing glimpse of Juan Carlos' casual, youthful callousness in its incongruous juxtaposition of saints' days with his terse, semi-literate descriptions of his exploits over a period of several months.

MARCH—TUESDAY 14, SAINT MATILDE, QUEEN. Hairy old memo book! I'm starting you off with a widow, who's already on the hook.
\* \* \*
SUNDAY, 19, SAINT JOSEPH. Shindig at the club. Paid two rounds for Pepe and Barrios Brothers. They owe me for next time.
WEDNESDAY, 22, SAINT LEA, NUN. Date at 7 P.M. Clarita.
THURSDAY, 23, SAINT VICTORIANO, MARTYR. Date at the Gaucho Inn, Amalia, produse car.
SATURDAY 25, THE ANNUNCIATION OF THE BLESSED VIRGIN MARY. Widow, 2 A.M.[84]

In Juan Carlos' notational script, the various women in his life— Clarita, Saint Lea, nun, the widow, the Blessed Virgin Mary, all lie comfortably alongside one another and are given equal status. They are discontinuous yet strangely simultaneous. Not only is the impropriety of entering his fornication with the widow beneath the rubric of the Virgin completely lost on him; he doesn't even grant their individual names the kind of presence or separateness that would allow such a rebuke to be uttered. They exist, except for an unavailable and therefore intriguing Mabel, only as items to be ticked off on a memo. His monosyllabic invocation of them effectively negates them for all purposes except his own. Ironically, he situates love and sainthood in literal proximity to each other, but they never threaten to become obverses of one another, as they are for Nené. Their metonymic juxtaposition doesn't imply, in his one-track mind at least, any metaphoric conjunction.

But by the time Juan Carlos arrives at the sanatorium, two years later, he has evolved as a lover to the point where he is ready to have a go at the writing genre most closely identified with the conventions and language of romance. Even here though, the authenticity of his gesture and its potential for granting Nené presence remain seriously open to question. In her June 22, 1947, letter to Mrs. Etchepare/Celina, Nené herself acknowledges, in effect, that the correspondence between her and Juan Carlos had been to a large extent devised by her. "Silly me got it into my head that he was dead set against the idea of corresponding with a girl . . . The letters addressed to me were all written on the same paper which I bought for him along with a fountain pen when he went away to Córdoba." Her need to fabricate the illusory sense of reciprocated love, which would grant her feminine presence as love object, leads her to furnish Juan Carlos with the necessary materials for creating her, rather than leaving this task to his own dubious initiative. Here is yet another version of letters from nowhere. One could say, in a certain sense, that she is writing to herself, and indeed she reflects on the futility of this enterprise, complaining "what use were the letters if we broke up just the same."[85]

Nené's identity is decidedly shaky, on account of Juan Carlos' refusal, despite his botched attempts at florid love language, to acknowledge her actuality. In that same letter, Nené puzzles over the fact that in the letters he sent to her "the heading changes sometimes, he wouldn't use my name because he said it was compromising, in case my mother found them I could say they were letters for another girl."[86] Nené doesn't realize how close to the truth she comes. For despite Juan Carlos' good-natured, semi-earnest dressing in the epistolary garb she has stitched together for him—he dutifully calls her "dearest darling," "Blondie," "my darling," and "light of my life"—he never goes very far toward granting her the existence as love object that she so vehemently desires.

In his first letter to her from the sanatorium, the only reciprocity he really seems concerned with is quantitative, receiving a specified number of pages to lessen the boredom of his convalescence. In the postscript he exhorts her to "write back immediately like you promised. I'm more bored than you think. At least three pages like I'm sending you." In the bit of prose that follows, the novel's narrator provides a further revealing detail. Juan Carlos has that same day written a total of three letters: "the first—seven pages long—addressed to a young lady, the second—three pages long—addressed to his family, and the third—also three pages long—addressed to another young lady."[87]

One is given to understand that despite his formulaic professions of devotion, Nené in fact comes third out of three in importance on his list of correspondents, or at best is a tie for second, accorded the same status as his family. (On another day, he arbitrarily makes Nené's the longer and devotes only half a page to the other "young lady," Mabel.) His amiable disregard for Nené's person is carried even further in the body of the letter. He has no compunction about informing her directly, after a pat pastoral description of his natural surroundings, that "I've put this same little paragraf in every letter because if not I'll get cramps in my brain from thinking so much."[88] This very first of his letters, though it doesn't, should shatter Nené's delusions about his epistolary authenticity. Juan Carlos is only at a very minor remove from the "lover" in Lydia Davis' story who sends the female protagonist a longhand copied-out French poem, which she in turn invests with authorial intent. Juan Carlos takes repeated stabs, tipped with sophomoric humor, at rhetorical gestures that are the most blunted and profane possible versions of what were once metaphysical conceits ("If only I was a pilow so I could be closer. And not a hot water bag because you might have dirty feet and I'd be done for.").

But, in Puig's canny use of restricted character consciousness, it is precisely through misspeakings and unintentional revelations, as a counterfeit courtier, that Juan Carlos lives as a character. Like most of the other male protagonists in the epistolary fiction I have been describing, his existence is assumed a priori, and therefore he can afford to proceed in a different fashion from his female counterparts. Borinsky formulates the issue in this way:

> What is the effect of such "bad writing" on the perception of Juan Carlos as a character? The most immediate one is the production of a strong novelistic presence for him. He sounds more pure, less literary, than the characters that mention him. He does not need to write about anything in a "good" way; his task is fulfilled merely by *presenting* himself.[89]

Because he forms the centerpiece of this epistolary cult, he is not governed by the rules that constrain the women who write about him. In fact, his violation of those rules is his "signature"—the assertion of self that is unattainable for them, even when they agree to carrying out to the letter their ancillary and expendable status as women, their mutual hatred, their obedience to sexual double standards, and their religious atonement for sins that they did not necessarily commit. The repeated result of these feminine oblations is to reinforce Juan Carlos' vibrancy and their status as nonentities. Pamela Bacarisse remarks of the women in *Boquitas pintadas* that "because of their adhesion to patriarchal ideology, they are stereotypes. ... They adhere to the rules of the game and go to great lengths, both practical and psychological, to conceal any failure to do so, and they are unquestioning believers in male superiority, cherishing unrealistic ambitions where men are concerned."[90] I would substitute the word "ciphers" where Bacarisse uses "stereotypes"; the women are colorful enough, distinct enough from one another in a novelistic sense, but what unites them is that in all cases, their various human attributes and idiosyncracies are like petrified accretions around a core of emptiness.

The one thing they can all agree on is the primacy of Juan Carlos, and since he, in life and death, remains at the center of their lives, they in effect agree on everything of importance to them, even though this cult following requires that they cut each other to verbal shreds. As Lucille Kerr says, Juan Carlos is "the organizing principle, the powerful figure, in or through whom everyone meets."[91] For him, they give their all; for one another, there is only enmity and the purple epithets that B-movie "tigresses" are expected to accord one another. Nené describes Celina to Mrs. Etchepare as, among other things, "such a bitch that daughter of yours" and verbally indicts the widow Elsa Di Carlo as "that stinking widow" and as "Juan Carlos's real murderess," "the possum-playing widow" who "sucked his blood." She critically reasons, with the sharpest soap-opera sophistry, that "since Celina is single and has free time, with no house of her own nor children to take care of, she could be of some use and help in the search for truth."[92] No matter that Nené despises her own actual marriage and children; her allegiance to the institutions and ideals of marriage remain intact within the social and sexual fantasies that are, in their turn, structured by the all-consuming conventions of romance. The codes in which she speaks are powerful, familiar, and readily understood by the other participants in this psychosocial drama. They dwell together in a world of tigresses, bitches, seductresses, temptresses, and most of all, actresses.

The devotion to Juan Carlos at her own and others' expense continues throughout Nené's life and those of the other women as well. Near the novel's end, the confessional mode of the epistolary conceit finds slightly different expression as literal confessions, to various priests, to God, and to the Virgin Mary. The confessees are respectively Mabel, an anonymous young girl whom Juan Carlos persuaded to have sexual relations with him when she was only thirteen, his mother, the widow Elsa Di Carlo, and Celina. All of them are ostensibly asking for forgiveness for their own "sins," but the person most of them seem bent on gaining absolution for is Juan Carlos. The girl who had sex with him at thirteen, even though afterward he wouldn't speak to her, prays to the Virgin Mary that "it wasn't his fault, it was I who let myself be tempted." His mother begs God "to let him enter your kingdom, because he didn't have time to confess," and makes excuses for his promiscuity, claiming that "it's [the girls'] fault more than his, Blessed Virgin, we both are women, we can't condemn a boy because he's like that, men are like that, isn't it true? it's the bad women who are to blame." Elsa Di Carlo, though he gambled her and her daughter's savings away, readily says in her prayers that "I forgive him, dear God, he was a scatterbrain . . . I'm going to take what's coming to me . . . because it's the punishment

I deserve." Finally, his sister, Celina, in a forgiving yet vindictive mood, wishes to attribute yet another facet of his venality to Nené and asks, "Jesus Christ, let there be justice, let that woman get her just deserts . . . I'm sure she was the one he stole for at the mayor's office, she must have asked him to!"[93]

Though Puig rarely provides overt authorial commentary, his brilliant juxtapositions are sufficiently illuminating by themselves. In this case, the aggregate of confessions leaves one with the distinct impression not merely of individual foibles or character flaws but rather of a social dynamic, a form of thought that is characteristic of a particular group. Elías Miguel Muñoz has rightly pointed out that Puig's novels "dialogically pose questions about the site of psychoanalytic confession, underlining one of [Argentine] society's most serious problems, with regard to the production of oppressive discourses about sex. . . . In *Boquitas pintadas*, the emphasis is on Christian confession."[94]

Even though Puig doesn't feature a psychoanalyst as a character in the text, as Schmid and Howe do, he nonetheless explores an oblique version of the transferential scene of psychoanalysis, wherein the correspondent receiving the letters of the penitent/patient acts as a confessor whose role is to ensure adherence to normative patriarchal standards. Bacarisse, too, remarks how Nené, in her letters to Mrs. Etchepare/Celina, "looks back with therapeutic longing."[95] And Celina, like the epistolary confessors of Schmid's and Howe's narrators, puts on the benign, sympathetic face of therapeutic quasi-concern for the "patient" in her forged letters to Nené. "I do hope that your marital life improves, what's going on between you two? Maybe with my experience I can give you advice, I think that a woman can be happy beside a man she doesn't love, as long as she knows how to understand and forgive. . . . I want to know more about your life, so that I can help you, although it be through my prayers only."[96] Like the therapist/confessors in Howe and Schmid, she urges the correspondent to reveal herself as intimately as possible, the better to annihilate her. In a single, contradictory stroke, Celina wishes to destroy Nené's marriage, yet all the same reinforce Nené's allegiance to the *ideal* that her devotion to patriarchal institutions can continue unabated, as long as she knows how to subjugate and sacrifice herself in the appropriate ways. (Another version of this occurs in episode 3, when an adolescent Mabel writes to an advice column in a women's magazine and is advised, in a telling oxymoronic cliche, to "wait for the knight on the white horse who is to everyone's taste.") Though the agendas of Celina and Nené are supposedly different, in that Nené wants to worship Juan Carlos

and Celina doesn't want her to, they really participate as complements in the maintenance of a social law. The vatic/phallic principle, here as in Howe, continues to regenerate itself, through both
its acolytes and its priestly enforcers.

Eventually, Nené, prompted by Celina's epistolary betrayal, leaves
her husband and makes a pilgrimage to the shrine—the room Juan
Carlos died in, at Elsa Di Carlo's boarding house—but, after living
alone for a time, is reconciled to her husband and returns to Buenos
Aires. The sixteenth and final episode begins with the announcement of Nené's own death, on September 15, 1968. Some years before, she had apparently instructed her attorney to bury her with a
packet of Juan Carlos' letters that Celina had returned to her, but on
her deathbed, she changes her mind and instructs her husband to
bury her with his engagement ring, a locket of her grandchild's hair,
and her son's wristwatch. She asks her husband to burn both sets of
letters, hers and Juan Carlos' and, after some hesitation, the husband
complies, dropping them into the incinerator. Her packet, as might
be expected, "fell into the fire and burned without scattering," so
that her cremation, her annihilation, is instantaneous and complete.
Juan Carlos, appropriately, has the last, fragmented word, as the
pages of his letters "broke loose and the flame that was to blacken
and destroy them first illuminated them fleetingly."[97]

The disembodied, decontextualized words, returned to their un-
mediated state as pure convention, take on a sudden paradoxical
charm and freshness, floating in the makeshift crematorium of the
incinerator: "Not to trust blondes, so what are you going to confide
to the pillow? . . . just a few crocodile tears . . . Doll, I'm running out
of paper . . . because now I feel that I love you very much."[98] Without
the illusion of an author to pen them, without a complicating, pre-
varicating human presence, they seem to speak themselves in a pe-
culiarly pristine fashion, returned to their origins, hovering on the
verge of authenticity. In their flicker of illumination, ashes to ashes,
these epistolary shreds seem to belong to no one so much as to language itself. Puig's affirmation in this final scene is one of conventionality in its strictest sense. In sickness and in health, for better
or for worse, in life and in death, the hackneyed prose of heartbreak
and love endures.

It should be underscored that Puig's attitude, not only here but
throughout the novel, is far from being one of pure critique. What
differentiates him from the women authors discussed in this chapter
is his more marked ambiguity concerning his assessment of the crippling effects of these "feminine" expressions of patriarchal language.
The popular cultural forms that inform the lives of his women char-

acters and the women's devotion to romance are both limiting and nourishing in the novelistic world of Puig. Like Howe, Schmid, and Davis, he offers little or no hope of direct escape from the constraints of feminine contingency, but he presents that status quo as a place that one doesn't *necessarily* need, or even want, to escape from. According to Pamela Bacarisse,

> He never provides solutions . . . He finds *cursilería* [lowbrow tastes and attitudes, as in a predilection for soap operas] touching, because it is born of "the desire to be better," and though his writings are often ironic, he employs what I have seen as "non-distanced irony." In spite of everything, he even sympathizes with the fact that countless generations of women have derived pleasure and happiness from their belief in male superiority.[99]

Puig demonstrates how he is, indeed, of two minds on this question when he speaks in an interview about his personal conception of feminism in Argentina and how that has been a continuing preoccupation in his writing.

> Around 1972, discussions of feminism became more frequent in Argentina. I was totally in agreement with the process. I was concerned, however, that people were only talking about the inconveniences of being oppressed women, and never of the advantages, since there had to be some for such an unnatural situation to last for centuries. I believe that in a war, one should never underestimate the enemy's weapons; therefore, I wanted to know what those weapons were. So I had an enormous desire to question some women and find out what could make them both happy and oppressed. I wanted to find such a woman, to turn her into the heroine of my next novel.[100]

In *Heartbreak Tango*, a pre-1972 novel, Puig has already mapped out this terrain to a considerable degree. His fascination with—in certain respects, one could almost say attraction to—the concept of a "benign patriarchy" puts him somewhat at variance with Schmid, Howe, and Davis, who present bleaker, more sharply adversarial social visions and who have also chosen to present them in a less spacious genre. All four of the writers treat the subject of epistolary subjugation for the most part in strikingly similar ways, but Puig comes closer than any of the women writers to offering his characters a cathartic deliverance that is something on the order of a good cry, on account of his ongoing flirtation with the pleasures of *cursilería*.

For centuries, letter writing seemed the only genre fully open to women who wrote. It is noteworthy that in the genre's contemporary reprise, women writers approach it with such hesitation. Howe, though she began by publishing fiction, is active chiefly as a poet, and Schmid devotes most of her artistic energies to playwriting. Even Davis, the "legitimate" fiction writer of the three women, writes stories that could be described as brief, notational, almost parenthetical, eschewing the more compendious fictionalizing of her male counterparts. Yet the illusion of a parenthesis, the methodical haste of this writing, is just what makes it so explosive and riveting. The fiction of Howe, Schmid, and Davis reads like the product of deliberate second thoughts, a suicide note found in a waste basket, scribbled and carefully crumpled so that the writer could return to her desk and get on with her next project.

# 6. Rioting Degree Zero: Radical Skepticism and the Retreat from Politics—Jorge Luis Borges, Luisa Valenzuela, Kathy Acker, and William Burroughs

Despite the marked styles and marked differences in style of Roland Barthes and Jorge Luis Borges, Barthes' insistence on a neutral writing, a language "no longer at the service of a triumphant ideology," which "reaches the state of a pure equation," is a preference shared by Borges. Barthes' notion of a zero degree of writing, first appearing in *Combat* in 1947, arose as an indirect refutation of Sartre's insistence in "What is Literature?" (his treatise of the same year) on a writer's "engagement."[1] In an interview, when questioned about "a writer's duty to his time," Borges too makes explicit his repugnance for Sartre's idea of engaged writing.

> I think a writer's duty is to be a writer, and if he can be a good writer, he is doing his duty. Besides, I think of my own opinions as being superficial. For example, I am a conservative, I hate the Communists, I hate the Nazis, I hate the anti-Semites, and so on; but I don't allow these opinions to find their way into my own writings . . . I am an antagonist of *littérature engagée* because I think it stands on the hypothesis that a writer can't write what he wants to.[2]

This formulation of "the writer's duty" itself appears ideological, stubbornly polemical, and even naive. Borges willfully distorts the notion of *littérature engagée* into its crudest lineaments. Nonetheless, his assertion of the marginal relevance of his political opinions to an assessment of his writing ought to be given serious consideration, if only as a speculative proposition. The appraisal of Borges' "political" status as a writer has been conducted publicly over the past half century in the often politically overdetermined atmosphere of the Latin American literary scene. That forum has tended to exaggerate the importance of Borges' often contradictory public opinions at the expense of his writing or has characterized his writing as cold, austere, intellectual, removed. Whichever of those tacks is taken, the ensuing discussion is usually to Borges' detriment. These emphases have precluded asking certain fundamental questions about Borges' fiction.[3]

The examples of this misapprehension are abundant, and rather than rehearse them here yet again, I will begin with what seems to me a representative instance. Angel Rama and Emir Rodríguez Monegal are two of the most noted critics of modern Latin American fiction, and Rodríguez Monegal has written with great sensitivity about Borges' work. In a radio dialogue between the two of them and Carlos Real de Azúa, in 1957, the three men engage in a heated exchange about Borges' relative merits as a writer and the relation of that writing to his political persona. This dialogue is one of countless discussions that have taken place over half a century in trying to reconcile the "reactionary" Borges with his dazzling parabolic tales. Real de Azúa complains in the radio dialogue that "the Borges who, in a recent polemical note, claims to believe that oligarchies, imperialism, and international consortiums are the only themes of [those devoted to] liberty-killing propaganda doesn't seem to me, honestly, a man who understands with his whole mind the world hemming him in. That much is clear and it spills over into his work."

Rodríguez Monegal, defending Borges, retorts, "You begin by talking about the man and then you turn to the work. But the work is . . . not written by the man on the I.D. card. If Borges aspired to have any validity as the creator of political theories . . . the argument would be impeccable. But the validity of Borges is as the creator of a world. . . . What aesthetic importance do the errors have that Borges commits as a citizen?"

Rama enters the fray by protesting "What confidence can we have in the 'literary' and apolitical vision, in the reality, of a man who, as you say, is oppressed, dogged, beaten down by it, and takes refuge within himself? . . . [Borges] is *disengaged* from the ultimate human condition."[4]

It would be as specious to exonerate Borges from his political opinions as it would be to fetishize them into the key to understanding his writings. One cannot, as Rodríguez Monegal suggests, make a neat distinction between the citizen and the creator. But if the identity on the I.D. card is a forgery, even a blank, then the terms of Rama's question are radically changed. Suppose one does, provisionally, grant Borges' writing the hypothetically "neutral" status he claims for it. What consequences would such a gambit have for coming to an understanding in Borges' writing of the "apolitical vision" of a man who might well be, as Rama suggests, oppressed, dogged, beaten down, taking refuge within himself, *disengaged?* Is it possible that this vision, rather than being an escapist cop-out from the human condition, could, by its very nature as a retreat from the vicissitudes of political strife, express the fundamental social attitude of its era?

Suppose that, beginning from Barthes' "zero degree," one uses the Borgesian neutral position of *littérature dégagée* as the gauge for contemporary forays into the political imagination by the celebrated and ostensibly more engagé experimental fiction writers Luisa Valenzuela, William Burroughs, and Kathy Acker. Proceeding in this fashion, it becomes clear that these writers, each in her or his own way, though presumably more "radical" than Borges, also set forth some form of neutrality as the state which must be experienced before new forms of collective political and cultural life can be imagined. My reason for grouping these four writers together is that they are all moral satirists about whom much wrongheaded criticism has been written. In all four cases, their visions of social strife are intense, often bleak, but their perspectives toward social change are essentially modest and conservative. It would be as erroneous to characterize Burroughs, Acker, and Valenzuela as "radicals" (an exercise often performed) as it would be to describe Borges as "reactionary" (which has also frequently been done). It is ironic that the qualities that have led to Borges' supposed "apolitical" or right-wing tendencies are the same qualities which have been mistaken for radicalism in the case of the others.

In "Pleasure: A Political Issue," Fredric Jameson characterizes *Writing Degree Zero* as Barthes' ingenious attempt to escape "from 'the nightmare of history,' namely the projection of a kind of writing from which all group or class signals had been eliminated: white or bleached writing, the practice of a kind of Utopian neutrality." But, he adds,

> even the flight from history and politics is a reaction to those
> realities and a way of registering their omnipresence . . . making
> it impossible to read [Barthes' later, related concept of *jouiss-*
> *ance*] except as a response to a political and historical dilemma,
> whatever position one chooses . . . to take about that response
> itself.[5]

Though Jameson, in his reversion to the classical, nineteenth-century Marxism he means to update, typically overstates the "impossibility" of alternative ways of reading Barthes' exploration of pleasure, he nonetheless suggests the plausibility of transposing Barthes' pristine, "bleached" definition of the zero degree into its social equivalent. In *Writing Degree Zero*, Barthes employs "a simile borrowed from linguistics," positing "between two terms of a polar opposition (such as single-plural, preterite-present) the existence of a third term, called a neutral term or a zero element: thus between the subjunctive and the imperative moods, the indicative is . . . an amodal form."[6] It seems licit, in turn, to borrow his borrowed simile and employ it as the social trope for the temporary stasis of those caught between the shaky subjunctive script of a doubting hand and an imperative manifesto calling for direct social transformation.

The neutral and the neuter are the signs under which all four of the abovementioned fiction writers attempt to formulate a certain anxiety experienced within their respective societies. In Borges' and Valenzuela's cases, it is the anxiety felt by the Argentine inhabitants of the interstice between chronic dictatorship and the perennial return to "democracy," a topic which I have been exploring in chapters 4 and 5. In the cases of Burroughs and Acker, the anxiety is felt by those in the U.S. caught in the cramped imaginative space that exists between a consumer society threatened by its own vicious, patriarchal logic and the "counterculture" it appears to absorb with such ease. Radicalism, in the work of these writers, takes the form of radical skepticism. Degree zero writing expresses the skepticism, in the wake of failed or crushed liberation movements, that overtook political radicals as a whole, while they searched for viable alternatives to the revolutionary politics formerly adhered to.

Luisa Valenzuela, a prolific novelist and short story writer, links her own writing, as well as that of her peers, to that of Borges in saying that "I don't think we would be the writers we are today if Borges had not existed first . . . [He] completely altered our view of literature."[7] And Acker, the author of *Blood and Guts in High School*, says "When I first started writing . . . I was working in a sex show, and [the] middle section [of that book] was based on diaries of sex shows. I was very influenced by Burroughs, so I was really writing out of a kind of 'third mind.' "[8] Yet the homages contained in the statements of Acker and Valenzuela are merely suggestive of similar preoccupations. Any attempt to trace the relationship among these writers cannot be neatly formulated in terms of literary genealogies.

The concept of a "third mind," for instance, did not, strictly speaking, originate with Burroughs. As I will explain later in this chapter, he and Brion Gysin borrowed the term from a self-help book, and Burroughs used it to effect a moral satire of consumer society. This sort of deliberate cribbing and travestying of ideas is central to an understanding of Burroughs' work. His own spurious "originality" complicates the question of his literary paternity or influence on Acker. Burroughs opts for the impersonality of an aleatory method which consists of combining large fragments of the writing of others with one's own text.

Borges, likewise, in much of his fiction, and especially in a story such as "Pierre Menard, Author of the *Quixote*," calls originality significantly into question. His clear unease with the nationalistic vogue of literary filiality in the early decades of the century raises some doubts about the appropriateness of flatly declaring him (as scores of contemporary Argentine writers seem eager to do at present) the father of modern Argentine literature. All four of these authors—Acker, Borges, Burroughs, Valenzuela—display their skepticism not least in a like-minded incredulity toward founding gestures. The inability to distinguish clearly enough to assign primacy to an original over its imitation, or to a desirable social state over its apparent opposite, is just what makes foundation (as in the founding of a modern literature or a new society, or even the oxymoron of "beginning anew") so difficult. The age-old art of plagiarism reemerges in modern writing as a more credible model than originality for aesthetic or social regeneration. In this vein, it would be difficult to trace the relationship among these four writers in terms of easy oppositions or unambiguous lines of filiation.

It therefore seems appropriate to begin with Borges not as mentor, but as a coordinate from which the other three coordinates can be plotted, or as a constant in a variable equation. Writing, as Barthes would have it, in this way presumably could then be "reduced to a sort of negative mood in which the social or mythical characters of a language are abolished in favor of a neutral and inert state of form . . . without being overlaid by a secondary commitment of form to a History not its own."[9]

But abolishing the social characters of language doesn't fully capture the relation among these writers either, since a "negative mood," an inert and "neutral" state, in this case has a social character. It describes the retreat from radicalism through which Borges, Valenzuela, Acker, and Burroughs seek to assess the possibility of radical thought. Or, to put it more succinctly, neutrality too has its history. Ambivalence toward the solutions of radicalism takes the form of the wish to find an intermediate, neutral, and seemingly less vulnerable social space. All four dégagé writers engage in a kind of passive resistance in their attempt to create an imaginative, contemplative refuge at a nourishing remove from societal violence. They are not a part of that violence, but their attention is focused on it with an almost monastic diligence. One might aptly call this attitude "rioting degree zero."

In the fiction of Borges, the search for an intermediate, neutral space can be located in the early decades of the first half of the twentieth century. Massive immigration from Europe to Argentina caused an enormous expansion of the working class, concentrated mostly in Buenos Aires. The political radicalization of these immigrants during the early decades of the century had a direct bearing on the modernization of what was to become Argentina's principal urban zone and the site, beginning in 1930, of cyclical struggles between the emergent dictatorial state and the more progressive, populist agenda of the constitutional republic.[10] Borges was deeply caught up in the vanguardist, ultraist aesthetic movements of modernity during the twenties and thirties yet fiercely attached to the themes and preoccupations of the previous century, particularly as they touched on his criollo military forebears, many of whom fought in the Wars of Independence.[11] Continually cited as the founding presence of modern Argentine literature, he nonetheless stands, among Argentine writers of the twentieth century, as the paragon of ambivalence toward modernity. Norman Thomas di Giovanni, who worked closely with Borges translating many of his stories into English, remarked in the early seventies that Borges is only "modern in spite of himself" and that even his "new stories are all set back in the Buenos Aires of fifty or sixty years ago." And Borges answered the question of how he dealt with modernisms by stating that "if I could write eighteenth-century English, that would be my best performance. But I can't."[12] As a result, he attempts to locate himself in an intermediate space.

In her book on the "peripheral modernity" of Buenos Aires during the twenties and thirties, Beatriz Sarlo attributes to Borges the literary creation of "the undecidable zone between the city and the country, almost vacant of personages ... The imaginary space of these borderlands seems little affected by immigration, by cultural and linguistic mixtures." Yet such mixtures, she says, are the very foundation and condition of "Argentinity." Faced with the dilemma of affirming a cohesive, stable national identity founded on the living ruins of its seeming negation—the chaotic, violent, politically radical flux of modernizing immigration, in reaction to which the modern authoritarian state takes shape—Borges tries to invent a form of literary "urbanity" that will remain untouched by these apparently incompatible demands.

Beginning in the latter half of the nineteenth century, at the moment a raw, insecure Argentina was founding itself as a constitutional republic, the government consciously devised and formally sanctioned a strategy of opening the country to European immigration in order to supply itself with a rural work force to cultivate its vast agricultural terrain and, if possible, to provide it with another kind of "cultivation"—the imprimatur of a cultural identity, via the importation of European high culture. The preamble to the 1853 constitution attests to the urgency of these needs, specifying that "the Federal Government shall stimulate European immigration, and shall not restrict, limit, nor burden with taxes those foreigners whose purpose is to cultivate the land, improve industry, and introduce the arts and sciences."[13]

But this elite plan to underpin democracy by dispersing a balanced immigrant work force throughout Argentina had unintentional consequences. Over the next several decades, immigrants, who quickly came to comprise as much as a third of the country's total population, almost as quickly gravitated in huge numbers to Buenos Aires, to make up more than half its population. "Immigration," says Leopoldo Rodríguez, "was demographically mostly an urban phenomenon . . . only a minority of the European peasants could settle down to stable work in the countryside . . . most ended up in the cities."[14] This nascent proletariat, which couldn't be absorbed economically or socially, soon began to participate in union movements and labor strikes, adhering to the tenets of both socialism and anarchism, even participating in attempts at armed revolution just after the turn of the century and helping to bring the populist, reform-minded Radical Party to power by 1916.

Already by the turn of the century, specific laws such as the Residency Law authorized the expulsion of foreigners who "threatened national security or public order," as well as provided for the extradition of—or flat denial of entry to—any foreigners who could be associated with the vaguely construed category of "common crimes." The law, says Orlando Lázaro, "whose end is to halt agitation, activists, and worker violence, only made specific reference to foreigners. This attests to the absolute majority of foreigners in the working class at the time."[15]

One governmental strategy was to try to assimilate these immigrants—at least in terms of culture and ideology—as quickly as possible. But the combination of their political radicalism (most often described by the authorities as "foreign agitation"), their upward mobility, and their range of ethnicity led to a serious backlash of conservatism, with racist overtones, which gathered force in the teens and early twenties. The backlash began to crystallize around opposition to the populist champion and longtime leader of the Radicals,

Hipólito Yrigoyen, just after he ascended to the presidency in 1916. Eduardo Crawley describes how

> among Yrigoyen's [traditional] enemies was a new breed, an admixture of élitist nationalism, ultramontane Catholicism, and supreme disdain for liberal democracy. They would oust Yrigoyen not only because he was Yrigoyen, but because he more than any other political figure embodied the vortex of rapid change that had swept away all the certainties of the old, pastoral Argentina. Not indeed the real Argentina of history, which had been changing unceasingly since its break with Spain, but a romanticised Argentina of strong, warlike, patriots . . . and a vision of future grandeur. Their journal *La Fronda* described Yrigoyen as "a resentful little Redskin who hates civilization," a man whose tenderness was evoked by tyranny, "especially if it is Central American, that is to say, run by mediocre and sickly little black men, who are of his own race and mentality."[16]

Crawley's analysis suggests how this racially charged backlash would eventually take the form of a nationalism defined in large part by its "rediscovery" of the country's foundational, Hispanic, criollo "origins" and its anti-liberal hostility toward urban immigrants and internationalism in general. The very lever of the modern state, of "progress," and of "Argentinity," became its bane. This ever-more-pervasive hostility, according to Leopoldo Rodríguez, was shared as much by intellectuals as anyone. "Many intellectuals began to reject positivist and cosmopolitan ideas in favor of other, nationalistic ones that defended traditional Hispanic culture, its values, habits, and heroes," eschewing the "cosmopolitan flood" and the "Babel of languages." These intellectuals cast themselves as heirs of the pre-republican, prelapsarian, national essence, and many of those who had ardently embraced European culture as a model now nostalgically "began a return to the *criollo* past, forgot Frenchification and civilization, to turn back to things Spanish and to what used to be called the barbarity of the countryside."[17]

Thus came about a blatant rupture with the ideology of the republican, immigrant-sympathetic "founders" of Argentina and Argentinity. The rural areas, against which the republic and "the nation" had heretofore necessarily defined themselves in order to come into being, were now embraced ardently by nationalistic intellectuals and artists, recuperated (to recall Barthes' phrase) in the service of a triumphant ideology. Gladys Onega remarks that

in the liberal dream, Europeans were in themselves the incarnation of civilization. Nonetheless, the hard facts were different,
because the immigrants came from the proletarian sectors and
the most dispossessed peasantry of their countries; because most
brought no more than their hands and their need; because they'd
had slight contact with the high cultural forms of their countries
or none at all, and were illiterate or semi-literate.[18]

These nationalistic, xenophobic precedents coalesced by the late
1920s into a growing sympathy toward the armed forces as the designated salvational instrument of an essentialized national culture,
perceived to be in disintegration due to a collapsing liberalism's tolerance—and in fact need and official encouragement—of "internationalism."[19] The first successful military coup, which would initiate a half-century cycle of coups, took place in 1930. Immigration
was abruptly and completely halted by the military government in
the same year.

The long era leading up to the Process began, in which the military
would perfect its ability to use republican democracy's own constitutional mechanisms to keep it in check. Donald Hodges comments
on the form of government which would supplant the immigrant
nation's brief experiment in open democracy:

> In Argentina military intervention became institutionalized. The
> Supreme Court set a precedent for the military era by ruling in
> 1930 that the armed forces may legitimately oust an elected gov-
> ernment because they alone have the task of protecting life, lib-
> erty, and property in the event the established order breaks
> down. The military may exercise this right when it states the
> reasons for its intervention, when it outlines its course of action,
> and when it swears under oath to obey the constitution and
> uphold existing legislation. . . . The effect of this court ruling
> was to legitimate prospective coups in advance, provided they
> were successful. . . . Beginning with the coup of September 1930
> and continuing through the coup of March 1976, military gov-
> ernments presented their case before the Supreme Court, which
> made them legal retroactively.[20]

It is in this context that the writing of the cosmopolitan criollo
Borges comes into print. The argument about whether Borges is a
"true" Argentine writer or a "Europeanized" one has been carried on
for even longer than the polemic over his political status. It is quite
easy to go back and trace, especially in Borges' early poetry and

fiction, themes and subjects that serve as plausible instances of a domestic topography and thereby earn him the badge of Argentinity. A story such as his 1933 "Hombre de la esquina rosada" features as its narrator an inhabitant of the borderlands who seems to be the "authentic" Argentine, the quasi-outlaw, half-gaucho, half-thief who inhabits the shady suburbs.[21] But since the very idea of Argentinity arises as manufactured and historically specific, with the domestic and the European mutually founded on one another, this kind of local-color "proof" seems specious. In his prologue to an edition of Borges' *Ficciones—El aleph—El informe de Brodie* Iraset Páez Urdaneta complains of the much-discussed question of Argentinity, saying that

> people demand nationality as if it were conceptually and materially possible . . . even if one has to resort to folkloristic falsifications. In Spanish America, where nationalisms have been invented on account of political insecurity, the tendency has continued to associate the national with local color, with the effete dormancy of an open plain, a jungle, or a sierra, considered to have been lost or never acquired.[22]

Borges provides his own dry, lucid insight to this effect in 1932, in his essay "The Argentine Writer and Tradition." In it he speaks about the dialectical relation between these two ostensibly opposed ideologies. "Gaucho poetry," he says, "is a literary genre as artificial as any other."[23] Though Borges means to make only an aesthetic point, he nonetheless frames it in historical terms.

> The idea that a literature should be defined by the differentiating features of its country is a relatively new idea; the idea that writers should seek themes about their countries is also new and arbitrary . . . the Argentine cult of local color is a recent European cult which the nationalists should reject as foreign.[24]

Borges, the "disengaged reactionary," rejects the resurgence of blind nationalism, in the early decades of the twentieth century, which created the social conditions for modern dictatorship—not because he is a partisan of radicalism, but because of a radical skepticism toward the essentializing, aesthetic foundational gestures of the modern republic. A participant in and "founder" of literary modernity himself, he yet remains keenly aware of the solipsism providing the flimsy conceptual ground for a liberal modernity bearing the seeds of its own destruction. Jaime Alazraki, in "Lo esencial argentino," indicates that Borges' "Argentinity resides precisely in having confronted [its] reality, in having presented it without local-color embellishments or nationalist genuflections."[25]

In his essay on tradition, Borges comments directly on the flawed logic of nationalism. "I want to point out another contradiction: the nationalists pretend to venerate the power of the Argentine imagination, but they want to limit the poetic exercise of that mind to a few poor local themes, as if we Argentines only knew how to talk about river banks and ranches, and not about the universe."[26]

Beatriz Sarlo remarks on Borges' use of "foreign language as the foundation of writing. . . . translations of translations, versions of versions . . . Borges proclaims the principle: originality is not a value."[27] The "criollization" of language he engages in is very different from that essentialized nationalism which served as a prolegomenon for dictatorship and which was fervently endorsed by such leading intellectuals as Borges' poetic idol Leopoldo Lugones. Luis Alén Lascano characterizes Lugones as the literary spokesman for a nascent militaristic nationalism driven by fear of the anarchic masses. In a 1923 tirade against pacifism, collectivism, and liberal democracy, "The Hour of the Sword," which Lascano describes as "a reflection of the entire ideological background of the new so-called nationalist groups," Lugones promoted the armed forces as the ultimate repository of the highest moral values of the Fatherland.[28] Lugones proclaimed that "the constitutional system of the nineteenth century is extinct. The army is the final aristocracy; by which I mean, the last possibility of hierarchical organization left before demagogic dissolution."[29]

An homage "To Leopoldo Lugones" written by Borges makes clear the mental rift that existed between the two writers, despite Borges' adulation of Lugones. He describes how, in a dream, he enters the Library, reminisces among the books, and is led to the door of Lugones' office, where he enters and speaks with Lugones but finds it difficult to progress beyond mutual pleasantries, due to their different casts of mind.

> We exchange a few conventional and cordial words, and I hand you this book. If I am not mistaken, you were rather fond of me, Lugones, and it would have pleased you to be pleased by some work of mine. That never happened, but this time you turn the pages and read approvingly some line or other.

Once the fantasy is dispelled, Borges can only speak with sadness and longing about an intellectual reconciliation that will have to

take place out of historical time, significantly naming the year before
the publication of his 1939 meditation on history and time, the story
"Pierre Menard, autor del *Quijote*," as marking this fact with catastrophic certitude.

> At this point my dream dissolves—like water in water. The vast
> library all around me is on Mexico Street, not on Rodríguez
> Peña, and you, Lugones, committed suicide around the begin-
> ning of 1938. My vanity and my wistfulness have set up an
> impossible scene. This may be so (I tell myself), but tomorrow I
> too will be dead and our times will become one, and chronology
> will be lost in a world of meaningless symbols, and in some way
> it may be true to say that I once handed you this book and that
> you accepted it.[30]

In the fiction of the wistful and alienated Borges, the non-
hierarchical Babel of language, in the crucible of translation, allows
Borges to differentiate himself into a third, neutral, dégagé modernity. His search is for a way of embracing the "internationalism" represented by immigration but in a fashion allowing "urbanity" to remain in the aesthetic realm, untouched, unaffected by the fatal,
suicidal exigencies of modernity that threaten the republic. Says
Sarlo, "The voice of translation and the voice of Buenos Aires: each
legitimates the other, and their co-presence opens up the possibility
of differentiating oneself from those new arrivals who don't possess
both voices as their own, as part of a heritage."[31] And also, one should
add, of differentiating oneself from the nationalists who reject the
voices of the new arrivals. Borges seeks not so much a political via
media (e.g., Barth's) as a zero degree of culture, exempt from those
warring, mutually implicated factions who make modernity such a
precarious enterprise.

Borges' story "Pierre Menard, autor del *Quijote*"—the farthest of
cries from folklorism—provides insight into Borges' attempt to fashion a neutral literary space as a disengaged retreat from the darker
political currents of Argentine modernization. Alazraki indicates it
as one of the stories that signal his movement in the mid-to-late
thirties away from Argentine creole themes, such as those expressed
in "Hombre de la esquina rosada," and toward more metaphysical
concerns.[32] "Pierre Menard, autor del *Quijote*" concerns the narrator's catalogue of, and apologia for, the "visible and invisible" literary remains of the polyglot, polymath, consummately European and
internationalist Menard. George Steiner, who has called this story
"the most acute, most concentrated commentary anyone has ever

offered on the business of translation," points to Borges' catalogue of Menard's "visible" works as an exemplum of a culturally non-specific, universalist approach to language.[33]

> The monographs on "a poetic vocabulary of concepts" and on "connections or affinities" between the thought of Descartes, Leibniz, and John Wilkins point toward the labors of the seventeenth century to construe an *ars signorum*, a universal ideo-grammatic language system . . . to reverse the disaster at Babel. Menard's "work shccts of a monograph on George Boole's symbolic logic" show his (and Borges's) awareness of the connections between the seventeenth century pursuit of an inter-lingua for philosophic discourse and the "universalism" of modern symbolic and mathematical logic.[34]

Borges, who, as Sarlo has suggested, sees foreign language as the "foundation" of writing and of Argentinity, eschews nationalistic, proto-militaristic means of "reversing the disaster at Babel," such as those endorsed by anti-cosmopolitan Argentine intellectuals. But Steiner's analysis goes awry in one important aspect. In the creation of Menard, Borges is not interested in negating Hispanic origins in order to merely replace them with more universal and cosmopolitan (i.e., European) ones—that is, in the official internationalism of the nascent Argentine republic, with its need to assimilate. Rather, his fascination with an "inter-lingua" remains a (fittingly quixotic) quest to *keep alive* the non-hierarchical character of Babel, rather than reverse it or resolve it. To resolve the question in a manner conferring primacy either on cosmopolitanism or on a more Hispanic Argentinity is to acknowledge, fatally, an origin, a definitive foundation for the modern state, literature, and so forth. Acknowledging these origins is for Borges tantamount to acquiescing in the pernicious myths that have enabled the emergence of the dictatorial state.

After listing the "visible" work of Menard, the narrator goes on to consider "his other work: the subterranean, the interminably heroic, the peerless. And . . . the unfinished." The unfinished—here consisting of Menard's rendition of "the ninth and thirty-eighth chapters of the first part of *Don Quixote* and a fragment of chapter twenty-two"—is what interests Borges, and the inconclusiveness of Menard's *Quixote* is a function of its dual, contradictory relation to its "original." Justifying this piece of "absurdity," says the narrator, "is the primordial object of this note."[35] Borges' deadpan recounting of Menard's ambition and of the narrator's scholasticism in interpreting it supplies him with the necessary balance of irony and genuine insight to probe into the thorny question of origins without succumbing to polemic or scholasticism himself.

Menard, says the narrator, was inspired to rewrite the *Quixote* by a meditation on "the theme of *total identification* with a given author." To have had Menard simply write a modern *Quixote* would only underscore and endorse a particular precedent for Argentine modernity, to cast it in one of the two definitive and interrelated molds I have described earlier—both of which lead to the same dictatorial social conclusion.

In an essay contained in a book devoted to exploring Borges' complex, ambivalent relationship to Spain, Blas Matamoro characterizes Borges first and foremost as a "traitor."

> The absence of . . . definitive authority makes Borgesian knowledge a perplexed and passionate exercise, where all can be pronounced and nothing can be said. . . . [His writing] tries not to give to the signifying qualities of words any power that yokes them to precise functions like demonstrating and guiding. On the contrary, it tries to deceive and disturb. In some cases, when the reader approaches the text in search of a strong paternal precision, it betrays that expectation.[36]

Borges complicates the question of origins by taking Menard's adherence to a "founding" text and figure to such an absurd extreme that the authority of the originating text over its "successor" crumbles; they become relational rather than hierarchical. Originality ceases to have value, when the two texts in question have become identical versions of one another.

> He did not want to compose another Quixote—which is easy—but *the Quixote itself*. Needless to say, he never contemplated a mechanical transcription of the original; he did not propose to copy it. His admirable intention was to produce a few pages which would coincide—word for word and line for line—with those of Miguel de Cervantes.[37]

Borges' choice of Cervantes is canny, since *Don Quixote*, often cited as the first novel in Western literature, looms as *the* authoritative founding text of modern Hispanic prose. Gregory Ulmer, who also makes a connection between Borges and Barthes in the two authors' mutual preference for an "impersonal creator," describes Borges' need, especially in "Pierre Menard," to reject an authority, a definitive point of origin, and to seek out instead a zero degree, a place of continual, evasive movement, where the question of allegiance dissolves.[38] Citing Barthes, Ulmer says that

> the obsession with infinite regression that permeates Borges' thought . . . reveals the similarity of his view of language to that of Barthes. Barthes' view of writing as an "hereditary process without end in a world of interconnecting codes" implies that "to explain a message, we are obliged to go over to another code, which in turn sends us to yet another code, and so on, in an infinite regress. This is ultimately a metaphysical conception, coming down to the irreducible fact of the non-origin of origins questioning the occidental idea that there are ultimate origins of a transcendental order."[39]

As Ulmer's last sentence implies, Borges' quixotic non-position of not declaring his definitive allegiance to either Hispanic or European origins is also a position, an "irreducible fact." The dégagé code of honor of the semiotic knight-errant Borges remains as much a stance as any other stance and presumably as subject to the fluxes of history. Yet Borges remains highly aware of the significance of this "fact" for his fiction: Menard's initial method of composition, which he *rejects*, attempts to bleach his enterprise of all history subsequent to Cervantes and would thereby have allowed him to become Cervantes. He would simply have to "know Spanish well, recover the Catholic faith, make war against the Moors or the Turks, forget the history of Europe between the years 1602 and 1918, *be* Miguel de Cervantes." This initial position, though a reductio ad absurdum, still hits strikingly close to the ethos of those Argentines like Lugones in the early decades of the twentieth century who wished to "forget" modernity in order to return to the Hispanicist, criollo essence of the past.

But Menard rejects the course of returning to the essence of the *Quixote* through Cervantes as a task both "impossible" and "easy." The narrator admits the impossibility of Menard's whole enterprise from the outset; but, he says, "of all the impossible ways of carrying it out, this was the least interesting. To be, in the twentieth century, a popular novelist of the seventeenth seemed to him a diminution."[40] In the case of Argentine letters, one could substitute *nineteenth* for *seventeenth* and arrive at an approximation of the atmosphere within which Borges wrote.

But Menard (like Borges), unconcerned with establishing "authentic" origins for his effort, opts to "reach the Quixote through the experiences of Pierre Menard." Rejecting the nationalized Argentine

(European) vogue of local color, Borges tellingly chooses as his contemporary author not an Argentine (who presumably could find
transmigrated Hispanicist "roots" in Cervantes' novel), nor even any
Spanish-language native, nor any exemplar of traditional Hispanic
culture, values, habits, or heroes. Rather, he chooses the seeming
antithesis of Argentinity and the Hispanic past.

> But why precisely the Quixote? our reader will ask. Such a pref-
> erence, in a Spaniard, wouldn't have been inexplicable; but it is,
> no doubt, in a Symbolist from Nîmes, essentially a devoté of
> Poe, who engendered Baudelaire, who engendered Mallarmé,
> who engendered Valéry, who engendered Edmond Teste.[41]

In attempting my own translation of this passage, I would be tempted
to translate Borges' *engendró* as *begat*, to emphasize the parodic Biblical quality in this genealogical litany. Menard, the Symbolist from
Nîmes, is not exactly the proper heir of the sacred Cervantine Hispanic tradition and so does not have the filial, national "right" to
appropriate him at all, much less in the fanatical, impossible way
that he attempts—that is, not unless one begins to think of this "hereditary process without end" in terms of the lateral displacements
and regressions that Barthes proposes. As Menard attests in a letter
to the narrator, for him "the Quixote is a contingent book, the Quixote is unnecessary." It doesn't have the same "inevitable" quality as
a single poetic line from Poe, which he "cannot imagine the universe
without." This violation of the standards of filiality, authenticity,
and originality is heightened—and the plagiarism made more
acute—by the offhand, indifferent, almost contemptuous tone of
Menard's remark.
   But the tone of casual yet anxious contempt is to a purpose. Borges,
the quixotic (but self-conscious) modernist *malgré lui,* with a subtle
mixture of poignance and irony tries to reconcile the demands of the
past with the inexorable pull of a modernity that allows him only
two choices. He must either negotiate modernity on his own terms
or simply succumb to it on its self-annihilating terms. His neutrality,
he is aware, lives in history. The measure of historical change, and
the price of modernity, might be gauged (in the spirit of translation)
by one's remarking on the anachronistic difficulty of trying to re-
capture Cervantes' usage of, say, the term *caballero*—the knight-
errant Don Quixote's term of self-definition. That is, one might say
that the modern Menard's attempt to write the *Quixote* while remaining himself is doomed by the fact that his remarks about

Cervantes' novel cannot be *chivalrous* but must instead be *cavalier.*
Menard complains of how

> my obliging predecessor did not refuse the collaboration of
> chance: he composed his immortal work somewhat *à la diable,*
> carried along by inertias of language and invention. I have taken
> on the mysterious duty of reconstructing literally his spontane-
> ous work. My solitary game is governed by two polar laws. The
> first permits me to essay variations of a formal or psychological
> type; the second obliges me to sacrifice these variations to the
> "original" text and reason out this annihilation in an irrefutable
> manner.

To these laws he adds a third "congenital" one: having written the
*Quixote* at the beginning of the seventeenth century should be considered "a reasonable undertaking, necessary, and perhaps even unavoidable; at the beginning of the twentieth, it is almost impossible.
It is not in vain that three hundred years have gone by, filled with
exceedingly complex events. Amongst them, to mention only one,
is the *Quixote* itself."[42] Though not truly the origin and begetter of
history, books such as the *Quixote* are *reconstructed* in retrospect
as exactly that by those who are attempting to establish a particular
(e.g., Hispanicist and xenophobic) version of modernity (and not, like
Borges, simply trying to keep at bay the darker aspects of modernity).
Cervantes' book, in the nationalist intellectual's attempt to negate
the Babel-like aspects of the nation, acquires the mystique of exis-
iting before or outside of history. Because the book is "necessary,
even unavoidable," existing (from the perspective of the present) in
the timeless Golden Age of Spanish literature, its author, Cervantes,
can compose complacently, *à la diable,* with spontaneity and without self-consciousness.

Menard, on the other hand, remains subject to the merciless polar
laws of filiation, which require that any variations on the gold standard set by the original ultimately be sacrificed to it. This stringent
standard, applied to modernity's own incursions on the past, seems
to ensure that modernity, and not the "original," will be decimated
in the end, and by its own hand. Menard adheres to the standard set
by these "polar laws." In assessing the *Quixote,* he adopts Cervantes'
cavalier tone—in the hope of demonstrating, however, that the earlier book *is* contingent and that his plagiaristic recreation is, in fact,
necessary, destined to survive.

From the retrospective perspective of the present, the *Quixote's*
seeming necessity in its own time allows its author, Cervantes, the

luxury of proceeding as if it were contingent; Menard (and Borges), because they stand at the cusp of a derivative modernity already precariously contingent within history, must compose with a literal-minded sense of necessity. But the plagiarism, unlike a mere recreation, is not undertaken, ultimately, in a spirit of reverence or devotion, even though Menard describes his reproduction as a "mysterious duty." By taking the constraints imposed on him a step further, to their logical extremes, Borges, in cavalier fashion, transforms filial, derivative literal-mindedness into a stay against the self-annihilating requirements of towering originality. For in spite of these exacting constraints, says the narrator, in the end "Menard's fragmentary *Quixote* is more subtle than Cervantes'," precisely on account of the passage of three hundred years of complex happenings.

Cervantes merely "opposes to the fictions of chivalry the tawdry provincial reality of his country." Menard, by choosing an alien time and century, could easily have fallen into such trivial "españoladas" (Hispanicisms) as gypsy folklore, autos da fe, and conquistadors, but he evades these pitfalls successfully and writes "with complete naturalness." Like Borges, the cosmopolitan criollo, he rigorously "neglects or eliminates local color." With great ingenuity, Menard opts for the zero degree, in which, as Barthes claims, language "reaches the state of a pure equation." His strategy of equating his text with that of Cervantes is effective not in spite of but *because of* the erosions and changes that history rings upon a "neutral" text. Unlike those who selectively recuperate history and consciously try to update it—e.g., Lugones and Co.—and end up with nothing more than a literature filled with the nationalistic impoverishment of *españoladas*, Argentinity, the cult of local color, and so forth, Menard's disengagement, buffeted by history, ironically gives his plagiarized text a potentially regenerative power. The narrator concludes that "Cervantes' text and Menard's are verbally identical, but the second is almost infinitely richer."

At this point, Borges makes his most ironic and devastating comment on attempts to essentialize history in its foundational aspect, when he compares a particular fragment of Cervantes' prose with an identical one from Menard's:

> . . . truth, whose mother is history, rival of time, depository of deeds, witness of the past, exemplar and adviser to the present, and the future's counsellor.

Written in the seventeenth century, by the "lay genius" Cervantes, this enumeration is a mere rhetorical praise of history. Menard, on the other hand, writes:

... truth, whose mother is history, rival of time, depository of deeds, witness of the past, exemplar and adviser to the present, and the future's counsellor.

History, the *mother* of truth: the idea is astounding. Menard, a contemporary of William James, does not define history as an inquiry into reality, but as its origin. Historical truth, for him, is not what happened; it is what we judge to have happened. The final phrases—*exemplar and adviser to the present, and the future's counsellor* —are brazenly pragmatic.[43]

The monomaniacal and peerless Menard's literal reproduction, through sheer force of will, of Cervantes' "rhetorical praise of history" takes to the extreme—"brazenly"—the rhetorical appropriation (as by Borges' nationalistic compeers) of history as the origin of truth and the key shaping force of the present and future. But unlike those compeers, "Pierre Menard" 's narrator openly acknowledges the constructed quality of truth and its origin and does not present history in the guise of a nostalgic lost essence. The definition of historical truth, like everything else, remains subject to the transforming flow of history, and Menard's attempt at deliberate anachronism has the paradoxical effect of recasting Cervantes' definition of history in Menard's contemporary pragmatic terms. Menard's peculiar brand of "devotion" to the original results in a necessary treason. History is not "what happened," but rather—in a William Jamesian, expedient, willful empiricism which rejects all transcendent principles, including truth—"what we judge to have happened." Borges believes that national culture is founded on "translations of translations, versions of versions." In this belief, he is as much of a traitor as Enrique Ossorio in Piglia's novel. Borges takes to new historical heights the old truism *traduttore, traditore*. The net result is what Mary Kinzie, in an essay on Borges' "recursive prose," refers to as "the changeability of the past under the magnetic effect of a present (or recent) writer."[44] Founding gestures are not even anachronisms—they are synchronisms. As Emir Rodríguez Monegal has put it, Borges, skeptical and even deliberately solipsistic, affirms both that

outside of the present, time does not exist and that this very present in which we live is by nature illusory. At the root of his speculations there is an intuition of the vanity of all intellectual knowledge and the conviction that it is impossible to penetrate the ultimate core of reality (if there is any).[45]

An ironic yet idealist space, negating time; a permanent hiatus on the cusp of modernity: that is the place the wistful and quixotic Borges would prefer to continue inhabiting ad infinitum. His stance resembles the "Utopian neutrality" which Jameson speaks of in relation to Barthes' flight from history and politics. But Borges' irony and radical skepticism instead carry "Pierre Menard, Author of the *Quixote*" to conclusions of "vanity." These conclusions are understandable given the political course that modern Argentina had already clearly taken by 1939, the date of the story's publication. The narrator remarks that "there is no exercise of the intellect which is not, in the final analysis, useless." Sooner or later it becomes "a mere chapter—if not a paragraph or a name in the history of philosophy." Even the glory of the "original" *Quixote*, the narrator remembers Menard saying, has dwindled into the book's having become "the occasion for patriotic toasts." Menard "set himself to an undertaking that was exceedingly complex and, from the very beginning, futile."[46]

There are difficulties, of course, in ascribing overt gloom or pessimism to the wry tone of a Borges fiction, given the emotional restraint of his writing. Mary Kinzie formulates the matter brilliantly when she observes that the metaphysical state present in the thought of his fiction

is a region seldom marked by pain, resentment, or failure, nor is there success or pleasure—not even anomie. In a body of work where even the subtleties of boredom are suppressed, character patently has never fully functioned: character, that is, which involves cupidity and doubt, devotion and revulsion, character which must be capable of breaks and jumps—discontinuities—in order to reflect the anomalous surface against which it balances itself, grounding its consistency. Borges' parallelisms, by contrast, claim nothing for character but its own permeability. There are neither civic nor private complexities in the lives of Borges' figures. . . . There are only further lateral displacements within selves which are initially isolated, inscrutably limited, and, above all, forgetful.[47]

Yet suppose one allows one of these "lateral displacements within selves," proposed by Kinzie, to take place within a larger context?

That is just the kind of displacement that Barthes, with his "hereditary process without end," would advocate in the realm of culture and semiotics. I would argue that though "pain, resentment, and failure," as Kinzie suggests, are *virtually* absent in the "characters" of Borges' prose and though civic and private complexities *seldom* exist for them one can yet, in this very straining toward an emotional degree zero, discover a clear anomie of the specific type I have been trying to describe. A muted pessimism, too, pervades the tone, taking the form of the "amodal form" and "negative mood" that Barthes (himself transforming grammatical categories into metaphysical states through the power of metaphor) says characterize the zero degree. The valences of this muted "mood" or tone might become more manifest precisely by my taking another metaphorical leap, laterally displacing the self represented in the neutral Borges of "Pierre Menard" onto one of the prose poems of his Peruvian compeer from the twenties and thirties, César Vallejo. Like Borges, Vallejo during that time struggled in his writing to reconcile his indigenous themes with a fervent devotion to European culture and internationalism. Fortunately Vallejo's cerebral and inscrutable qualities have not blinded critics to the feeling that suffuses his poetry. A brief displacement of Borges' persona onto one of Vallejo's poems may help dispel the notion of Borges' emotional aridity.

In many important respects, Vallejo seems at the furthest possible remove from Borges. An avowed Communist and engagé (though often hermetic) poet and writer and the author of the overtly partisan, Spanish republican *España, aparta de mí este cáliz,* he became enmeshed (a scant few years before Borges published "Pierre Menard") in a quixotic enterprise very different from those which could have concerned Borges or his apocryphal Symbolist, Menard—namely, his active support of the Loyalists in the Spanish Civil War. His poems from *España, aparta de mí este cáliz* circulated in the trenches during the war. Yet there remains at least one striking parallel between the two writers. Much of Vallejo's poetry, beyond any explicitly engagé quality that might be found in some of it, is strongly marked by the striving for disengagement, for a neutral or neuter space exempt from the ravages of history, time, and filiality; a space in which (to reiterate Barthes' dictum) "the social or mythical characters of a language are abolished."

This striving is especially salient in the ironically titled "I am going to speak of hope," a prose poem of Vallejo's from the 1920s. One can imagine the speaking voice as a laterally displaced self of the emotionally austere narrator of Menard. But Vallejo's version of the impersonal poetic self, rather than inhabiting a realm seldom marked by pain, resentment, or failure, is steeped in all three and tries to wring from them an amodal negative mood, a metaphysical state approaching the absolute of the zero degree.

> I do not suffer this pain as César Vallejo. I do not ache now as an artist, as a man or even as a simple living being. . . . If my name were not César Vallejo, I would still suffer this very same pain. If I were not an artist, I would still suffer it. If I were not a man or even a living being, I would still suffer it . . .
> I ache now without any explanation. My pain is so deep, that it never had a cause, nor does it lack a cause now. What could have been its cause? Where is that thing so important, that it might stop being its cause? Its cause is nothing . . . For what has this pain been born, for itself? My pain comes from the north wind and from the south wind, like those neuter eggs certain rare birds lay in the wind . . .
> I believed until now that all the things of the universe were, inevitably, parents or sons. But behold that my pain today is neither parent nor son. It lacks a back to darken, as well as having too much chest to dawn and if they put it in a dark room, it would not give light and if they put it in a brightly lit room, it would cast no shadow. Today I suffer no matter what happens. Today I am simply in pain.[48]

This unfilial and unaffiliated universe, where pain is "neither parent nor son," can, if transposed, become the universe of Borges. His fiction, reluctant to acknowledge either political discomfiture or personal uneasiness, would scarcely consent to containing a litany of self-incriminating words like "pain" and "suffering." Even the immoderate and seemingly shameless Borges of innumerable interviews, who holds forth without restraint on a panoply of subjects, would doubtless find them distasteful and an embarrassment. Yet his fiction, in its revealing reticence, can almost be said, like Vallejo's poetry, to speak of hope.

The protagonist of Luisa Valenzuela's "Other Weapons," Laura, also inhabits a region marked by pain and nullity. But her internment is so complete that neither hope nor hopelessness form part of her severely reduced vocabulary. The bald facts of the story, which remain unavailable to the protagonist until the story's end, are the following: Laura, who belonged to a resistance movement, attempted to assassinate a colonel in the military, who then, after breaking her nose and torturing her to near insanity, married her and now keeps her sequestered and under guard in an apartment, in a drug-induced torpor, where he subjects her to a combination of paternalistic pampering and sexual and emotional degradation. But this roughly familiar, almost cliche topos of the torture-victim story, as Marta Morello-Frosch points out, is of only minor interest in itself. Rather, "what sets this narrative apart is the mode of entrapment and the structure of isolation it reveals ... the structuring of the barriers imposed to [Laura's] recall" of how she came to be abducted and imprisoned.[49]

Laura's psychic neutrality is so complete, because she has been so effectively "neutralized," that her amnesia-reinforced cell of deprivation becomes for her a retreat she doesn't want to give up. Cloistered within four walls, she embodies in a different way the pain of which Vallejo says "if they put it in a dark room, it would not give light and if they put it in a brightly lit room, it would cast no shadow." Stripped of all but the bare remnants of language, identity, and will, "so-called Laura" is reluctant to relinquish her atopia of pain because, she reflects, "that pain is the only thing that really belongs to her."[50] Morello-Frosch describes her as "severed totally from her past, reduced to the condition of psychological tabula rasa, zero degree of consciousness."[51]

This is another version of Barthes' and Borges' rioting degree zero. But unlike the personae of Borges, Laura has indeed already attained a nightmarish version of neutrality from the outset, and the story's movement, roughly inverse to that of Borges, is her fitful, feeble attempt to make her way back from it, whether she wills it or not. Laura is not a cipher in the enduring, speculative Borgesian sense that Kinzie describes but rather a character temporarily stripped of all her character-like qualities. The existential Borgesian attributes Laura possesses appear to be more by default than by design. In the more traditional and less philosophical modality of Valenzuela's fiction, which flirts with parabolic qualities without fully embracing them, it is understood that Laura wishes to recover those qualities of full-blown character and feeling as quickly as possible, that they exist in a heuristic, exploratory suspended animation.

But in "The Words," the opening vignette of "Other Weapons," it appears premature to speak of Laura's volition, since her incipient struggle to recover language has only brought her, a detached observer, to the edge of that unfamiliar linguistic precipice called *will*. "The Words" begins in this way:

> She doesn't find it the least bit surprising that she has no memory, that she feels completely devoid of recollections. She may

not even realize that she's living in an absolute void. She is quite concerned about something else, about her capacity to find the right word for each thing and receive a cup of tea when she says I want (and that "I want" also disconcerts her, that act of willing) when she says I want a cup of tea.[52]

This title story is taken from Valenzuela's *Cambio de armas* (Other Weapons), first published in 1982, the book which serves as her most direct fictional commentary on the dictatorial Argentine Process.[53] The book and its title story provide fictional commentaries on the radical stasis of a political left finally paralyzed by its own inefficacy vis-à-vis the successive shocks of military social violence over the course of the twentieth century.[54] In contrast to Borges, Valenzuela does not present the zero degree of consciousness as a state to be aspired to. Her story, fully immersed in a wayward modernity and separated from his by a political span of more than forty years, rests at the other end of the half-century cycle of Argentine military coups whose most recent incarnation was (or is) the Process. With yet another return to "so-called" democracy imminent, Valenzuela gives voice to radicalism's necessary and imposed, however undesired, arrival at a social void of spent initiatives. An immense difficulty besets the collective imagination, making it almost impossible for radicals to conceptualize, much less act on, renewed versions of social transformation. Her skepticism is toward the depressing results and limited alternatives of the modernity that vexed Borges in its early stages. The narrator of "Other Weapons" describes Laura's reaction to a ring of keys left hanging on the wall by the door in plain view.

> She, so-called Laura, is on this side of the so-called door, with its so-called locks and its so-called key begging her to cross the threshold. But she can't; not yet. Facing the door, she thinks about it and realizes she can't, although no one appears to care much. Suddenly the so-called door opens and the man we will now call Hector [the colonel-torturer] walks in, proving that he also has his set of so-called keys and uses them quite freely.[55]

In the larger social realm, as in Laura's individual instance, action remains contingent on regenerating the more basic powers of cognition and naming. Desirable and undesirable states must first be distinguished successfully from one another—a task made unimaginably arduous by the fact that all discourses are permeated with, and seeming functions of, dictatorial consciousness. Morello-Frosch comments that "the speaking or uttering subject can . . . be opposed to the consensus or the dominant discourse. But the subject needs to establish differences between views, between perceptions, among beings and among periods . . . The subject needs a collective and subjective memory that will furnish a context for his or her own practice."[56]

The analysis of Morello-Frosch strikes me as limited only in the respect that she seems to suggest that Laura's reconnection with the outside world could in and of itself provide access to a successful "space of resistance." But the crisis of Argentine radicalism is precisely a crisis of consensus in that outside world, of a "collective memory" in search of a suitable context, led to the impasse of neutrality by its inability to differentiate among perceptions.[57] Radical failure, perforce, is therefore most aptly traced in personal, experiential terms.

Other voices, in post-Process Argentina as well as Uruguay and Chile, have expressed similar doubts. One broadly based, recent group of Latin American intellectuals, faced with this crisis, has dedicated its energies to a wholesale reconceptualization of radicalism. They have employed the working term "political culture" in their attempt to assess the failed solutions provided by traditional left initiatives. The definition the group gives to this term and the specific changes the group proposes significantly remain somewhat vague. In the introduction to an anthology entitled *Cultura política y democratización*, comprised of writings by adherents of this group (and including analyses of the Argentine situation), Norbert Lechner takes pains, in fact, to make clear the group's hesitancy toward giving (or inability to give) a definition. "What do we understand by political culture? The fact is, a clear, precise meaning doesn't exist."

What does become clear in the collective position taken by these "radical" intellectuals is their frustration with radicalism—their reluctant yet profound skepticism toward it. Lechner locates the origin of Latin American society's reawakened interest in "political culture" (as opposed to the instrumental concepts of electoral politics and direct revolutionary political action) in "that phenomenon which today comes again to be closely linked to our concerns: modernity." Modernity, he says, finds its most vibrant historical expression in "the experience of authoritarianism," and Lechner suggests that the widespread collapse of representative democracies, and the unexpected breadth of support for military dictatorships, raises doubts about virtually all the going ideologies of progress and social change. He suggests that the skepticism of many radicals toward the too-often-repeated foundational gesture of beginning anew and the rejection of a whole spectrum of ideologies—especially those allied with orthodox Marxist, economic- and institution-based analysis and praxis (superstructure, infrastructure, etc.)—are partly driven by the successful co-optation of those ideologies by the militaristic state.

> The attempt to found an authoritarian State, shutting down the classic sites of politics (political parties, parliament) also gives impetus to a revision of the very notion of politics. Today, the usual identification of politics with the state and the public domain is widely rejected. Critics take up liberal arguments afresh, but without accepting the marketplace as the organizing principle of society. Politics is not rejected, but its instrumental conception is. The very violence of the attempt to impose the laws of the marketplace throws into greater relief the ethical dimension of politics. The defense of human rights and, in a more diffuse sense, of social identity opens the way to a re-politicization which makes evident the continuity between the political and the non-political.[58]

This left-based critique of orthodox Marxism, its attempt to de-institutionalize the political, and its heavy emphasis on such sites of engagement as human rights and a dispersed "social identity" might not appear especially striking in the context of Western European social philosophy, where the unified "subject of history" and the efficacy of the basic tenets of the many varieties of Marxist thought and their institutions have been under revision (and outright assault) from the left for decades. Nor, for different reasons, might this situational strain of ideation seem striking in the U.S. context, where Marxism has held only sporadic sway in mainstream arenas of political praxis (in its brief hold on labor unions during the thirties and forties, for instance) and where European poststructuralism has come to fill a void among U.S. intellectuals who have for some time felt isolated from participation in the premises and promises of liberalism. Even the more radical partisan (communist, socialist) left in the U.S. has shifted its emphasis these days almost entirely to coalition-building with activist groups around specific focal issues such as human rights, nuclear disarmament, and the right of other countries to self-determination.

But in Argentina, Uruguay, and Chile, this sort of issue- and culture-oriented emphasis and rhetoric has for decades been dismissed, often with great trenchancy, by the militant left (the Tupamaros or Montoneros, for instance), who have used the deprecatory adjectives "progressive" (*progresista*) and "reformist" (*reformista*) to describe the shortcomings of liberal thought. At best, "progressive" initiatives have been accepted with misgiving as pragmatic short-term strategies, with the understanding that they are theoretically subsumed, ultimately, within more "far-reaching" and orthodox economic analyses. Lechner's specific suggestion that such arenas of activity as human rights (e.g., the Mothers of the Plaza de Mayo in Argentina) can comprise more fruitful long-term bases for reconstructing political life than failed guerrilla movements is certainly open to question. Some commentators indeed suggest that such issue-oriented groups, by definition, are short-lived. John Simpson and Jana Bennett were already remarking in 1985 that a nominal change in power was sufficient to make the Mothers a much less formidable force for change than they were a couple of years earlier. "With the military government gone, and the No Name graves opened, there is little for the Mothers to campaign for except the punishment of the people who carried out the torture and killing of their children. . . . They devoted seven years of anger and courage to the organization, and now there are few outlets for either quality."[59]

All the same, the emphasis of Lechner and others on exploring the parameters of a more diffuse social identity indicates a mighty striving toward a wholesale reimagination of political consciousness. While decidedly not millenarian, intellectuals ache for change and try to keep faith during a time in which the social sphere and the psyches of its inhabitants are conspicuously fragile. I would argue that in Argentina, the experience of the Process and its ambiguous "end" mark the crystallization of modern radical skepticism, a state of mind which should not be confused with political quietism.

In his introduction to a 1987 collection of essays on mass media and social transformation, Oscar Landi echoes this sense of a fundamental shift. He argues that the 1983 return to democracy after the Process can't be thought of as the mere resumption of a dialogue interrupted by a parenthetical coup.

> Politics "returned," but accompanied by a critique of politics; one of the principal cultural confrontations to be unleashed concerned (and concerns) the interpretation of our past and our collective memory. Under these circumstances, certain basic questions have to be asked: what does it mean to "practice" politics; what links exist between the new themes of democracy and the traditional parties; what should be the role of the State,

parties, social movements; and also, in what sense can one speak anew of politics in communication and culture?[60]

Significantly, in Valenzuela's "Other Weapons," the ex-guerrilla Laura has fallen to the "basic" cognitive level at which the ability to conceptualize can no longer be taken for granted. In the second vignette of the narrative sequence, entitled "The Concept," Laura reassures herself that "crazy she is not" but goes on, in completing that sentence, to qualify her affirmation: "although she sometimes wonders and even asks Martina [the housekeeper] where she gets that concept of insanity and why she's so sure." What Valenzuela offers here is not simply a portrait of the torture victim per se but a political pathology, the sense of suffering an "unspeakable" social disease instilled in individual political dissidents *and the society at large* by the logic of dictatorship. The isolated disjunctiveness experienced by Laura designates precisely what she holds in common with that outside world from which she is sealed off.

The conclusions of a group of women psychiatrists, who devoted their labors to analyzing the psychological effects of the Argentine Process on "disappeared" people and their families, underscore important continuities between the psychic torments suffered by disappeared victims and by those close to them. The ego dissolution of the direct victim of disappearance is brought about in part by her having "no contact with the outside world; not knowing where [she] is . . . and knowing that people on the outside don't know where [she] is; and by her absolute uncertainty about [her] future."[61] In the case of the families (also friends, acquaintances) of the disappeared dissidents, they, like Laura—even though they may not be involved in active dissidence themselves—are encouraged to question their sanity (and that of others). These "outsiders," in an increasingly desperate attempt to deny their own collective imprisonment, are "induced to consider political dissidence a lack of social adaptation, and therefore a type of mental illness." They are also "induced to forget," to develop social amnesia. Their capacity to imagine alternative forms of society's life and the means for arriving at them will hopefully thereby atrophy. Diana Kordon and the other psychiatrists describe the motive of the 1976 dictatorship in pursuing this particular form of collective malaise: "To create a consensus in its favor, the dictatorship undertook a campaign of specific psychological action, based on individuals' feelings of social belonging, and on the need for these individuals to develop the appropriate attitudes concerning their social demands."[62] The political and individual crises of consensus are together brought about by the coercive manufacture of a single normative "consensus." One of the ways in which military leaders instilled this generalized obedience and fear of deviance in the civilian population was by concocting definitions of subversion that could, at whim, include virtually any member of the civilian populace.

> By subversion was understood considerably more than the armed operations of ERP [the People's Revolutionary Party] and the Montoneros. As defined by General L. A. Jáuregui in a press conference in April 1977, "subversion is any concealed or open, insidious or violent action that attempts to change or destroy a people's moral criteria and way of life, for the purpose of seizing power or imposing from a position of power a new way of life based on a different ordering of human values." . . . In this perspective the guerrillas constituted only the tip of the iceberg, below which it became imperative to dig out and expose the civilian elements directly and indirectly responsible for social unrest.[63]

The definition of aberrance is a catchall, infinitely flexible and infinitely menacing. All places are equally unsafe. That is why Laura's individualized case of social amnesia presents such a conundrum and what accounts for the seductive, lotus-like allure that her neutral retreat holds for her, despite its sadistic component. If the social sphere is apparently unitary and self-identical, what better place may Laura turn to? Even near the story's end, when her lover-tormentor has rushed out of the apartment after being given news of a counter-coup in progress (something new, or more of the same?) and Laura's "freedom" is imminent, she clings steadfastly to her retreat. The voices she hears outside, during the exchange, are perceived as a "hopeful sound which she doesn't try to interpret. Interpret? What for? Why should she try to interpret something that's beyond her meager capacity to understand?"[64]

The ingenuity of the story lies in Valenzuela's appreciation of the timeliness of that lotus-like conundrum. Her presentation of it as a crisis of atrophied cognitive ability allows her to treat the precarious subject matter of gender, torture, and sexuality without—as most stories of this kind unwittingly do—fetishizing the erotic charge of the physical violence done to the woman's body. In fact, Valenzuela seems highly conscious of the potential for sensationalizing her subject matter and is careful to make the connection between Laura's socially induced psychic inability to differentiate and the consequent, perverse aesthetic appeal of her masochistic retreat. In a scene in which Laura examines one of the wounds resulting from her captivity and torture, her disengaged reverie takes this turn:

> She feels strange, foreign, different. Different from whom? From other women? From herself? So she runs back to the bedroom to look at herself in the big wardrobe mirror. There she is, all of her: rather sad, pointy knees; in general, not much is rounded. Then there's that long, inexplicable scar that runs down her back, that she can only see in the mirror. A thick scar, apparent to the touch, sort of tender even though it's already healed and doesn't hurt. How did that long seam get to that back that seems to have suffered so much? A beaten back. The word beaten, which sounds so pretty if you don't analyze it, gives her goose pimples.[65]

The erotic appeal of the body in conventional terms is carefully underplayed: "sad, pointy knees . . . not much is rounded." The scar, not the body itself, is lingered over; it, not she, has suffered. Its fascination derives from the failure of her mental attempt to locate herself in either personal memory or social imagination. The severe limits on her analytical capability to differentiate throw her back into the immediate flow of language's pure sensory appeal. Significantly, not her body or even the scar, but the prettiness of "the word beaten" (*la palabra azotada,* which could also be translated as "whipped") gives her goose pimples.

Language, for her, has reached the state of pure equation. Still, that state of equation need not be equated in its turn with absolute passivity. As I have said, the movement of the story is her attempt, by reclaiming language, to find her way out of the perpetual "return to softness, letting oneself be." In the fourth brief section, "The Names," Valenzuela even employs that state of equation as Laura's first significant act of passive resistance. Lying in bed with the Colonel, admiring the length of his body, she pillow-talks to him by reciting an ever-changing roster of male names, renaming him at every instant rather than using his real name. His attentive listening, with a smile "not altogether sincere," is motivated, the narrative implies, by his hope that the tone of her voice, through its emphasis, will unwittingly betray which ones in the list are the names of her former guerrilla accomplices. Her passive act of non-differentiation, as she recites to her wary listener, seems to be made up of equal parts inertia and calculation and signals the possible beginnings of a new and more complex relationship to language.

Something's on edge behind [his] peace, something's crouching, ready to pounce at the slightest tremble in her voice when she pronounces a name. But her voice is monotonous, with no apparent feelings or hesitations. She recites like a litany: José, Francisco, Adolfo, Armando, Eduardo, and he can let himself slip into sleep feeling he's all of them to her, he fulfills all their roles. Except that all is equal to none, and she keeps on reciting even after she knows he's asleep, while playing with the listless, sad remains of the wonder of him. She recites names, exercising her memory with some delight.[66]

The state of equation—the neutral place where "all is equal to none"—holds two contradictory valences, each embedded in the other: first, the dictatorial presence which co-opts all roles, and second, the abolishment of that presence into nullity. The possibility is hinted at that the phallic dictatorship might peter out, one might say, into nothing more than its "listless, sad remains," precisely because it is so cocksure. Valenzuela here captures the longing of the post-Process Argentine "political culture" to use its hiatus into skepticism as a site of renewal, rather than as a slide into sheer pessimism. My attempt in characterizing post-Process Argentina as skeptical is not by any means to suggest that stasis has paralyzed the possibility of radical politics with any kind of finality. Rather, I mean to acknowledge that the Argentine dictatorship still has a hold on the social imagination and suggest that the knowledge of that fact, to a significant degree, tempers the brittle euphoria occasioned by the return to partisan politics. Hence the ambiguity in Valenzuela's portrayal, up to the very last sentence, of Laura's process of "liberation" from seclusion.

At a later stage on the way to this return, by degrees, from the zero degree, Laura vacillates between the desire to recuperate the "secret" of her existence and the desire to be bathed in forgetfulness. "What is being forbidden? Where does fear end, where does the need to know begin, or viceversa? The price of knowing the secret is death . . . Wanting, not wanting to know. Wanting and not wanting to be, at the same time."[67] Even when the game is up and the Colonel, before fleeing, shows her the still-loaded gun with which she tried to assassinate him and recounts to her the details of her torture and forced seclusion, to make her "pop out of your sweet little dream," she resists the revelation of this secret. The vehemence of that resistance, in reaction to the overwhelming reality of the facts of her former existence as they rush into the void of her mind, signals the imminence of her active return to the world of memory.

In "The Revelation," he tells her in a final burst of fury that his counter-strategy to her political hatred of him was to "force you to love me, to depend on me like a newborn baby, I've got my weapons, too." But despite this revelation and his insistence that as of tomorrow she can "walk out, stay, tell everyone, do as you please," she can only reiterate her plea for him to "come on, stay with me. Come on to bed." The precipitous thrust back into memory and society alone does not serve to break the spell of dependence, and Valenzuela moves Laura in the last three sentences to a final and more violent act with her own weapon, the identical weapon that occasioned her retreat in the first place.

> She sees his back move away and feels like the fog is beginning to clear. She starts to understand a few things—what that black instrument is for, that thing he calls a gun.
> She lifts it and aims.[68]

This reluctant re-enactment of the original, intended crime of political assassination remains fraught with ambiguity—an ambiguity certainly reinforced by the depressing contexts in which the murders in the other stories of the book *Other Weapons* take place. Laura's having begun to "understand a few things" might suggest that her act of violence will catapult her back into a clarity of understanding and somehow begin to resolve the difficulties of the social amnesia in which she has been trapped. But the reluctance with which she arrives at this step and the cyclical and inconclusive nature of the story, as well as its title and its tone, seem wholly dissonant with an optimistic conclusion of that kind. It is not for mere dramatic effect that Valenzuela truncates "Other Weapons" at the very moment Laura takes aim. The recovery of the inhabitants of Argentina from the social amnesia imposed under the Process does require the recovery of memory and will doubtless, as it already has, lead to further violence. But the definitive vindication of Argentines remains contingent on the invention of other political weapons.

The frustrating search for a cultural weaponry adequate to the rumored demise of left politics has been equally intense, if more diffuse, north of the border. Contemporary fiction criticism in the U.S. seems as anxious to find its revolutionary as Emerson was to find his poet. The more easily dismissed forms of attempt could include the oft-reproduced photographs, under literary auspices, of William Burroughs brandishing various pistols, like a more gangsterish version of the images of Che Guevara that still adorn taxi cabs (along-side miniature icons of the Virgin Mary) throughout Latin America today. The U.S. vogue in revolutionary pop literati includes accounts such as the abomination of a Burroughs biography entitled *Literary Outlaw: The Life and Times of William S. Burroughs*, in which Burroughs is exalted as a literary bad boy, a deranged cross between Arthur Rimbaud and Johnny Cash. Kathy Acker, too, has been enshrined as a cultural outlaw, a punk queen, by a New York "intelligentsia" as much enamoured of her tattoos, her body-building, and the fact that she worked for a time as a stripper in sex shows as it is of the visceral shock of her prose. I won't linger over these forgettable facets of the two authors' respective writing careers except to say that both "outlaws," Acker and Burroughs, have remained conspicuously distant from any public engagement with political radicalism.

Even were this not the case, the iconic subversive status they have attained through the respective public images they have cultivated would seem to have closest affinities with the Yippie type of "lifestyle" counterculturalism professed by Jerry Rubin in his heyday. In his coyly titled *Growing (Up) at Thirty-Seven*, Rubin's effortless transition from sixties radical to other forms of "life experience" speaks for itself. "We activists of the sixties lost touch with ourselves," he proclaims in the name of the aggregate. His antidote for the seventies comes in the form of an inane cultural dilettantism, which he sees as a logical outgrowth of his early personal journey through radical consciousness. "In five years, from 1971 to 1975, I directly experienced est, gestalt therapy, bioenergetics, rolfing, massage, jogging, health foods, tai chi, Esalen, hypnotism, modern dance, meditation, Silva Mind Control, Arica, acupuncture, sex therapy, Reichian therapy, and More House—a smorgasbord course in New Consciousness."[69] The limitations of this brand of "radicalism" are fairly obvious and well documented, and I won't rehearse them here.

Yet both Acker and Burroughs have been held up as radicals on other, more sophisticated grounds that have little or nothing to do with their public personae —namely, their fiction and their writing methods. The claims made for these methods and their revolutionary effects on consciousness are more intricate but just as open to question. Acker and Burroughs, it is true, savagely critique a crippling capitalist culture. And their writing methods do struggle with the stranglehold of consumer society on consciousness. But they, in ways similar to Borges and Valenzuela and even more starkly, end up constructing a "third mind" as a temporary but not really satisfactory refuge of radical skepticism in a dystopian maelstrom. The only real breakthrough possible in their fiction is the breakthrough to a zero degree of consciousness.

Robin Lydenberg's claim in "Beyond Good and Evil: 'How To' Read *Naked Lunch*" that Burroughs' "radical aesthetics of silence" frees him from the moral duality of Western metaphysics seems to me grossly overstated. He says that Burroughs rejects "allegory and moral satire" and instead "lay[s] bare the abstract mechanisms by which metaphor and morality insinuate themselves into our thinking," thereby "throw[ing] the reader into a horizontal world of meaning and materiality."[70] But both Acker and Burroughs elide semiotic structures with metaphorical and metaphysical states. Lydenberg is certainly correct in claiming that "Burroughs' purpose is not to incite reform;" but, as I will detail, what Burroughs' (like Acker's) "horizontal" constructs offer instead are the retreat into a state of radical skepticism.

Ecstatically dubbing Acker a "literary criminal," Larry McCaffery, in a vein similar to Lydenberg's, makes overtly radical claims for Acker's fiction, availing himself of the rhetoric of revolutionary politics. Her chief interest, according to him, lies in

> developing a literary aesthetic capable of rendering a radical, brutally honest exploration of female identity, role-playing, and sexuality—and of the ways these relate to wider social, political, and linguistic structures. . . . [Her] deliberately crude, violent, obscene, disjointed . . . methods are designed to force a confrontation between readers and *all* conventions (literary and otherwise), to shock them out of their complacent acceptance of hierarchies, received traditions, meanings, stable identities.[71]

What Acker actually offers, in lieu of this confrontation, is an apocalyptic account of the "radical" splintering of female sexual identity, time and again, against the reinforced wall of those "social, political, and linguistic structures." Acker's method of studied unoriginality is a last-ditch attempt to salvage feminine identity, paradoxically by succumbing to "convention." She is a transvestite Pierre Menard, garishly clothed in the deliberately unconvincing, shoddy conventions and trappings of femininity. The question lingers, however, whether her deliberately haphazard jettisoning of originality (as opposed to the conscious reappropriations and "plagiaristic" recraftings of Borges, Piglia, and Benjamin, for instance) doesn't perhaps make her fiction, in the end, too inchoate to accomplish its darkly satirical aims.

Acker's 1986 novel *Don Quixote* seems to come into secondary being in the wake of Elizabeth Hardwick's reflection, in a contemporary social sphere hyper-conscious of its own failings and diminishment, on the eclipse of the possibility of morally unified character for fiction:

> Awareness turns contrivance into a self-conscious jest. But without it the novelist is hard-put to produce what everyone insists on—a novel. It is easy to imagine that all possibilities are open, that it is only the medium and not life itself that destroys the branches one by one. Caprice, fashion, exhaustion, indulgence: these are what the novelist who has not produced a circular action of motive and resolution is accused of. Meanwhile he looks about, squinting, and he sees the self-parodying mirror and this is his present, now, in its clothes, makeup, with its dialogue, library of books read, his words, his memory of old spy stories, films, baseball scores, murders, revolutionaries, of *Don Quixote* to be rewritten.[72]

The malaise one detects in Acker's fiction is indeed largely about "life itself," and her struggle is to find a medium adequate to that malaise. For all her surface unconventionalities, she opts to work within the venerable and hallowed conventions of parody and moral satire. The self-parodying contrivance that Hardwick speaks of seems characteristic of the anxieties of the modern epoch, with the literature of caprice and exhaustion (that spoken of by Barth and Sontag) being only its most recent incarnation. In this respect, Acker is of a piece with the writers of her age. In *The Parodistic Episteme*, Margaret Rose employs parody as the defining term of modern identity. Discussing both Cervantes' *Don Quixote* and Borges' rewriting of it, she observes that "so many parodies—such as Borges' admired *Don Quixote*—can be described as having played a role not only in changing the course of literary history, but [as] the episteme of their age."[73]

Citing Foucault's analysis of *Don Quixote* as a landmark of transition into modernity, Rose remarks how Cervantes' novel "shows the negative aspect of the Renaissance world in which writing no longer represents the world, but leads to the searches for identities which must necessarily end in absurdity, and so, also to lead to the criticism of [Renaissance] discourse. Parody—through carrying out this criticism through a new form of discourse—shows how the latter may be the carrier of both its own transformation, and dialetical continuation." This ability of parody to renew "discourse" is, she says, what gives it a "broader historical function . . . in times of epistemological crisis."[74] One can easily see in this description of the function of parody yet another version of the cultural rhetoric of entropy, silence, and the literature of exhaustion. Parody is here set forth as a source of artistic and social renewal, and this dilemma is one that even Acker, in her novel of knight-errancy, has girded her loins to contend with.

The remark of Hardwick above goes a good ways toward defining Rose's "epistemological" crisis in twentieth-century terms, and I have tried to suggest that Borges' understated parody, in his particular time and context of 1930s Argentina, served estimably in the transformation and dialetical continuation of the discourse opposed to Argentine nationalism. It remains open to question, however, to what extent Acker's "revolutionary" rewriting of *Don Quixote* possesses that sort of dialectical and transformative power. Her style of parody—if one can speak of a style at all—is, to begin with, decidedly at odds with McCaffery's claim about the "liberating feel of Acker's fiction because she is affirming a freedom to say and be anything her imagination can invent or plagiarize."[75]

As I have already suggested, Acker is bound by a specific set of literary conventions, ones she doesn't always seem completely cognizant of. Rather than "liberation," she offers a mournful travesty that feels less than fully in command of its own reckless impulses. Her aesthetic is one of desperate evasions, decked out in the gay apparel and funereal accouterments of Hardwick's "books read" and the "self-conscious jest."

The pervasive and sometimes nondescript flatness of Acker's *Don Quixote*, however, does not entirely belie a calculated, even earnest, deliberation on her part. Acker gives some insight into her method of constructing her female Quixote's madness early on in the novel, in a brief section baldly titled "Another Insert":

> The Arabs (in their culture) have no (concept of) originality.
> That is, culture. They write by cutting chunks out of all-ready
> written texts and in other ways defacing traditions: changing
> important names into silly ones, making dirty jokes out of mat
> ters that should be of the utmost importance to us such as
> nuclear warfare.[76]

She is a grave woman, one without much mercurial wit, yet still an advocate of Mercutial wit. When faced with destruction, she rails against the foundational "traditions" of power. Yet as in Mercutio's grave case, she is aware, for all her offhandedness in the face of calamity, that bad jokes alone will not resuscitate the dead. Nor will the patched-together protagonist's "liberation" into what Larry McCaffery calls "visionary flights into a realm of pure madness," in and of itself, negate the social madness which engendered those flights.[77] *Don Quixote* begins in an abortion clinic, where the protagonist and patient, in a parodic naming ceremony, is "delivered" into her new name and identity (prerequisites for what she calls her "Grail quest") by the paradoxical and highly ambiguous gesture of having an abortion. The opening sentences signal the yearning toward the redemptive power of love—but also acknowledge the pessimistic underpinnings of, and severe constraints on, Don Quixote's "abortive" quest.

> When she was finally crazy because she was about to have an abortion, she conceived of the most insane idea that any woman can think of. Which is to love. . . . She would love another person. By loving another person, she would right every manner of political, social, and individual wrong: she would put herself in those situations so perilous the glory of her name would resound. The abortion was about to take place.
> From her neck to her knees she wore pale or puke green paper. This was her armor. She had chosen it especially, for she knew that this world's conditions are so rough for any single person, even a rich person, that person has to make do with what she can find: this's no world for idealism. Example: the green paper would tear as soon as the abortion began.[78]

The preoccupation of Acker with "righting" political and social wrong does not confine itself to that plane of "writing"—self-referential and structuralist—that McCaffery and Lydenberg are eager to claim as the exclusive site of artistic radicalism and which they oppose to metaphoristic moral allegory. The plane of radical writing is claimed to be metonymically textual (Lydenberg calls it a "horizontal world of meaning and materiality"; McCaffery calls it a "lexical space of free play"), but even this claim turns out to be, as in the case of Barthes, *metaphorically* social. Acker is no exception. Her partial reliance on overt metaphorizing and moral, allegorical satire is patent in the above opening passage. A critical exaggeration of her "metonymical" tendencies seems strange in light of it. Moral feeling and moral skepticism in Acker's fiction dovetail with the self-conscious creation of a semiotic universe; neutrality and the zero degree have distinct emotional overtones. In this case, she stages a lament. Passages such as the abortion scene, where her thematizing is most traditional and straightforward, are ironically those in which Acker comes closest to being articulate about the subjects that appear to matter to her the most.

To a limited extent, Acker recognizes herself in Hardwick's self-parodying mirror of sheer actuality, but even more, I am suggesting, she is plagued by uncertainty about whether "it is only the medium and not life itself that destroys the branches one by one." A sober assessment of Acker's writing and of its would-be transformative power must regard her first and foremost as a moralist manqué. An updated version of Hardwick's lament about the disappearance of morally unified character appears in the second section of *Don Quixote*, when two women are conversing about their disappointments not only in love but in writing and reading. "Who, then, 're you reading now?" one asks. The other complains, "I have a theory we're at the end of a generation. Semiotics's no longer applicable. At the moment there's nothing."[79] A credible set of guiding ideals, like a good man, is hard to find. Elegiac impulses, under the rubric of the parodic episteme, are necessarily displaced onto semiotics, for lack of a more suitable object.

This ambivalent writerly attitude is displayed in the punning, self-conscious definition of the nature of the writing task when the nameless female protagonist, en route to becoming Don Quixote, mounts the Rocinante/wheelchair that is to take her to the operating room. "It was dying. It had once been a hack . . . the same as all the hacks on grub street. . . . Her wheeling-bed's name was 'Hack-kneed' or 'Hackneyed,' meaning 'once a hack' or 'always a hack' or 'a writer' or 'an attempt to have an identity that always fails.' "[80] The multiple literal and metaphorical valences of *hack*—cab, horse, penny-dreadful writer, the life about to be chopped out of her body, personal failure—are asserted, given emotional weight, and then just as quickly dissected, themselves "hacked" to bits. Acker freely evokes the pain of personal and social trauma, but the evocative power of the narrator's own metaphors seems spent to her, second-hand, even as she utters them. She realizes that the elaboration of chilling, poignant metaphors will fall short of capturing the degradation of the "attempt to have an identity which always fails" that she wishes to represent. Instead, she opts for a deliberately degraded, "hackneyed" language as the only serviceable one. Under the pressure of these conflicting and attenuating impulses, she, like her author, has no choice but to write like a hack.

Acker's protagonist sets herself to a quixotic quest in a "borrowed" language, an undertaking futile from the very beginning. The abortive quest for language and the abortive quest for love complement one another. In a manner equivalent to Pierre Menard's (though in fundamental ways dissimilar to his), Acker's Don Quixote wishes to affirm and reform the present, to reject an essentialized culture and tradition, by plagiarizing and ultimately subverting Cervantes' master text. But unlike Menard's, her language really is borrowed; she believes, with fatal certitude, that she is barred a priori by her gender from the possibility of writing the *Quixote* while remaining herself. Her "self," as far as she is concerned, does not exist. As a female plagiarist of an oppressive tradition, it would never occur to her to describe Menard's initial, rejected course of action as "easy": the attempt to "forget the history of Europe between the years 1602 and 1918; *be* Miguel de Cervantes." From her perspective, it is the luxury and prerogative of the male writer to dispense casually with three centuries of a tradition he has already mastered and with which he can identify wholly (or not, as he chooses). The genealogy that Menard dismisses out of hand has an alienating stranglehold on Acker's female Don Quixote, preventing her from forming an identity as a basis from which to appropriate wholesale (and thereby annihilate) the original *Quixote*.

These gender-bound facts become clear in a vignette from the novel's first section entitled "History and Women." In it, Don Quixote reflects that her quest for love is frustrated by a contradiction of her gender: "She was both a woman therefore she couldn't feel love and a knight in search of Love. . . . She could solve this problem only by becoming partly male." This expedient abdication of her feminine identity leads her to undertake a broader, masculine historical perspective of her personal situation, to attempt the long view, to seize the problem in its entirety, and to formulate more properly philosophical questions: "What was a woman? Was a woman different from a man? . . . Of course I'm not interested in personal identity. I mean: what is it to be female?"

These broader speculations, in their turn, cause her to hit on the identical passage about history and time, from *Don Quixote*, that the narrator of "Pierre Menard" reproduces. Acker's Quixote, tellingly, reproduces Cervantes' "rhetorical praise of history" not identically but with a difference. "If history, the enemy of time, is the mother of truth, the history of women must define female identity." Wishing to affirm her identity in the sweeping manner of her male counterpart, she tries to apprehend the "mother of truth" in its entirety and draw therefrom the pertinent lessons for herself. Perhaps there is another tradition, one written by women, parallel to Menard's. If so, she could do with it what Menard has done with his. In the process of trying to locate that counter-tradition, she plucks from *Don Quixote* a passage from an Arab text written by a chronicler who is one of the characters in Cervantes' novel: "Cid Hamete Benengeli, a man."

At this point, the "abortive" failure inherent in her pose of masculine philosophizing, on account of her gender, begins to emerge. Benengeli's book begins with the proclamation that "'the history of women is that of degradation and suffering' ('True,' she said to herself, rubbing her wounded cunt.)" Here, finally if depressingly, is a premise she can identify with! The irony builds as she continues to recite the "appropriated" text and to realize her absolute alienation from its second major premise. Benengeli's text states that "history shows us that no woman nor any other person has to endure anything: a woman has the power to choose to be a king and a tyrant." As examples, the text cites how Amadia, the first woman recorded by human history, "fell into the clutches of her mortal enemy, Arcalus. Arcalus made her prisoner. Then he stuck two knives into her thigh flesh. Then he bound her to a pillar in his court-yard" and "lashed her body two hundred times with his horse's reins solely for her own pleasure." Her own pleasure? Other atrocities such as these, Acker's Don Quixote says, were recorded by "a certain female chronicler, anonymous or dead as women in those days had to be."[81]

By now, Don Quixote has fully convinced herself that as a woman, given the dubious quality of these textual assurances and exemplifications of a woman's "power to choose," she cannot appropriate wholesale—not even as a plagiarist—a hostile, misogynistic tradition that, as far as she can see, remains ruthlessly bent on her punishment and negation. No less can she simply dismiss this "mother of truth," since it alone has served to define her female identity, albeit negatively and in terms of female degradation. The only alternative left to her is to plagiarize from that masculine tradition piecemeal, revising and defacing it as best (or rather, as worst) she can. She passes from the position of the "dead or anonymous" female scribe of the male tradition's degradation of woman to the "neutral" state of plagiarism, which rejects the foundational aspects of this tradition. The second section of *Don Quixote* begins with this incipit: "Being dead, Don Quixote could no longer speak. Being born into and part of a male world, she had no speech of her own. All she could do was read male texts which weren't hers."[82] But both Acker and her protagonist seem at a loss in the book's second half about what to do with this bleak insight, other than to assert it. However hypothetically resonant with "subversive" potential, the incipit, by the time one finishes *Don Quixote*, reads like an epitaph.

The second section, chronicling Don Quixote's passage from absolute "deadness" to the spurious refuge of non-originality, consists of Acker's rewritten pastiche of a promiscuous mélange of texts. Douglas Shields Dix identifies some of them: "Andrei Biely's *Petersburg* (and the poems of Catullus), Giuseppe di Lampedusa's *The Leopard*, Godzilla movies, Frank Wedekind's Lulu plays."[83] Others include Shakespeare, George Bernard Shaw, Rigoberto López (the slayer of Somoza), General Smedley D. Butler, prose from an amendment to the Monroe Doctrine, Milton. Yet only a very attenuated pleasure can be had, or importance attached, to the tracking down or "discovery" of the individual sources of these references. In many cases, Acker herself supplies the source (text 4, for instance, is baldly entitled "Wedekind's Words"). At other times, it is difficult to perceive at all where the words in question might have come from or how they have been changed. Acker makes liberal use of allusions and parodic techniques, but a reader never receives anything near the insight yielded by the subtle allusiveness of a Yeats or the brilliant mythical parody and rigorous experimentation of a Joyce. As Ellen Friedman puts it, "her work does not feel quite 'literary' . . . Her surfaces are almost anti-literary, despite their allusiveness."[84]

Therein lies both Acker's modest achievement and her limitation. Friedman's comment about Acker's literary surfaces is decidedly an understatement. The abovementioned assertion about writing and feminine identity made in the epigraph to part 2 of Acker's novel is of keen interest as a *proposition,* a speculative possibility, but the often tedious pages that follow it are rarely speculative in their own right, not even in "anti-philosophical" fashion. Her failure to make good on the possibilities of imaginative ideation she sets up in her portentous literary premises sets her apart not only from Borges but also from feminist writers such as Howe, Schmid, and Davis, who skillfully travesty the epistolary genre and the drama of psychoanalysis to their own specific and clearly discernible ends.

Acker, on the other hand, largely settles for copping an attitude. Richard Walsh, meaning to praise Acker, says, "At first sight, Acker's *Quixote* owes little to Cervantes' original . . . Her use of Cervantes . . . is at one remove."[85] But there are many ways of being "at a remove" from an author, and Acker too often chooses to use Cervantes' source text as a mere evocative occasion, something in the manner of how Gordon Lish makes use of Peru in his novel. A reader is left with Acker's professed, somewhat grandiose initial literary conceits, followed by a mass of ostensibly illustrative but apparently unrelated text, and asked to reconcile the disjunction.

In his book on the modern satiric grotesque, a tendency of which Acker is decidedly a part, John Clark makes a useful distinction when he reminds us that the seeming "clutter and disarray" of satiric form "results from the fact that the satiric artist renders an 'imitation' of the excessive, the imperfect, and the negative." And, says Clark, the satiric artist "accomplishes these imitations of the defective with a simulated naiveté that requires, in fact, considerable artistry."[86] For someone who has built her career on flamboyant plagiarism, Acker frequently displays only the sketchiest understanding of the idea of imitation, and one suspects that her naivete, in certain regards, may be lacking in simulation. Most often, Acker seems to find the authenticity that she yearns for in the form of literary excess.

Yet there is an undeniable modicum of calculation in her fiction. The non-dimensional dimension of her writing, at its most provocative, produces something of a deliberately flat and anti-climactic effect. But unlike Borges' tightly wrought plagiaristic parables, with their symmetrical structures and neat pseudo-philosophical formulations, Acker's brand of plagiarism really *is* sprawling, borrowed, and largely haphazard and ragged. The third portion of the novel even includes a section entitled "Intrusion of a Badly Written Section" (a judgement which may have already crossed the reader's mind once or twice well before page 190, on which the "badly written" portion is said to begin). "Each thing had no meaning, other than itself, or meant nothing. The room was existing surfaces, as TV." Back-cover blurbs, never noted for their coherent relation to the books they refer to, seem especially inappropriate in Acker's case. One of several gracing *Don Quixote*'s back cover describes her as having "an unmistakable voice that's brash, feisty, sexy, smart."

But Don Quixote, with her "wounded cunt," is smarting rather than smart. In contrast to the phallic tradition she defaces, her intellectual and philosophical concepts, which proliferate throughout, often simply dissipate. If one goes to Acker's novel with the whetted expectation of a dialectical or symbiotic recasting of *Don Quixote* into a contemporary or intermediate idiom, the result is bound to be disappointment, even dismay. One really need not have read the "original" novel, nor in fact any of the other "original" texts, to be a party to her brand of plagiarism.

To say so is not to dismiss the novel outright but to recognize its modality and the limitations it is subject to because of that modality. There is a certain pleasure to be had in her particular trashing approach to artistic and social dilemmas, but the pleasure is fairly predictable and short-lived. And yet, there is, all the same, an unmistakable drift to her seemingly aimless drifting. The non-epic quest is to encounter, through plagiarism, a space of no allegiance. As Don

Quixote puts it in her "First Battle against America": "I will be a mercenary . . . For what other kind of soldier is there who isn't an owner, even of ideas? I don't own anything."[87] This mercenary stance finds its expression both in Acker's process-oriented writing and in her thematizing of the psychic and social punishments—associated with the withholding of female identity and the frustrated, quixotic quest for "love"—that drive a woman to this necessary borrowing. In explaining the genesis and method of *Don Quixote*, in an interview with Friedman, Acker makes explicit this elision between the textual and the social.

> What I was interested in was what happens when you just copy something, without any reason . . . it was the simple fact of copying that fascinated me. . . . I came to plagiarism from another point of view, from exploring schizophrenia and identity, and I wanted to see what pure plagiarism would look like, mainly because I didn't understand my fascination with it. I picked up Don Quixote as a subject really by chance. . . . I wrote the second part of *Don Quixote* first by rewriting texts . . . Then I actually had an abortion. While I was waiting to have the abortion, I was reading *Don Quixote*. Because I couldn't think, I just started copying *Don Quixote*. Then I had all these pieces and I thought about how they fit together. I realized that *Don Quixote*, more than any of my other books, is about appropriating male texts and that the middle part is very much about trying to find your voice as a woman.[88]

This discussion of the personal circumstances of her abortion is not of interest simply as a biographical or psychological detail. In her remarks, one can see how Acker forges the "chance" confluence of personal trauma and its casual companion text into a logic of necessity. Acker's claims to be interested in copying "without any reason" and to have been reading *Don Quixote* "really by chance," while true in the most immediate sense, do not belie the inexorability of the social logic which draws those disparate elements together. *Don Quixote* in a profound sense explains the fact of her abortion, just as her abortion begins to illuminate for her the inexplicable "fascination" she feels with plagiarism. Her remarks about the novel's genesis bring to mind the refuge within nullity sought by Tardewski in Piglia's *Artificial Respiration*. But in Acker's *Don Quixote*, one seldom encounters the plagiaristic nuance that Tardewski begins to articulate when, after his personal debacle and the cultural obliteration of his Polish homeland, he takes a job as a backwater bank clerk and begins to copy out verbatim the Spanish translation of his own text, resolving "not to write anything I could think of myself, nothing mine, no ideas of my own."

In an apparently similar fashion, Acker's protagonist, "being born into and part of a male world . . . had no speech of her own." Yet despite the apparent equivalencies between her situation and Tardewski's, as well as the all-important differences, her process of dispossession as a woman offers a protracted exercise in mechanical textual appropriation. Though Walsh, like Larry McCaffery, wishes to characterize Acker as "radical," he allows as how "her plagiarism does not engage the original texts directly or coherently enough to constitute a critique of their perpetuation of 'harmful stereotypes of women.' "[89] In the third part of the novel, instead of relying on teasing out the methodical intricacies of plagiarism, she gives her version of womanhood in the shape of androgyny. The attempted passage from femaleness to a metaphorical "neuter" state parallels the writerly passage from dead scribe to neutral plagiarist.

The depiction of this passage takes place largely on the conventional terms of moral satire, especially in its use of the grotesque. Bernard McElroy's characterization of modern grotesque fiction and art provides a roughly accurate characterization of Acker's *Don Quixote* as well. He says that the "pervasive effect of . . . animalism and corporeal degradation in grotesque art is to direct our attention to the undignified, perilous, even gross physicality of existence, and to emphasize it by exaggeration, distortion, or unexpected combination."[90] McElroy further remarks that "literature of the modern grotesque usually focuses on the struggle between the self and . . . a hostile environment, and the most common theme . . . is dominance and submission."[91]

Much of Acker's novel answers to that description, consisting of relentless permutations of dependent, violent, excessive, animalistic, sadomasochistic relations, the fruit of a social logic in which compulsory heterosexuality, coupled with intense misogyny, is carried to its furthest degree. In a portion entitled "Heterosexuality," Don Quixote's sidekick, an anthropomorphized dog (a "bitch," of course) alternately named Saint Simeon and Villebranche, explicates both the urgency and the ultimate failure of attempted flights away from compulsory heterosexuality into androgyny, when she recounts to Don Quixote her affair with an androgyne named De Franville. The bitch, Villebranche, refers to herself in the third person, since she has no identity of her own. Her life has consisted of constant rejection as a woman, and thus she envies De Franville, whose gender is ambiguous. Because the dog is still female, therefore "oversexed," she explains the allure that the androgynous position holds for her and for others in conventional terms, while noting the difference in the "neuter" attitude of the androgyne toward others:

> Both men and women adored this creature who, by his/her sexual void, like a magnet, attracted mostly those whose sexual desires were the fiercest. He/She seemed to be magnificently sexual. For De Franville, wanting a self he/she could love, needed with a desperation that seemed sexual . . . He/She, being nothing, was incapable of anything including sexuality.[92]

Even this neuter position is untenable, since De Franville's sexual "void," though expressed as an actual need for identity, is incorrectly perceived by both sexes as doubly sexual and temptingly virginal. Androgyny's failure lies in its forced reinsertion into the dynamic of heterosexuality. Despite the ruthlessness of De Franville and the obvious unhappiness underlying it, Villebranche admires his/her description of his/her unattainability.

> I happen to be unreachable because everybody wants me and I don't want anybody. Because my father kept trying to control me brutally, I became untouchable. I will not be a male like my father. Moreover, I am what I am not, for I have to control people, especially lovers, in order to ensure they don't get too close to me and I despise control. For this reason, I can't abide sexuality. At the same time, I despise the women I control who, like my mother who put up with my brutal father, are weak. I can be with a woman only in my thoughts. My sexuality, fixed or inert, is dead, therefore beautiful.[93]

This bleak alternative approach to being "dead" is about as close to affirmation as Acker comes in this "brash, feisty, sexy, smart" novel. The wish for an alternate space of retreat and identity is voiced but never comes into being, not even as a sustained textual fantasy. Naomi Jacobs' assertion of the subversions that Acker's "plagiarized self" might be capable of certainly has faint echoes in *Don Quixote*, but Jacobs' claim that fixed or dead selves are eluded in Acker's prose requires too sanguine a leap of faith on the reader's part and seems at odds with the tenor of the above passage. Jacobs says that "only a fixed and thus dead self is recognizable; only a recognizable self is useful, locatable, controllable . . . Complete lack of definition is nothingness; but it is also perfect potentiality, complete freedom to redefine, to experiment, what Cixous has called 'permanent escapade.' "[94]

It is true that Acker is capable of cracking jokes at the crack of doom, as when she has the bitch's Job-like lamentation about the unending torments of women take this deadpan turn: "The next question about my sexuality is: Why am I lower than Jesus Christ?" But the overwhelming drift of the lamentation as a whole seems very un-Cixousian in its abhorrence of the "permanent escapade": "Unlike Jesus Christ, I can't find any joy in wanting to not exist or in suffering."[95] The gambit of plagiarism as identity seems, finally, to offer as high a potential for regression into nothingness as do the social forces to which it opposes itself.

This regression into nothingness, which is anything but escapade, finds its most precise expression in the structure of certain scenes, in the form of repetition. It is in these isolated cases that Acker's largely unimaginative and mechanical notion of plagiarism, almost by serendipity, seems suddenly suited to her aims. This conjuncture is most apt to occur when she is working squarely within the tradition of the satiric grotesque, and it is because of that continuity with tradition, rather than any innovation on Acker's part, that she is sometimes able to depict the extreme vicissitudes of female sexuality within patriarchy with a sort of numbing accuracy.

Clark comments on a double-edged, potentially troublesome aspect of form in the satiric grotesque. He observes that authors who employ it are fond of "inserting a clutter of seemingly mindless repetitions in their narratives, arranging insidious circularities in their storylines. In fact, the most deplorable kind of plotting . . . is the kind that engineers duplication, redundancy, reiteration. . . . This might seem comic and amusing at first, but at its worst it suggests a hellish repetition."[96] Despite being plagued by this tendency, Acker on occasion matches the hellishness of her repetition to the hellish collective psyche of her characters. Near the end of the novel, the bitch recounts to Don Quixote a didactic sexual initiation rite she was made to participate in at the girls' school where she received her education. The purpose of the rite, according to her teacher, is to learn to resist those forms of education that "rather than teaching the child to know who she is or to know, dictate to the child who she is. Thus obfuscate any act of knowledge." The teacher proposes that to counter this tendency, "we must react against our opinions; we must act exactly in those ways of which we don't approve." The taboo action proposed is the bitch's acquiescence in an all-female orgy, participated in by students and teachers, the idea being that a return to the immediacy of sensory experience—including whips and leather bonds—followed by analysis of that experience will break through the "bonds" of masculine education.

The failure of this visceral approach, of moving beyond the logic of degradation by assuming its parodic, violent physical trappings, is signaled in the discussion leading up to the sadistic sexual encounter. Through the simple stylistic ploy of repetition, Acker reaches new plagiaristic heights. Rather than defacing male texts, the participants begin the illusory "breakthrough" to the zero degree of consciousness by plagiarizing verbatim their own statements as they utter them. This regressive plagiarism thus becomes a solipsistic nightmare, rather than a liberating taboo mode of thought. The exchange between the teacher Delbène and the doubting bitch is rendered in this way:

Delbène said: "We must do what we consider crimes in order to break down our destructive education."
"But *crimes* are evil because they're human acts by which humans hurt other humans."
"But *crimes* are evil because they're human acts by which humans hurt other humans."
"But *crimes* are evil because they're human acts by which humans hurt other humans."
"A good reply," answered my teacher, "according to the world."
"A good reply," answered my teacher, "according to the world."
"A good reply," answered my teacher, "according to the world."
"Wrong," my teacher thundered, "for any answer that seems to be the correct answer denies this world whose nature is chance and unreliability. There is no correct answer."
"Wrong," my teacher thundered, "for any answer that seems to be the correct answer denies this world whose nature is chance and unreliability. There is no correct answer."
"Wrong," my teacher thundered, "for any answer that seems to be the correct answer denies this world whose nature is chance and unreliability. There is no correct answer."[97]

The dog, still lusting after a satisfactory answer, is instructed to take off her clothes, so that she can arrive at the body—the "first ground of knowledge." She begins to experience the ecstasy of "a finger stuck into my asshole. A dildo thrust into my asshole and a dildo thrust into my cunt. Both dildos squirted liquid into me which

I saw was white." She comes violently and is asked by the perpetrators to judge which orifice has caused her more excitement. When she replies that her intense excitement has blurred her ability to judge, the response of one of the participants, with its implications of ad infinitum and ad nauseam, indicates the abject failure of the endlessly repetitive, plagiaristic attempt to achieve the zero degree "beyond" thought by inhabiting the self-identical "pure" realm of the senses.

> Volmar said, "That thought is barely the beginning of thought. You must perceive exactly what it is. We will do it all over again so you can try to begin to perceive just what is."
> Volmar said, "That thought is barely the beginning of thought. You must perceive exactly what it is. We will do it all over again so you can try to begin to perceive just what is."
> Volmar said, "That thought is barely the beginning of thought. You must perceive exactly what it is. We will do it all over again so you can try to begin to perceive just what is."
> Volmar said, "That thought is barely the beginning of thought. You must perceive exactly what it is. We will do it all over again so you can try to begin to perceive just what is."[98]

Rather than self, she is offered the selfsame degradation, to be repeated as necessary. Delbène grandiosely claims that she is offering the bitch an antidote to "the overlays of culture in Europe, culminating in a decayed seaside hotel whose walls peel away from themselves into the literature they think is supporting them." But this "teacher," though she no longer plagiarizes (or so she says) the European literary tradition that has resulted in those cultural overlays, instead simply plagiarizes herself—to no end. The exacting price of this "liberation" is revealed in the way that the bitch internalizes the lesson. She in her turn immediately degrades another, younger student named Laure whom she desires, referring to her as, among other endearments, "twat, tart-face, fish-teats, vomit bag" and then replicating a parodic, equally dictatorial version of that social logic which insists on "dictating to the child who she is." The bitch tells Laure that

> I'll whip you by breaking you down by breaking through your virginity or identity. As soon as you're no longer a virgin, you're going to leak. You'll keep on leaking so you won't be able to retain any more of their teachings.[99]

But this grotesque and brutal revolutionary leakage of the logic and traditions of patriarchy appears to have fatal consequences. In the midst of being sexually violated with a rod by the bitch, Laure sums up the circular outcome of this supposed passage from the status of dead scribe to author of a new consciousness: "This's the true state of female human knowledge . . . I'm going to die." In the aftermath of this anecdote, Acker's Don Quixote makes a final, brief, somewhat feeble and unconvincing attempt at suggesting belief in an eternal present as a way out of the parallel textual and sexual hells of patriarchy and *écriture féminine*. Retorting that the dog's lengthy tale "all took place in the past. It's all past and gone," she exhorts her companion to realize that "we have to decide about the present. You and I. I mean: what we're going to do now." But the dubious affirmation she offers seems to try to split the difference between rational refutation of universal doubt, à la Descartes, and the retreat into regressive plagiarism. "In the beginning of me, I am. Therefore I am."[100] The grail quest for identity, for the zero degree of consciousness, ends in solipsism. Splitting the difference is the same as splitting hairs. Ellen Friedman's assessment of the fundamental pessimism in Acker's fiction seems to me to capture accurately the blatant apocalyptic strain that surfaces in the most compelling portions of *Don Quixote*. Friedman says that

> Acker's questers' searches for identity and a new healing myth lead to silence, death, nothingness, or reentry into the sadomasochism of patriarchal culture. As she said in an interview, "You can't get to a place, to a society, that isn't constructed according to the phallus." The attempts to subvert male texts and thus male culture result in revelation rather than revolution, the path to an alternate site of enunciation blocked by the very forces this path is meant to escape.[101]

In *Don Quixote*, Acker's last-ditch attempt to salvage femininity— as that famous, dead, male author Shakespeare's invention Mercutio might have put it in his dying breath—offers only a stark, plain view of the last ditch.

William Burroughs' fiction offers a resting place scarcely more hospitable. Lydenberg contends that Burroughs' "horizontal" fiction, in *Naked Lunch* and in general, rigorously avoids the moral dualisms that "establish 'word locks' or 'mind locks' which dictate our ways of thinking and feeling, stifling spontaneous life and change." But this view ignores the metaphorical continuity between Burroughs' writing method and his portrayals of the consumeristic society against which his concept of the "third mind" comes into being as a reaction. Throughout his writing life and especially in his later fiction, Burroughs has given as much attention to thematizing social ills as he has to discussion and implementation of non-linear writing methods such as the cut-up.[102] In a 1974 interview, in response to a question about the proportion of cut-up in his books *The Wild Boys* and *Exterminator!*, Burroughs answered, "Small, small. Not more than five percent, if that."[103] Burroughs' attention to method cannot be ignored, but nor is it sufficient evidence for granting him a questionable "revolutionary" status. His concept of the third mind, as I will demonstrate, has all the makings of a moral category and expresses another instance of radical skepticism, in the desire to find an "interzone," a neutral place beyond the grimly comic machinations of a savage, authoritarian society.

This utopian wish—along with an attendant hopelessness—comes through clearly in the story "International Zone," the key piece in Burroughs' provocatively titled volume *Interzone*. This "definitive" *Interzone* (hard cover 1989, paperback 1990), recouping some of his earliest work, serves at present in some ways as the consummate volume of Burroughs, the relentless recycler of his own prose, who has frequently described all his books as one unending book. In a more immediate sense, *Interzone* is an early draft of *Naked Lunch*, the book that brought Burroughs the verbal innovator to worldwide attention.[104] In "International Zone," Burroughs creates a dystopian refuge of neutrality, a hellish, depressing version of a free-market consumer society taken to its ultimate degree of "freedom." In it, one can see thematized the preoccupation with oppressive "mind locks" that led Burroughs to experimentation with the writing methods described by Burroughs and Brion Gysin in their volume *The Third Mind*.

"International Zone" consists of Burroughs' satirical description of Tangier, an outpost of free-market capitalism carried to the nth degree, where the chilly social temperature is decidedly zero degrees.

> A miasma of suspicion and snobbery hangs over the European Quarter of Tangier. Everyone looks you over for the price tag, appraising you like merchandise in terms of immediate practical or prestige advantage. The Boulevard Pasteur is the Fifth Avenue of Tangier. The store clerks tend to be discourteous with you unless you buy something immediately. Inquiries without purchase are coldly and grudgingly answered.[105]

This artificial International Zone, because it represents "pure" capitalism, is even more subject than most consumer societies to the plagues of cyclical prosperity and depression. At present, Tangier seems to have fallen into an economic depression, which is accompanied by a collective psychological depression. The politically reclusive narrator, who cherishes the purity of this inert and neutral retreat as much as he abhors it, retreats even further from the pervasive economic distress into "a fashionable bar, one of the few places that continues prosperous in the present slump." But even in there, the merciless logic of capitalism adheres. Rather than creating oversouls or numina, the consciousness of these inhabitants finds its more palpable expression as sheer commodification. "If a woman sits there long enough with that expression of rich discontent and sourness, a Cadillac simply builds itself around her. A man would probably accrete a Jaguar." The narrator's failed attempt to establish a shred of emotional contact with another patron by starting a conversation is characteristically described in the lingo of commodity exchange: "I . . . allowed my shaky option on his notice to lapse."

Burroughs offers not a study in alternative consciousness but a moral study of the "interzone" as the zero degree of consciousness existing between a rock and a hard place, where the all-too-human wish for asylum can only be expressed as consumer society's all-consuming parody of humanity's deepest desires. His writing acknowledges overtly the metaphorical slippage among moral, financial, and verbal "economies":

The market of psychic exchange is as glutted as the shops. A nightmare feeling of stasis permeates the Socco, like nothing can happen, nothing can change. Conversations disintegrate in cosmic inanity. People sit at the café tables, silent and separate as stones. No other relation than physical closeness is possible. Economic laws, untouched by any human factor, evolve equations of ultimate stasis.[106]

Eric Mottram's comparison between Kafka and Burroughs is apt in illuminating the pessimism in Burroughs' marking out of the emotional coordinates of this in-between, neutral social space. Kafka wrote in a letter, quoted by Mottram, that

capitalism is a system of dependencies, which run from within to without, from without to within, from above to below, from below to above. All is dependent, all stands in chains. Capitalism is a condition of the soul and of the world.

And citing from one of Kafka's diary entries—"I have but very rarely crossed out of this borderland between loneliness and community; I have taken root in it more than in loneliness itself"—Mottram observes that Kafka "might have been describing the melancholy within the border lands . . . in the work of William Burroughs."[107]

Burroughs and Gysin, in *The Third Mind*, describe the methodological equivalent of this borderland, the amalgamating practice of writing by together combining borrowed texts, eschewing the prerogatives of authorial unity and self-sufficiency. "It is not the history of a literary collaboration but rather the complete fusion in a praxis of two subjectivities that metamorphose into a third; it is from this collusion that a new author emerges, an absent third person, invisible and beyond grasp, decoding the silence."[108] This "praxis" is conceived with seeming ebullience as holding the potential for breaking through oppressive notions of the author as "the geometrist who clings to his inspiration as coming from divine inspiration, a mission, or the dictates of language." But a closer look at the specific etymology of the "third mind" reveals a preoccupation with the pervasiveness of the dictates and dictators of language in capitalistic society and suggests conclusions in the spirit of Kafka's description of capitalism's numbing effects. Like Acker, Burroughs undergirds his comic appropriations with grim social appraisals. Even ebullience is expressed in terms of the zero degree, as the radically skeptical wish for "an absent third person, invisible and beyond grasp."

As is the case with many of Burroughs' amalgamations, the concept of the "third mind" derives from a curious but appropriate source, one that reads like a version of "International Zone" as written by Horatio Alger. Burroughs and Gysin name the source of the phrase's derivation as

Burroughs: A book called *Think and Grow Rich*.
Gysin: It says that when you put two minds together . . .
Burroughs: . . . there is always a third mind . . .
Gysin: . . . a third and superior mind . . .
Burroughs: . . . as an unseen collaborator.
Gysin: That is where we picked up the title.[109]

*Think and Grow Rich*, written by Napoleon Hill, a popular and cheery "inspirational" book about the secular religion of making money, sold hundreds of thousands of copies during the fifties and has continued to sell widely ever since, running perhaps into the millions. It has circulated not only among business executives but among white-collar workers such as insurance agents and other salesmen as a kind of bible, the equivalent of books like Lee Iacocca's *Talking Straight,* with the difference that the materialistic idealism expressed in Hill's self-explanatory title openly advocates living a pious "Christian" life as the basis for accumulating massive personal wealth.

Like Burroughs and Gysin, Napoleon Hill engaged in his own collusion and fusion of two subjectivities in his equally popular sequel to *Think and Grow Rich.* Written in collaboration with insurance tycoon W. Clement Stone, "who turned $100 into a multi-million dollar international business organization," *Success through a Positive Mental Attitude* was published only a year after *Naked Lunch.* In a gesture that Burroughs and Gysin would doubtless approve of, Hill and Stone recycle much of the material from Hill's earlier book. Cast in the mold of its predecessor, *Success* on the cover of its first edition bullishly boasts "over 420,000 copies in print." Despite their impressive personal credentials, neither Hill nor Stone wishes to claim as his own the ideas promulgated since the method, not they themselves (inspirational though they are), is responsible for the many triumphs enumerated within the book's covers. Like their experimental counterparts, Hill and Stone have their notions about the merits of derivativeness as a methodology, and they put forth stirring claims about its social effectiveness. These entrepreneurs seem to meet the rather qualified standard that Burroughs and Gysin erect as the aim of their own "collusion": "The negation of the book as such—or at least the representation of that negation." Like Hill and Stone, Burroughs and Gysin actually do accept de facto authorship and are credited unambiguously as co-authors on the cover of *The Third Mind* (even though others, e.g., a contributor named Gérard Georges Lemaire, wrote portions of the book's contents).[110] Their interest lies rather in "representing" the negation of authorship, in using the principle of citation as a working hypothesis. Likewise, the first page of *Success through a Positive Mental Attitude* addresses the reader in these terms:

> When you read this book . . . underscore sentences, quotations, and words that are meaningful to you. Memorize quotations.
> Keep in mind that this is a book to motivate you to action.
>   Abraham Lincoln developed the habit of trying to learn from the books he read. . . . He was able to *relate, assimilate and use them as his own.*[111]

The italic-ridden prose insists here that even Abraham Lincoln did not write books, he only "assimilated" them toward a particular end. As is no doubt obvious, a wide gap nonetheless separates the aims of Burroughs and Gysin from those of Hill and Stone. But that gap cannot merely be described as the a priori assumed "radicalism" of the literati versus the "conservatism" of the businessmen. Nor would it be accurate to say that Burroughs and Gysin appropriate Hill's idea of a "third mind" for the simple and simpleminded exercise of subjecting Hill's book to parodic ridicule. Describing Burroughs as a straightforward parodist seems a drastic diminishment of his writing, and as for his "radicalism"—that is exactly what is in question here. Rather, I would argue that Burroughs is highly aware of the frightening persuasiveness and pervasiveness of Napoleon Hill and W. Clement Stone's rather crude collaborative social logic, its "generic" quality in every sense of the word, and the disillusioning continuity and "collusion" of this peculiar primer of capitalism with Burroughs' own cut-ups. This realization fires his utopian but skeptical wish for a remote "third person, invisible and beyond grasp, decoding the silence." The presence of that neutral third person runs throughout his fiction and is clearly anticipated in the narrator of "International Zone," which could be subtitled *A Stab at Success through a Skeptical Mental Attitude*. The difference between Hill/Stone's book and Burroughs' story lies not so much in the difference in their fundamental premises but in the relative sanguinity or gloom with which they assert them.

*Success through a Positive Mental Attitude* makes no bones about its tone. Chapter 6, for instance, assures the reader with the title "You've Got a Problem? That's Good!" The reason behind this uncautious optimism is explained in a single acronym, which gets invoked throughout the book so often that it acquires the status of a mantra: "Repeated victories over your problems are the rungs on your ladder of success. With each victory you grow in wisdom, stature, and experience. You become a better, bigger, more successful person each time you meet a problem and tackle it with PMA."[112]

Not underestimating the innate and lingering pessimism of their readers, the authors provide as proof of the powers of PMA the true-life exemplary tale of Charlie Ward, a down-and-out guy and inmate of Leavenworth Penitentiary, who could easily have hailed from the ranks of the "full-time professional spongers" with their "dead, hopeless eyes, drooping shoulders, clothes beyond mending," who inhabit Burroughs' interzone.[113] Born in poverty and traveling with the wrong company as an adult, yet always wishing that things might be otherwise, Charlie Ward dwells in his own version of

Burroughs' border lands. "His companions," say the authors of *Success*, "were hard-bitten men. He gambled, associated with riffraff-men of the so-called 'Border Legion.' Soldiers of fortune, fugitives, smugglers, cattle thieves, and the like were his companions." In retrospect, Charlie realizes that "My major sin was in associating with people who were bad."[114]

Suggestive of the types who populate "International Zone," and Burroughs' fiction in general, is Burroughs' description of one of the men in the bar, Robbins. "With the face of a Cockney informer, the archetypal 'Copper's Nark' . . . Robbins looks like some unsuccessful species of *Homo non Sapiens*, blackmailing the human race with his existence." The unsuccessful Robbins' indefinite residence in the interzone stems from the fact that "he had all his money in his wife's name to evade income tax, and his wife ran away with a perfidious Australian." Like Charlie Ward, Robbins admits only to guilt by association, attributing his fall from wealth to the fact that he was "betrayed and cheated by dishonest associates." Other hopeless hopefuls like Robbins hang out endlessly, stymied by the circumstance that "there are no jobs in Tangier, and smuggling is as overcrowded as any other line."[115]

But unlike the indeterminate beings in the interzone, Charlie Ward has the chance to bring his malaise to a concrete resolution, occasioned by his fortunate fall, on narcotics smuggling charges, into the ultimate planned dystopia: prison. An embittered Charlie, interned in Leavenworth Penitentiary, spends his time scheming about ways to escape. But luckily for him, he is in a perfect position to learn the true meaning of the premise "You've Got a Problem? That's Good!" Hill and Stone recount his miraculous transformation by sheer dint of mental effort in the hazy terms of a religious conversion experience. "Then something happened! Charlie chose to change his attitude from negative to positive. He met the challenge to *change* with PMA." But the specific valences of this mantra become clear in their subsequent description of the particular ways in which Charlie *changes*.

> Something within him told him to *stop being hostile* and to become the best prisoner in the the prison. From that very moment the entire tide of his life began to flow in the direction most favorable for him. By the simple *change from negative to positive thinking*, Charlie Ward began to master himself.
>
> He changed the direction of his aggressive personality. He forgave the federal agents who had brought about his plight. He quit hating the judge who sentenced him. . . . He looked around

for ways to make his stay in prison as pleasant as possible. . . . In his prison cell he began to read *the Bible.* [116]

Charlie Ward is a far cry from the unrepentant junky William Lee at the end of *Naked Lunch,* who flees to Interzone and, when pursued by narcotics agents, squirts alcohol into their eyes and then kills them. Charlie's magical transformation involves his total, passive acquiescence in and capitulation to the contradictory and punitive logic of a capitalistic society of economic booms and drug busts—an economy that encourages unlimited personal acquisition, claims that it is available to anyone who desires it ardently enough, withholds it from most, and exacts severe penance from those whose ardent desires take non-sanctioned forms. To invoke once again the words of Kafka (who, it seems appropriate to recall here, wrote *In the Penal Colony*), "All is dependent, all stands in chains. Capitalism is a condition of the soul and of the world." Unlike Burroughs' text, *Success* never acknowledges the fact that capitalism itself spawns the parodic, dysfunctional economy inhabited by the "Border Legion" and the "soldiers of fortune." This symptomatic secondary economy must, of course, be denied at all costs. Charlie Ward's salvation lies in his acceptance that the prison forged by consumerism already *is* paradise. One succeeds there, as on the outside, by "becoming the best prisoner in the prison." Once he has discovered that premise, it is not so difficult "to make his stay in prison as pleasant as possible."

The heavenly qualities of the penitentiary—which is after all only a microcosm of the paradisical consumer society where a man "can turn $100 into a multi-million dollar international business organization"—quickly become apparent. The prison library has self-help books on electricity, just the books he will need to help identify and learn his vocation in life. Another fortuitous coincidence, combined with Charlie's PMA and the fact that the penitentiary, like capitalism, provides jobs, puts him into a slot as superintendent of the prison power plant, where he not only accepts but helps to propagate the passive terms of his social imprisonment on a larger scale. As plant superintendent, "with one hundred and fifty men under him," Charlie "tried to inspire each one of them to make the best of his situation."

But these leaps in consciousness are mere preliminaries for the most fortuitous and fateful happening of all. "When Herbert Hughes Bigelow, president of Brown & Bigelow of St. Paul, Minnesota, arrived at Leavenworth on a conviction of income tax evasion, Charlie Ward befriended him. In fact, he went out of his way to motivate

Bigelow to adjust himself to his environment." Charlie, now the consummate ideologue and zealot of a consumer society based on the contradictory principles of unlimited gratification and limitless punishment, makes true believers out of those border legions—and their mainstream counterparts—maladjusted to the oppressive realities and by-products of rampant consumerism. His sophistry is rewarded by Bigelow's promise to offer Charlie a job in St. Paul (the patron saint of those with PMA) upon Charlie's release from prison.[117]

Bigelow the income-tax evader, who like Burroughs' Robbins was presumably betrayed and cheated by dishonest associates, is eventually set free, five weeks before the model-prisoner Charlie Ward—the white-collar crime of income-tax evasion doubtless a lesser offense than drug smuggling. When Charlie follows, he reaps his reward in a sequence that neatly recapitulates his successes within the prison. He begins as a laborer, quickly becomes a foreman on account of his PMA, then a vice president, then finally the president of Brown & Bigelow upon the happy demise of Mr. Bigelow, and he builds sales from three million dollars a year to fifty million. But his success, outside of prison as in, remains contingent on his continuing as an ideologue of strict conformism to consumerism's punitive paradise. He systematically employs ex-cons, who "continued their rehabilitation under his stern and understanding guidance and inspiration." The two spheres merge into a single, cosmic prison, with Charlie as its warden.

But in Burroughs' distorting mirror of the pure consumer society, success evades even the believers who dwell among the border legion. Fortuitous coincidence never seems to fall their way as it does repeatedly for Charlie. For some, their attempt to adhere to the tenets of capitalism manifests itself as the mere attenuated symptoms of capitalism. "It is typical of these people that they all believe in some sort of gambling system, usually a variation on the old routine of doubling up when you lose, which is the pattern of their lives. They always back up their mistakes with more of themselves." Others take the practical lessons and logic of building a multi-million-dollar organization from one hundred dollars more to heart. Yet for them too, there waits only repeated failure, as they act out grotesquely unsuccessful parodies of the self-made man. Chris, for instance,

> is the type who gets involved in fur farming, projects to raise
> ramie, frogs, cultured pearls. He had, in fact, lost all his savings
> in a bee-raising venture in the West Indies. He had observed that

all the honey was imported and expensive. It looked like a sure thing, and he invested all he had. He did not know about a certain moth preying on the bees in that area, so that bee-raising is impossible.[118]

The most telling and disconsolate failures, though, are those who seem to possess the unmistakable makings of PMA, who seem worthy of keeping company with the likes of the mature Charlie Ward. Brinton, for instance, were he reincarnated into Hill and Stone's text, would appear a prime candidate for the exemplary life, almost destined for conversion and success by the hand of fate owing to his sheer mental mettle. In Burroughs' interzone, however, he languishes inexplicably, trapped in the interstice between faith and reward.

He has intelligence, the rare ability to see the relations between disparate factors, to coordinate data, but he moves through life like a phantom, never able to find the time, place and person to put anything into effect, to realize any project in terms of three-dimensional reality. He could have been a successful business executive, anthropologist, explorer, criminal, but the conjuncture of circumstances was never there. He is always too late or too early. His abilities remain larval, discarnate. He is the last of an archaic line, or the first here from another space-time way—in any case a man without context, of no place or time.[119]

The conjuncture of circumstances never seems to be there for any of these forever wayfaring, forever waylaid types. In Burroughs' fictional universe, capitalism inexorably defrauds and mocks its adherents, forging its illusory myths of success at everyone's expense. Eric Mottram points out that "his work is restricted to undermining the dystopia and not extended to setting up alternative, even anarchist, systems."[120] The only reward to be had in this intermediate space is the neutral reward of intermediacy itself. The narrator of "International Zone" wrings a scant drop of relief from the arid landscape by recounting Tangier's attractions as a place of political and moral neutrality. It is, for him at least, a kind of halfway house between enclosure and consolation, a place where its non-residents may dwell for an indefinite period.

Americans are exempt from the usual annoyances of registering with the police. . . . No visa is required for Tangier. You can stay

as long as you want, work, if you can find a job, or go into business, without any formalities or permits.[121]

The absence of violent crime, the timelessness of Arabic music,
and the sense of a hazy eternal present created by smoking hashish
enhance the feelings of refuge and reclusiveness. But the closing passage of "International Zone" underscores again the ambiguity of this
dubious sanctuary. It expresses both Burroughs' yearning toward the
zero degree of consciousness and his reluctant, melancholy acknowl-
edgement, much in the vein of Kafka, that this ineffectual place of
hiatus, however freestanding and detached, replicates in its own be-
nignant architecture the laissez-faire structures of the consumeristic
social prison.

> Tangier is a vast penal colony.
> The special attraction of Tangier can be put in one word:
> exemption. Exemption from interference, legal or otherwise.
> Your private life is your own, to act exactly as you please. . . .
> No legal pressure or pressure of public opinion will curtail your
> behavior. The cop stands here with his hands behind his back,
> reduced to his basic function of keeping order. That is all he
> does. He is the other extreme from the thought police of police
> states, or our own vice squad.
> Tangier is one of the few places left in the world where, so
> long as you don't proceed to robbery, violence, or some form of
> crude, antisocial behavior, you can do exactly as you want. It is a
> sanctuary of noninterference.[122]

The sanctuary isn't much, or even real, but given the evanescence
of the alternatives, one can understand its dark attractions.

Borges, Valenzuela, Acker, and Burroughs, all by different paths,
make the secular pilgrimage to a sanctuary of noninterference.
Borges strives to escape the increasing polarization over national literature versus European literature that accompanied the transition
into the dictatorial modern state. In its stead, he offers a wistful
parable of plagiarism, suggesting that a nation, like literature, can
only be founded on a language already at a remove—translations of
translations and versions of versions. In his hall of infinitely repeating mirrors, he nourishes the hope that his image will not be located
among the multitude and that he will thereby not be asked to pledge
an allegiance.

Jean Franco, cribbing a phrase from Borges and calling this space of illusion and elusiveness "the utopia of a tired man,"[123] astutely points out that his fiction is "an exercise in which the world must be read skeptically in order to provide the motor force for spiritual withdrawal and privatized intensity." But her categorical insistence that his "fictions hold out no possibility of solidarity" does their subtlety a disservice. As Franco acknowledges, Borges in his writing "has unmasked the disinterested and apparently universal knowledge of the metropolis as an exercise of power, and has brought the destructive force of parody to bear on these knowledge effects."[124] Given the competing ideologies in circulation during the years preceding and during his writing of "Pierre Menard," Borges' thoughtful acts of evasions seem in retrospect to possess a more than modest worth. As of many a tired utopian intellectual since, it can surely be said of him, with no more than a touch of irony, that he is not really dead, just resting.

Luisa Valenzuela proves less wistful than Borges and more than willing to depict in agonizing detail the psychological brutality and sadism of military dictatorship. Nonetheless, Valenzuela presents Laura's cloister, removed from revolutionary militancy, to be in some respects as inevitable as it is perverse. In a political climate where the left has been reappraising and rejecting precedents to an astonishing degree, Valenzuela's psychic appraisal of the shambles left by dictatorship comprises a worthwhile taking of stock. Kathy Acker's *Don Quixote* offers an even scanter refuge than does Valenzuela from the sadistic onslaughts of recent and historical patriarchal tyranny. Acker's plagiarisms cast a thin shadow of shelter from the rough stylistic beast of her apocalyptic vision, with its gaze blank and pitiless as the sun. Yet, as with Borges' more quietly steadfast stare, this vision does at times illuminate the exercise of power in its nakedness. William Burroughs' interzone, because it is, in Franco's phrase, a knowledge effect of an all-encompassing consumer capitalism, can differentiate itself from that capitalism only through the grotesque distortions of parody. The interzone supplies a hideout scarcely more alluring, a provisional place in which the only mental alternatives to collusion with one's imprisonment are opium sedation or painstaking reflection. Burroughs, the renowned junkie, opts for painstaking reflection.

Relentless social and political violence can diminish perspectives toward the future, making it unthinkable, at least for a time, to utter the word *revolution* under any auspices. This stasis may seem unfortunate, perhaps regressive, to political temperaments more given to voicing a telos of social change with wishful, peremptory certitude. Yet there is much value in exploring the more modest possibilities of healing and succor to be had in epochs of desperation. Whatever social regeneration might occur will have to begin, in any case, with the barest touch of balm.

# Notes

## Introduction

1. Jorge Luis Borges, "La supersticiosa ética del lector," *Obras completas,* 202.

## 1. Conquest of the New Word: U.S. Experimental Fiction, Gabriel García Márquez, and the Latin American Boom

1. John Barth, "The Literature of Exhaustion," in *Surfiction,* ed. Raymond Federman, 19, 28.

2. Stephen Koch, "Premature Speculations on the Perpetual Renaissance," *TriQuarterly* 10 (Fall 1967): 5.

3. Barth, "Literature of Exhaustion," 23.

4. Susan Sontag, "The Aesthetics of Silence," *A Susan Sontag Reader,* 183.

5. Sontag, *Reader,* 187. For more on the "zero degree" as part of a cultural rhetoric, see Chapter 6 here.

6. I use the phrase "experimental fiction," here and throughout, chiefly as a descriptive term, rather than an evaluative one. The term has been much bandied about, in both mindlessly celebratory and unjustifiably prejudicial ways. More lately, it has been abandoned as outdated or passé. I find it useful, however, for its "historical" import; that is, it was the term widely employed in the sixties and seventies to describe the fiction of John Barth and many of his fellow fiction writers.

7. Sontag, *Reader,* 187–188.

8. See Borges' essay, "Kafka y sus precursores," from *Otras inquisiciones,* reprinted in *Obras completas.*

9. Barth, "Literature of Exhaustion," 25.

10. John Barth, "The Literature of Replenishment," *Atlantic,* January 1980, 71.

11. Barth, "Literature of Replenishment," 71.

12. Tzvetan Todorov, *The Conquest of America,* trans. Richard Howard, 247.

13. R. Z. Sheppard, "Where the Fiction is *Fantástica,*" *Time,* 7 March

1983, 78. More complete information about the size of editions (both in Spanish and in various translations) of this novel and other boom novels is available in Sarah Castro-Klarén and Héctor Campos, "Traducciones, tirajes, ventas y estrellas: El 'Boom,' " *Ideologies and Literature* 4, no. 17 (September-October 1983): 319–338, and in Angel Rama's "El Boom en Perspectiva," *La novela en América Latina.*

14. Larry McCaffery, ed., *Postmodern Fiction: A Bio-Bibliographical Guide,* xxvi. María Gowland de Gallo, in an article in *Américas,* describes García Márquez's novel as "the great allegory of Latin America." In "Latin American Literature: A Rising Star: The Novel," *Américas* 28, no. 2 (February 1976): 40.

15. Alain Robbe-Grillet, "On Several Obsolete Notions," *For a New Novel: Essays on Fiction,* trans. Richard Howard, 25.

16. McCaffery, *Postmodern Fiction,* xxvi.

17. Andreas Huyssen, *After the Great Divide: Modernism, Mass Culture, Postmodernism,* 170–172.

18. Roberto Fernández Retamar, *Caliban and Other Essays,* trans. Edward Baker, 30–31.

19. Fernández Retamar, *Caliban,* 7.

20. "Treinta preguntas a un Tupamaro," in *Contribución a la historia del Movimiento de Liberación Nacional,* vol. 2, 219. This volume provides a thorough record of the main documents and position papers published by the Tupamaros during their years of greatest activity. All translations from the Spanish throughout this book are mine, except where noted.

21. *Contribución a la historia,* and Eleutero Fernández Huidobro, *Historia de los Tupamaros,* vols. 1, 2, and 3. Fernández Huidobro, one of the prominent Tupamaro guerrillas and one of the prisoners involved in the abortive negotiations between the MLN and members of the armed forces, provides a highly personal but thorough account of the guerrilla struggle. See too his *La tregua armada.*

22. William Gass, "The Medium of Fiction," reprinted in *Fiction and the Figures of Life,* 30.

23. See also the polemic between Gass and Gardner in *Anything Can Happen,* ed. Tom Le Clair and Larry McCaffery, 20–31. For Gardner, fiction ideally puts the reader into a "vivid and continous dream, living a virtual life, making moral judgements in a virtual state." He acidly compares Gass' fiction to his own by saying, "The difference is that my 707 will fly and his is too encrusted with gold to get off the ground." His metaphor here comes straight out of the cultural narrative of Western technological progress, to say nothing of the scarcely more subtle macho overtones of being able to "get it up." In Gardner's later treatise, *The Art of Fiction,* which emerged as a cult book on the creative-writing workshop scene, he attempts to tame and hiply trivialize the impulse toward metafiction and artifice by describing and acknowledging most novelists' occasional necessity to "jazz around"—a tinkering not to be confused with the serious business of writing fiction.

24. Sheppard, "*Fantástica,*" 78. This kind of cursory approach has been

widespread. Robert Mead quotes, among other examples, a perceptive passage in a review by *Atlantic* critic Melvin Maddocks, who states that the boom novelists are "the latest blips on our cultural radar screen . . . Reputations circulate instead of the books themselves . . . Latin American novelists inhabit their nonreaders' minds as I.D. cards with space only for a name, nationality, and one or two irrelevant facts: Carlos Fuentes, Mexican. Friend of Norman Mailer's. Visa Problems. Miguel Angel Asturias, Guatemalan, Nobel Prize. Hates United Fruit. Julio Cortázar, Argentine. Lives in Paris. Author of the short story from which *Blowup* was derived." In "After the Boom: The Fate of Latin American Literature in English Translation," *Américas* 30, no. 4 (April 1978): 5.

25. Sarah Crichton, "El boom de la novela latinoamericana," *Publisher's Weekly*, 24 December 1982, 26–30.

26. Gabriel García Márquez, "Latin America's Impossible Reality," *Harper's*, January 1985, 13.

27. García Márquez, "Impossible Reality," 14.

28. Ibid., 14.

29. Todorov, *Conquest*, 43–44.

30. Ibid., 44.

31. "The Quality of Imagination," advertisement, *Harper's*, January 1985, 12.

32. Angel Rama, *La novela en América Latina*, 240. Some writers and critics have strongly dissented from assessments of the boom such as Rama's, notably the Chilean novelist José Donoso. Donoso begins his reminiscence and book-length demurrer by branding the denomination El Boom as "a creation of envy, hysteria, and paranoia." He characterizes critics and writers who have used the term as "slanderers . . . who jabber," "hostile," "pedants . . . bent over texts and brandishing names in their flaccid, sweaty hands," "dangerous personal enemies," "envious," "failures: a professor who wanted to be a novelist and failed, a decayed bureaucrat in his little international job," and on and on. Donoso seems less interested in critical dissent or analysis of a personally lived cultural moment than in the settling of perceived scores. In *The Boom in Spanish American Literature: A Personal History*, trans. Gregory Kolovakos, 1–6.

33. Rama, *La novela en América Latina*, 236.

34. Ibid., 288–289. Examples of this celebrification of Latin American novelists abound, such as the 1984 *Newsweek* cover story on Vargas Llosa or a PBS special on Carlos Fuentes, aired in 1989, complete with shots of the "genius" celebrity Fuentes on the set with Jane Fonda and Gregory Peck, actors in the film version of the English translation of his novel *Gringo viejo*. The program depicts Fuentes as the quintessential literary lion, the vigorous and potent patriarch who exclaims, "I eat critics for breakfast," and describes himself as a "Don Juan." Discussion about his work alternates with shots of him accompanied, for instance, by his glamorous yet demure young wife, who works for Mexican television. This made-for-TV Fuentes resembles no one so much as the larger-than-life patriarch Artemio Cruz, the macho megalomaniac and apotheosis of capitalism who is alternately

vilified and lionized in his novel *La muerte de Artemio Cruz.* Vargas Llosa's initial impressive showings in his race for the presidency of Peru in 1990 derived to a great degree from his status as a celebrity abroad—especially his high visibility as a novelist in the U.S.—and the perception that he would therefore be capable of delivering on his supply-side monetary promises to woo foreign capital to Peru's hopelessly depressed economy.

35. Ibid., 250. This account of the mechanisms of literary publishing, though it may seem overstated, is in its essentials common knowledge by now and widely borne out in various quarters, from frequent reports about mergers in the financial pages of various U.S. newspapers (such articles, too numerous to mention, are a staple of the *New York Times* business section), to commercial editor David Lehman's somewhat grim account, "On the Publishing Scene," in *Partisan Review* 3 (1988). Lehman takes great pains to assert that no worthwhile works have to go begging for a publisher today, but his statement is clearly an attempt to foist the large publishing houses' perceived cultural responsibility onto small presses. His guarded optimism smacks of a kind of literary New Federalism.

36. Alastair Reid, "The Latin American Lottery," *New Yorker,* 26 January 1981, 109.

37. Eduardo Galeano, *Las venas abiertas de América Latina,* 75 and 206–207. The English version of this book is *Open Veins of Latin America,* trans. Cedric Belfrage.

38. Robert G. Mead, "After the Boom," 5.

39. Thomas Weyr, "Daisy Goes Latin," *Publisher's Weekly,* 17 July 1981, 69–72.

40. Weyr, "Daisy," 69.

41. Ibid., 69.

42. Tony Cartano, "Latin America's Golden Age: The 'Boom' of the Hispanic-American Novel," *World Press Review,* April 1984, 59.

43. Rama, *La novela en América Latina,* 235.

## 2. Primers of Power: Nelson Marra's "El guardaespalda" and the Uruguayan Military

1. *Diccionario de literatura uruguaya,* vol. 2, ed. Wilfredo Penco, 55.

2. Nelson Marra, "José Arcadio Buendía," *Vietnam se divierte,* 69–80.

3. William Shakespeare, "The Tempest," *The Complete Works of Shakespeare,* ed. William Aldis Wright, 1312.

4. Juan Carlos Onetti, *Cuentos secretos: Periquito el Aguador y otras Máscaras* 26–27.

5. Onetti, *Cuentos Secretos,* 28.

6. Onetti, *Cuentos Secretos,* 29–30.

7. Hugo Alfaro, *Navegar es necesario,* 112.

8. Alfaro, *Navegar,* 112–115.

9. Selva López Chirico, *El estado y las fuerzas armadas en el Uruguay del siglo XX,* 9.

10. López Chirico, *Uruguay del siglo XX,* 105–109.

11. Alfaro, *Navegar*, quoting Arturo Ardao, 98.

12. François Lerin and Cristina Torres, *Historia política de la dictadura uruguaya, 1973–1980,* 130–132.

13. Lerin and Torres, *Dictadura uruguaya,* 9–10.

14. López Chirico, *Uruguay del siglo XX,* 194.

15. Ibid., 179–182.

16. Ibid., 182.

17. Oscar Bruschera, *Las décadas infames: Análisis político 1967–1985,* 114.

18. Bruschera, *Décadas infames,* 121.

19. Ibid., 124.

20. Hernán Vidal, "Hacia un modelo general de la sensibilidad social literaturizable bajo el fascismo," in *Fascismo y experiencia literaria: Reflexiones para una recanonización,* ed. Hernán Vidal, 30.

21. The English text is taken from my translation of Marra's story, "The Bodyguard," which appeared in *Central Park* 13 (Spring 1988): 49–61. The passage cited appears on p. 52. The original Spanish text of "El guardaespalda" appears in Marra's *El guardaespalda y otros cuentos.*

22. Marra, "The Bodyguard," 58.

23. Manuel Puig, *Kiss of the Spider Woman,* trans. Thomas Colchie, 53. The original text appears in *El beso de la mujer araña,* 60.

24. Marra, "El guardaespalda," 33.

25. Marra, "The Bodyguard," 58.

26. Marra, "El guardaespalda," 33–34.

27. Marra, "The Bodyguard," 58.

28. Gass, *Figures of Life, 101.*

29. Donald Barthelme, "Paraguay," *Sixty Stories,* 127–134.

30. Mary Pratt, "Fieldwork in Common Places," in *Writing Culture: The Poetics and Politics of Ethnography,* eds. James Clifford and George E. Marcus, 36.

31. Barthelme, "Paraguay," 128.

32. Ibid., 129.

33. Larry McCaffery, "Donald Barthelme: The Aesthetics of Trash," *The Metafictional Muse: The Works of Robert Coover, Donald Barthelme, and William H. Gass,* 110.

34. Barthelme, "Paraguay," 129.

35. Ibid., 129.

36. Bruschera, *Décadas infames,* 95.

37. Ibid., 95.

38. Barthelme, "Paraguay," 130.

39. López Chirico, *Uruguay del siglo XX,* 191.

40. Barthelme, "Paraguay," 131–132.

41. Vidal, "Hacia un modelo general," 36–37.

42. Marra, "The Bodyguard," 50.

43. Vidal, "Hacia un modelo general," 37.

44. Marra, "The Bodyguard," 53, 57.

45. Ibid., 53.

Notes to Pages 61–76

46. Gordon Lish, *Peru*, 11.

47. Lish, *Peru*, 13.

48. Ibid., xiii.

49. Ibid., 17.

50. Ibid., 17.

51. Fredric Jameson, "Postmodernism, or the Cultural Logic of Late Capitalism," *New Left Review* 146 (August 1984): 57–58.

52. Jameson, "Postmodernism," 65.

53. Marra, "The Bodyguard," 61.

54. Ibid., 50.

55. Ibid., 50.

56. Marra, "El guardaespalda," 21.

57. Marra, "The Bodyguard," 50.

58. Klaus Theweleit, *Male Fantasies*, vol. 2, *Male Bodies: Psychoanalyzing the White Terror*, trans. Erica Carter, Chris Turner, and Stephen Conway, 304–305, 309.

59. Marra, "El guardaespalda," 31; "The Bodyguard," 57.

60. Elaine Scarry, *The Body in Pain: The Making and Unmaking of the World*, 4.

61. Marra, "El guardaespalda," 32.

62. Marra, "The Bodyguard," 57.

63. Theweleit, *Male Bodies*, 166–168.

64. *Diccionario Karten ilustrado*, 985.

65. Avenir Rosell, "El habla popular montevideana," *Texto crítico* 6 (Xalapa, Mexico, January–April 1977): 87–112.

66. Marra, "El guardaespalda," 19, 22.

67. Ibid., 22.

68. Marra, "The Bodyguard," 51.

69. Marra, "El guardaespalda," 22–23; "The Bodyguard," 51.

70. Marra, "El guardaespalda," 26; "The Bodyguard," 53.

71. Marra, "The Bodyguard," 50, 54, 55.

72. Ibid., 49.

73. Ibid., 61.

74. Ibid.

75. Quoted in Gerardo Caetano and José Rilla, *Breve historia de la dictadura: 1973–1985*, 112.

76. John Felstiner, *Translating Neruda: The Way to Machu Picchu*, 5.

77. Felstiner, *Neruda*, 5–6.

78. Ibid., 199–200.

79. Jorge Luis Borges, *Borges on Writing*, eds. Norman Thomas di Giovanni, Daniel Halpern, and Frank MacShane.

## 3. Cutting Up History: The Uses of Aleatory Fiction in Teresa Porzecanski and Harry Mathews

1. Jorge Albistur, "Buenos cuentos bajo el título equívoco," *El Día* (Montevideo), 17 November 1987, 12.

2. Teresa Porzecanski, "Inoportuno," *Ciudad impune*, 73.

3. Charles Bernstein, "Blood on the Cutting-Room Floor," in *What Is a Poet?* ed. Hank Lazer, 135–137.

4. Teresa Porzecanski, "Construcciones," *Construcciones*, 39–40.

5. Rómulo Cosse, "Teresa Porzecanski: Cuentos en luz," *El Día*, 31 October 1980, 5.

6. George Steiner, *After Babel: Aspects of Language and Translation*, 298.

7. Fredric Jameson, "Postmodernism, or the Cultural Logic of Late Capitalism," *New Left Review* 146 (August 1984).

8. Charles Bernstein, "Writing and Method," *Content's Dream*, 221.

9. This statement came up in a conversation I had with Porzecanski (late 1988). The delicate and complicated question of intellectuals in exile is taken up in chapter 4 (in the Argentine situation, but the circumstances are quite similar in Uruguay). For more on Uruguay's exiles during the dictatorship, see also Juan Carlos Fortuna, Nelly Niederwok, and Adela Pellegrino, *Uruguay y la emigración de los 70*, and César Aguiar, *Uruguay, País de emigración*. I mention Porzecanski's statement not as a value judgement against other intellectuals, but rather to suggest that continued contact with daily life in Montevideo, even given the prevailing social climate, was and is important to Porzecanski as a writer and that her fiction is deeply informed by this circumstance. Though she has often described Montevideo as having few charms and offering few attractions, she seems much less willing or able than some others to write from the perspective of exile.

10. François Le Lionnais, "Second Manifesto," in *Oulipo: A Primer of Potential Literature*, trans. and ed. Warren F. Motte Jr., 30.

11. Noël Arnaud, "Et naquit l'ouvroir de littérature potentielle," in *OuLiPo: 1960–1963*, ed. Jacques Bens, 7.

12. Motte, *Oulipo*, 61.

13. Harry Mathews, "Mathews's Algorithm," in Motte, ed., *Oulipo*, 126.

14. Fredric Jameson, *The Ideologies of Theory: Essays 1971–1986*, vol. 2, *Syntax of History*, 149–150.

15. There are, of course, many Marxisms, but I limit my analysis here to the claims staked by Jameson for Marxist thought—his particular structuralist version of dialectical method as represented in his books *Marxism and Form* and *The Prison House of Language*.

16. Theodor Adorno, *Minima Moralia: Reflections from Damaged Life*, trans. E. F. N. Jephcot, 150.

17. Adorno, *Minima Moralia*, 151.

18. Teresa Porzecanski, "Implacable Ancestors," trans. Johnny Payne, *Stanford Humanities Review* 1, no. 1 (Spring 1989): 25–32. Original text, *Invención de los soles*. Chapters of Porzecanski's novel in my translation also appear as follows: "Family's End," *Paper Air* 4, no. 3 (Summer 1990): 79–82; "Witchcraft of the Tribe," *Black Warrior Review* 18, no. 2 (Spring 1992): 126–134.

19. Harry Mathews, "Notes on the Threshold of a Book," *Review of Contemporary Fiction* 8, no. 3 (Fall 1988): 86–90.

20. Mathews, "Notes," 90.

21. Steve McCaffery, *North of Intention: Critical Writings 1973–86*, 15.

22. Motte, *Oulipo*, 28.

23. Harry Mathews, *The Conversions*, 70.

24. Mathews, *Conversions*, 70.

25. Georges Perec, "Avez-vous lu Harry Mathews?" *Review of Contemporary Fiction: Harry Mathews Number* 7, no. 3 (Fall 1987): 82–83.

26. Mathews, *Conversions*, 81.

27. Steiner, *After Babel*, 300–301.

28. Mathews, "Mathews's Algorithm," 126.

29. Motte, *Oulipo*, 61.

30. Teresa Porzecanski, "Ficción y fricción de la narrativa de imaginación escrita dentro de fronteras," in *Represión, exilio, y democracia: La cultura uruguaya*, ed. Saul Sosnowski, 225.

31. Porzecanski, "Ficción y fricción," 223–229.

32. Porzecanski, *Invención de los soles*, 5.

33. Ibid., 33, 47.

34. Porzecanski, "Ficción y fricción," 226.

35. Eric Mottram, "'Eleusions Truths': Harry Mathews's Strategies and Games," *Review of Contemporary Fiction: Harry Mathews Number* 7, no. 3 (Fall 1987): 154–155.

36. Mathews, *Conversions*, 124.

37. Mottram, " 'Eleusions Truths,' " 171–172.

## 4. Epistolary Fiction and Intellectual Life in a Shattered Culture: Ricardo Piglia and John Barth

1. Beatriz Sarlo, "El campo intelectual: Un espacio doblemente fracturado," in *Represión y reconstrucción de una cultura: El caso argentino*, ed. Saul Sosnowski, 101.

2. Osvaldo Bayer, "Pequeño recordatorio para un país sin memoria," in *Represión y reconstrucción*, ed. Sosnowski, 205–206.

3. Sarlo, "Campo intelectual," 104.

4. Tomás Eloy Martínez, "El lenguaje de la inexistencia," in *Represión y reconstrucción*, ed. Sosnowski, 187–188.

5. Sarlo, "Campo intelectual," 101.

6. Having the name Martínez would be much like having the name Smith in the U.S. Even though it is his actual name, the use of this surname, especially without the first surname, would provide a degree of anonymity.

7. Martínez, "Lenguaje," 189.

8. Sarlo, "Campo intelectual," 106.

9. Janet Gurkin Altman, *Epistolarity: Approaches to a Form*, 211. Three articles, by Carolyn Williams, Linda Kauffman, and Alicia Borinsky, on contemporary epistolary fiction do appear in Elizabeth Goldsmith's 1989 collection *Writing the Female Voice: Essays on Epistolary Literature*. See also Ruth Perry, *Women, Letters, and the Novel*.

10. Altman, *Epistolarity*, Acknowledgments.

11. Ernesto Sábato and Jorge Luis Borges, for instance, were two notable writers permitted and encouraged to express themselves "freely," as part of a consciously crafted and sometimes ostentatious display of the society's "openness."

12. Perry, *Women, Letters,* 117.

13. Ricardo Piglia, *Respiración artificial,* 38.

14. Martínez, "Lenguaje," 191–192.

15. Piglia, *Respiración,* 39.

16. Ibid., 40.

17. Ibid., 43–47.

18. Altman, *Epistolarity,* 128–129.

19. Piglia, *Respiración,* 94.

20. Ibid., 97.

21. Alberto Kohen, *Crisis política y poder armado,* 50–54.

22. Kohen, *Crisis política,* 55.

23. Beatriz Sarlo, "Política, ideología y figuración literaria," in *Ficción y política: La narrativa argentina durante el proceso militar,* ed. René Jara and Hernán Vidal, 38.

24. Bayer, "Recordatorio," 224–225.

25. Ibid., 204–205.

26. Piglia, *Respiración,* 102.

27. Juan Francisco Guevara, *Argentina y su sombra,* 19–22.

28. For more on the construction of Argentine nationalism in the nineteenth century, see Nicolas Shumway, *The Invention of Argentina.*

29. Piglia, *Respiración,* 103–104.

30. Sarlo, "Figuración literaria," 32.

31. Piglia, *Respiración,* 124–126.

32. Daniel Balderston, "El significado latente en Ricardo Piglia y Luis Gusman," in *Ficción y política,* ed. Jara and Vidal, 113.

33. Jorge Lafforgue, "La narrativa argentina, 1975–1984," in *Represión y reconstrucción,* ed. Sosnowski, 157–158.

34. For more on the relationship of Tardewski and *Respiración artificial* to translation, cultural obliteration, and Central European writing, see my essay "Translating the Unspeakable" in *Open Magazine* #5 (Westfield, NJ, Summer 1990): 35–41.

35. Piglia, *Respiración,* 227–228.

36. Ibid., 229.

37. Martínez, "Lenguaje," 190–191.

38. The composite also borrows doubtless elements from the Polish/ Argentine writer Gombrowicz. Biographically, there even appears to be closer proximity to Gombrowicz, but the intellectual profile seems to me to derive more from Benjamin. In 1987 telephone conversations with Piglia, who was at the time doing a teaching stint at Princeton, he indicated to me that there were elements of both. However, Piglia, like his narrator, is a game player in conversation, and it was clear that, like James Joyce, he wants to keep the critics guessing for another fifty years. So readers will simply have to take their choice. It was instructive to me that at that time, after

he and I had corresponded and I had sent him some sample English translations of mine of *Respiración artificial,* he enthused to me about them over
the phone and agreed that I should and would be the novel's translator into
English. The morning before he left for Argentina, he called me up to con-
firm the arrangement and gave me the telephone number of his literary agent
in NYC, Rosario Santos. That was the last I heard of Piglia. When I called
Santos about a month later to make arrangements, she said "I don't even
know where he is. I think maybe France, but I really don't have a clue. If
you hear from him, would you let me know?" At that moment, I felt a bit
like Renzi when he shows up in Entre Ríos in search of his uncle, only to
discover that the uncle has departed for parts unknown. *Respiración artificial* is forthcoming in English translation from Duke University Press, translated by Daniel Balderston, though no precise date has been given.

39. Walter Benjamin, *Illuminations,* ed. Hannah Arendt and trans. Harry
Zohn, 3.

40. Piglia, *Respiración,* 233.

41. Benjamin, *Illuminations,* 4.

42. Piglia's idea of plagiarism and the status of the intellectual in Argentina also has marked affinities with Borges' "Pierre Menard, Author of the
Quixote" which I do not examine here but discuss in a separate chapter.

43. Benjamin, *Illuminations,* 59.

44. Gershom Scholem, ed., *The Correspondence of Walter Benjamin and
Gershom Scholem: 1932–1940,* trans. Gary Smith and Andre Lefevere, letter
19, 40.

45. Scholem, *Correspondence,* letter 32, 74.

46. Santiago Kovadloff, *Argentina, oscuro país,* 17.

47. Kovadloff, *Argentina,* 18.

48. Benjamin, *Illuminations,* 60.

49. Ibid., 60.

50. John Barth, *LETTERS,* 88–89.

51. Barth, *LETTERS,* 89.

52. In interviews, Barth has baldly professed his allegiance to the
Tragic View. See, for instance, Barth, *The Friday Book: Essays and Other
Nonfiction.*

53. John Barth, "The Literature of Exhaustion," in *Surfiction,* ed. Raymond Federman.

54. Charlie Reilly, "An Interview with John Barth," *Contemporary Literature* 22, no. 1 (Winter 1981): 15.

55. Reilly, "Interview," 16.

56. Ibid., 10.

57. Barth, *LETTERS,* 87.

58. Richard Flacks, "Revolt of the Young Intelligentsia: Revolutionary
Class-Consciousness in a Post-Scarcity America," in *The New American
Revolution,* ed. Roderick Aya and Norman Miller, 223.

59. Kenneth Keniston, *Young Radicals: Notes on Committed Youth,*
304–306.

60. Keniston, *Radicals,* 309.

61. Flacks, "Revolt," 226–227.
62. Todd Gitlin, *The Sixties: Years of Hope, Days of Rage*, 12–13.
63. Gitlin, *Sixties*, 27.
64. Flacks, "Revolt," 230.
65. Gibson Winter, *Being Free*, 85–87.
66. Quoted in Winter, *Being Free*, 150–151.
67. Staughton Lynd, *Intellectual Origins of American Radicalism*, 17–18.
68. Lynd, *Origins*, v–vi.
69. Reilly, "Interview," 10.
70. Paul Kress, "Revolution, Liberation, and Utopia," in *The New American Revolution*, ed. Aya and Miller, 312–313.
71. Barth, *LETTERS*, 324.
72. Charles Harris, *Passionate Virtuosity: The Fiction of John Barth*, 162.
73. Barth, *LETTERS*, 674.
74. Alan Friedman, *The Turn of the Novel*, xi–xiii.
75. Barth, *LETTERS*, 772.
76. Ibid., 765.
77. Reilly, "Interview," 10.
78. Barth, *LETTERS*, 324.
79. Gerald Graff, "Under Our Belt and Off Our Back: Barth's *LETTERS* and Postmodern Fiction," *TriQuarterly* 52 (Fall 1981): 160–161.
80. Reilly, "Interview," 5.

## 5. Letters from Nowhere: Epistolary Fiction and Feminine Identity— Fanny Howe, Silvia Schmid, Lydia Davis, and Manuel Puig

1. See Kate Millet, *Sexual Politics*, for an illuminating take on Genet's aesthetic bisexuality. Though Millet is perhaps too eager to appropriate Genet's writing wholly for purposes of offering it as a distorting mirror of heterosexual relations, she nonetheless makes a convincing argument for this aspect of it. Puig may be even closer to Williams, in the sense that he most often writes explicitly about heterosexual romance.

2. Bonnie Zimmerman, "Feminist Fiction and the Postmodern Challenge," in *Postmodern Fiction: A Bio-Bibliographical Guide*, ed. Larry McCaffery, 175–188.

3. For a specific breakdown of the woeful representation of women experimental writers, see the preface to Ellen G. Friedman and Miriam Fuchs, eds., *Breaking the Sequence: Women's Experimental Fiction*, xi. Puig's case is somewhat different. He has often complained of his exclusion by many of the boom writers and their refusal to take him seriously because of his allegiance to popular culture. While there is some truth to these complaints, Puig has always been, at the least, a succès de scandale and went on fairly quickly and painlessly to be accorded international respect and success, much on the model of the boom writer laid out in chapter 1. One can say that Puig was a relative latecomer to that stature, but only when measured by the prodigy standards of his male compeers in Latin America.

4. Friedman and Fuchs, *Breaking the Sequence,* 27.

5. Introduction, *Feminism and Psychoanalysis,* ed. Richard Feldstein and Judith Roof, 3.

6. Fanny Howe, *Forty Whacks,* 3–4.

7. Howe, *Whacks,* 14.

8. Jerry Aline Flieger, "Entertaining the Ménage à Trois: Psychoanalysis, Feminism, and Literature," in *Feminism and Psychoanalysis,* ed. Feldstein and Roof, 197, 185–208.

9. Howe, *Whacks,* 2.

10. Ibid., 3.

11. Ibid., 19.

12. Ibid., 11–12.

13. Shirley Nelson Garner, "Feminism, Psychoanalysis, and the Heterosexual Imperative," in *Feminism and Psychoanalysis,* ed. Feldstein and Roof, 164.

14. Howe, *Whacks,* 21.

15. Ibid., 9.

16. Ibid., 10.

17. Ibid., 27.

18. Ibid., 35–36.

19. Ibid., 46.

20. Flieger," Ménage à Trois," 198.

21. Howe, *Whacks,* 1.

22. Fanny Howe, "Artobiography," in *Writing/Talks,* ed. Bob Perelman, 200.

23. Edward Dahlberg, "From *The Sorrows of Priapus,*" in *Writers in Revolt,* ed. Richard Seaver, Terry Southern, and Alexander Trucchi, 277.

24. Howe, "Artobiography," 201.

25. Christine Brooke-Rose, "Illiterations," in *Breaking the Sequence,* eds. Friedman and Fuchs, 55–56.

26. Claire Kahane, "Hysteria, Feminism, and the Case of *The Bostonians,*" in *Feminism and Psychoanalysis,* eds. Feldstein and Roof, 280.

27. Kahane, "Hysteria," 280–281.

28. Howe, "Artobiography," 201.

29. Edward Dahlberg, *Because I Was Flesh,* 153.

30. Edward Dahlberg and Herbert Read, *Truth Is More Sacred,* 11–21.

31. Howe, "Artobiography," 203.

32. Silvia Schmid, "Viva Freud!" *Mabel salta la rayuela,* 21.

33. Schmid, "Viva Freud!" 21–22.

34. Emiliano Galende, "Psiconanálisis: Institucionalización y/o cambio," in *Cuestionamos 2,* ed. Marie Langer, 67.

35. Marie Langer, "La mujer: Sus limitaciones y potencialidades," in *Cuestionamos,* ed. Langer, 268.

36. Langer, "La Mujer," 269.

37. Schmid, "Viva Freud!" 22.

38. Ibid., 23.

39. Marie Langer, "Carta a Einstein," in *El psicoanálisis frente a la guerra*, ed. Marie Langer, 134.

40. Schmid, "Viva Freud!" 25–27.

41. Ibid., 28.

42. Langer, "Carta a Einstein," 129.

43. Schmid, "Viva Freud!" 29.

44. Elizabeth Goldsmith, ed., *Writing the Female Voice: Essays on Epistolary Literature*, viii.

45. Adrienne Rich, "Snapshots of a Daughter-In-Law," in *The Norton Anthology of American Literature*, 2nd edition, 2531.

46. Mariana Alcoforado, "The Portugese Letters: Love Letters of Mariana to the Marquis de Chamilly," trans. Donald E. Ericson. They are included as an appendix to Maria Isabel Barreno, Maria Teresa Horta, Maria Velho da Costa, *The Three Marias: New Portuguese Letters*, trans. Helen R. Lane, 408, 410.

47. Alcoforado, "The Portugese Letters," 409.

48. Lydia Davis, "The Letter," *Break It Down*, 50–51.

49. Marjorie Perloff, "Fiction as Language Game: The Hermeneutic Parables of Lydia Davis and Maxine Chernoff," in *Breaking the Sequence*, ed. Friedman and Fuchs, 208.

50. Iris Marion Young, "Impartiality and the Civic Public," in *Feminism as Critique: The Politics of Gender*, ed. Seyla Benhabib and Drucilla Cornell, 63.

51. Young, "Impartiality," 75.

52. Ibid., 67.

53. Charles Bernstein, *Content's Dream*, 221.

54. Davis, "The Letter," 54.

55. Ibid., 54.

56. Ibid., 55–56.

57. Ibid., 56.

58. Or so it might be called, although it contains, in addition to the many letters, much poetry and a rather loose structure. Nonetheless, Helen Lane, in her preface to the volume in English, states that "it has a collagelike quality, varying as it does in tone from acute intellectual analysis to utterly personal revelation, which is close to that of today's "new novel."

59. Helen R. Lane, "Translator's Preface," Barreno, Horta, and Velho da Costa, *The Three Marias*, 7.

60. Barreno, Horta, and Velho da Costa, *The Three Marías*, 40.

61. Ibid., 114–115.

62. Ibid., 200.

63. Ibid., 203.

64. Ibid., 206.

65. Ibid., 163.

66. Davis, "The Letter," 51.

67. Barbara Johnson, "Supplementary Reading," Jacques Derrida, *Dissemination*, trans. Barbara Johnson, xiii.

68. Monique Bosco, in Jacques Derrida, *L'Oreille de l'autre,* ed. Claude Lévesque and Christie V. McDonald, 200.

69. Derrida here, and in his sometimes arcane treatise "Des Tours de Babel," plays with the language of Benjamin's justly famous, brief, dense essay "The Task of the Translator." See "Des Tours de Babel," in *Difference in Translation,* ed. Joseph F. Graham, trans. Gina Michelle Collins and Walter Verschueren (into English; French version in the Appendix), 165–207, 209–248.

70. Derrida, *L'Oreille de l'autre,* 202.

71. Davis, "The Letter," 53.

72. Ibid., 54–55.

73. Manuel Puig, *Heartbreak Tango: A Serial,* trans. Suzanne Jill Levine, 32. It should be noted that this epigraph is supplied by the translator, in lieu of Puig's use of tango lyrics, which read "Deliciosas criaturas perfumadas/ quiero el beso de sus boquitas pintadas" (Delicious perfumed creatures, I long for the kiss of your painted lips). Levine supplies the publicity blurb in keeping with her strategy of foregrounding, throughout the novel, Puig's use of movie and TV conventions, e.g., her choice of the word *episode* for "entrega" at the beginning of each chapter. It has been suggested by Douglas C. Thompson that the word *installment,* to accentuate the novel's link to serialized magazine fiction, might be an equally appropriate translation. See Thompson, "Manuel Puig's *Boquitas pintadas:* 'True Romance' for Our Time," *Critique: Studies in Contemporary Fiction* 23, no. 1 (1981): 37–44. But I think Levine's use of the movie publicity blurb in this particular case, as a translative equivalent, accurately points to the self-defeating mutual enmity and suspicion among the female characters, who are in part inspired to behave as "tigresses" by their immersion in the belief systems generated by popular culture's romantic conventions—movies, songs, magazines, soap operas.

74. Puig, *Heartbreak Tango,* 11.

75. Ibid., 14.

76. Ibid., 10.

77. Ibid., 13.

78. Ibid., 18.

79. Ibid., 206.

80. Stephanie Merrim, "For a New (Psychological) Novel in the Works of Manuel Puig," *Novel: A Forum on Fiction* 17, no. 2 (Winter 1984): 141–157.

81. Alurista, *"Boquitas pintadas:* Producción folletinesca bajo el militarismo," *Maize: Notebooks of Xicano Art and Literature* 4, nos. 1–2 (Fall/Winter, 1980–1981): 23.

82. Puig, *Heartbreak Tango,* 13. In the original Spanish, the word for "sky-blue" is *celeste,* which has obvious connotations of heaven—i.e, celestial.

83. Alicia Borinsky, "No Body There: The Politics of Interlocution," in *Writing the Female Voice,* ed. Goldsmith, 247–248.

84. Puig, *Heartbreak Tango,* 41–42.

85. Ibid., 16.

86. Ibid., 16.

87. Ibid., 92.

88. Ibid., 91.

89. Borinsky, "No Body," 249.

90. Pamela Bacarisse, "Manuel Puig: *Boquitas pintadas*," in *Landmarks in Latin American Fiction*, ed. Philip Swanson, 212.

91. Lucille Kerr, "The Fiction of Popular Design and Desire: Manuel Puig's *Boquitas pintadas*," *MLN* 97, no. 2 (March 1982): 415.

92. Puig, *Heartbreak Tango*, 28–31.

93. Ibid., 196–200.

94. Elías Miguel Muñoz, "*Boquitas pintadas:* Una zona de resistencia en el discurso literario novelístico de Manuel Puig," *Explicación de textos literarios* 16, nos. 1, 4 (1987–1988): 1–7.

95. Bacarisse, "Manuel Puig: *Boquitas pintadas*," 211.

96. Puig, *Heartbreak Tango*, 202.

97. Ibid., 224.

98. Ibid., 224.

99. Bacarisse, "Manuel Puig: *Boquitas pintadas*," 218. The phrase "the desire to be better" is Puig's, which I have here translated from the Spanish.

100. Marie-Lise Gazarian Gautier, *Interviews with Latin American Writers*, 224.

## 6. Rioting Degree Zero: Radical Skepticism and the Retreat from Politics—Jorge Luis Borges, Luisa Valenzuela, Kathy Acker, and William Burroughs

1. Roland Barthes, *Writing Degree Zero and Elements of Semiology*, trans. Annette Lavers and Colin Smith, 77–78, and Susan Sontag, Preface, *Degree Zero*, xiv–xvi.

2. Jorge Luis Borges, *Borges on Writing*, ed. Norman Thomas di Giovanni, Daniel Halpern, and Frank MacShane, 59.

3. A good overview of Borges' longstanding status as the object of polemics within Argentina is provided by María Luisa Bastos, *Borges ante la crítica argentina: 1923–1960*. For a more general synthesis of Borges criticism from the twenties to the seventies, see the first section of Gabriela Massuh, *Borges: Una estética del silencio*.

4. This radio dialogue was published as *Evasión y arraigo de Borges y Neruda* (Evasion and Engagement in Borges and Neruda), 18.

5. Fredric Jameson, "Pleasure: A Political Issue," *The Ideologies of Theory: Essays 1971–1986*, vol. 2, *Syntax of History*, 68–69.

6. Barthes, *Degree Zero*, 76.

7. Luisa Valenzuela, interviewed in Evelyn Picon Garfield, *Women's Voices from Latin America: Interviews with Six Contemporary Authors*, 147.

8. Ellen G. Friedman, "A Conversation with Kathy Acker," *Review of*

*Contemporary Fiction: Kathy Acker, Christine Brooke Rose, Marguerite Young* Number 9, no. 3 (Fall 1989): 13.

9. Barthes, *Degree Zero*, 77.

10. This date is widely recognized by scholars and political analysts as the beginning of chronic military intervention in civilian affairs.

11. See, for instance, his 1923 poem "Rosas," in *Fervor de Buenos Aires*, or "El General Quiroga va en coche al muere," in the 1925 *Luna de enfrente*, contained in *Obra poética 1923–1977*.

12. Borges, *Borges on Writing*, 109.

13. Gladys S. Onega, *La inmigración en la literatura argentina: 1880–1910*, 9–10.

14. Leopoldo F. Rodríguez, *Inmigración, nacionalismo, y fuerzas armadas: Antecedentes del golpismo en Argentina 1870–1930*, 26.

15. Orlando Lázaro, "Inmigración y sociedad," in *La inmigración en la Argentina*, ed. Lucía Piossek de Zucchi, 188–189.

16. Eduardo Crawley, *A House Divided: Argentina 1880–1980*, 43–44.

17. Rodríguez, *Inmigración*, 46–55.

18. Onega, *Inmigración en la literatura*, 19.

19. Rodríguez, *Inmigración*, 92–93.

20. Donald C. Hodges, *Argentina's "Dirty War": An Intellectual Biography*, 20–21.

21. First published in 1933 as "Hombre de la orilla," in *Crítica: Revista multicolor de los sábados*, no. 6 (Buenos Aires, 16 September 1933). Collected in *Historia universal de la infamia*.

22. Iraset Páez Urdaneta, prologue to Jorge Luis Borges, *Ficciones-El Aleph-El Informe de Brodie*, xxii.

23. Jorge Luis Borges, "El escritor argentino y la tradición," *Obras completas*, 268.

24. Borges, "El escritor argentino," 270.

25. Jaime Alazraki, *La prosa narrativa de Jorge Luis Borges*, 136.

26. Borges, "El escritor argentino," 271.

27. Sarlo, "Figuración literaria," 48.

28. Luis C. Alén Lascano, *La Argentina ilusionada: 1922–1930*, 154–155.

29. Leopoldo Lugones, cited in Rodríguez, *Inmigración*, 93, and Lascano, *Argentina ilusionada*, 154.

30. Jorge Luis Borges, "To Leopoldo Lugones," *TriQuarterly: Prose for Borges* 25 (Fall 1972), 186.

31. Sarlo, "Figuración literaria," 49–50.

32. Alazraki, *Prosa*, 123.

33. George Steiner, *After Babel: Aspects of Language and Translation*, 70.

34. Steiner, *After Babel*, 70.

35. Jorge Luis Borges, "Pierre Menard, Author of the *Quixote*," trans. James Irby, *Labyrinths*, ed. Donald A. Yates and James Irby, 38–39.

36. Blas Matamoro, "Borges el traidor," in *España en Borges*, ed. Fernando Lafuente, 113–122, 114.

37. Borges, "Pierre Menard," 39.

38. The South African novelist J. M. Coetzee uses "Pierre Menard" to make a cogent point about the subtly political qualities of literature in another context of oppression (Poland of the 1950s). "Writing under censorship, the writer may produce a text identical in all respects to the text he would have produced in a state of ideal freedom; in this sense he has been unaffected by the censorship. But to say that such a writer has transcended or overcome or escaped the censorship depends on an ahistorical and simplistic notion of what writing, and indeed the institution of literature, is. Aside from the fact that what one would have written under different circumstances is unknowable; aside even from the fact that a work written under one historical dispensation must be different from the 'same' work written under another, even if the two texts should be word for word identical (this is the point of Jorge Luis Borges' well-known fable, 'Pierre Menard, Author of *Don Quixote*'); we are left with the fact that work *brought out* under censorship has a different social existence from a work brought out in conditions of free expression." "Zbigniew Herbert and the Figure of the Censor," *Salmagundi* 88–89 (Fall–Winter 1991): 158–175, 161.

39. Gregory L. Ulmer, "Borges and Conceptual Art," *boundary 2* 5, no. 3 (Spring 1977): 850–851. For a very different, more strictly semiotic discussion of Borges, Barth, and *écriture*, see David William Foster, "Para una caracterización de la *Escritura* en los relatos de Borges," *Revista iberoamericana* no. 100–101 (1977): 337–357.

40. Borges, "Pierre Menard," 40.

41. Ibid., 40.

42. Ibid., 41–42.

43. Ibid., 43.

44. Mary Kinzie, "Recursive Prose," *TriQuarterly: Prose for Borges* 25, 38.

45. Emir Rodríguez Monegal, "Borges: The Reader as Writer," *Triquarterly: Prose for Borges* 25, 108.

46. Borges, "Pierre Menard," 43–44.

47. Kinzie, "Recursive Prose," 11.

48. César Vallejo, "I am going to speak of hope," *The Complete Posthumous Poetry*, trans. Clayton Eshleman and José Rubia Barcia, 17 (bilingual edition).

49. Marta Morello-Frosch, " 'Other Weapons': When Metaphors Become Real," *Review of Contemporary Fiction: Luisa Valenzuela Number* 6, no. 3 (Fall 1986): 82.

50. Luisa Valenzuela, "Other Weapons," trans. Deborah Bonner, in *Women's Fiction from Latin America*, ed. Evelyn Picon Garfield, 289.

51. Morello-Frosch, "Metaphors," 82.

52. Valenzuela, "Other Weapons," 288.

53. The re-edition from which I am working is Valenzuela, *Cambio de armas* (Hanover, N.H.: Ediciones del Norte, 1988).

54. All of the stories in *Cambio de armas* treat in different ways the problem of this "neutralized" social space and are, I would argue, self-

conscious variations on or permutations of the same story. "Cuarta versión," for instance, concerns a banned actress' affair with an ambassador to her country who uses the embassy to provide internal asylum to political dissidents. This "neutral" space of temporary liberation, in the end, gets shattered when soldiers storm the embassy during a party, and the actress is killed. "De noche soy tu caballo," in part a gender critique of left politics, deals with the lover of a guerrilla who uses her as a sexual refuge from his political activities while excluding her from any specific knowledge of them. This refuge, too, is destroyed when he gets captured by military authorities and thrown from a helicopter, and she, despite her ignorance, is imprisoned as an accomplice. "Other Weapons" seems to me to come the closest of all the stories to enacting successsfully, in its style and structure, the precarious nature of radical consciousness.

55. Valenzuela, "Other Weapons," 289.

56. Morello-Frosch, "Metaphors," 82.

57. See chapter 4, concerning Piglia's *Artificial Respiration,* in particular the comments of Tomás Eloy Martínez about the 1983 return to democracy in Argentina.

58. Norbert Lechner, "El nuevo interés por la cultura política," *Cultura política y democratización,* 7–9.

59. John Simpson and Jana Bennett, *The Disappeared: Voices from a Secret War,* 169–170.

60. Oscar Landi, ed., introduction, *Medios, transformación cultural y política,* 10.

61. Diana Kordon, Lucila Edelman, et al., *Efectos psicológicos de la represión política,* 94. For another moving and psychologically acute treatment of this phenomenon, see the autobiographical account of Alicia Partnoy, *The Little School: Tales of Disappearance and Survival in Argentina.*

62. Kordon, *Efectos,* 33–36.

63. Hodges, *Argentina's "Dirty" War,* 181. Hodges also cites the celebrated, oft-cited threat of General Ibérico Saint-Jean: "First we will kill all the subversives; then we will kill their collaborators; then their sympathizers; then ... those who remain indifferent; and finally we will kill the timid!"

64. Valenzuela, "Other Weapons," 306.

65. Ibid., 292.

66. Ibid., 291.

67. Ibid., 302.

68. Ibid., 310.

69. Jerry Rubin, *Growing (Up) at Thirty-Seven,* 198, 20.

70. Robin Lydenberg, "Beyond Good and Evil: 'How to' Read *Naked Lunch,*" *Review of Contemporary Fiction: Williams S. Burroughs Number* no. 1 (Spring 1984): 75–79. Lydenberg puts forth these claims even more extensively and strongly in *Word Cultures: Radical Theory and Practice in William S. Burroughs' Fiction.*

71. Larry McCaffery, "Kathy Acker and 'Punk' Aesthetics," in *Breaking*

*the Sequence: Women's Experimental Fiction,* ed. Ellen G. Friedman and Miriam Fuchs, 218.

72. Elizabeth Hardwick, "The Sense of the Present," *Bartleby in Manhattan & Other Essays,* 263.

73. Margaret A. Rose, *Parody/Metafiction: An Analysis of Parody as a Critical Mirror to the Writing and Reception of Fiction,* 130–131.

74. Rose, *Parody,* 131–132.

75. McCaffery, "Kathy Acker," 223.

76. Kathy Acker, *Don Quixote,* 25.

77. McCaffery, "Kathy Acker," 223.

78. Acker, *Don Quixote,* 9.

79. Ibid., 54.

80. Ibid., 9–10.

81. Ibid., 29–30.

82. Ibid., 39.

83. Douglas Shields Dix, "Kathy Acker's *Don Quixote:* Nomad Writing," *Review of Contemporary Fiction: Kathy Acker, Christine Brooke Rose, Marguerite Young Number* 9, no. 3 (Fall 1989): 58.

84. Ellen G. Friedman, " 'Now Eat Your Mind': An Introduction to the Works of Kathy Acker," *Review of Contemporary Fiction: Kathy Acker, Christine Brooke Rose, Marguerite Young Number* 9, no. 3 (Fall 1989): 39.

85. Richard Walsh, "The Quest for Love and the Writing of Female Desire in Kathy Acker's *Don Quixote,*" *Critique: Studies in Contemporary Fiction* 32, no. 3 (Spring 1991): 149.

86. John R. Clark, *The Modern Satiric Grotesque and Its Traditions,* 51–52.

87. Acker, *Don Quixote,* 104.

88. Friedman, "A Conversation," 13.

89. Walsh, "The Quest," 163.

90. Bernard McElroy, *Fiction of the Modern Grotesque,* 11.

91. McElroy, *Fiction,* 17.

92. Acker, *Don Quixote,* 129.

93. Ibid., 132.

94. Naomi Jacobs, "Kathy Acker and the Plagiarized Self," *Review of Contemporary Fiction: Kathy Acker, Christine Brooke Rose, Marguerite Young Number* 9, no. 3 (Fall 1989): 52.

95. Acker, *Don Quixote,* 149.

96. Clark, *Modern Satiric Grotesque,* 90.

97. Acker, *Don Quixote,* 166–167.

98. Ibid., 169.

99. Ibid., 173.

100. Ibid., 175–176.

101. Friedman, "Now Eat Your Mind," 44.

102. Lydenberg, "Beyond Good," 76.

103. Phillipe Mikriammos, "The Last European Interview," *Review of Contemporary Fiction: Williams S. Burroughs Number* 4, no. 1 (Spring 1984): 16.

104. James Grauerholz, in his introduction to the 1989 edition, calls *Interzone* "the working title of the book that, in somewhat different form, was to become *Naked Lunch*." In William S. Burroughs, *Interzone*, x.

105. William S. Burroughs, "International Zone," *Interzone*, 47.

106. Burroughs, "International Zone," 49.

107. Eric Mottram, *William Burroughs: The Algebra of Need*, 17.

108. William Burroughs and Brion Gysin, *The Third Mind*, 18.

109. Burroughs and Gysin, *The Third Mind*, 19.

110. Ibid., 18.

111. Napoleon Hill and W. Clement Stone, *Success through a Positive Mental Attitude*, introductory page.

112. Hill and Stone, *Success*, 69.

113. Burroughs, "International Zone," 50, 52.

114. Hill and Stone, *Success*, 70.

115. Burroughs, "International Zone," 51.

116. Hill and Stone, *Success*, 70–71.

117. Ibid., 71.

118. Burroughs, "International Zone," 50.

119. Ibid., 50.

120. Mottram, *William Burroughs*, 26.

121. Burroughs, "International Zone," 55.

122. Ibid., 59.

123. The phrase is the title of Borges' story "Utopía de un hombre cansado," previously published in *El libro de arena*. The story appears in translation in *The Book of Sand*, trans. Norman Thomas di Giovanni.

124. Jean Franco, "Utopia of a Tired Man: Jorge Luis Borges," *Social Text* (Fall 1981): 53–55.

# Bibliography

Acker, Kathy. *Don Quixote*. New York: Grove Press, 1986.

Adorno, Theodor. *Minima Moralia: Reflections from Damaged Life*. Translated by E. F. N. Jephcot. London: Verso, 1978.

Alazraki, Jaime. *La prosa narrativa de Jorge Luis Borges*. Madrid: Gredos, 1974.

Alfaro, Hugo. *Navegar es necesario*. Montevideo: Ediciones de la Banda Oriental, 1984.

Altman, Janet Gurkin. *Epistolarity: Approaches to a Form*. Columbus: Ohio State University Press, 1982.

Alurista. *"Boquitas pintadas:* Producción folletinesca bajo el militarismo." *Maize: Notebooks of Xicano Art and Literature* 4, nos. 1–2 (Fall/Winter 1980–1981): 21–26.

Aya, Roderick, and Norman Miller, eds. *The New American Revolution*. New York: Free Press, 1971.

Balderston, Daniel, ed. *The Historical Novel in Latin America: A Symposium*. Gaithersburg, Md.: Ediciones Hispamérica, 1986.

Barreno, Maria Isabel, Maria Teresa Horta, and Maria Velho da Costa. *The Three Marias: New Portuguese Letters*. Translated by Helen R. Lane. Garden City: Doubleday, 1975.

Barth, John. *The Friday Book: Essays and Other Nonfiction*. New York: Putnam, 1979.

———. *LETTERS*. New York: Putnam, 1979.

———. "The Literature of Exhaustion." In *Surfiction*. Edited by Raymond Federman. Chicago: Swallow Press, 1981.

———. "The Literature of Replenishment." *Atlantic*, January 1980, 65–71.

Barthelme, Donald. *Sixty Stories*. New York: E. P. Dutton, 1981.

Barthes, Roland. *Writing Degree Zero and Elements of Semiology*. Translated by Annette Lavers and Colin Smith. Boston: Beacon Press, 1967.

Bastos, María Luisa. *Borges ante la crítica argentina: 1923–1960*. Buenos Aires: Ediciones Hispamérica, 1974.

Benhabib, Seyla, and Drucilla Cornell, eds. *Feminism as Critique: The Politics of Gender*. Minneapolis: University of Minnesota Press, 1987.

Benjamin, Walter. *Illuminations*. Translated by Harry Zohn and edited by Hannah Arendt. Frankfurt: Schocken, 1969.

Bens, Jacques, ed. *OuLiPo: 1960–1963*. Paris: Christian Bourgois, 1980.

Bernstein, Charles. *Content's Dream*. Los Angeles: Sun and Moon Press, 1986.

Borges, Jorge Luis. *The Book of Sand*. Translated by Norman Thomas di Giovanni. New York: E. P. Dutton, 1977.

———. *Borges on Writing*. Edited by Norman Thomas di Giovanni, Daniel Halpern, and Frank MacShane. New York: E. P. Dutton, 1973.

———. *Fervor de Buenos Aires*. Buenos Aires: Emecé Editores, 1969.

———. *Ficciones—El aleph—El informe de Brodie*. Caracas: Biblioteca Ayacucho, 1986.

———. *Historia universal de la infamia*. Buenas Aires: Emecé Editores, 1958.

———. *Labyrinths*. Edited by Donald A. Yates and James Irby. New York: New Directions, 1964.

———. *El libro de arena*. Buenos Aires: Emecé Editores, 1975.

———. *Obra poética 1923–1977*. Buenos Aires: Emecé Editores, 1977.

———. *Obras completas*. Madrid: Ultramar, 1977.

———. "To Leopoldo Lugones." *TriQuarterly: Prose for Borges* 25 (Fall 1972): 186.

Bruschera, Oscar. *Las décadas infames: Análisis político 1967–1985*. Montevideo: Librería Linardi y Risso, 1986.

Burroughs, William S. *Interzone*. Edited by James Grauerholz. New York: Viking, 1989.

Burroughs, William, and Brion Gysin. *The Third Mind*. New York: Viking, 1978.

Caetano, Gerardo, and José Rilla. *Breve historia de la dictadura: 1973–1985*. Montevideo: Ediciones de la Banda Oriental, 1989.

Cartano, Tony. "Latin America's Golden Age: The 'Boom' of the Hispanic-American Novel." *World Press Review*, April 1984, 59.

Castro-Klarén, Sarah, and Héctor Campos. "Traducciones, tirajes, ventas, y estrellas: El 'boom.'" *Ideologies and Literature* 4, no. 17 (September–October 1983): 319–338.

Cervantes Saavedra, Miguel de. *Don Quijote de la Mancha*. Buenos Aires: Centro Editor de América Latina, 1968.

Clark, John. *The Modern Satiric Grotesque and Its Traditions*. Lexington: University Press of Kentucky, 1991.

Clifford, James, and George E. Marcus, eds. *Writing Culture: The Poetics and Politics of Ethnography*. Berkeley: University of California Press, 1986.

Coetzee, J. M. "Zbignew Herbert and the Figure of the Censor." *Salmagundi* 88–89 (Fall–Winter 1991): 158–175.

*Contribución a la historia del Movimiento de Liberación Nacional*. Vol. 2. Montevideo: Ediciones MZ, 1986.

Crawley, Eduardo. *A House Divided: Argentina 1880–1980*. London: C. Hurst, 1984.

Crichton, Sarah. "El boom de la novela latinoamericana." *Publisher's Weekly*, 24 December 1982, 26–30.

Davis, Lydia. *Break It Down.* New York: Farrar, Straus, Giroux, 1986.

Dahlberg, Edward. *Because I Was Flesh.* New York: New Directions, 1963.

Dahlberg, Edward, and Herbert Read. *Truth Is More Sacred.* London: Routledge, 1961.

Derrida, Jacques. *Dissemination.* Translated by Barbara Johnson. Chicago: University of Chicago Press, 1981.

———. *L'Oreille de l'autre.* Edited by Claude Lévesque and Christie V. McDonald. Montreal: VLB Editeur, 1982.

*Diccionario Karten ilustrado.* Buenos Aires: Karten Editora, 1978.

Dix, Douglas Shields. "Kathy Acker's *Don Quixote:* Nomad Writing." *Review of Contemporary Fiction: Kathy Acker, Christine Brooke Rose, Marguerite Young Number* 9, no. 3 (Fall 1989): 56–62.

Donoso, José. *The Boom in Spanish American Literature: A Personal History.* Translated by Gregory Kolovakos. New York: Columbia University Press, 1977.

*Evasión y arraigo de Borges y Neruda.* Montevideo: Ligu, 1960.

Feldstein, Richard, and Judith Roof, eds. *Feminism and Psychoanalysis.* Ithaca: Cornell University Press, 1989.

Felstiner, John. *Translating Neruda: The Way to Machu Picchu.* Stanford: Stanford University Press, 1980.

Fernández Huidobro, Eleutero. *Historia de los Tupamaros.* 3 vols. Montevideo: Tupac Amaru Editores, 1987.

———. *La tregua armada.* Montevideo: Tupac Amaru Editores, 1980.

Fernández Retamar, Roberto. *Caliban and Other Essays.* Translated by Edward Baker. Minneapolis: University of Minnesota Press, 1989.

Foster, David William. "Para una caracterización de la *Escritura* en los relatos de Borges." *Revista iberoamericana* no. 100–101 (1977): 337–357.

Franco, Jean. "Utopia of a Tired Man: Jorge Luis Borges." *Social Text* (Fall 1981): 52–78.

Friedman, Alan. *The Turn of the Novel.* New York: Oxford University Press, 1966.

Friedman, Ellen G. "A Conversation with Kathy Acker." *Review of Contemporary Fiction: Kathy Acker, Christine Brooke Rose, Marguerite Young Number* 9, no. 3 (Fall 1989): 12–22.

———. " 'Now Eat Your Mind': An Introduction to the Works of Kathy Acker." *Review of Contemporary Fiction: Kathy Acker, Christine Brooke Rose, Marguerite Young Number* 9, no. 3 (Fall 1989): 37–49.

Friedman, Ellen G., and Miriam Fuchs, eds. *Breaking the Sequence: Women's Experimental Fiction.* Princeton: Princeton University Press, 1989.

Fuentes, Carlos. *La muerte de Artemio Cruz.* Mexico City: Fondo de Cultura Económica, 1962.

Galeano, Eduardo. *Las venas abiertas de América Latina.* Buenos Aires: Siglo Veintiuno, 1971.

———. *Open Veins of Latin America.* Translated by Cedric Belfrage. New York: Monthly Review Press, 1973.

———. *Memory of Fire.* Vol. 3, *Century of the Wind.* Translated by Cedric Belfrage. New York: Pantheon, 1988.

García Márquez, Gabriel. *Cien años de soledad.* Buenos Aires: Sudamericana, 1967.

———. "Latin America's Impossible Reality." *Harper's,* January 1985, 13–
16.

———. *One Hundred Years of Solitude.* Translated by Gregory Rabassa.
New York: Avon, 1971.

Gardner, John. *The Art of Fiction.* New York: Knopf, 1984.

———. *On Moral Fiction.* New York: Basic Books, 1978.

Garfield, Evelyn Picon. *Women's Voices from Latin America: Interviews
with Six Contemporary Authors.* Detroit: Wayne State University Press,
1987.

———, ed. *Women's Fiction from Latin America.* Detroit: Wayne State
University Press, 1988.

Gass, William. *Fiction and the Figures of Life.* New York: Knopf, 1970.

Gazarian Gautier, Marie-Lise. *Interviews with Latin American Writers.*
Elmwood Park, Ill: Dalkey Archive Press, 1989.

Gitlin, Todd. *The Sixties: Years of Hope, Days of Rage.* New York: Bantam,
1987.

Goldsmith, Elizabeth, ed. *Writing the Female Voice: Essays on Epistolary
Literature.* Boston: Northeastern University Press, 1989.

Gowland de Gallo, María. "Latin American Literature: A Rising Star: The
Novel." *Américas* 28, no. 2 (February 1976): 37–41.

Graff, Gerald. "Under Our Belt and Off Our Back: Barth's *LETTERS* and
Postmodern Fiction." *TriQuarterly* 52 (Fall 1981): 150–164.

Graham, Joseph F., ed. *Difference in Translation.* Ithaca: Cornell University
Press, 1985.

Guevara, Juan Francisco. *Argentina y su sombra.* Buenos Aires: Edición del
Autor, 1970.

Hardwick, Elizabeth. *Bartleby in Manhattan and Other Essays.* New York:
Random House, 1983.

Harris, Charles. *Passionate Virtuosity: The Fiction of John Barth.* Urbana:
University of Illinois Press, 1983.

Hill, Napoleon, and W. Clement Stone. *Success through a Positive Mental
Attitude.* Englewood Cliffs, N.J.: Prentice-Hall, 1960.

Hodges, Donald C. *Argentina's "Dirty War": An Intellectual Biography.*
Austin: University of Texas Press, 1991.

Howe, Fanny. "Artobiography." In *Writing/Talks,* edited by Bob Perelman,
192–206. Carbondale: Southern Illinois University Press, 1985.

———. *Forty Whacks.* Boston: Houghton Mifflin, 1969.

Huyssen, Andreas. *After the Great Divide: Modernism, Mass Culture, Postmodernism.* Bloomington: Indiana University Press, 1986.

Jacobs, Naomi. "Kathy Acker and the Plagiarized Self." *Review of Contemporary Fiction: Kathy Acker, Christine Brooke Rose, Marguerite Young
Number* 9, no. 3 (Fall 1989): 50–55.

Jaffe, Harold, and John Tytell, eds. *The American Experience: A Radical
Reader.* New York: Harper and Row, 1970.

Jameson, Fredric. *The Ideologies of Theory: Essays 1971–1986.* Vol. 2, *Syntax of History.* Minneapolis: University of Minnesota Press, 1988.

———. *Marxism and Form.* Princeton: Princeton University Press, 1971.

———. "Postmodernism, or the Cultural Logic of Late Capitalism," *New Left Review* 146 (August 1984).

———. *The Prison House of Language.* Princeton: Princeton University Press, 1972.

Jara, René, and Hernán Vidal, eds. *Ficción y política: La narrativa argentina durante el proceso militar.* Buenos Aires: Alianza, 1987.

Keniston, Kenneth. *Young Radicals: Notes On Committed Youth.* New York: Harcourt, Brace and World, 1968.

Kerr, Lucille. "The Fiction of Popular Design and Desire: Manuel Puig's *Boquitas pintadas.*" *MLN* 97, no. 2 (March 1982): 411–421.

Kinzie, Mary. "Recursive Prose." *TriQuarterly: Prose for Borges* 25 (Fall 1972): 11–51.

Koch, Stephen. "Premature Speculations on the Perpetual Renaissance." *TriQuarterly* 10 (Fall 1967): 4–19.

Kohen, Alberto. *Crisis política y poder armado.* Buenos Aires: Anteo, 1983.

Kordon, Diana, Lucila Edelman, et al. *Efectos psicológicos de la represión política.* Buenos Aires: Sudamericana, 1986.

Kovadloff, Santiago. *Argentina, oscuro país.* Buenos Aires: Torres Agüero, 1983.

Lafuente, Fernando, ed. *España en Borges.* Madrid: Arquero, 1990.

Landi, Oscar, ed. *Medios, transformación cultural y política.* Buenos Aires: Editorial Legasa, 1987.

Langer, Marie, ed. *Cuestionamos 2.* Buenos Aires: Granica Editor, 1973.

———, ed. *El psicoanálisis frente a la guerra.* Buenos Aires: Rodolfo Alonso Editor, 1970.

Lascano, Luis C. Alén. *La Argentina ilusionada: 1922–1930.* Buenos Aires: Ediciones La Bastilla, 1975.

Lazer, Hank, ed. *What is a Poet?* Tuscaloosa: University of Alabama Press, 1987.

Lechner, Norbert, ed. *Cultura política y democratización.* Buenos Aires: Consejo Latinoamericano de Ciencias Sociales, 1987.

Le Clair, Tom, and Larry McCaffery, eds. *Anything Can Happen.* Urbana: University of Illinois Press, 1983.

Lehman, David. "On the Publishing Scene." *Partisan Review* 3 (1988): 371–386.

Lerin, François, and Cristina Torres. *Historia política de la dictadura uruguaya, 1973–1980.* Montevideo: Ediciones del Nuevo Mundo, 1987.

Lish, Gordon. *Peru.* New York: E. P. Dutton, 1986.

López Chirico, Selva. *El estado y las fuerzas armadas en el Uruguay del siglo XX.* Montevideo: Ediciones de la Banda Oriental, 1985.

Lydenberg, Robin. "Beyond Good and Evil: 'How to' Read *Naked Lunch.*" *Review of Contemporary Fiction: Williams S. Burroughs Number* 4, no. 1 (Spring 1984): 75–85.

————. *Word Cultures: Radical Theory and Practice in William S. Burroughs' Fiction.* Urbana: University of Illinois Press, 1987.

Lynd, Staughton. *Intellectual Origins of American Radicalism.* New York: Pantheon, 1968.

Marra, Nelson. "The Bodyguard." Translated by Johnny Payne. *Central Park* 13 (Spring 1988): 49–61.

————. *El guardaespalda y otros cuentos.* Stockholm: Förlaget Nordan, 1981.

————. *Vietnam se divierte.* Montevideo: Editorial Alfa, 1970.

Massuh, Gabriela. *Borges: Una estética del silencio.* Buenos Aires: Editorial del Belgrano, 1980.

Mathews, Harry. *The Conversions.* New York: Carcanet, 1987.

————. "Notes on the Threshold of a Book." *Review of Contemporary Fiction* 8, no. 3 (Fall 1988): 86–90.

McCaffery, Larry. *The Metafictional Muse: The Works of Robert Coover, Donald Barthelme, and William H. Gass.* Pittsburgh: University of Pittsburgh Press, 1982.

————, ed. *Postmodern Fiction: A Bio-Bibliographical Guide.* New York, Greenwood Press, 1986.

McCaffery, Steve. *North of Intention: Critical Writings 1973–1986.* New York: Roof Books, 1986.

McElroy, Bernard. *Fiction of the Modern Grotesque.* Basingstoke: Macmillan, 1989.

Mead, Robert. "After the Boom: The Fate of Latin American Literature in English Translation." *Américas* 30, no. 4 (April 1978): 2–8.

Merrim, Stephanie. "For a New (Psychological) Novel in the Works of Manuel Puig." *Novel: A Forum on Fiction* 17, no. 2 (Winter 1984): 141–157.

Mikriammos, Phillipe. "The Last European Interview." *Review of Contemporary Fiction: Williams S. Burroughs Number* 4, no. 1 (Spring 1984): 12–18.

Millet, Kate. *Sexual Politics.* New York: Avon, 1969.

Morello-Frosch, Marta. " 'Other Weapons': When Metaphors Become Real." *Review of Contemporary Fiction: Luisa Valenzuela Number* 6, no. 3 (Fall 1986): 82–87.

Motte, Jr., Warren F., trans. and ed. *Oulipo: A Primer of Potencial Literature.* Lincoln: University of Nebraska Press, 1986.

Mottram, Eric. " 'Eleusions Truths': Harry Mathews's Strategies and Games." *Review of Contemporary Fiction: Harry Mathews Number* 7, no. 3 (Fall 1987): 154–172.

————. *William Burroughs: The Algebra of Need.* Buffalo: Intrepid Press, 1971.

Muñoz, Elías Miguel. "*Boquitas pintadas:* Una zona de resistencia en el discurso literario novelístico de Manuel Puig." *Explicación de textos literarios* 16, no. 1 (1987–1988): 1–7.

Nida, Eugene. *Toward a Science of Translating.* Leiden: E. J. Brill, 1964.

Onega, Gladys S. *La inmigración en la literatura argentina:* 1880–1910. Buenos Aires: Centro Editor de América Latina, 1982.

Onetti, Juan Carlos. *Cuentos secretos: Periquito el Aguador y otras máscaras.* Montevideo: Biblioteca de Marcha, 1986.

Partnoy, Alicia. *The Little School: Tales of Disappearance and Survival in Argentina.* Pittsburgh: Cleis Press, 1986.

Penco, Wilfredo, ed. *Diccionario de la literatura Uruguaya.* Vol. 2. Montevideo: Arca, 1987.

Perec, Georges. "Avez-vous lu Harry Mathews?" *Review of Contemporary Fiction: Harry Mathews Number* 7, no. 3 (Fall 1987): 82–83.

Perloff, Marjorie. *The Poetics of Indeterminacy: Rimbaud to Cage.* Evanston: Northwestern University Press, 1981.

Perry, Ruth. *Women, Letters, and the Novel.* New York: AMS Press, 1980.

Piglia, Ricardo. *Prisión perpetua.* Buenos Aires: Sudamericana, 1988.

———. *Respiración artificial.* Buenos Aires: Sudamericana, 1988.

Prossek de Zucchi, Lucía, ed. *La inmigración en la Argentina.* Tucuman: Universidad Nacional de Tucumán, 1979.

Porzecanski, Teresa. *Ciudad impune.* Montevideo: Monte Sexto, 1986.

———. *Construcciones.* Montevideo: Arca, 1982.

———. "Family's End." Translated by Johnny Payne. *Paper Air* 4, no. 3 (Summer 1990): 79–82.

———. "Implacable Ancestors." Translated by Johnny Payne. *Stanford Humanities Review* 1, no. 1 (Spring 1989): 25–32.

———. *Invención de los soles.* Stockholm: Förlaget Nordan, 1982.

———. "Witchcraft of the Tribe." Translated by Johnny Payne. *Black Warrior Review* 18, no. 2 (Spring 1992): 126–134.

Puig, Manuel. *El beso de la mujer araña.* Barcelona: Seix Barral, 1976.

———. *Boquitas Pintadas.* Buenos Aires: Sudamericana, 1970.

———. *Heartbreak Tango: A Serial.* Translated by Suzanne Jill Levine. New York: Penguin, 1991.

———. *Kiss of the Spider Woman.* Translated by Thomas Colchie. New York: Vintage, 1991.

Rama, Angel. *La novela en América Latina.* Veracruz: Fundación Angel Rama, 1986.

Reid, Alastair. "The Latin American Lottery." *New Yorker,* 26 January 1981, 106–111.

Reilly, Charlie. "An Interview with John Barth." *Contemporary Literature* 22, no. 1 (Winter 1981): 1–23.

Rich, Adrienne. "Snapshots of a Daughter-in-Law." In *The Norton Anthology of American Literature,* 2nd edition. New York: W. W. Norton, 1984.

Robbe-Grillet, Alain. *For a New Novel: Essays on Fiction.* Translated by Richard Howard. Evanston: Northwestern University Press, 1989.

Rodríguez, Leopoldo F. *Inmigración, nacionalismo, y fuerzas armadas: Antecedentes del golpismo en Argentina* 1870–1930. Mexico City: Ediciones de Impresora Internacional, 1986.

Rodríguez Monegal, Emir. "Borges: The Reader as Writer." *TriQuarterly: Prose for Borges:* 25 (Fall 1972): 102–143.

Rose, Margaret A. *Parody/Metafiction: An Analysis of Parody as a Critical Mirror to the Writing and Reception of Fiction.* London: Croom Helm, 1979.

Rosell, Avenir. "El habla popular montevideana." *Texto crítico* 6 (Xalapa, Mexico, January–April 1977): 87–112.

Rubin, Jerry. *Growing (Up) at Thirty-Seven.* New York: M. Evans and Co., 1976.

Scarry, Elaine. *The Body in Pain: The Making and Unmaking of the World.* New York: Oxford University Press, 1985.

Schmid, Silvia. *Mabel salta la rayuela.* Buenos Aires: Editorial Legasa, 1987.

Scholem, Gershom, ed. *The Correspondence of Walter Benjamin and Gershom Scholem: 1932–1940.* Translated by Gary Smith and Andre Lefevere. New York: Schocken, 1989.

Seaver, Richard, Terry Southern, and Alexander Trucchi, eds. *Writers in Revolt.* New York: Frederick Fell, 1963.

Shakespeare, William. *The Complete Works of Shakespeare.* Ed. William Aldis Wright. New York: Doubleday, 1936.

Sheppard, R. Z. "Where the Fiction is *Fantástica.*" *Time,* 7 March 1983, 78–82.

Shumway, Nicolas. *The Invention of Argentina.* Berkeley: University of California Press, 1991.

Simpson, John, and Jana Bennett. *The Disappeared: Voices from a Secret War.* London: Robson Books, 1985.

Sontag, Susan. *A Susan Sontag Reader.* New York: Vintage, 1983.

Sorrentino, Fernando. *Seven Conversations with Jorge Luis Borges.* Troy, New York: Whitston Publishing, 1982.

Sosnowski, Saul, ed. *Represión, exilio, y democracia: La cultura uruguaya.* College Park: University of Maryland, 1987.

———, ed. *Represión y reconstrucción de una cultura: El caso argentino.* Buenos Aires: Eudeba, 1988.

Steiner, George. *After Babel: Aspects of Language and Translation.* London: Oxford University Press, 1975.

Swanson, Philip, ed. *Landmarks in Modern Latin American Fiction.* London: Routledge, 1990.

Theweleit, Klaus. *Male Fantasies.* Vol. 2, *Male Bodies: Psychoanalyzing the White Terror.* Translated by Erica Carter, Chris Turner, and Stephen Conway. Minneapolis: University of Minnesota Press, 1989.

Thompson, Douglas C. "Manuel Puig's *Boquitas pintadas:* 'True Romance' for Our Time." *Critique: Studies in Contemporary Fiction* 23, no. 1 (1981): 37–44.

Todorov, Tzvetan. *The Conquest of America.* Translated by Richard Howard. New York: Harper and Row, 1984.

Ulmer, Gregory L. "Borges and Conceptual Art." *Boundary* 2 5, no. 3 (Spring 1977): 845–861.

Valenzuela, Luisa. *Cambio de armas.* Hanover, N.H.: Ediciones del Norte, 1988.

Vallejo, César. *The Complete Posthumous Poetry.* Translated by Clayton

Eshleman and José Rubia Barcia. Berkeley: University of California Press, 1980.

Vázquez, María Esther. *Borges: Imágenes, memorias, diálogos*. Caracas: Monte Avila, 1977.

Vidal, Hernán, ed. *Fascismo y experiencia literaria: Reflexiones para una recanonización*. Minneapolis: Society for the Study of Contemporary Hispanic and Lusophone Revolutionary Literatures, 1985.

Viñas, David, et al. *Más allá del boom: Literatura y mercado*. Mexico City: Marcha Editores, 1981.

Walsh, Richard. "The Quest for Love and the Writing of Female Desire in Kathy Acker's *Don Quixote*." *Critique: Studies in Contemporary Fiction* 32, no. 3 (Spring 1991): 149–168.

Weyr, Thomas. "Daisy Goes Latin." *Publisher's Weekly*, 17 July 1981, 69–72.

Winter, Gibson. *Being Free*. New York: Macmillan, 1970.

# Index